JAMES SILAS CALHOUN

———

SHERRY ROBINSON

═══

James Silas Calhoun

═══

FIRST GOVERNOR

OF NEW MEXICO TERRITORY

AND FIRST

INDIAN AGENT

═══

University of New Mexico Press ◆ Albuquerque

Founded in 1889, the University of New Mexico sits on the traditional homelands of the Pueblo of Sandia. The original peoples of New Mexico—Pueblo, Navajo, and Apache—since time immemorial have deep connections to the land and have made significant contributions to the broader community statewide. We honor the land itself and those who remain stewards of this land throughout the generations and also acknowledge our committed relationship to Indigenous peoples. We gratefully recognize our history.

ISBN 978-0-8263-6305-3 (cloth)
ISBN 978-0-8263-6306-0 (e-book)

Library of Congress Control Number: 2021939769

COVER ILLUSTRATIONS

James Silas Calhoun, #000–742–0026, William A. Keleher
Pictorial Collection, Center for Southwest Research,
University of New Mexico Libraries

"Western States," *Black's Atlas Of North America*, by Adam and
Charles Black, engraved by John Bartholomew, 1856.
Courtesy of the David Rumsey Historical Map Collection.

COVER AND TEXT DESIGN Mindy Basinger Hill

TO *Steve*

CONTENTS

ILLUSTRATIONS

INTRODUCTION

James Silas Calhoun and I have been acquainted since 2012, when I made him the subject of a talk. New Mexico was celebrating its statehood centennial, and I had come across Calhoun, the first governor of New Mexico Territory, in my reading. What jumped out was that he took a coffin with him on his last journey across the plains on the Santa Fe Trail. What kind of person does that?

The answer to that question soon faded in importance as I discovered more about the man in his native Georgia and during his brief but crucial tenure in New Mexico. History recognizes the giants who lead governments and armies and movements, but it doesn't always recognize change agents, the people present at a critical time who have the knowledge and powers of persuasion to move the current of events in the right direction. It may not be a solo performance. Often the change agent relies on others of like mind to make change palatable. From his years in business and politics in Georgia to his service in New Mexico, Calhoun was a change agent, grounded in the present but always driving toward a better future, whether it was transportation for Georgia or statehood for New Mexico. He said as much in his inaugural address: "Our business is with the future."

Calhoun arrived during a turbulent period in New Mexico, after it was torn from Mexico and made an American possession and prize of the unpopular Mexican War. New Mexicans were struggling with the changes thrust upon them—unsure of their allegiance to a new sovereign but intrigued by the possibilities. There had already been one uprising that cost the life of a military governor and rumors of others persisted for years. The Americans didn't inspire confidence. Although American traders, residents for decades, had embraced New Mexico and New Mexicans, the war delivered a new wave of Americans intent on making their fortunes in New Mexico. They championed military governance and territorial status and had no love for Hispanic New Mexicans,

FIGURE 1. James Silas Calhoun, a native Georgian, rose in business and politics, served in the Mexican War, and became the first territorial governor of New Mexico. #000–742–0026, William A. Keleher Pictorial Collection, Center for Southwest Research, University of New Mexico Libraries.

although a few of the newcomers, also ambitious, saw New Mexicans as worthy allies in a campaign for statehood.

Into this raucous setting, Calhoun entered with his family and a party of Georgia friends in 1849. A self-made man, he was tempered by his life experiences in Georgia and well prepared to serve the government in New Mexico. He was a far better man, in fact, than New Mexico might have expected from a political appointee. And he spoke Spanish.

Almost everything we think we know about James S. Calhoun is wrong, beginning with his name. He's often misidentified as a relative of the well-known South Carolina political lion John C. Calhoun. They are not related, but he's so frequently given John Calhoun's middle initial that I took to calling him by his entire name, James Silas Calhoun.

James Silas Calhoun came to New Mexico in 1849 as the first Indian agent, a political appointee sent from Washington, DC. He won his post on the basis of influential friends—not President Zachary Taylor, as is often reported, but Georgia congressmen Alexander Stephens and Robert Toombs, two of the most powerful men in political office at the time. The president charged Calhoun with doing what he could to move the statehood process in New Mexico.

After eighteen months of demanding service, Calhoun was tapped by President Millard Fillmore to be governor of the newly created New Mexico Territory, not because of agitation by New Mexico's delegate, as it's been reported, but because of Stephens, Toombs, and Calhoun's close friend Congressman William C. Dawson of Georgia.

Calhoun brought a great deal to the position. Born into poverty and orphaned, Calhoun had been a farmer, lawyer, judge, merchant, banker, cotton broker, and a real estate and shipping magnate. (This side of the man struck a chord with me. I've spent most of my career as a business journalist and interviewed hundreds of people like him.) Calhoun started his first businesses and ran for his first political offices in Milledgeville, then Georgia's capital. In his early thirties he moved west to the frontier boomtown of Columbus. "Few names figured more conspicuously in the early history of Columbus than that of Col. James S. Calhoun," wrote the *Columbus Daily Enquirer* nearly a half century after his death.[1]

A committed Whig, he served in both chambers of the state legislature and was mayor of Columbus twice. Well-liked and widely respected, Calhoun counted some of Georgia's most influential people as personal friends. "It was the peculiar good fortune of Gov. Calhoun to retain the confidence, esteem and friendship of his fellow citizens in every condition and amidst every vicissitude of his life," wrote the *Enquirer*. After his death the newspaper called him "candid, honorable, generous and charitable in all his dealings with men."[2]

During the Panic of 1837 Calhoun lost nearly everything and never recovered financially. After a stint as US Consul in Havana, where he learned to speak Spanish, he was a newspaper editor for a time before volunteering at age forty-seven to fight in the Mexican War. During his two tours as an officer, he was still the newspaperman, sending regular dispatches home that revealed more hardships than heroics for the Georgia volunteers. His two years south of the border introduced him to Mexican people, improved his Spanish, transformed the businessman into a military officer, and gave him a taste for what he called "the novelty and excitement of an active life as a colonel commanding a mounted regiment."[3]

Stepping out of his wagon into the ancient, dusty streets of Santa Fe, the new Indian agent shouldered his duties—governing singlehandedly the occupied territory's forty thousand plus Indian people. These were not the Five Civilized Tribes of the southeastern United States but so-called wild Indians—Navajos, Apaches, Utes, Comanches, and others who had been at war with New Mexico's Hispanic people for two centuries. His charges also included hundreds of peaceful Pueblo and Hopi Indians. "Although Calhoun must have realized the enormity, perhaps the futility, of the task, nevertheless he courageously shouldered the burden that had been entrusted to him," wrote historian William Keleher.[4]

Calhoun can't entirely be described as an enlightened agent—he was as inclined toward punishment as he was toward diplomacy in his relations with the tribes—but he was honest and conscientious. Fresh from the Mexican War, he saw military solutions to New Mexico's Indian problems and annoyed commanders with his opinions. "Calhoun's whole administration, his every report and suggestion, show that he was in spirit the military man first and the civil official afterward," wrote Leo Crane, an Indian agent in the 1900s.[5] On the other hand, Calhoun was forthright with tribal leaders. He spent the government's money—and much of his own—to accommodate a steady stream of visiting tribal members, communicate with far-flung pueblos and tribes, snuff rumors started by troublemakers, and distribute gifts intended to cement peaceful relations.

He diligently pursued his responsibilities despite the active hostility and interference of two military commanders, while his superiors in distant Washington, DC, ignored his pleas for guidance and money. In truth, the bureaucrats really didn't know what to do. Indian policy, such as it was, hadn't advanced much from signing treaties and moving tribes to distant, vacant lands, and the concept of a reservation system was still years away. A war-weary Congress didn't want to spend money on New Mexico.

Crane found Calhoun "a trifle indolent and fastidious" for needing a teamster to "wrangle his field equipment" but thought it unconscionable that the government dispatched Calhoun to toil alone on a small salary and ignored his pleas for guidance and help. No federal bureaucrat gave a thought to the difficulties of sending Calhoun to such a remote place. Crane was offended that government auditors nitpicked Calhoun's expenditures "while turbulent New Mexico fomented around him."[6]

Annie Heloise Abel, who compiled Calhoun's letters as Indian agent and superintendent into *The Official Correspondence of James S. Calhoun*, said he "proved himself a thoroughly capable and honest official. Not a single scandal, not a single suspicion of peculation tarnished his record and, in his time, at least, that was a singularly rare experience in the United States Indian Service."[7]

The letters show us a diligent public servant who supplied the Indian Department with valuable new information about the Native populations and politics in New Mexico. He described his collisions with the army, reported on the politics of statehood, and documented Indian raids. Still the newspaperman, he was an astute observer of events and not without a sense of humor.

For all I learned about Calhoun in Georgia, in the Mexican War, and in New Mexico, much remains unknown. I was often annoyed that he never penned a few words about his life. Certainly he understood that he had a place in history, but maybe the press of duties didn't allow time. Maybe he wondered what he would write about. His birth on Boggy Gut Creek? His rags to riches to rags story? His role in the Creek land frauds? His soul-trying misadventures in New Mexico?

I found his family in Jefferson and Burke Counties, but his birth—even his mother's name, eluded me. The federal government lost the first three census schedules for Georgia, from 1790 to 1810. General Sherman and his infamous march to the sea contributed to this rip in the historic fabric by burning courthouses and vandalizing the statehouse.

I also came up empty handed regarding his schooling. Obviously, Calhoun was educated, but I found no institution that claims him as an alumnus. Even his headstone in Kansas City bears the wrong date of birth. But for one small portrait obtained from descendants by historian Ralph Emerson Twitchell, we wouldn't know what he looked like.

I found no physical description of Calhoun. Historian Calvin Horn once described him as "dignified, heavyset" but that's pure conjecture.[8] The portrait shows us an intelligent face, a receding hairline, a long nose, and a hint of smile. It's safe to assume Calhoun sat for the small painting when he became a colonel during the Mexican War; his epaulets are visible. He was forty-eight and would have been quite fit after marching hundreds of miles with his infantry regiment just months before. Had he been a big man, like his friend Toombs, or a small man, like his friend Stephens, some political enemy would have invoked that in the petty criticisms of the day, and so we can assume he was an average height for his time.

Of his personal life, we know that Calhoun was twice a widower and the doting father of two daughters who came with him to New Mexico at a time when few American women could be seen on the Santa Fe Trail. For them and the aunt who raised him, he championed women's property rights, but he was swimming against the current. Calhoun liked women—not in a skirt-chasing way but in healthy admiration—and yet he never remarried after the death of Anna, his second wife.

Much of what I learned came from newspapers and Calhoun's correspondence. As a journalist I was interested in what the newspapers had to say about issues and people. Georgia newspapers were well established by the early 1800s and followed politics and business closely. New Mexico struggled to keep one newspaper alive, and few early issues survive, but before wire services, newspapers routinely picked up each other's stories, ran letters from distant correspondents, and commented on matters far from their doorsteps. As an editor in Columbus, Calhoun weighed in on the controversies of the day and revealed a bit of himself. In New Mexico, Calhoun and the Georgians with him kept the *Columbus Enquirer* informed. The Missouri newspapers, at the head of the Santa Fe Trail, took a keen interest in New Mexico, as did Washington, DC, newspapers. After John Greiner became an agent for Calhoun, he kept the Ohio newspapers posted on all New Mexico subjects and, like his mentor Calhoun, wrote lively letters home.

Readers should be aware of word usage in this book. I use the term "Indians" and not "Native Americans" because this is the usage of the period. "Pueblo," capitalized, refers to Pueblo people, while "pueblo" refers to their village. "Americans" refers to the Anglo (white) newcomers, even though New Mexicans were technically Americans. "New Mexicans" refers to Hispanic people long in residence before the Americans came. Fellow historians often use "Nuevo Mexicanos," but Georgia readers may not be familiar with this usage.

Calhoun was governor for only fourteen months. Historians have opined that although Calhoun was honorable and intelligent, his task was so overwhelming, so burdened by difficulties, that he can't be remembered for his accomplishments.[9] I disagree. It isn't necessary for a change agent to be in place for long periods of time or to accomplish great feats; it's only necessary that they be present at the right time, that they tighten a bolt at the right juncture to make the frame strong.

One of New Mexico's most famous writers, Eugene Manlove Rhodes, read Calhoun's letters and concluded: "If ever any man was set to make robes of sand, Calhoun was the man. Without means, without instructions and without power, he was set to bring order out of chaos. On no single day, as agent or as governor, did he have one free dollar to expend for the government's business. When any money came, it was already long due and overdue. When he became governor, there was not one cent in the territorial treasury."[10]

Regardless, Rhodes said, Calhoun did his best to protect the Pueblos and instruct them on their rights. He signed treaties with the Navajos, Utes, Comanches, and Apaches that became a basis for future relations and delivered periods of peace. Hampered by treachery, "by intrigues of unbelievable cunning, opposed and thwarted at many points by the military powers, who refused him, at times, escort, subsistence or transportation on public business—without money, without a single rifle at his command, he managed with discretion and unexampled resolution to accomplish much of lasting benefit to his country."[11]

In 1929 Rhodes wrote to Governor R. C. Dillon: "The most interesting figure I have found in New Mexico history—the most interesting figure I have found in all history—bar Camille Desmoulins [a participant in the French Revolution] and Marco Polo—is your predecessor Calhoun, first American civil governor of New Mexico."[12]

I agree with Rhodes that despite harrowing interference, Calhoun did make a lasting contribution to New Mexico. By his own honesty, character, and personal relationships with mostly Hispanic citizens, he set the tone of government. He was the first US appointee to validate native New Mexicans' hopes and expectations that they could be participants in a democracy. As he told them in his inaugural speech, "The fate of New Mexico, under Providence, is in the hands of her own sons, and if wise and patriotic counsels prevail, a brilliant destiny awaits her."

He drew on his knowledge as an attorney, judge, and legislator to guide the first two legislative sessions. Together, he and the territory's new legislators produced an impressive set of laws. He befriended the territory's first judges. As in Georgia, Calhoun's personal warmth and charisma won him influential friends who helped advance his priorities. Finally, he did it all knowing that he wouldn't be rewarded financially. Calhoun may not have spent a great deal of time on the historical stage, but he was a vital and passionate player.

1

EARLY LIFE

The tea-colored Ogeechee River twists and curls for 245 miles from its headwaters on the southeastern edge of the Piedmont to the Atlantic Ocean below Savannah. In the places where it spreads languidly to embrace miles of swamps, tannins from decaying vegetation give the Ogeechee the hue scientists call *blackwater*. Mirroring tree trunks, the inky water might conceal a snag or an alligator. Oak and hickory crowd raised banks, tupelo and cypress stand in swamps, and they're all fringed generously with Spanish moss. The Ogeechee and its woods harbor game animals as well as pests and parasites. Even today, visitors find it primordial.[1] It was here along the Ogeechee that the Calhoon (later, Calhoun) family made its start in Georgia.

After the Revolutionary War, seekers from North Carolina and Virginia swarmed into Georgia to claim land and start a new life. The majority, like the Calhoons, were Scots-Irish—Scottish by blood, Irish by relocation, Protestant by faith—who hoped to practice their religion far from the heavy hand of the Anglican Church and to prosper far from the heavy boot of the English government.[2]

Most of the new residents built one-room log houses with floors of packed clay. Nobody had glazed windows. Even nails were a luxury. They raised corn and livestock on small- or medium-sized farms and hunted deer and wild turkey. Their enthusiastic letters back home delivered new waves of immigrants, but to become successful landowners, they had to survive malaria and attacks by the Creek Indians they had displaced. Mosquitoes may have been the bigger danger.[3]

The Calhoons

Two of James's uncles, Philip and Aquilla Cohoon (also written Cahoon and Calhoon), along with his cousin James, were the first of their family to arrive in Georgia, probably from North Carolina. Three brothers, a sister, and several cousins would follow. (For more detail on the family, see appendix 1.)

Burke County, one of Georgia's oldest counties, drew settlers of modest means—"plain, unpretentious, religious people," wrote historian George Gilman Smith. They built their log houses, grew corn, and raised livestock on the fertile, rolling lands between the Ogeechee and Savannah rivers. Philip, Aquilla, and their nephew James were settled by 1787. A man of some means, Philip had 1,200 acres, including 700 acres at Bark Camp, a settlement that predated the revolution. Aquilla and James were typical new settlers who located their tracts and began building even before they had head rights. Beginning in 1782, the state of Georgia awarded 200 acres to the head of a family, plus 50 acres for each additional member of his family, up to 1,000 acres. It was a way of discouraging speculation. Aquilla and James each had 200 acres in 1787 and acquired head rights in 1790. Burke County then had 9,467 people, and 2,392 of them were slaves.[4]

In 1796, the state carved a hilly expanse from Burke County to create Jefferson County and made Louisville, the hub of the new county, Georgia's third capital. By then, Philip was living in Jefferson County on Williamson's Swamp Creek southeast of present-day Wadley. The creek is a substantial tributary of the Ogeechee. Philip was one of 636 landowners in the county and one of the few (26 percent) who owned slaves. By 1799 he owned fourteen slaves.[5] Philip's neighbor was Solomon Wood, a captain in the Revolutionary War who built a fortress-like house for defense against Indian attacks. He equipped it with a loud bell that warned his neighbors at the first sign of trouble so they could take shelter within his walls. Creeks raided Jefferson County as late as 1788. After four Creeks chased four men and a boy in Williamson Swamp, shooting and scalping one and burning a house, Wood petitioned the Georgia governor for help.

Living nearby, also on Williamson's Swamp Creek, was Philip's brother John Cohoon (also Calhoon) and his family.[6] John was not as well-heeled as his brother. After he died in early 1797, the sheriff sold John's two hundred acres to settle his debts.[7] Next to appear in the records were Aquilla's son William and John's son Elbert, who became landowners in Jefferson County. William in 1796 owned three hundred acres on the Ogeechee and would keep expanding his acreage. He also had a home in Louisville. Elbert Calhoon had eighty acres.[8]

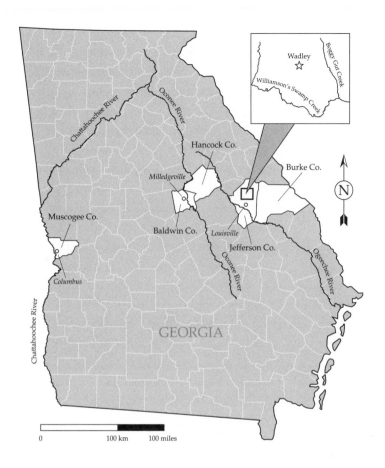

FIGURE 2. The Calhoons settled along Williamson's Swamp Creek
in the late 1700s. Michael Calhoon's land was nearby on Boggy Gut Creek.
This was James Calhoun's birthplace.

In 1799, a fourth brother, Michael Calhoon, settled on Boggy Gut Creek, a
tributary of Williamson's Swamp Creek. He owned 250 acres and one slave.
That year, his son, James Silas, was born. Michael's brief presence in Jefferson
County establishes James S. Calhoun's birthplace. Despite the hopes of a few
relatives, he was not born in South Carolina nor was he related to John C.
Calhoun.[9] A second son, Philip T., would come along in 1804.[10] A fifth brother,
Irwin Calhoon, bought 40 acres near Aquilla and the other James in 1801. Irwin
was probably the youngest of the five brothers.

The state of Georgia was as eager for settlement as newcomers were to turn a shovel on land of their own. With settlement concentrated in the east, it had a vast interior to fill. After a peace treaty ended the Revolutionary War in 1783, the pace of immigration quickened and demand rose. Distribution of bounty lands to veterans began in 1784. The state allotted land to every veteran by rank, from 230 acres for a private in the Georgia line to 1,955 acres for a militia general. It also awarded land to "refugees," or men belonging to regiments from North and South Carolina who fought in Georgia. An estimated two thousand veterans, including many from out of state, were granted some 750,000 acres in Georgia. When the application deadline expired for soldiers, the remaining land was available to settlers under the head-right system, and state laws encouraged emigrants from other states to come to Georgia and take out free head-right grants. To discourage speculation, Georgia revised its system in 1803, surveying former Indian lands and laying out tracts of 202.5 or 490 acres, depending on value. The land was then distributed by lottery.[11] The Calhoons probably owed their new status as landowners to both systems of land grants.

After a few years, small farms gave way to larger farms. With the cotton gin—Eli Whitney set up one of his first machines in Burke County—large plantations multiplied, along with the slave population.

Fortunate Drawers

James S. Calhoun's early life is largely unknown. His name enters written records for the first time in 1805, when six-year-old James and his baby brother were registered to draw in the land lottery in neighboring Washington County. Because widows and orphans were eligible to draw, it means that James and Philip had lost their parents, probably to repeated outbreaks of malaria that carried away many people in the county. Their uncle Irwin was also registered to draw. A year later James drew in the 1806 land lottery of Hancock County with his aunt, Patience Calhoon. Maybe the boys were living with their Uncle Irwin or Aunt Patience, but they also spent time in an orphanage. James's obituary would say "his youth [was] encumbered with every disadvantage."[12]

The 1805 Georgia Land Lottery, the first of its kind in the United States, was a grand experiment, intended to end the land fraud and corruption of the 1790s. Names of eligible participants were placed in one drum and lot numbers of properties in another drum. The lottery transformed ordinary people into large landowners in a single draw. The 1805 lottery distributed more than a million acres, although James wasn't a "fortunate drawer," as the winners were called, nor were his Uncle Irwin or brother Philip. (James Calhoun was still unlucky when he drew in the 1827 lotteries in Baldwin and Jefferson Counties.) Subsequent lotteries would deliver about three-quarters of the state to some 100,000 families and individuals for token payments.[13]

The land parceled out in these drawings had been taken from the Creeks. Once the most powerful tribe in the South, they lived from the Atlantic Ocean to the Mississippi River. From 1733 to 1826, white colonists armed with treaties separated the Creeks from their lands and pushed them west, from one river to the next. In 1802 Georgia gave up its claims to 86 million acres, which became Alabama and Mississippi, in return for $1.25 million and the federal government's promise to extinguish Indian titles in Georgia. On June 16, 1802, the Creeks ceded two strips of land, one in central Georgia just west of the Oconee River, and the other in the southeast corner.[14] In later years, hostilities pitted friendly Creeks against more traditional Creeks, and in August 1814 General Andrew Jackson forced the Creeks to surrender territory that would form half of Alabama. When they refused to give up any more land, President James Madison's appointees negotiated the fraudulent Indian Springs Treaty with minority leader William McIntosh and thirteen chiefs who ceded 25 million acres—their remaining lands—to the state of Georgia. The other thirty-six chiefs condemned the thirteen, and in 1825 warriors killed McIntosh. The government nullified the Indian Springs Treaty and replaced it with the 1826 Treaty of Washington, which affirmed Creek possession of their remaining lands.[15]

Creek and Cherokee lands not only provided an outlet for Georgia's swelling population but also an economic steppingstone, and each lottery stoked demand for more such giveaways.[16] As the population shifted westward, Louisville lost its luster. It was too far from the new counties, and the pull westward was irresistible.[17]

Milledgeville

Yet another treaty pushed the Creeks from land west of the Oconee River, and farmers poured into Middle Georgia. Milledgeville grew at the edge of the frontier, where the Upper Coastal Plain rises into the Piedmont, a plateau region that stretches from New Jersey to Alabama. Legislators in 1804 made Milledgeville in Baldwin County the new state capital. Modeled after Savannah and Washington, DC, Milledgeville was carefully laid out with a great square designated for the Capitol, and yet it was a typical frontier town of clapboard houses, taverns, brothels, and inns, its residents given to gambling, dueling, and violent political feuds. Gamblers played their hands in the streets, prostitution flourished, and liquor was sold without restriction. "Milledgeville, as the capital city, was . . . the scene of much gayety and much dissipation," wrote Smith. Like Jefferson County, Baldwin County's small farms gave way to large cotton plantations. In the autumn, the quiet agricultural town grew noisy as legislators arrived from around the state and planters converged to market their cotton.[18]

By 1808 James's Uncle Irwin joined the migration to Baldwin County. That year, on May 16, Irwin Calhoon married Martha Lawrence. He lived only another two years. The likely killer was malaria, also prevalent in Baldwin County. In a sale on June 6, William Calhoun received a silver watch, Patsey Calhoun received some stock, Philip received one lot of corn, and Irwin's widow, Martha, received one negro boy. She had in her care their daughter Susan, along with Irwin's nephews James and Philip.

As a widow, Martha couldn't expect much. The laws provided only that a man provide for his wife during his life. A man might leave his property to his wife, but if he died intestate and without children, half the estate went to the widow and the rest to his next of kin. Not until 1829 was a widow recognized as the sole heir of her husband under any circumstances. Eleven-year-old James and his aunt were named administrators for the humble estate. Martha and the boys, in 1810, were listed among Baldwin County's first thousand taxpayers and slave owners.[19] No doubt, Martha struggled to survive. The family would have worked in the fields along with their one slave. Out of those trying years, James's love and respect for his aunt grew into a lifelong solicitude for women.

Life may have eased in 1813 after the boys' Uncle Philip and cousin Elbert Calhoun (the family was now spelling its name this way) moved to Baldwin County. Philip owned 506 acres six miles above Milledgeville. Elbert, who had served in the War of 1812, was a lawyer and judge, and his presence may be the reason James became a lawyer.[20]

The Calhouns were Methodists. Many Georgians converted to Methodism at camp meetings in the 1790s, and it was the biggest religious group in Baldwin County by 1808, when the first Methodist church organized in Milled-

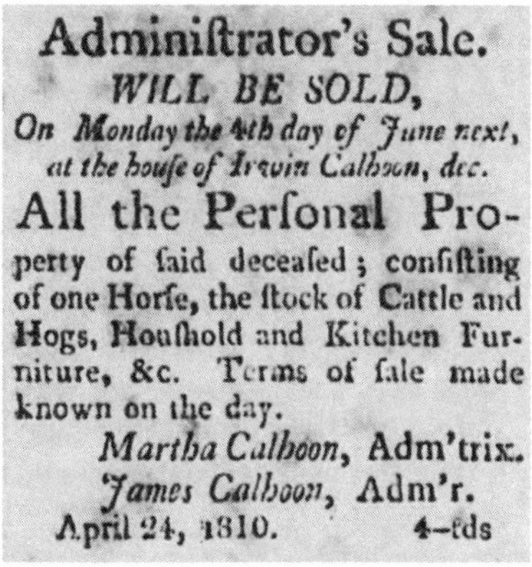

Administrator's Sale.

WILL BE SOLD,

On Monday the 4th day of June next, at the house of Irwin Calhoun, dec.

All the Personal Property of said deceased; consisting of one Horse, the stock of Cattle and Hogs, Houshold and Kitchen Furniture, &c. Terms of sale made known on the day.

Martha Calhoon, Adm'trix.
James Calhoon, Adm'r.
April 24, 1810.   4—tds

FIGURE 3. This administrator's sale advertisement from the *Georgia Argus*, May 29, 1810, indicates that Irwin's widow Martha, Calhoun's aunt, received very little.

FIGURE 4. An early view of Milledgeville shows the capitol on the right and two hotels on the left. In the center are the Presbyterian, Methodist, Baptist, and Episcopal churches. The image appears in *Our Whole Country; or The Past and Present of the United States, Historical and Descriptive*, 1861.

geville. The church's missions included education, health care, social reform, prison reform, and temperance.[21] James Calhoun was a life-long Methodist and championed those causes.

As the wealthy and powerful gravitated to the new capital and market center, Milledgeville began to gain respectability. The more affluent residents had plantations in the county and homes in Milledgeville, and their homes gave the town a new face. Newcomers included the families of James Calhoun's friends and future associates: the Lamars and Joneses. In neighboring Hancock County he met the Holts and Flournoys. "Few parts of the state were settled more rapidly and with a better class of people, and none of the middle Georgia counties were more rapidly worn out and sooner abandoned by the large planters," Smith wrote.[22]

Coming of Age

James Calhoun disappears from public records as an adolescent and young man. From his writing and the positions he held—lawyer, judge, merchant, banker, cotton broker—we know he was educated, but his alma mater remains a mystery. Men who were his lifelong friends were University of Georgia alumni. William C. Dawson, a year older, graduated in the class of 1816 and received his master's degree in 1824. Hines Holt Jr. graduated in 1824. Robert Alexander was enrolled in 1828 but didn't graduate. After the graduation of Dawson's small class, the university president resigned, and the school closed for two months. During 1817 and 1818, when Calhoun might have been a student, an acting president kept the doors open and taught "the few students who remained in attendance." For two years the university was all but suspended, faculty members departed, students dwindled to a handful, and records were poorly kept. In 1819, when Dr. Moses Wadel became president, the school had one junior, one sophomore, four freshmen and two "irregulars." After the summer break that year, it could count twenty-five college students. Commencement exercises began again in 1820, but Calhoun isn't among graduates from 1820 through 1824. Georgians hoped the institution's revival meant they would no longer need to send their sons off to New York, Pennsylvania, or Europe.[23]

Calhoun could have been educated outside Georgia. Because his first wife was from Charleston, South Carolina, the College of Charleston is a possibility, but he isn't on record there or at the University of South Carolina. Other possibilities were Washington and Lee University in Virginia and Union College in Pennsylvania, where southerners often sent their sons. He was not a student in either place, nor was he at Yale, Princeton (College of New Jersey), the College of William and Mary, the University of North Carolina, West Point, Transylvania University in Kentucky, Union College in New York (Congressman Robert Toombs' alma mater), or Columbia University (King's College). We also know that Calhoun's friends Dawson and Holt attended Litchfield Law School in Connecticut, where many southern young men trained, but Calhoun's name doesn't appear in records.[24]

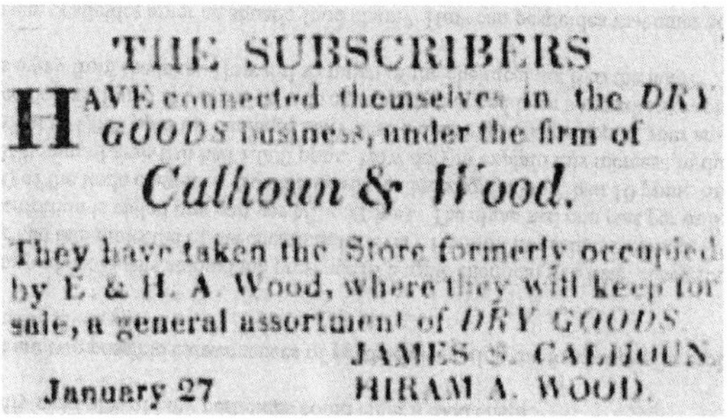

THE SUBSCRIBERS

HAVE connected themselves in the *DRY GOODS* business, under the firm of

Calhoun & Wood.

They have taken the Store formerly occupied by E. & H. A. Wood, where they will keep for sale, a general assortment of *DRY GOODS.*

JAMES S. CALHOUN.

January 27 HIRAM A. WOOD.

FIGURE 5. This modest advertisement in the February 18, 1823, *Georgia Journal* herald's James Calhoun's first foray into business, Calhoun & Wood.

Uncle Philip died at age sixty on November 13, 1820. James reappeared that year. He and his friend Burton Hepburn, a New Yorker one year older, helped incorporate the Milledgeville Thespian Society. Its first performance was a comedy, *The Poor Gentleman*.[25] That year, Hepburn, who would be a friend for years, opened a law practice and became a merchant in town.[26] Aunt Martha Calhoun remarried in 1821, becoming the third wife of the Methodist minister Charles Malone.[27] Her only child, Susan, died five months later.[28]

The following year, James Calhoun married Caroline Ann Simmons, of Charleston, South Carolina, on December 19, 1822. The nuptials were held in Hancock County, where Calhoun was probably living. Created in 1793, Hancock County's heavily timbered red hills and river valleys lay between Jefferson and Baldwin Counties. Some of its first settlers came from Jefferson County.[29]

Calhoun's younger brother Philip lived in Milledgeville, but the two may not have been close. In 1823 James placed this ad: "The Public Are cautioned against trading for Notes said to be signed by my brother, P. T. Calhoun, as there is not one given to a citizen of Georgia for a valuable consideration." Philip died in 1825 at age twenty-one, leaving few earthly goods. James sold his brother's gold watch, clothing, books, and personal belongings to settle his debts.[30]

When Calhoun returned to Milledgeville, he was a lawyer, but he quickly gravitated to business. At age twenty-four in January 1823 he joined Hiram A. Wood to open a dry goods store, Calhoun & Wood. After Wood died in October, Calhoun continued the business, but in March 1825 he auctioned off "the residue of my stock of goods" and a month later asked debtors "to settle their notes and accounts without delay." (By "notes" he meant promissory notes—any written promises to pay. These notes then circulated in the local economy like currency.) In 1826 he tried again with a dry goods and hardware store next to the State Bank. Milledgeville's rising tide finally lifted Calhoun's boat. In

1828, when the population had grown to 1,599, he seemed to be everywhere. He was a judge in Baldwin County and performed marriages in Hancock County. He was a cotton broker. At a time when shipping was a challenge and most freight arrived overland by wagon, Calhoun began shipping cotton to Savannah on poleboats. He forged a new mercantile partnership with R. W. Fort for a larger, more sophisticated establishment. In a large advertisement, they offered a selection of fabrics, as well as Carolina hoes, hardware, crockery, teas and spices, powder and shot, saws and shovels. In 1929 Calhoun took a big step, investing in a bank in the distant frontier boom town of Columbus, Georgia. He established a pattern he would maintain for years. Not satisfied with just being a lawyer, he entered business, and not just one business but many. And not just safe businesses but increasingly risky businesses like shipping, banking, and real estate.[31]

Calhoun became an enthusiastic Mason, organizing lodge festivals and helping raise money to build Masonic halls, first in Milledgeville and later in Columbus. In 1825 Calhoun and four other Masons greeted a fellow Mason, the Marquis de Lafayette, the French hero of the American Revolution, when he came to Milledgeville on a tour of the southern states. Seaborn Jones, a rising political star and aide to the governor, escorted the great man. Lafayette also attended the Methodist Church and a Georgia barbecue on the capitol grounds. After a military ball that lasted until 3 a.m. Lafayette departed Milledgeville.[32] Calhoun so revered the old general that he named his first child for him. Sadly, Frances Lafayette Calhoun died in Hancock County at eighteen months on August 29, 1825.[33] Said the death notice:

So fades the lovely blooming flower,
Frail smiling solace of an hour,
So soon our transient comforts fly,
And pleasures only bloom to die.[34]

James and Caroline would have two more children—Carolina Louisa, born in 1826, and Martha Ann, born in 1827. By 1827 they were living on two hundred acres five miles from Milledgeville, an indication of his success, but tragedy struck in 1828 when Caroline died at age twenty-five. "For the last 11 years of her life she was a member of the Methodist Episcopal Church and a monument to the profession she had made," according to cemetery records. "She left to mourn with her husband two little daughters." After a suitable period of mourning, Calhoun remarried on February 2, 1830, to Anna V. Williamson, of Greene County, Georgia, who was a close friend of William C. Dawson's wife, Henrietta.[35]

Siren Song of Politics

At age twenty-five the fledgling merchant became a Milledgeville town commissioner, igniting a lifetime passion for politics. In the persuasions of the day, one was either a Troup man or a Clark man, and Calhoun was a Troup man. George M. Troup, a states' rights firebrand, led a faction of the more affluent; his adversary was John Clark, whose followers were farmers and frontiersmen.[36]

Troup in 1824 pressured the federal government to remove the Creek Indians, arguing that it had been more than twenty years since Georgia gave up its claims to territory that would become Alabama and Mississippi in exchange for the government's promise to buy Georgia's remaining Indian lands. The government had done this for other states, but Creeks and Cherokees still held half of Georgia's land. When President James Madison's appointees couldn't extract further concessions from the tribes, they instead negotiated the fraudulent Indian Springs Treaty; the government nullified and replaced it with one affirming Creek possession of their remaining lands. Troup then tangled with the federal government over the nullified treaty and Creek removal. Calhoun and other Troup men viewed President Adams's handling of the treaty as unconstitutional and unprecedented because it reduced the states "to mere provinces" and established a "Splendid National Government."[37]

Calhoun was an up and comer, fraternizing regularly with the town's influential men. Some, like Hines Holt Sr., who had known him since he was a fatherless boy, seemed to be mentoring him. At a Fourth of July celebration in 1826—the all-day celebrations honored Revolutionary War veterans and featured speeches, processions, prayers, and dinner—Calhoun made a toast to Congressman John Forsyth, a fellow champion of states' rights who became governor in 1827. Forsyth gave Calhoun his first political appointment in 1829 as a prison inspector. The Georgia Penitentiary, completed in Milledgeville in 1816, was one of the first in the South. Reformers believed confinement, and not whipping, ear-cropping, or branding, would allow prisoners to contemplate the error of their ways, and prison shops would train them in such vocations as tailoring and blacksmithing. It would also bring in revenue. With eight other

FIGURE 6. In the halls of Georgia's former state house in Milledgeville, Calhoun served as both a senator and representative. Sherry Robinson photo.

inspectors, who governed the penitentiary, Calhoun swore he would not abuse convicts.[38]

Calhoun and two other inspectors wrote in 1829 that "to reform and to deter, to punish rigidly but preserve life, to give trades and industrious habits to those who have been raised in idleness and vice, to produce reimbursement and revenue and other ends of justice and moderation" were praise-worthy goals. However, they noted that punishments often didn't match the crimes; penalties for property crimes were often greater than those for assault. And the cells were in poor repair.[39]

In 1830, as Troup-Clark factionalism subsided, Calhoun ran successfully for state representative. As a freshman legislator he served on the Banking and Penitentiary committees. He won reelection the following year on the States Rights ticket of the Democratic Party.[40] Calhoun joined a legislative body whose members were notable for their individuality—evidence, wrote a German nobleman, "that they had been reared separately and apart from the civilized world."[41]

Lawmakers were bent on hastening the tribes' removal and distributing their lands. In 1829 they extended Georgia's laws over the Cherokees, which meant the state had the right to survey lands occupied or formerly occupied by the Cherokees. After Calhoun took his seat in November 1830, the legislative Committee on the State of the Republic declared that Georgia had jurisdiction over its soil and the right to regulate tribes, and it introduced a bill to divide Creek lands. A House memorial urged the president to relocate the Cherokees to the "wilds of Mississippi," where they would be happier, and register Cherokees willing to sell their improvements and immigrate. Debating as a fireplace in each wall of the two chambers kept them warm, legislators passed a bill authorizing the survey and disposition of land once occupied by Cherokees, along with vacated Creek lands, and called out a military force to protect surveyors and Indian people in peaceful possession of their improvements.[42]

Calhoun added his voice to the vehement rhetoric against the Tariff of 1828, which southerners called the "Tariff of Abominations." Intended to protect northern manufacturing, the tariff was burdensome to the South, which now had to pay more for manufactured goods, as Britain reduced its cotton imports. Calhoun considered the United States Constitution a compact between the states and the federal union; it should be interpreted literally, he believed, and the federal government should carefully avoid trampling any right not surrendered by the states. In the legislature he joined with others in condemning the tariff as "manifestly unconstitutional and unjust." At a Fourth of July celebration in 1828, Calhoun made a toast: "To the national government: you are authorized for your defence to draw on us for our lives, and for your support, on our treasures; but if you draw on us for the support of a protecting tariff, your bills will be returned, noted for non-acceptance, 'Don't tread on me.'"[43]

South Carolina wanted to defy the federal government by nullifying the act, and the Troup party leaned in that direction. Considering Georgia's faceoff over the Indian question and its bitter opposition to the tariff, the state might have supported nullification, but most Georgians firmly supported the union. The Georgia legislature passed resolutions condemning the tariff but otherwise tabled any wild-eyed proposals. In February 1832, Calhoun attended a large antitariff meeting and stated: "Relax not your energies until justice shall resume her place and your violated federal constitution be restored to its original purity." His friend William Dawson attended the meeting, along with a future political ally, Robert Toombs.[44]

In July 1832, the president signed a new tariff bill, reducing some rates but not enough to placate South Carolina. In September Calhoun helped organize a meeting of Baldwin County citizens opposed to the tariff. After a South Carolina convention voted to nullify both tariffs and declare them unenforceable, Georgia held an antitariff convention. Calhoun served on a central committee, and his friends Dawson and Hines Holt Jr., were delegates, but they were swimming against the current. Nullification was still repugnant to Georgians, and even Forsyth came to believe federal authority superseded state authority. The nullification movement died, and the Troup party became the State Rights Party, which later became the Whig Party. Calhoun joined the State Rights Party. Historian Fletcher Green believed that political independence would be a hallmark of Calhoun's career, but Calhoun would always be an ardent southern Whig.[45]

In September 1832 Calhoun was reelected to a third term as state representative. During his first three years, he helped increase appropriations for the University of Georgia. As a member of the Banking Committee, Calhoun urged a more liberal policy of incorporation but more strict supervision of banks by the state; had the legislature acted, it might have avoided the financial disasters to come. On the Penitentiary Committee, Calhoun tried to reorganize the penitentiary according to current reform philosophies, advocating productive labor under close supervision, solitary confinement at night, and trained personnel. And he supported reform of the state constitution. He urged reapportionment on the basis of population and a broader base of voters. In 1832 Calhoun was also a lottery commissioner, supervising drawings of the Milledgeville Street Lottery. Tickets were $10.[46]

In the first thirty-three years of his life, Calhoun became more than a self-made man. Soaring above the poverty of Jefferson County's swamps and the loss of his parents and closest uncle as a young boy, Calhoun managed an education and on his return to Milledgeville, turned his abundant energies to law and business. Friends like Burton Hepburn and Hines Holt Jr. were cut from the same cloth. Calhoun took up the political pennant he would carry in public office for years, and with his prison work exhibited his first stirrings as a reformer.

2

COLUMBUS

At the foot of the Chattahoochee River's falls, where the Spanish once built a mission and fort, the Georgia legislature, on Christmas Eve 1827, located the new "trading town" of Columbus. Months before the sale of lots, nine hundred people were already on site, busy as ants, creating houses, many built on wheels for their eventual move to permanent locations. Established in 1828, Columbus sprouted into a frontier boomtown. In its early days, a dozen springs provided Columbus with good water, and stately groves of trees graced the riverbanks. Governor Forsyth preferred camping there to the town's hotels when he attended the sale of lots in 1828. The river, which forms the Georgia–Alabama border, ran clear and offered a variety of fish; newcomers enjoyed watching Creek fishermen catch shad every spring using bark nets. "Progress" would soon eliminate springs, Indian people, shad, and wilderness, and the Chattahoochee would run muddy. Steamboats coursed up and down the river, carrying cotton downstream and returning with cargo for merchants. Columbus was now the "Queen City of the Chattahoochee."[1]

Within months, new residents—many from Milledgeville, 128 miles away—erected two-story houses, hotels, and shops, and the population of more than seven hundred lived mostly without the benefits of law enforcement. River traffic and prime cotton country made Columbus a major commercial center, and it drew entrepreneurs, speculators, and fortune seekers. In 1828 Mirabeau Buonaparte Lamar, member of a prominent family and future president of the Republic of Texas, established the first newspaper, the *Columbus Enquirer*, and used it to promote the town.[2] The broad streets of Columbus, he wrote, gave the town "an elegant and airy appearance." Before long, it was graced with big grassy parks, a block-long square with Baptist and Methodist churches, and an elegant courthouse square.[3]

In 1832 the *Enquirer* congratulated citizens for creating "a handsome town,

FIGURE 7. "Chutes de la Chattahoutchie" is an 1838 lithograph
by Francis de la Porte. The Columbus Museum, Georgia G.1983.74

FIGURE 8. Captain Basil Hall captured "The Embryo Town of Columbus"
in *Forty Etchings From the Sketches Made by the Camera Lucida, in North America
in 1827 and 1828.* He was amazed to find throngs of settlers awaiting the official
start of the city at auction. Courtesy The Columbus Museum, Georgia;
The Evelyn S. and H. Wayne Patterson Fund G.2007.14

with a population of 1,800 souls" from a "howling wilderness." Three banks were operating, warehouses braced for the next cotton crop, and a bridge across the Chattahoochee was under construction. The town boasted three churches, a theater, a bookstore, a library, and a public garden. Within two more years, prosperity could be measured by the bales of cotton rolling down the street, and "sacks of salt and coffee, hogsheads of sugar, barrels of strong drink and all manner of merchandise" moving along on stout wagons and wheelbarrows, wrote the *Enquirer*.[4]

Calhoun moved to Columbus in 1833 at age thirty-four and became a justice of the peace.[5] Within three years, he had his hands in banking, cotton brokering, retail, transportation, and real estate, and he counted many of the town's leading citizens among his friends and business associates.

Eye for Opportunity

One early incident illustrates the temper of the town Calhoun now called home. On October 14, 1833, future congressman Seaborn Jones[6] rode into town and conversed briefly with business associates before striding into his bank, the Bank of Columbus. He was deep in a discussion of bank affairs when he heard two shots fired nearby, dashed out of the bank without his hat (several witnesses commented on his hatless appearance), and ran toward the victim, Major Joseph T. Camp. A Clark man, Camp had been exchanging written barbs in the newspaper with Colonel John Milton, a Troup man, and Milton heard that Camp had vowed to shoot him in the street. Because Camp had recently killed General Sowell Woolfolk in a duel, Milton had reason to feel threatened. Standing on a Columbus street outside a store, Milton saw Camp coming down the street in his direction. He stepped into the store, picked up a double-barrel gun, and shot Camp in the chest, and, as he fell, shot him again in the back. Jones, a prominent lawyer, successfully defended Milton in court.[7]

Jones's bank was the town's first, opened in 1831, three years after he moved from Milledgeville. Calhoun became a major shareholder while still living in Milledgeville, having bought 300 shares for $15,000; he later increased his position to 350 shares, second only to Jones. Arthur B. Davis was cashier; he would be a city commissioner in 1838, the year Calhoun was mayor. Other shareholders included merchant Hampton Smith, Daniel McDougald, and Samuel K. Hodges, a Columbus warehouseman and Methodist minister.

FIGURE 9. Seaborn Jones was a business associate of James Calhoun for several years in Columbus. Courtesy, Georgia Archives, Small Print collection, spc03–016.

Calhoun became its acting president in 1834.[8] Columbus drew men with an eye for opportunity, wrote historian John H. Martin. The boldest could be found in banking.

The second bank was Farmers' Bank of Chattahoochee. When organizers began selling stock in June 1831, a large crowd gathered early in the morning and rushed the doors. "We have before seen men eager to get hold of money; but here they were possessed with a rage to get rid of it," wrote the *Columbus Democrat*. Two rival groups emerged—one controlled by attorney and civic leader James C. Watson, Daniel McDougald, and Robert Collins, and the other by Judge Eli Shorter, future congressman Alfred Iverson, and Edward Cary.[9] After a struggle, Shorter's group prevailed; Shorter became president, and Cary, a lawyer and a friend of Calhoun's in Milledgeville, was cashier. Undeterred, in 1832 Watson opened a third financial institution, the Insurance Bank of Columbus, and became its president. Calhoun's good friend Burton Hepburn, who had moved from Milledgeville to Columbus to help open the bank, was cashier. Daniel McDougald was a shareholder of this bank too.[10] These were some of the most substantial businessmen in Columbus, and Calhoun would join them in a variety of ventures—all legitimate with one dreadful exception.

McDougald and Hepburn, both in their early thirties, became Calhoun's regular business associates until one killed the other. A native of North Carolina, McDougald moved to Columbus in 1832. There, "his fine abilities and popular manners made him at once a favorite of the people" and one of the shrewdest and most influential members of the legislature, wrote Martin. A big, coarse-looking man with a bald head, McDougald was generous and impulsive. He could count many devoted friends and a number of enemies. McDougald was so charismatic that he once persuaded a New York financier he didn't know to lend him $100,000. Hepburn, a lawyer, merchant, and landowner, like Calhoun, had been an officer in the branch Bank of Darien in Milledgeville. When the newly formed Russell County, across the river in Alabama, was ready for a bridge to Columbus, McDougald, Hepburn, Robert Collins and Watson owned the land for the western abutment. With the blessings of the Alabama legislature they built that portion of the bridge and split tolls with the county. Georgia and Alabama fought for years over ownership of the bridge's western abutment, and the court ultimately decided in Georgia's favor.[11]

Before he left Milledgeville, Calhoun also plunged into the shipping business in Columbus. In June 1830 he became part owner of a steamboat, the *Georgian*, which arrived in December to a booming cannon and cheering citizens. It was a beautiful boat—120 tons and 114 feet long. His co-owners were Seaborn Jones, John Fontaine, and six other Columbus men. Fontaine was a successful merchant, planter, and manufacturer known for "conscientiousness and uprightness in all his dealings." River navigation was still hazardous, and in December 1833 the *Georgian* struck a snag and sank on its way upriver with a load of dry goods and groceries for Columbus merchants. The following year Calhoun, Hepburn, and Fontaine partnered with other investors in another handsome steamboat, the *Eloisa*. Such boats, wrote the *Columbus Enquirer*, were "evidences of our prosperity, and we shall be glad to see them and many more plying our river." Weeks later, fire consumed the elegant *Eloisa* and her valuable cargo of cotton and furniture on her first voyage down the river from Columbus.[12]

In 1835, Calhoun organized Calhoun & Bass Shipping Company with young Charles L. Bass.[13] Their line of boats operated on the Chattahoochee and Coosa Rivers to Rome and the Gulf. Bass was another friend from Milledgeville who was an officer of the Bank of Columbus. In Bass, Calhoun found not only a worthy business partner but also his political double. A fellow member of the State Rights Party, Bass made a toast that year: "Nullification and State Rights, may they spread like the Asian Cholera."[14]

Calhoun was buying and shipping up to ten thousand bales of cotton a year to markets in New York and Liverpool. He was the first to ship cotton in 1835—three hundred bales aboard two barges and traveled regularly to deliver cotton to customers in New York. The next year, "the House of J. S. Calhoun & Co." bought the entire crop of Sterling Bass, his partner's father, for 15.25 cents a pound. "Our friends at Macon will have to bid up, or the planters Beyond the Flint will gang this way," taunted the *Enquirer*.[15]

J. S. Calhoun & Co., at the corner of Oglethorpe and Randolph Streets, advertised bacon, bagging, hemp, rope, sugar, coffee, flour, whiskey, molasses, lard, pork, beef, mackerel from New York and New Orleans, and dry goods, which they would sell for cash or "on time for approved paper." Calhoun's partner was Edward Cary until mid-1835, when Cary withdrew, and Calhoun merged the business with Calhoun & Bass. In October Thomas C. Evans, a future alderman and legislator, became a partner. During 1836 the store offered twenty-five thousand pounds of Georgia cured ham and two hundred barrels of stone lime, "which will be sold low for cash." Calhoun joined McDougald, Alfred Iverson, Asa Bates, Hodges, Fontaine, and Smith to buy the wharves at the Port of Columbus. By then Calhoun owned, individually or in partnerships, at least thirty-two lots in Columbus alone.[16]

In early 1836 Columbus was booming. Heavily laden steamboats—one of them was the *Anna Calhoun*, which Calhoun named for his wife—arrived and departed "while the wagons of the planters have rolled in without number," the *Enquirer* reported. The *Anna Calhoun* was a 133-ton paddle wheeler built the year before. Calhoun & Bass added a new steamer, the *Hyperion*, to their line between Columbus and Apalachicola, Florida. "The Hyperion was built expressly for this trade, and in point of strength, is not surpassed by any boat on the river. She is supplied with a water tight snag room, and a fire engine and hose, that will reach to any part of the boat, which can be instantly applied in case of fire," the advertisement said.[17]

Down the Chattahoochee in Apalachicola, Florida, Calhoun partnered in a warehouse and commission operation that received cotton shipped to New York or New Orleans. He was also doing business in St. Joseph, Florida. Calhoun was among businessmen from Columbus, New York, and Charleston who contracted to build sixty fire-proof brick buildings in Apalachicola in 1836. Others included James C. Watson, Edward Cary, William H. Harper, Alfred Iverson, Moore & Tarver, Burton Hepburn, and Daniel McDougald. He was selling lots at New Echota, a planned town in northern Georgia, in partnership with John Bethune, former Georgia surveyor general and future Columbus city treasurer and alderman; future *Enquirer* publisher Thomas Ragland; and Samuel Rockwell.[18]

This would have been more than enough for most businessmen, but Calhoun's energies seemed unlimited, and he was always driving toward the future. When construction began on the Western and Atlantic Railroad, the Chattahoochee Railroad and Banking Company in 1836 planned a line to connect with it. (Because the market for railroad securities was thin, many states allowed railroads to function as banks to finance construction.) Although it was later said to be a fraud, never intending to build a railroad, the Who's Who list of principals and investors argues otherwise. Its officers were James Watson, president; Wiley Williams, cashier; Allen G. Bass (Charles's brother), teller; and as bookkeeper, John E. Davis. Directors were Calhoun, Watson, future alderman and state representative John W. Campbell, hotelier Nicholas Howard, Judge William Mitchell, James R. Jones, and state senator and town alderman John L. Lewis. The company proposed that the city issue $750,000 in bonds, which it would borrow to build the railroad. And in 1836 Calhoun incorporated the Columbus Canal and Water Company with Charles Bass, Alfred Iverson, and Edward Cary, and the legislature authorized the company to build a canal on the Chattahoochee above Columbus, dam the river, and supply water.[19]

Unfortunate Bank

An unusual transaction ruffled the community in early March 1836: Calhoun and Eli Shorter swapped banks. Shorter got the better deal. It began with disgruntled shareholder Albert Iverson selling his stock in the troubled Farmers' Bank of the Chattahoochee to Calhoun and "other gentlemen of large capital in this place." Calhoun became president and Bass, cashier; Calhoun, Edward Cary, and Thomas Evans were elected to the board of directors. The three largest shareholders were Calhoun, Burton Hepburn, and Bass. Under the "able management of Calhoun (whose financial talents and business habits are too well known to the community to need commendation) we have every assurance that the Chattahoochee Bank will again be put upon a solid basis," said the *Georgia Journal*. The *Southern Recorder* chimed in: "We consider the

FIGURE 10. This bank note was issued by the Bank of Columbus, which was
the town's first bank when it opened in 1831. Calhoun was a major shareholder.

President of the Bank one of the most accomplished merchants in the state."
The *Enquirer* had confidence in the "future management of this hitherto unfortunate Bank." It was capitalized in specie (gold and silver) at $180,000, which
Daniel McDougald, president of the Insurance Bank of Columbus, agreed
to redeem. Simultaneously, Calhoun, Seaborn Jones, and Samuel K. Hodges
withdrew from the Bank of Columbus and sold all their stock. Eli Shorter and
his associates took their places as directors.[20]

Banks then were a relatively new development and far riskier enterprises
than they are today. They were slow in coming to Georgia's interior, so until 1818 merchants accepted deposits and issued their own notes, script, and
change bills for customers. The federal government didn't yet provide paper
money, so banks issued banknotes, which came in all shapes, colors, sizes, and
designs. Georgia banks might back their notes with gold and silver, but typically they used their own deposits; there was no standard. Banknotes usually
circulated at a discount, or less than their face value. Businessmen had to keep
up with news and rumors to avoid holding the notes of overextended banks.
If they learned that a bank's financial condition had weakened, the discount
would increase. Speculation was rampant. Banks also used banknotes (and not
deposits as they do now) to finance their loans, so the more notes they printed,
the more they could lend.

The US Treasury issued coins, as did private entities, but because coins
were in short supply, banks and some businesses issued paper money in small
denominations so that they could make change. These "change bills" also be-

came a currency of sorts if others accepted them. So "every local economy had a distinctive currency which originated from scores of businessmen who held disparate assets—and consciences," wrote historian Lynn Willoughby Ware. In the Apalachicola–Chattahoochee valley, a variety of paper bills, along with foreign and American coins, made up the local currency. Spanish pesos and reales and English sterling pounds circulated, as did French, Scandinavian, and German coins. Buyers and sellers had to calculate in multiple currencies. Merchants kept tables to help them convert and tracked debits and credits in ledgers, settling up once a year, at the end of cotton season.

Now consider how this worked in the Southern cotton economy. Each year when cotton came to market, brokers shipping cotton received bills of exchange, foreign and Northern buyers' assurance they would pay in the future. Brokers sold these bills of exchange to banks and used the money to pay planters for their cotton. The planters would then pay local merchants who had extended them credit for supplies. The merchants then paid their own suppliers. So banking was not only seasonal, it also depended on the price of cotton and the yield. Calhoun, as merchant, cotton broker, shipper, and banker, was squarely in the middle of this merry commerce.[21]

Wholesome Laws

Calhoun would have found the politics in Muscogee County as exciting as the business climate. To his delight, the Troup faction dominated. In 1834, Calhoun and newspaperman Mirabeau Lamar were vice presidents of the newly organized State Rights Auxiliary Association.

Lamar, former personal secretary to Troup, believed passionately in state rights and was also a staunch nullifier who thought states had the right to nullify any federal law they regarded as unconstitutional. The association counted among its members some of the town's best-known men, including a few of Calhoun's business associates, although his frequent partners Hepburn, McDougald, and Watson were all Democrats, evidence that, to Calhoun, business was business.[22]

In July 1835, the State Rights Party submitted Calhoun's name for both the town commission and state representative. The *Enquirer* called him a "public spirited citizen who, during the business season, gave an impulse to the commerce of our Town, and long prices for the short staple of the Farmers." In

October 1835, Calhoun was elected state representative, Burton Hepburn was elected state senator, and merchant John Fontaine was elected mayor. "No expense was spared to entertain and care for the voters," wrote John E. Lamar years later. "Carriages were sent out, two hotels were opened, one for each party; good tables spread, free bars with waiters to attend to their every want, faithful guards to watch over them, and at the proper time a procession was formed and all marched to the polls, with safe watchers to see they were not molested, and then all voted as free men."[23]

FIGURE 11. Mirabeau B. Lamar, in an engraving by J. Sartain, was a newspaper editor in Columbus, Georgia, before becoming president of the Texas Republic. Image 1987/097–1, Courtesy of Texas State Library and Archives Commission.

As a legislator, Calhoun was all about business—often his own. Nobody then worried about conflicts of interest. He introduced bills to incorporate Planters' Bank of Columbus, authorize a lottery to raise $25,000 to build a Masonic hall in Columbus, incorporate the Columbus Wharf Company, incorporate a railroad company and authorize construction from Columbus to a point on the Flint or Ocmulgee Rivers, amend the charter of the Bank of Columbus, authorize trustees of the Muscogee Academy to sell a portion of the Female Academy lots, and appropriate money for the improvement of the Chattahoochee River for navigation.[24]

As 1836 was ending, the *Enquirer* editorialized that "in the great flood of prosperity that has poured in upon the city," property was well protected but not lives. The newspaper wanted city fathers who would enact and enforce "wholesome laws." And it wanted the officials to maintain "a free bridge to Alabama planters and traders" and pass an ordinance confirming the legislature's charter of a railroad with banking privileges. The *Enquirer* endorsed Calhoun to become the second mayor of Columbus, and he prevailed.[25]

Calhoun was now a tycoon with interests in every aspect of business the booming city had to offer. Nothing, it seemed, was beyond his intellect, his interest, or his financial reach. That would change.

CREEK WAR

Many thousands of Native people once inhabited the region that became Georgia and Alabama. They lived in groups, each with its own language and culture. Years of war with white interlopers and disease reduced their numbers, weaker groups merged with stronger groups, and they often relocated. Together, they formed a loose confederacy that the English called the Creeks for one particular group on the Ochese Creek near present-day Macon. Creek country lay south of the Cherokees, east of the Choctaws and Chickasaws, and west of the English settlements. The Upper Creeks, the dominant group, lived on the Coosa and Tallapoosa Rivers. The Lower Creeks lived along the Chattahoochee and Flint Rivers. By 1825, the Creek Nation numbered around twenty-two thousand, organized into about seventy towns of several hundred people each and governed by a *micco*, or headman.[1]

Creeks were hunters and farmers who grew or gathered maize, squash, beans, sunflower seeds, and honey. A matrilineal society, Creeks traced their descent through their mothers and belonged to their mother's clan. They grew up in clan compounds or neighborhoods close to their mothers, her sisters, and other female relatives. Women headed the households, managed property, and did the farming. By 1800 the Creek hunting grounds were exhausted, and they depended more on farming, adopting the plow, spinning wheel, and loom. They also cultivated a taste for sweet potatoes, poultry, pork, and beef. Most were subsistence farmers but a few owned large farms and even cotton plantations. In 1818 they codified and wrote down their laws, but despite all their efforts to acculturate, white newcomers would always covet the tribes' fine agricultural lands.[2]

The booming cotton market devoured new acreage at the same time the lottery triggered a land rush. In some places settlers moved onto land still occupied by Creeks, built their homes nearby, and began clearing forests and plowing, which deprived the Native people of game, nuts, and china briar roots they used to make flour; the newcomers' nets and fish traps harvested fish from the rivers. After suffering a crop failure in 1831, hungry Creeks tried to hunt, but game was scarce, and smallpox added to their misery. Living on roots and bark, they begged at homes in Columbus. "It is really painful to me to see the wretched creatures wandering about the streets, haggard and naked," said a letter writer. Columbus was edgy with fear, and citizens agitated for Indian removal.[3]

In the treaty of March 24, 1832, the Creeks ceded to the United States their remaining 5.2 million acres in eastern Alabama, between the Coosa and Tallapoosa Rivers and the state's eastern border. The government allotted 320 acres to the head of each Creek family and 640 acres to ninety chiefs and headmen. They could sell their allotments and move west to land the government promised beyond the Mississippi River or keep their property and remain in Alabama. They had five years to decide. Meanwhile, the government promised to protect tribal lands from encroachment by intruders. The Creeks understandably believed they could stay, but the government really intended for them to sell and move to a new reservation in the west.

In Columbus, adjacent to the Creeks' waning territory, citizens saw only glorious opportunities. Land speculators multiplied like gnats in the summer. "Lawyers, preachers, doctors, merchants and bankers were all buying plots, grants and soldiers' warrants and selling them at an advance," wrtes historian George Gilman Smith. It was easy to get credit from the town's new banks. Census takers greased the wheels by identifying men as heads of families and owners of land, contrary to Creek tradition.[4]

Speculators

Seduced by the land frenzy, Calhoun jumped in. Less than two weeks after the treaty signing, on April 5, 1832, twenty men, led by banker Eli Shorter and attorney Seaborn Jones, capitalized the Columbus Land Company to acquire Creek lands. Calhoun, still living in Milledgeville, was one of the original investors. They were all well-known businessmen, such as attorney and future congressman Alfred Iverson, attorney and merchant Edward Cary, and cotton broker and warehouseman M. W. Perry.[5] Investors each put up $500 with the understanding that their money would be used to buy land, each would receive an equal share, and their stake would be refunded. Shorter and his partners,

Benjamin P. Tarver, M. W. Perry, and their agent John S. Scott, ran day-to-day operations. Others, like James C. Watson, Daniel McDougald, and Burton Hepburn, formed their own combinations to buy land. "Events . . . do not warrant a belief that the white contracting parties or the influences that controlled them were concerned with an honest performance of (the treaty's) terms for the protection of the Indians," wrote historian Grant Foreman. "If the government had deliberately sought to accomplish the complete ruin and demoralization of the Creeks, a more vicious measure could hardly have been devised" than to let them sell their lands utterly unprotected by the government. Businessmen sent agents into Alabama to establish stores, sell to Creeks on credit, and, after the Creeks were in debt, demand payment in bonds for title to their lands.[6]

When the War Department decided to buy Creek allotments to expedite removal, Columbus speculators who had already spent heavily on bonds objected. President Andrew Jackson sent Francis Scott Key to Alabama in 1833 to find common ground among conflicting interests. Key saw the speculators' underlings at work among the Creeks and warned that speculators had acquired property rights for a pittance that gave them possession until the government issued deeds. He predicted the speculators would present bogus receipts for whiskey and other goods and exchange the debts for land. Most of

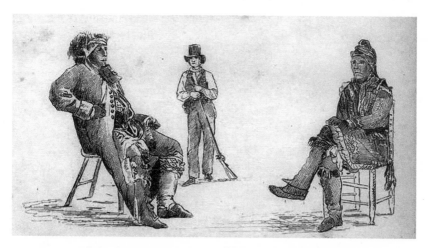

FIGURE 12. "Chiefs of the Creek Nation and a Georgian Squatter" by Captain Basil Hall. Although drawn separately, the figures are accurate in showing the Creeks shadowed by squatters who wanted their land. Courtesy, Alabama Department of Archives and History.

the Creeks were starving. Few had harvested any corn, and nearly all had sold their land two or three times over. "I met crowds of them going to Columbus with bundles of fodder on their heads to sell, and saw numbers of them in the streets where they exchanged everything they carried for whiskey," Key wrote.[7]

In early 1834, with surveys complete, the Creeks could legally sell their land, but the Jackson administration refused to recognize previous transactions, so thousands had to be redone by the government's certifying agents— General John W. A. Sanford, James Bright, Leonard Tarrant, and Dr. Robert W. McHenry, who were directed to vet the contracts. As soon as the agents opened their doors, buyers filled their offices. The government's minimum was $1.25 an acre, unless the agent believed a lower price was justifiable. McHenry soon reported that speculators were making a brazen, organized effort to deceive agents and "introduce the wrong Indian to certify or approve contracts."[8]

Speculators had a large bag of tricks and a posse of minions to secure land. They paid Creeks to tell the agent a certain parcel was theirs and then they took back their money. They paid in banknotes of dubious value. They employed "strikers" who married Creek women and feigned friendships in order to claim land. If Creeks resisted selling, the speculators found more cooperative individuals. Shopkeepers and whiskey sellers offered easy credit, and Creeks paid their debts with land. The most ruthless land grabbers forced the Creeks from their cabins and stole their crops and livestock; tribal members disappeared or were found dead. Another tactic was to offer high prices for the land to drive off other bidders and then refuse to comply with the contract. The judge would then order a resale, where they bid again at lower prices. In this way Calhoun's partner, John G. Worsham, a state representative and Baldwin County deputy sheriff, bought the reserves allotted to five Creeks. As long as a single parcel was left, the speculators discouraged the Creeks from emigrating. Desperate, some Creeks began to steal from whites; others asked to live with the Cherokees. A few Creek men went into the woods and hanged themselves with grapevines.[9]

Secretary of War Lewis Cass believed that once the contract was certified, the Creeks could do what they wanted with their money. Agents shouldn't complain about fraud, he said, because the Indians were at fault for allowing themselves to be swindled. When Seaborn Jones, now a congressman, received a list of land buyers (Calhoun appears on the list) in April 1834, he told Cass that some of the contracts belonged to his friends and acquaintances.[10] Jones had frequently advocated for them with the War Department and that year received $500 for his services from the Columbus Land Company, which he cofounded. Agent Sanford wrote indignantly: "What! A member of Congress paid for the indiscriminate defence of a landjobbing co. thro right and thro wrong.—paid, Sir, to tell or disguise the truth, to disclose or discolor facts so as to misguide one of the Departments of Government in its investigations."[11]

"Steal all we can"

In October 1834, the Columbus Land Company began to auction 320-acre plots of "the most valuable land in the Creek Territory adapted to the culture of cotton, corn, etc." It was well watered, in healthy locations, and convenient to market, stated the advertisement. Interested parties could apply to the executive committee: Edward Cary, John G. Worsham, and Thomas Hoxey, all friends of Calhoun. Shorter and his partners ran similar ads. However, by year end, Columbus Land Company was in trouble, and the schemes began to unravel. In December 1834, investor James Wadsworth warned in a newspaper advertisement against trading for his promissory note to the company because it couldn't prove the titles, and he was "determined not to pay."[12] Also in trouble was Farmers' Bank of Chattahoochee. Bank president Eli Shorter and his businesses ran up debts of $55,080, nearly half the bank's capital. Late in 1833 bank directors fired him and cut off his use of the bank's money. In a furious exchange of letters published by local newspapers, bank shareholder Alfred Iverson wrote that Shorter was "notorious for his love of money." Shorter had furnished nearly all the money for his various partnerships to buy Creek land.[13]

Shorter, who was also a judge and merchant, pressured his subordinates in January 1835 to close contracts. Indians who refused to sell, he rationalized, were better off trusting white buyers like himself without receiving a dollar than be "cheated out of their rights" by the government. On March 1 Shorter left Columbus Land Company men at the agency and had "four hundred Indians hid out all around the hill." He instructed: "Camp your Indians out of sight of the road. You need give yourself no trouble about the value of the land; I will arrange all that. Stealing is the order of the day; and out of the host of Indians at the agency, I do not think there were ten true holders of land," he wrote. The same day, Shorter's partner, merchant Benjamin Tarver, wrote, "There is nothing going on at this time but stealing of land with about

FIGURE 13. Opothle Yoholo, a Creek chief,
was drawn by Charles Bird King and published
in 1838. Library of Congress.

fifty Indians. Pay them $10 or $5 when certified, and get all the balance back, and 400 or 500 contracts certified with fifty Indians, is all the game." He later wrote, "Hurrah, boys! Here goes it! Let's steal all we can. I shall go for it, or get no lands! Now or never!"[14]

In February 1835, Creek Headman Opothle Yaholo and six other headmen complained to Cass about the frauds and asked for an investigation. Angry Creeks, determined to stay, were beginning to fight back, and newspapers stoked growing white hysteria with reports, not entirely true, of ambushes, massacres, and stolen slaves. "It is high time these blood-thirsty beings should be hunted up and made to suffer for their crimes," the *Columbus Enquirer* thundered. Land speculator Daniel McDougald, in his capacity as general in the state militia (a title he would hold from 1832 to 1849), assured the governor that he would promptly "render such aid as I can command to put down these worthless savage robbers." He warned that they must expect more frequent outrages "and of a more aggravated character" unless the federal government adopted energetic measures for their removal west of the Mississippi. "They are a wandering tribe destitute of all the comforts of life," he wrote, without acknowledging his own role in their destitution. "The Indians are favourably disposed towards immigration and nothing is necessary to consummate this most desirable object but a decided movement on the part of the government." McDougald would begin selling his properties that year.

On February 28, 1835, citizens gathered at the Columbus courthouse for a large meeting chaired by Calhoun's friend Dr. Thomas Hoxey. Burton Hepburn proposed a memorial to the president on "the state of our relations with the Indians and the probable consequences which may result from delay in removing them to their destined homes beyond the Mississippi." Calhoun, Hepburn, McDougald, and two others drafted the memorial and recommended former Indian agent John W. A. Sanford as emigrating agent.[15] Sanford, now living in Columbus and allied with some of the speculators, informed Cass that Shorter and one or two others "had the chief direction" of the Columbus Land Company, "wielding a capital of about $150,000 in cash . . . No frauds were practiced by this company on the Indians but by some of the managers on distant stockholders, a part of whom, seeing how things were going, sold out their shares for cost, losing all the interest that would have accrued on the money paid in." If there were profits, they were small, he said. When chiefs of the Upper Creeks reluctantly resolved to emigrate, the government contracted with Sanford's company to serve as emigrating agent. His partners included such familiar players as Alfred Iverson, James C. Watson, and McDougald.[16]

Alabama governor John Gayle asked the Secretary of War to send soldiers to maintain order. "I entertain no doubt that the outrages which have been committed by the Indians upon the innocent settlers and the innocent travelers have been provoked by the injuries they have received from the speculators and if they alone could be selected as the victims of revenge, they would meet but little sympathy from the honest part of the community," he wrote. The *Enquirer* protested that all of the town's residents were branded as land pirates and yet some acted in good faith.[17]

On August 25, 1835, Creeks wrote the president that they would like to begin moving west but couldn't sell their land and needed money to move and start again. The president suggested appointing another special agent, and Secretary Cass chose Colonel John B. Hogan, of Mobile, to investigate. Hogan reversed contracts and, after being vilified in the Columbus press, the incriminating letters were published.[18] Shorter and his fellow buyers, including Calhoun, protested to Cass in October that they had acted according to terms of the treaty and instructions from the agents. There were no problems, they said, until February, when Creeks, growing anxious about their impending departure, sold a great deal of land, and many contracts were made and certified with certain individuals and companies, which caused others to complain. "Thousands of innocent persons have purchased and paid for their lands, built their houses and opened plantations; and if those titles are thus to be assailed, a scene of confusion and ruin will ensue discreditable to the government, and too intolerable to be borne," they wrote. Reliance on Indian testimony was illegal in Alabama, they said, and because of the Creeks'"present degraded and fallen state . . . no confidence can be placed in their veracity, especially when their interest is at stake." They urged Cass to submit their contracts to the president for approval.[19]

A month later, Shorter and his cronies complained to the president about Cass's "mistaken opinions and policy." Transactions had gone well, "the Indians had gold and were selling rapidly" and looking forward to their journey west, "when a hungry and disappointed company of the most inveterate speculators in the nation" (a rival group in Alabama) leveled charges of fraud. In two short months, contracts between "hundreds and thousands of substantial and honest farmers" and the Indians were thrown into doubt. Now the farmers were afraid to continue improvements and others were reluctant to buy. "Further delay is almost certain ruin; for some of us have nearly our all at stake."[20] They wrote again to Cass claiming the chiefs, influenced by white men, made false allegations. "The Indians are not now what they once have been, or what you believe them to be. There are few 'respectable Indians' in the whole nation. They have lost their original character, and have sunk into a state of degradation of which you have no conception." The Columbus men were outraged that Cass could "treat as trifles contracts solemnly made" and "large sums of money actually paid." They adamantly denied "fraud in any contract in which any of us have any manner of interest."[21]

Great Alarm

The Columbus Guards entered the state's service in December 1835 under Major General Daniel McDougald. Speculators Robert A. Ware and Burton Hepburn were officers. Calhoun's close friend Hines Holt and business partner Charles Bass also signed up, as did his two future sons-in-law. Calhoun is conspicuously absent from the list, probably owing to the press of business.[22] McDougald chaired a big meeting on January 19, 1836, at which Calhoun presented resolutions for the safety and protection of Columbus and Georgia's southwestern frontier and proposed asking the governor for troops and requesting that a citizen-supported volunteer force be accepted for service. He joined a committee to organize citizens to guard the city and became one of the citizen guards. McDougald wrote Governor William Schley: "The citizens of Columbus and the adjoining country are in great alarm. Several valuable citizens have fallen today in an engagement with the Indians about fifteen miles below this place. We are in want of guns. Will you furnish me with three hundred muskets and whatever other munitions of war you may have at your disposal?"[23]

Forty or so armed Creeks—a messenger warned of five hundred—crossed the Chattahoochee at Bryant's Ferry, fifteen miles below Columbus. On January 26, a small detachment led by John H. Watson, son of speculator James Watson, pursued them into a ravine, exchanged fire, and retreated without retrieving the bodies of two dead. A larger party descended the river on the *Anna Calhoun* and returned with the bodies. The Creeks scattered. "Too much praise cannot be bestowed on our fellow citizen Judge Calhoun, for his praiseworthy tender of the steam boat *Anna Calhoun*, to convey forces to the assistance of our suffering fellow citizens below," wrote the *Enquirer*.[24]

McDougald wrote again to Governor Schley that residents were fleeing, "and a great alarm pervades the whole country." The same day Calhoun wrote a pointed letter to Schley saying they were disappointed that his knowledge of "the many and continued acts of aggression by the Indians upon our frontier" had not prompted his action to prevent hostilities in Columbus, and now two respected citizens were dead. "Last night the steamer *Anna Calhoun* with a company of men hastened to the battleground and returned this morning with the bodies of the two killed." McDougald ordered more volunteers, "but what are we to do without arms and ammunition?" McDougald subsequently appointed Calhoun commissary; his boats, especially the swift *Anna Calhoun*, would see more service in the war. The town's two banks quickly made $5,000 credit available to him as a loan to the state. On February 1, McDougald met Eneah Micco, his brother Efau Emathla, and other Lower Creek town chiefs, who agreed to keep their young men from entering Georgia and committing depredations and to arrest and bring marauders to justice. McDougald promised that Creek horses taken to Georgia would be restored. The chiefs' promises eased tensions, and McDougald discharged troops from two counties, stationed remaining men near Bryant's Ferry, and bought weapons.[25]

The negotiations bought some time, but crowds of speculators dogged agent Hogan's every move. He could see anger festering among the southernmost Lower Creeks, who had ties to Florida Seminoles. Every Creek man attended council fires armed and ready for battle. The mixed bloods among them who could read and write kept them informed of the Seminoles' successes in their Florida war. Fear spreading along the Chattahoochee River Valley prompted settlers from Russell and Barbour Counties in Alabama, across from Columbus, to petition their governor for troops. Two of the petitioners were Columbus Land Company members Anderson Abercrombie and Edward Cary. McDougald warned, "A war with the Creeks is inevitable."[26]

Citizens met again on April 25 to discuss the "numerous aggressions upon the property of citizens of Georgia, and their inhuman massacre of several unoffending individuals," and Shorter and McDougald addressed them at length. They wanted McDougald to command the Georgia troops, but Governor Schley appointed the more level-headed Sanford to the command and declared that if McDougald crossed the Chattahoochee in temporary command, he would be arrested. In Alabama, authorities agreed with James Belser, editor of the *Montgomery Advertiser*, who wrote: "The Creek war is all a humbug. It is a base and diabolical scheme, devised by interested men, to keep an ignorant race of people from maintaining their just rights, and to deprive them of the small remaining pittance placed under their control, through the munificence of the government."[27]

The Creek rebellion boiled over on May 5, 1836, when warriors overran Glennville, Alabama, and attacked homesteads and communities in the area, burning structures, killing livestock, and capturing slaves. Two days later, Calhoun, then in Russell County, Alabama, signed onto a letter to Major General Gilbert Shearer describing the Creeks' murder of a young man. "The Indians have assumed a bold and decided hostile attitude and have avowed their determination to drive out every man from the nation or murder them." Families below the old Columbus-Montgomery Federal Road were fleeing to Georgia, leaving their crops, livestock, and belongings. Without action, they feared the hostilities would expand and "require much blood and treasure to subdue it." Cosigners included Calhoun's friends Robert Alexander, Edward Cary, William H. Mitchell, and Thomas Hoxey. The editor of the newspaper carrying the story was less sympathetic. There was abundant evidence that "the Indians are not the only persons at fault," he wrote. In Creek country were "unprincipled and avaricious adventurers who it is well known have cheated and defrauded the Indians out of the last foot of their paternal soil, and who ... would be willing to see them driven in poverty, ignominy and wretchedness from the homes (or rather the graves) of their forefathers, and even to be butchered like beasts of prey, and totally exterminated."[28]

As the Lower Creek hostilities, led by Neah Emathla and Eneah Micco, burned across the area, settlers and slaves fled toward Montgomery or Columbus. At the *Enquirer*, editor Samuel Flournoy angrily blamed Hogan and even threatened him. The *Enquirer* stubbornly maintained that Hogan's investigation and the resulting refusal of Creeks to leave were at the heart of the conflict, not anger at speculators. On May 8 former Creek agent John Crowell sent word that Eneah Micco said his people would fight; they urged Crowell to warn Columbus. In the next several weeks, Creeks destroyed farms and plantations below the federal road, killed livestock, tortured and killed settlers, carried off slaves, waylaid stagecoaches, and severed communications between Columbus and Montgomery. Word of the conflict drew more Creeks, and they attacked larger settlements, pillaging shops and homes, which yielded more guns. They hid supplies in the swamps.[29]

A slave who escaped the Creeks said mixed-blood firebrand Jim Henry, who was raiding near Columbus, had three hundred men, and they had amassed money, plunder, and slaves intending to join the Seminoles in Florida. Henry was known to Calhoun, having clerked for three years with merchants Stewart & Fontaine; for a time he was a striker for their land acquisitions. The son of a Chehaw Indian woman and a Scottish trader, Henry was educated at Asbury Methodist Mission School near Fort Mitchell and described as intelligent and well dressed. He was about twenty years old. The *Enquirer* considered Henry "one of the most troublesome and active of the hostile Indians in the neighborhood of Columbus." The *Columbus Herald* wrote that Henry and his men, "all like himself choking for the blood of white men, has been prowling the nation like a hungry wolf, and committing depredations wherever he went."[30]

On May 15, Creeks stormed the village of Roanoke, south of Columbus, burning every building but one and killing twelve people. Warriors fired on two of Calhoun's boats; the *Georgian* got away, but they killed the pilot of the *Hyperion* and wounded the engineer and one or two others. The boat drifted to the Georgia shore, and the passengers and crew escaped. The *Columbus Sentinel* charged that the rich, who had everything to lose, were uninvolved in the town's defense, while the poor and volunteers were defending everyone's lives and property. The newspaper urged the governor to force every man from his warm feather bed to serve in the militia. At the *Enquirer*, Flournoy countered that the wealthy (he could have been speaking for Calhoun) had shouldered their share of responsibilities and "engaged in almost every expedition."[31]

Two thousand refugees streamed into Columbus, already crowded with speculators, volunteers, and regular troops, and occupied any available building. On rumors of attack, citizens headed for Calhoun's unfinished hotel, the Oglethorpe House. For weeks, many women and children spent the night there and returned home the next day. When President Jackson ordered General Winfield Scott to take charge of operations against the Seminoles in Florida and the Creeks in Georgia, the Oglethorpe House became Scott's military headquarters and barracks. Scott was technically in command, but Brigadier General Thomas S. Jesup got to the field first. With help from sixteen hundred Upper Creek warriors under Opothle Yaholo and Jim Boy, Jesup's forces, by the end of June, captured or killed all the hostiles' leading headmen. Jim Henry, badly wounded, was captured. (He would later become a Methodist minister in Oklahoma.) Jesup started the first sixteen hundred Creeks on their journey to Indian Territory on July 2, 1836, some of the men in chains, women weeping as they walked or rode in wagons. "To see the remnant of a once mighty people fettered and chained together forced to depart from the land of their fathers into a country unknown to them, is of itself sufficient to move the stoutest heart," wrote the *Montgomery Advertiser*. Except for isolated actions, the war was over. Removal continued through 1836, and white parasites preyed on them until the very end. Ultimately, 17,798 Creeks, including 3,089 who voluntarily left before September 1835, relocated.[32]

"Difficulties between land speculators"

Now it was time to sort out the land purchases. "I would prefer to fight all the Indian warriors in the Creek Nation [than] have any agency in settling the difficulties between the land speculators of this country," Jesup wrote. He allowed the friendly chiefs to reclaim more than 200,000 acres that were fraudulently purchased from them and resell them on August 28, 1836, to James C. Watson and Company for $75,000. Some of Watson's partners got back land they had lost and for a lot less money, 37.5 cents an acre. Calhoun wasn't a member of Watson's company; he and Worsham had six contracts. When the War Department sent two more commissioners, T. Hartley Crawford and Alfred Balch, to conduct yet another investigation, they found "acts that make the blood of a just man mount to his cheeks for shame that he and the perpetrators of them belong to the same community." If the Indians had been treated honestly, Balch concluded, they would probably have departed peacefully in spring of 1835. During this investigation, Seaborn Jones represented the Alabama company, Thomas G. Gordon was Calhoun's attorney, and James C. Watson represented himself and others. Calhoun, Irwin Lawson, and others argued that the Watson contract was made "in a private room, and after the hour of midnight" with little notice to competing buyers or Indians. Alabama speculators argued that the chiefs had no right to sell land for their people. Calhoun and others said they bought Creek lands believing the Indians had a right to sell.[33]

The commissioners recommended rejecting the Watson contract, and Watson appealed to the secretary of war. The president approved as long as the Indian landowners approved. Watson then tried to include holders of second contracts, which were less tainted by fraud. By April 1837, his group included all the principal Columbus speculators, their Alabama allies, and many influential Indian traders, but not dissidents Calhoun and Lawson. The Shorter group reached a separate compromise. Joel R. Poinsett, President Van Buren's secretary of war, again investigated. In May 1839, there was a compromise. Patents to all the lands in question would be issued to Watson's company, which would relinquish land contracted by the Alabama group and settle half-and-half with everyone else. The Creek chiefs and Poinsett signed off, and President Van Buren approved nearly all of the contracts. The Creeks received $890,400 for 774,400 acres. About 209,920 acres, nearly a tenth of the lands covered by the Creek allotments, were partitioned among the speculators. Worsham and Calhoun

FIGURE 14. "The Great White Father,"
drawn in 1830 by Thomas Nast, captures
the relationship between the southeastern
tribes and President Andrew Jackson. It was
published in *Harper's Weekly*.

ultimately received 21,979 acres.
By comparison, Shorter's land
company held 312,574 acres.
Shorter personally held about
fifty thousand acres and sold
about half at a profit of 62 percent
before he died on December 14,
1836, of "bilious pleurisy."[34] Calhoun and Bass submitted claims
of $15,000 for damages suffered
during Creek hostilities, which
Congress disallowed along with
all other such claims.[35]

Not one speculator was ever
prosecuted except in the court
of public opinion, and there the
judgment was harsh. In a memorial to Congress in 1836, 640 citizens of East Alabama and West
Georgia blamed land companies
for the war. Citizens vented their
anger for the most part at Eli
Shorter and Benjamin Tarver as
the leading "land pirates" and war

mongers and for sullying the reputation of Columbus. "While the American
people generally were convinced in the 1830s that it was the destiny of the
Indian to be removed from the path of the white man's advance, they believed
with equal conviction that he must be fairly treated," wrtes historian Mary E.
Young. "The allotment policy was the instrument through which these incom-
patible convictions were to be reconciled, and its failure was the inevitable
failure of self-deception." The Creeks not only lost their land, they also lost
everything of value. In the end, 87 percent of land ended up in the grip of
speculators and not with the farmers President Jackson had envisioned.[36]

How involved was James Calhoun in this sorry business? He was a founding
member but not an organizer of the Columbus Land Company. Because of his
many other business ventures, he probably relied on John Worsham, who was

more of a presence in Alabama, to handle the land purchases. Calhoun was involved enough to add his name to Eli Shorter's three letters to Washington and to coordinate with Daniel McDougald in writing to Georgia's governor. However, by March 4, 1836, Calhoun was sufficiently dissatisfied with the Columbus Land Company to question its decisions and call for a meeting to review its actions. This is also when he took over Shorter's ailing bank and separated himself from Shorter in business dealings.

When agent John Sanford said that Shorter and others practiced fraud on distant stockholders who "seeing how things were going, sold their shares for cost," he was probably referring to Calhoun. Sanford and Calhoun knew each other well enough for Calhoun to recommend Sanford as emigration agent and for Sanford to have a seat on Calhoun's bank board. As the government attempted to settle claims, it was clear that Calhoun had not only parted company from Shorter and the other speculators but also believed he had purchased Creek lands in good faith. His name was not on the lips of investigators as one of the egregious offenders. Columbus citizens apparently didn't blame him because in December 1836 they elected him mayor. Calhoun never again worked with John Worsham, but he would continue to do business with Hepburn, McDougald, and Edward Cary. To sum up, Calhoun obviously hoped to profit off the sale of Creek lands, had no sympathy with the plight of the Creeks, and shared some responsibility for the Creek War, but in the big picture, he was a minor player. If he made money on Creek lands it would soon not matter.

4

FINANCIAL TURMOIL

The Panic of 1837 blew like a financial hurricane through the nation, capsizing businesses, closing banks, and destroying jobs, shops, and farms. Many a substantial man was ruined, and neither Georgia nor Columbus was spared. Economists and historians have blamed the collapse on unbridled land speculation, easy bank credit, and the policies of President Andrew Jackson, who had no use for the central banking system. In 1833 he stopped depositing government money in the Second Bank of the United States and instead placed new proceeds from land sales and revenue from taxes in various state banks, often owned by his friends; he called them his "pet banks." Larger deposits encouraged state banks to make more loans just as speculation in former Indian lands boosted land prices, so speculators borrowed more. States and local governments sold bonds to build roads, canals, and other public improvements. Railroad and canal builders borrowed to finance construction. To dampen speculation, the Treasury Secretary, after August 15, 1836, required buyers of government land to pay in gold and silver, which devalued paper money. Banks called in loans, and people lost their property. Prices plunged, bankruptcies rippled across communities, and trade halted. Merchants marked down their goods, sold what they could, and closed their doors.[1]

Georgia banks limped on by suspending specie (gold and silver) payment, which relieved some pressure. They could avoid calling in loans, and commerce could continue without disruption. But without the backing of specie, banknotes—functioning as the local currency—lost value, affecting everyone. Banks were withholding coins, but because people still needed to make change, they relied on change bills of one dollar and less, known as "shinplasters" from an incident during the American Revolution when a soldier used worthless Continental currency to bandage his wounded leg. The change bills passed from hand to hand but were only as reliable as their source, and the region was saturated with them.[2]

FIGURE 15. "The Times," 1837. A cartoon by Edward W. Clay takes aim at the Panic of 1837. Blamed on the treasury policies of Andrew Jackson, represented by the sun in a top hat and spectacles. Clay shows hopeless working people in the streets near a pawn broker called "Shylock Graspall." The busy drawing includes a bank run, a debtors prison and an almshouse. A punctured balloon, labeled "Safety Fund," falls from the sky. Library of Congress.

Strict Justice

Calhoun and Charles Bass became heroes when they acquired the ailing Farmers' Bank of the Chattahoochee in February 1836. On April 8, Calhoun posted the bank's condition and assured the governor that it would soon resume business. The partners were confident that once shareholders propped up the bank by paying in an additional 20 percent, the bank could exchange discounted banknotes for current banknotes. Their friend Daniel McDougald, president of the Insurance Bank of Columbus, was even willing to redeem Farmers' banknotes in specie. Calhoun was grateful for "this act of courtesy and liberality." They spent the rest of 1836 attempting to stanch red ink. At year's end, they were trying to collect debts owed J. S. Calhoun & Co. and Calhoun & Bass, and Calhoun was selling a plantation. Calhoun would later try to sell all his land in Florida, Alabama, and Georgia "on reasonable terms for good notes, or Negroes at fair prices," along with land belonging to Calhoun & Bass.[3]

As the Panic of 1837 enveloped them, they liquidated their stores, giving debtors the option of paying quickly with bills of Farmers' Bank. Remarkably, four businesses advertised that they would accept Farmers' Bank bills for goods. Merchant E. Sigourney Norton offered to sell his wares for the bank's bills, not because he had loans but "because I believe every dollar will be redeemed in a short time." Bass held out hope that if the bank could be "tolerably successful" in collecting bills of exchange and promissory notes, it "would be able to pay every cent it owed in a short time." The bank stopped payment in late April, but the *Columbus Sentinel* observed that "we believe it to be entirely solvent." The *Sentinel* didn't share Calhoun's politics, and yet, "justice, bare justice" moved its editor to observe that Calhoun was "an energetic business man who had worked as hard as anyone for his wealth and fame . . . and in prosecuting his own private views, he has never left the public good behind him . . . Such a man ought to be prized in a community, and we do prize him and many have come forward determined to receive his bills . . . relying altogether on his honor and integrity." The paper predicted that Calhoun would pay off the bank's bills, "even to the last dollar (should it be necessary) of his private funds." On May 2, Farmers' Bank's statement of condition showed capital stock of $295,525 and assets of $953,058. Calhoun held 449 shares, Bass 400, and Hepburn 706. Soon after, banks in Columbus and across the country suspended specie payment.[4]

Calhoun was in New York among the crowds milling around Wall Street on May 10, 1837, the day every bank in the city suspended specie payments. "It is indeed an anxious moment," he wrote. "The military are ordered to hold themselves in readiness for all emergencies . . . The magistrates, constables, and indeed every police officer is mingling in the crowd, soothing and attempting to keep it within proper bounds. I hope they may succeed—but fear they will not. The streets—Wall Street in particular—are immensely crowded, and go where you will, you find angry and turbulent spirits, and by their side a policeman." He reported that the banks were trying to maintain business as usual and paying in bank notes rather than specie. That afternoon the New York Stock Exchange "unanimously resolved to sustain and aid the Banks in the suspension."[5]

Bass advised bank creditors to not give up their claims because bills of exchange and promissory notes were coming due, and if the bank could be "tolerably successful in making collections," it could pay every cent owed, but in July the bank had to pursue its debtors. By June 1840, Farmers' Bank closed. In October, Calhoun wrote: "We are steadily progressing in winding up the affairs of the Bank, and trust we shall be able to do so without loss to any one." The *Sentinel's* "last dollar" prediction was prophetic. When Farmers' Bank failed, it was the only institution in the state to do "strict justice to its creditors," wrote a friend of Calhoun's. "Every bill and every liability of said bank was redeemed without discount or diminution." Calhoun could have walked away—many in his position did and still do—but he exhausted his personal fortune to assure that nobody lost a dollar in his bank. It's a remarkable statement of character.[6]

His Honor

As Calhoun struggled to keep his enterprises afloat, he was elected mayor of Columbus. Two priorities, said the *Enquirer*, were maintaining a free bridge to Alabama planters and traders and building a rail link to Columbus. "Men of enterprise, as well as good financiers, are required to do justice to the town in this matter," said the newspaper as it endorsed the ticket headed by Calhoun. In early January 1837, he succeeded John Fontaine to become the second mayor of Columbus. Within weeks Mayor Calhoun and the council passed an ordinance guaranteeing free use of the bridge to Columbus citizens who were farming in Alabama and for wagons carrying building materials for Columbus. And they approved the sale of stock in the Chattahoochee Railroad and Banking Company, which Calhoun helped organize to build a branch connecting Columbus to the Western and Atlantic Railroad then under construction. The *Enquirer*, noting that Savannah and Macon were pursuing rail connections, advised that "now is the time to do it."

Calhoun and the council tightened the ordinances regulating slaves to prohibit any slave from hiring out his own time in the city or living away from his owner. Free persons of color couldn't live on a different lot than their guardians. And they levied personal and property taxes on citizens, even taxing carriages, lottery vendors, inventories, and auction sales. The following year, they added taxes for billiard tables, blacksmith forges, and stallions. When Governor William Schley refused to convene the legislature because the state was as poor as

FIGURE 16. During the economic collapse in 1837, Calhoun and his partner Charles Bass opened a hotel, the Oglethorpe House, advertised in the *Macon Telegraph* on April 13, 1837.

its citizens, Mayor Calhoun called a public meeting to consider measures that might provide some relief. For the next two years Calhoun would be at odds "with a few of our wise and most influential citizens," who had not advanced the destiny of the town, he later wrote. "After my first election, my anxiety to be useful was greater than my ability," but because of "the sickening disasters" that afflicted him as much as his fellow citizens, his "omissions of duty were manifest and frequent during the first year."[7]

In the slumping economy that April, Calhoun and Bass opened the Oglethorpe House on the corner of Oglethorpe and Randolph streets. Referred to informally in 1836 as the "Calhoun hotel," the Oglethorpe House was the first brick building in Columbus and for years was one of the largest buildings in Columbus, well known for its famous guests and gala receptions. The first floor was taken up by shops, and one of Calhoun's businesses occupied a corner. A year later Calhoun and Bass sold the hotel. Its new owner described the hotel as "new, large, airy and convenient" and boasted about its well-stocked bar, a hint that the previous owners did not. Calhoun was a teetotaler, as were most Methodists of the day. The following year he would add his name to a letter asking the legislature to prohibit spirituous liquor within the state.[8]

A government contract for the use of his boats might have been a lifeline during the downturn. It wasn't. Calhoun had leased the *Anna Calhoun* and the barges *Mary Elizabeth* and the *Antoinette* to the army for use in transporting troops and supplies from September 12, 1836, to October 1, 1837, at $300 a day for the steamboat and $50 each per day for the barges. Instead of returning the boats to Columbus as promised on October 1, 1837, the army discharged them weeks later in Apalachicola. Calhoun had contracted to ship 4,381 bales of cotton to three New York cotton merchants for subsequent shipment to Liverpool aboard two brigs that would wait for the cargo at a fee of $50 a day. When his boats didn't return, he spent $1,000 to build cotton boxes, to no avail. By the time the army released his boats, the water had dropped in the Chattahoochee. The barges didn't return until November 17, and the steamboat not until December 22. Calhoun filed a claim for $154,155.85 for time, expenses, and losses. Congress would deny the claim twice and, finally, in 1843, pay Calhoun a trifling $15,900 in rent owed and nothing for the loss of his cotton.[9]

The only glimmer of good news was a land rush in the neighboring counties of Alabama in fall 1837. "We daily see large numbers of strangers going West to purchase land and build new homes," reported the *Enquirer*. "The Oglethorpe House ... is crowded every night with travelers in search of lands and fortunes. The City Hall, too, under the management of our worthy fellow-citizen, Mr. James Calhoun, is in a like manner filled, with sojourners. This is all indicative of better times, and shows the spirit of enterprise which nothing can subdue in the Southern people. Columbus will soon be herself again."[10] Calhoun too had joined that land rush. With A. Cary, probably Edward Cary's stepson Adolphus,[11] he filed for thousands of acres across the river in Russell County.[12]

Internal Improvements

Calhoun's friends talked him into a second term as mayor. Thanks to a new ordinance, it carried a salary of $1,000 a year. He was devoting his energies to internal improvements—what we now call infrastructure. On January 29, 1838, Mayor Calhoun and the council authorized $750,000 in bonds for the Chattahoochee Railroad and Banking Company. The city also subscribed for two thousand shares and mortgaged its toll bridge to secure its payment. In June the railroad negotiated a $300,000 loan at 7 percent but postponed seeking the remaining $350,000 it needed. Citizens had high hopes for a rail connection, but it was a slow process, and in the lingering economic downturn interest rates climbed. Opponents campaigned for a shorter line and challenged the legality of the bonds, so the city didn't issue all the bonds it promised. The last straw was a flood March 11, 1841, that carried away the bridge. A few days later, the company suggested that the city withdraw its subscription. Historian Joseph B. Mahan lamented the loss of "the far-sighted project that would have endowed Columbus with an early strategic position in the developing system of regional railroads. The fall of the Chattahoochee Railroad changed the course of the city's history." The bridge was rebuilt within months, but a railroad wouldn't enter Columbus until 1853.[13]

Calhoun's decision to run for the Georgia Senate, together with his "multiplied and complex private obligations," required him to decline a third term as mayor, he said. "My private affairs must now have my undivided attention."[14] As usual, the *Enquirer* endorsed him: "His personal enterprise and energy are as proverbial as his public spirit and private worth. Who has done more, who can do more, to promote the prosperity of our City and advance it to the rank it is destined to hold, than this man?" In fall 1838 Calhoun won his election, and John H. Howard prevailed in his campaign as state representative.

Calhoun was then deeply involved in the Columbus Canal, which Howard would eventually build. During his many trips north, Calhoun had seen how the Erie Canal contributed to New York City's success as a port and commercial center. Completed in 1825, it launched the nation's canal era, as state after state built canals to reduce transportation costs, link markets, and even generate waterpower for manufacturing. Georgia wouldn't be left behind. Beginning in 1826, boosters built the Brunswick Canal and the Savannah, Ogeechee, and Altamaha Canal for transportation. In 1836 Calhoun incorporated the Columbus Canal and Water Company, with Charles Bass, Alfred Iverson, and Edward Cary. The legislature authorized the company to build a canal on the Chattahoochee above Columbus, dam the river, and supply water. In 1838, as a member of the legislative Committee on Internal Improvements, Calhoun introduced a bill authorizing the Columbus mayor (himself) and city aldermen to lease or sell waterpower and to incorporate the Chattahoochee Company to improve navigation of the river. Subsequently, the city would sell thirty-seven water lots to Howard and a partner on the condition that they would build the canal.[15]

In September 1839, Calhoun bowed out of another senate race, "having been compelled by his private affairs to decline the nomination." His Columbus real estate had shrunk to one small property, and he was hemorrhaging properties in sheriffs' sales in other counties, but he was acting as agent for at least twenty-eight parcels.[16] The State Rights Party nominated instead Calhoun's friend Hampton S. Smith. Another friend, William H. Mitchell, president of the railroad company, was on the ticket for state representative. (Mitchell would go to New Mexico with Calhoun.) Cotton prices then hovered at just four or five cents a pound, and commerce was nonexistent. The state of Georgia was nearly a million dollars in debt, and its treasury was empty.[17]

Harrison Campaign

The economy dominated the 1840 presidential campaigns of William Henry Harrison, a Whig, and incumbent Martin Van Buren, a Democrat. Each promised debt-ridden voters that they would deliver a sound economy and higher cotton prices. The State Rights Party, now calling itself the Whig party, and a majority of Columbus citizens supported Harrison, and the Union Party backed Van Buren.

Calhoun ran again for state senate as a Harrison Whig. Like his fellow Whigs, he believed the federal government had limited powers, but he advocated a national bank to collect, transfer, and disburse revenue, equalize exchange, and support sound currency. Jackson and his successor, Van Buren, opposed a national bank. The right to incorporate banks belonged to the states, argued the Unionists, who feared the power of a federal bank. The question loomed large in legislative elections. Calhoun also said that returning fugitive slaves was of "vital importance to the slave holding states—one which admits of no Compromise." And he believed that Congress couldn't lawfully pass a tariff to protect domestic manufacturing. Calhoun ardently defended Harrison in the newspapers, arguing and clarifying his views. He occasionally took a swipe at the "Van Buren pretenders to Democracy" who tried to discredit Harrison.[18]

In a Fourth of July speech, Hines Holt Jr.[19] described his friend Calhoun as "the man in whose political course there has been 'no shadow of turning.' We trust that he is, as he always has been, ready to honor us by his faithful and efficient services." Holt, six years younger than Calhoun, dabbled in politics but wasn't tempted by business, preferring to practice law. He was a life-long friend; his father, Hines Holt Sr.,[20] was a friend of Calhoun's family and was probably Calhoun's mentor. Harrison won Georgia by a large majority, and Calhoun prevailed in his race. His good friend Robert B. Alexander[21] was elected representative. Alexander had arrived in Columbus a few years after Calhoun and, although he shared Calhoun's zeal for politics, he, like Holt, stuck to his law books.

In October 1840, there was a movement to make Calhoun senate president. "As a presiding officer, he is prompt and decisive, courteous in his deportment, and conciliatory in his manners," wrote Muscogee. When it appeared that friends might disagree over the office, Calhoun kept the peace by nominating someone else "with magnanimity of conduct greatly characteristic of the man." Calhoun instead chaired the powerful Committee on the State of the Republic and sat on the Internal Improvements Committee.

In the legislative session, Calhoun threw himself into the heated debate over how to resolve the banking crisis. Governor Charles McDonald, a Democrat, wrote that even though the state had given the banks latitude, they remained in suspension, "an evil which has subjected the community to great losses." He asked for and received a deadline for banks to resume specie payments.[22] Columbus citizens sent a memorial through Calhoun asking the legislature to help the town's banks.[23] He introduced four measures to free the hands of unchartered banks and private bankers, permit the circulation of change bills and bank notes, reign in bank profiteering, and deregulate rates of exchange. Calhoun also advocated for the establishment of a Supreme Court, but the bill was defeated. "Remove all restrictions, and unfetter the energy and industry of the State," urged the Enquirer.[24] Late in the session, Governor McDonald called attention to the near failure of the cotton crop and the resulting "pecuniary distress of the people" and asked the legislature to provide relief. The Central Bank, already burdened, couldn't help. Calhoun in the Senate and Robert Toombs in the House asked the governor what, exactly, he suggested they do. The senate debated long into the night. In Congress, Whigs pushed for a national bank, but just as the bill passed in 1841, Harrison died, and his successor, John Tyler, vetoed it.[25]

The local economy worsened in 1841. Columbus banks suspended specie payment again in March. Daniel McDougald resigned as president of Planters and Mechanics Bank. Calhoun and his partners in the Franklin Land and Apalachicola Lot Company (James Watson, McDougald, and Burton Hepburn) divided the properties in Apalachicola, Florida, among themselves and put them up for sale: 600 feet of wharfs, 56 lots, 50 acres adjacent to the town, and 320 acres within three miles of the town. The Chattahoochee Railroad and Banking Company returned the city's bonds and mortgage on the bridge, allowed shareholders to cash out, and closed its doors. Hines Holt Jr. wrote, "All over the Apalachicola-Chattahoochee River valley men were embarrassed at not being able to repay their loans." Few had any credit, and if they did, they

FIGURE 17. Calhoun's home, later sold to Daniel Griffin and then to Col. Randolph L. Mott, looks out on the Chattahoochee River. Artist Esther "Mollie" Mealing sketched historic homes in the Columbus area to help preserve their memory. It's a good thing; the house burned in 2014. Courtesy of Columbus State University Archives, Mollie Mealing Collection (MC 72).

didn't dare use it. His friends, he said, were "used up . . . They may recover but for my life I can't see how."[26]

That year, Calhoun built a red-brick mansion along the river front, where his peers also had stately homes. In the architectural style of the Second Empire, the elegant three-story home featured high dormer windows in a mansard roof with lacy, wrought-iron edges, and wrought-iron balconies. In the center of the roof was a prominent cupola. It had two enclosed chimneys on each end. "The house represented prominent wealth, the commitment to Columbus and the faith in the potential of Columbus," said local historian and retired Columbus State University professor John Lupold in 2014. It also said Calhoun might be down, but he wasn't out.[27]

"Shadow of Death"

We know very little about the women in Calhoun's life. A woman only earned a mention in print when she married. If she lost a child, as Caroline Calhoun did, the newspaper wrote up the loss as the father's. Women commonly sat in the gallery of the legislature, and we can assume Caroline and Anna were present while they lived in Milledgeville. Women also attended political celebrations, dinners, and balls. Outside of church and her husband's public interests, however, a woman was often lonely and isolated. The Calhoun women probably didn't know the joys of extravagant *Gone with the Wind* dresses because the Methodist Church frowned on gay apparel, big bonnets, and ruffles as well as jewelry. Not until 1845 were young women brazen enough to wear ribbon and artificial flowers on their bonnets. Antebellum Georgia girls were expected to get married, and schools were expected to make them attractive to prospective husbands. Daughters Carolina and Martha attended the Columbus High School for Young Ladies, where they learned literature, science, music, drawing, and French. They also took piano lessons.[28]

In 1834, four years after Calhoun married Anna, the *Columbus Enquirer* published a *Dictionary for Ladies* with this advice: Avoid contradicting your husband. Occupy yourself only with household affairs. Wait until your husband confides important matters, and don't offer advice until he asks. Never censor your husband's morals or read lectures to him. Command his attention by being attentive. "Never exact anything, and you will obtain much. Appear always flattered by the little he does for you, which will excite him to perform more. All men are vain. Never wound this vanity not even in the most trifling instances. A wife may have more sense than her husband but should never seem to know it."[29]

James Calhoun was probably charming and attentive when he was home, but he was often absent for long stretches on business, traveling to New York, Florida, Alabama, and Washington, DC. That left Anna to manage what was probably a substantial home with his two daughters and thirty-five slaves. The symbol of her authority and her complex duties was the large bunch of keys she usually carried.[30]

In 1841, Calhoun lost his wife, and his teen-aged daughters lost their stepmother. Anna Calhoun died of dysentery July 16 at the Greensboro home of William Crosby Dawson, whom Calhoun had just entertained at a dinner in his honor. Dawson, like Calhoun a lawyer and judge, would be a faithful friend and key ally throughout Calhoun's life. Dawson jumped into politics at age twenty-two, served twelve years as a state representative and two as state senator. He served in the US House of Representatives from 1836 to 1841 and in the US Senate from 1847 to 1855.[31] He was known for his kindness and elegant manners, as was Calhoun.[32]

Anna was healthy and in good spirits when she left Columbus to visit Dawson's wife Henrietta and expected to spend two or three weeks. Calhoun, then out of state, was to join her on his return. Her physician later described her constitution as "extremely delicate and fragile" and said she was often in pain, and yet she masked her condition with spirit, vivacity, and dignity. When he arrived at the Dawson home, Anna said calmly, "I see, doctor, you are alarmed at my condition." He was, he said, and informed her she was unlikely to recover. She replied, "I have no fears about the future. The religion I have been so long professing and living up to will carry me triumphant through 'the dark valley of the shadow of death.'"[33]

Anna said she would have liked a little more time to see her family, and especially "her dear husband, whom she loved most ardently, but that she would not complain at the ways of Providence." She died in the arms of Henrietta, who was like a sister to her. Her funeral procession was the largest ever seen in Greensboro. She was the "light and joy" of her family, said the *Enquirer*, recalling her "amiable deportment," "suavity of manners," "natural vivacity," and "talent for conversation."[34]

In four years, Calhoun lost his wealth and his wife and must have been as despondent as he'd ever been. It's telling that as his great wealth slipped away in a tempest beyond his control, his friends and adversaries alike held him in such great esteem that he had to decline a third term as mayor. He could continue living in Columbus and look everyone in the eye because no one lost money in his bank. Characteristically, he involved himself in new endeavors, like a railroad and canal, that promised to benefit the town. The unexpected loss of Anna was another matter. Calhoun would never marry again.

5

CUBA

Calhoun's hearty campaigning for William Henry Harrison earned him an appointment as consul at Havana in early 1841. The *New York Herald*'s Washington correspondent wrote that the president promised the appointment to Congressman William Dawson. "Mr. Calhoun was a speculator in Georgia, and, it is said, was one of those whose operations in that way caused the Seminole war." The writer named the wrong war and misreported the extent of Calhoun's involvement but wasn't entirely incorrect. The *Columbus Enquirer* took the *Herald* to task for "a miserable slander against one of the most valued and highly esteemed citizens of Georgia, Judge Calhoun... The contemptibility of the charge is exceeded only by its falsity." New England newspapers protested the appointment of a judge. Because the consul would have important mercantile duties they demanded to know if he was knowledgeable about the commerce between the two countries or familiar with mercantile transactions and shipping interests. Could he speak the language? He was, and he would learn Spanish.[1]

When well-wishers asked to honor him with a public dinner at the Oglethorpe House, Calhoun, then at the resort in Indian Springs, responded: "I have, at all times, and under all circumstances, attempted an honest, faithful, and zealous discharge of the various duties I owed them as a citizen—as the Chief Magistrate of the City of Columbus—and as their Representative in the Legislature of this, my native State." The thought of leaving the home of his childhood, youth, and manhood filled him with grief because he wanted to live and die in Muscogee County, he wrote. He thanked them but knew they would understand why he must decline, "when I remind them of the solemn and afflicting scenes through which I have recently passed, and the sad duty which I must yet discharge, before I can feel myself at liberty to leave the country. These totally disqualify me for social intercourse."

Just months after the death of Anna, James Calhoun and his daughters, then fourteen and fifteen, packed their grief and belongings and left for Havana on November 10, 1841, traveling compliments of the stage line and the Monroe Railroad, which was "evidence of a high regard entertained for Judge Calhoun by all classes of our citizens," wrote the *Enquirer*. Calhoun named Josiah Morris, a young employee well acquainted with his affairs, along with his friends Hines Holt Jr. and Robert Alexander as his agents and attorneys to represent him in business dealings during his absence. As they passed through Milledgeville, more friends greeted Calhoun. "He has the warmest wishes for his welfare," wrote the *Georgia Journal*. The Calhouns reached Havana on December 3.[2]

Cuba

Calhoun arrived in Cuba, called "a perfect paradise" and one of the loveliest islands on the face of the earth by a New York newspaper, at a time when the island seethed with racial tension and international intrigue. Cuba was Spain's last remaining colony, and Spain owed money to Great Britain, the dominant foreign power in Central and South America. The United States, conscious of Cuba's importance economically and strategically, wanted to annex Cuba but feared that Spain would sell Cuba to Great Britain. The Brits saw Cuba as a barrier to US expansion southward. Another monumental complication was the matter of slavery. As Cuba became a major supplier of sugar, coffee, and other tropical staples, planters demanded more slaves, and slave traders obliged, ballooning the island slave population from 39,000 in 1774 to some 436,000, or 45 percent of the population. With 153,000 free people of color—more than any other Caribbean island—slaves and free blacks were 58 percent of the population. Both the numbers of black people and their potential to organize was unsettling to white people in Cuba and the South; free blacks had already led several rebellions since 1795. Great Britain had abolished slavery in its Caribbean territories in the 1830s and tightened its blockade of slave traders. British consul David Turnbull, an outspoken abolitionist, was promoting Cuban independence and an end to slavery, to the consternation of Cuba's merchants, planters and bureaucrats. Southerners feared that Great Britain would not only interfere with American shipping but instigate a revolt in Cuba that could lead to slave rebellions in the South.[3]

The year Calhoun was appointed, the *Amistad* affair commanded public attention. The United States Supreme Court in 1841 decided to free fifty-three

FIGURE 18. *above*
Alameda de Paula, by
Frederic Mialhe in 1840,
was one of Havana's most
important social and
cultural spaces.

FIGURE 19. *right*
Daniel Webster was
Calhoun's boss twice—
the first time when he was
a consul in Havana and
the second time as governor
of New Mexico. Currier & Ives
lithograph, 1852. Library
of Congress.

slaves who were taken from Africa to Cuba, where they rebelled aboard the schooner *Amistad*, killed the captain and a cook, and held two other white people captive. They intended to return to Africa but mistakenly reached Long Island and were jailed by the US Coast Guard. Abolitionists in the United States and Britain took up their cause. Spain demanded that the ship and its mutineers be returned to Cuba, but the British consul testified that the slaves had been abducted from Africa in violation of Spain's trade agreements.[4]

The *Amistad* controversy prompted Georgian John Forsyth, then US secretary of state, to warn Britain and Spain that the United States would not permit British forces to occupy Cuba. The British foreign secretary and abolitionists accused Calhoun's predecessor, consul Nicholas Trist,[5] of plotting to annex Cuba and participating in Cuba's slave trade. Trist, a Southerner who had served in Cuba for eight years, invested in at least one sugar plantation and helped legitimize the sale of ships to Americans in Cuba who represented slave traders. In 1840 President Martin Van Buren sent Alexander Everett to Cuba to manage the consulate while Trist defended himself in the United States. Everett was also to investigate allegations and assess Cuba's political climate. After Van Buren lost the election, the Whigs removed Trist and appointed Calhoun.[6]

Vice President John Tyler succeeded President Harrison when he died after a month in office. His secretary of state, Daniel Webster, supported the status quo in Cuba and tried to improve relations with Britain. Webster insisted the United States had no plans to take control of Cuba and sought the same assurance from Britain. Rumors of British agitation to emancipate slaves refused to die. Cuban landowners and merchants, fearing Spain would hand them over to Great Britain, pleaded for annexation to the United States. Webster turned them down and promised Spain he would continue to do so as long as Spain retained Cuba.

That's how matters stood as Calhoun took his post. In December 1841 an uneasy Tyler wrote to Webster, "Has our new consul yet gone to Cuba—if not he ought to be ordered forthwith to repair to his post—with special instructions to report from time to time the condition of things." Tyler enclosed a letter describing evidence of British plans for an insurrection through Turnbull and agents in Jamaica.[7] Calhoun saw to his routine duties but also reported widespread tension to Webster in February 1842.[8] A slave revolt had broken out near Baracoa on the eastern end of Cuba, and stories circulated about the slaughter of whites in Jamaica. Calhoun didn't believe the British government was plotting to take the island but said Turnbull was "perfectly willing to engage in any scheme, having for its object the abolition of Slavery here or elsewhere."[9]

In one of several letters to Georgia Congressman Thomas Butler King, Calhoun wrote in March: "If you could be abroad as I am and be compelled to witness the discord of our cherished government, so little confidence is placed in our fixedness of purpose and everything considered so uncertain and disjointed in the United States. The consequence is our credit is not appreciated," and drafts on the Navy Department were discounted.[10]

Deteriorating relations between Texas and Mexico fueled speculation that if England seized Cuba, she might ally herself with Mexico against the United States. One congressman believed it was time to prepare for war with Mexico and England. Others were convinced that Cuba would separate from Spain but not become part of England because its economy relied on slavery. In April 1842 the *Columbus Enquirer* reported that "the black and brown subjects of Queen Victoria" in Jamaica had forced the governor and commander in chief to flee. Rebels were also planning to move against Cuba's southern shores, and the captain general of Cuba had readied transports and troops. "The rising is supposed to have been instigated by certain English fanatics, the better to cloak their designs on Cuba." In May Washington expected Great Britain to gain possession of Cuba by a treaty with Spain, which would result in emancipation of slaves and "afford further means of suppressing the African slave trade," said the *Georgia Telegram*. Cuba was often mentioned in the same breath with Texas and Mexico.[11]

Envoy Alexander Everett kept a divisive hand in Cuban affairs. Everett's good friend Domingo del Monte, a Cuban planter, warned that Great Britain was determined to ruin Cuba and that Spain suspected nothing. Island authorities were incompetent to meet the crisis, he said, and the situation was dangerous and critical. He said British agents in large numbers were trying to free slaves and create a black military republic under British protection. Everett criticized Whigs, including Calhoun and Webster, for trusting Great Britain. The *New York Herald*, quoting an anonymous source, wrote: "The real project of the British Government has been discovered at last in Havana—and we are informed their intentions are to get possession of Cuba . . . and to abolish slavery . . . and thus to menace the Southern United States." Tyler was growing increasingly jittery, and in late September he recalled Calhoun. Webster instructed Calhoun's successor, Robert Blair Campbell, that the president was "exceedingly anxious to be well informed ... at the earliest practicable moment" about the situation in Cuba. Campbell, a former congressman from South Carolina, reported that the British were not prepared to take Cuba.[12]

On the eve of his departure, all the Americans in Havana signed a letter to Calhoun dated November 22, 1842, "to offer to you our acknowledgments and thanks for the impartial and courteous manner our interests have been regarded by you and our intercourse with your office made satisfactory and pleasing." While Calhoun supported the authority of shipmasters, every difficulty between officers and men or between Americans and Cubans had ended amicably and to the satisfaction of the parties "both as regards kindness on your part to our countrymen and justice to all." The Havana correspondent of the *New Orleans Tropic* reported that Calhoun's replacement "seems to know as much of his duties as Consul as a mummy 2000 years old might be expected to know of the polite usages of modern society." Calhoun's departure "will be regretted by everyone." Georgia Whigs were furious. Tyler is "thoroughly disgusting to us," the *Southern Recorder* declared. Tyler had by then broken with Whigs to begin building his own states' rights party. Whigs, who called Tyler "His Accidency," expelled him from the party.[13]

When Calhoun returned to Columbus in December, the *Enquirer* welcomed him back. "Almost any man could be better spared from our city than Judge Calhoun. . . No man in all this section has more or truer friends than Mr. Calhoun. They sympathise with him, that in the embarrassments which his own generous heart has brought upon his fortunes, he has been removed from a station in which he might have somewhat repaired them." The *Savannah Georgian* was less kind: "A gentleman is appointed to the fat office of U.S. Consul at Havana. He repairs thither to discharge his duties, and to pocket the shiners. The President who has appointed him dies, and it so happens that the Vice President who succeeds him in office is opposed to the Consul upon every question of national policy. Is it incumbent upon the Consul to resign forthwith?" Calhoun pronounced the statement "false in every particular." He said he was appointed not by Harrison but by "President Tyler, about three months after 'His Accidency' assumed the reins of government."[14]

For Calhoun, the recall must have been a humiliating blow, and yet the appointment whisked him away from a place with many sad memories to lovely

Havana, gave him some valuable experience, and sparked an appreciation for adventure. He polished his diplomatic skills and gained a valuable new skill: he learned to speak Spanish.[15] It would serve him well in the future.

"Deepest Gloom"

Calhoun and his daughters had scarcely unpacked when, on January 5, 1843, one of his business associates killed the other, to the shock of everyone in the region. In the directors' room of the Insurance Bank shortly after 9 a.m., Daniel McDougald shot Burton Hepburn. The two had quarreled the day before over an old cotton transaction, which McDougald refused to settle, according to one account. Hepburn told friends that unless it was settled in two days, one of them would die. Then he armed himself. When Hepburn, armed with two pistols, entered the office in what McDougald perceived to be a threatening manner, he shot Hepburn through the heart. Hepburn died in minutes. He was forty-five. A large procession followed his remains to the grave. McDougald was acquitted soon after an inquest found the shooting to be an act of justifiable homicide.[16]

Calhoun related more of the story to the New York *Evening Post*. Hepburn and McDougald "had been attempting the adjustment of some business transactions," Calhoun wrote. Hepburn told Calhoun that he was dissatisfied with the outcome but would meet with McDougald on January 3. Hepburn parted, saying the general would hear from him the next day. Hepburn talked to friends, who discouraged him from challenging McDougald. "He reluctantly yielded and then determined he would notify the General of his intention to make an expose to the public, for which purpose he prepared a note, which he designed delivering in person," but never had the opportunity to deliver. The next night someone warned McDougald in an anonymous note that Hepburn intended to attack him. Calhoun believed that when Hepburn called on Mc-Dougald to deliver his note and without "the slightest intention of making an attack then, or at any other time," he was shot and died instantly. "Not a single witness was present. Our city now is in the deepest gloom," Calhoun wrote.[17]

Hepburn's death cooled the friendship between Calhoun and McDougald, and the fortunes of both continued to slide. McDougald "labored on under an immense load of debt to the day of his death," wrote a friend. Six years later, when Calhoun learned of McDougald's death, he wrote, "The peculiar relations which existed between Gen. McDougald and myself, caused it to be a matter of the deepest concern that I should take him by the hand once more in life, but as this cannot be done, I can now only grieve that my friend is dead!" Mc-Dougald died September 8, 1849, at fifty-one. The home occupied by his wife, Ann, was sold to satisfy debt.[18]

The shadow of economic downturn still darkened Columbus in 1843. Cotton prices were down, crops failed, and in March, a fire blazed through town, destroying stores and homes. Owners had little insurance, and Columbus didn't have a single fire engine. Calhoun was poorer by several town lots, buildings, storehouses, and a home, which were sold that year to satisfy his own debts and those of Calhoun & Bass. While he was in Cuba, he lost another eleven lots in Lumpkin County, auctioned to satisfy debts. Congress finally compensated him a token amount for keeping his steamboat and barges past the contract deadline. To make a living, Calhoun obtained charters for insurance companies. After an accusation that he used his privileges in the legislature to obtain a charter for Western Insurance & Trust Company, he explained that the charter was given to thirteen people, including Bass, and he was not then serving in the legislature. "It is intimated that I am quite an expert in obtaining charters, and somewhat shrewd in selling them advantageously—this may be true," he wrote immodestly.[19]

Political Integrity

Calhoun's political candle burned brightly. In 1843 Whigs circulated his name as a candidate for governor for his "universal popularity with his party." An unnamed admirer wrote that his "suavity of manners, and spotless private character, have gained him a large circle of warm and ardent friends among his political opponents." Many agreed, but Calhoun withdrew his name and urged delegates to "provide for the women and children of Georgia" instead of looking for "the cause of the evils with which we have been and are yet summoned." In June, at the Whig and State Rights convention, he was appointed to the Committee of 21 to consider matters brought before the convention. And he was chosen as a delegate to the national convention, along with such prominent Georgians as John Berrien, Robert Toombs, and Thomas Butler King.[20] That year he ran for state senate on the Whig ticket: Henry Clay for president, George W. Crawford for governor, Alexander H. Stephens for Congress, and his friend Robert B. Alexander for the state house. Democrats carried the election

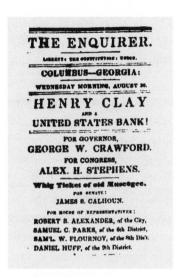

THE ENQUIRER.

LIBERTY: THE CONSTITUTION: UNION.

COLUMBUS—GEORGIA:

WEDNESDAY MORNING, AUGUST 30.

HENRY CLAY
AND A
UNITED STATES BANK!

FOR GOVERNOR,
GEORGE W. CRAWFORD.
FOR CONGRESS,
ALEX. H. STEPHENS.

Whig Ticket of old Muscogee.
FOR SENATE:
JAMES B. CALHOUN.

FOR HOUSE OF REPRESENTATIVES:
ROBERT B. ALEXANDER, of the City,
SAMUEL C. PARKS, of the 6th District,
SAM'L. W. FLOURNOY, of the 9th Dis't.
DANIEL HUFF, of the 9th District.

FIGURE 20. In 1843 Calhoun ran for the Georgia senate on the Whig ticket headed by Henry Clay. This political endorsement appeared in the *Columbus Enquirer* on August 30, 1843.

in October, and Calhoun lost to Albert Iverson, 905 to 833 votes. Alexander was the only Whig to win.[21]

Calhoun set politics aside for the delightful duties of marrying off his older daughter. On October 26, 1843, seventeen-year-old Carolina Louisa Calhoun married William E. Love, twenty-three. Calhoun would have considered this a good match. Love was an active Whig and part-owner of Oglethorpe House with Seaborn Jones, Daniel McDougald, and Charles Cleghorn. Carolina was young by today's standards, but the marriageable age for a Georgia woman was then fifteen to twenty-six.[22]

In January, miserable weather couldn't keep Henry Clay's many admirers away from a meeting to form the Muscogee Clay Club. Kentuckian Henry Clay, a political giant of the day, had been a long-serving member of Congress and secretary of state. He unsuccessfully butted heads with Andrew Jackson over rechartering the Second Bank of the United States to stabilize currency and control credit. Calhoun wrote the club's constitution and became president by acclamation; his friends Thomas Hoxey, Hines Holt Jr., J. A. L. Lee, and George W. Martin were officers. (Martin and the sons of Hoxey and Lee would travel to New Mexico with Calhoun.) The club vigorously opposed Van Buren's position that government funds should be held in an independent subtreasury and not in state banks. That, said Calhoun, "would enable the government and the rich to combine against everyone else." Whigs preferred a central bank that would regulate exchanges, currency, and state banks. When Clay accepted the club's invitation to speak, a large crowd met him at the bridge, and a carriage drawn by six cream-colored horses conveyed Clay to the Oglethorpe House through crowds shouting their welcomes. Hundreds of people waited at a platform erected in front of the hotel and hung on to every word of Clay's hypnotic baritone voice. He stayed two days.[23]

Newspapering beckoned in 1845. Calhoun became editor of the *Columbus Enquirer*. Publisher Samuel W. Flournoy expected Calhoun to stimulate interest in the *Enquirer*. The newspaper had changed hands several times since Mirabeau Lamar started it, but it remained the town's Whig voice. His counterpart at the competing *Columbus Times* was gratified to deal with someone who "will appreciate and practice the courtesies and amenities of our professional and gladiatorial warfare."[24]

Calhoun spent the next fourteen months gleefully championing Whigs and their causes, jousting with editors of Democratic newspapers, and pressing his own pet causes, namely transportation and women's property rights. He assured readers that his object would be "to elevate the social condition of man . . . to guard the rights of the strong . . . to succor and protect the weak." In reporting on the city's interests, he would advocate measures that would "advance prosperity without injury to anyone." He intended to preserve the goodwill of his political opponents "and to reclaim them, if possible, from the error of their ways." Subscriptions increased.[25]

The new editor enjoyed the perks of the job. He often thanked a citizen for their garden produce—on one occasion "a fine mess of green peas"—and local merchants dropped by with samples of their wares. Calhoun, then forty-six, revealed himself as something of a merry widower: "The ladies—may they

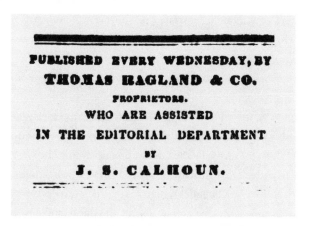

FIGURE 21. With this change in the *Columbus Enquirer's* masthead, Calhoun became a newspaper editor.

live always—are the appreciating better half of mankind, and since they have exhibited an interest in our behalf, we feel that many of the obstacles to our success are removed." Commenting on a New Yorker's observation that Washington society featured an abundance of widows, he wrote, "It is a delightful fact, and the idea of it makes me laugh in my sleep . . . I am bound to confess that I consider a young widow, that is, one under sixty, to hold the superlative degree in the comparison of female excellence." However, in New Orleans "the most charming widows upon the face of the earth may be found."[26]

Calhoun devoted his first editorial to the looming war with Mexico. It was the Democrats' policy "to involve the country in a war," he wrote, and yet property holders, planters, and farmers didn't favor a war. "What will the Merchants and Mechanics do when the Planters and Farmers are without a market for the cotton? When the honor of the country requires it; when the happiness of the present generation and the happiness of unborn millions shall seem to demand it, it will be time enough to draw the sword and sound the war clarion." The cry for war, he concluded, came chiefly from the big cities and from people with nothing to lose. At the time, Mirabeau B. Lamar was visiting from Texas "and we are happy to inform his numerous friends that he is in exceeding fine health."[27]

He filled many a column with Whig positions on the political questions of the day. "We are still the State Rights men we used to be," he wrote. Whigs were faithful to the Constitution, opposed to a protective tariff, and opposed internal improvements by the federal government. Revealing himself as moderate, he found equally contemptible the Southern Democrats' hatred of the North and "the wild fanaticism of the most wicked Abolitionists." He favored "a just medium, an appropriate ground, upon which every American interest may rest. The North must not expect to control, nor should the South attempt to dictate."[28]

The *Enquirer* followed the US annexation of Texas closely, and its editor began to modify his opposition to war with Mexico. "The consequences of the Annexation scheme . . . are now inevitable and impending," he wrote on August 20, 1845. "War, with all its incidental horrors and evils, individual suffering, privation and death—a national debt, high taxes, the interruption of commerce, and last, though not least, the corruption of the public morals, are the bitter fruits . . . [of] the premature and indecent annexation of Texas." He conceded that a war with Mexico was inevitable, but annexation would "benefit Texas land speculators over national honor" (he now had no use for land speculators, a distaste that remained the rest of his life), while the people would "fight the battles and bear the burdens of the war." Calhoun was seriously considering relocating to Texas. When a Democratic paper accused Whigs of opposing the Texas annexation, Calhoun fired back that Whigs had never opposed the admission of Texas if a majority were in its favor. Once the citizens decided to admit Texas, the Whigs "declared for its favor, and professed their readiness to fight for it."[29]

He examined Democrat John C. Calhoun on just one occasion and wrote: "We regard him not exactly as a 'walking calculation,' but as a talking abstraction. The remark of an intelligent friend long ago made to us is true, with one qualification, that 'Mr. Calhoun is as cold and as abstract as conic sections—he loves nobody, he hates nobody . . .' The qualification we have to make is that Mr. Calhoun is in love with the Presidency. That has been the passion, and the only passion, of his life. It has determined his course at every turn of his zigzag career."[30] Calhoun made no mention of the man as a relative.

Editor Calhoun expounded on the benefits of railroads. Despite the failure of the Chattahoochee Railroad, Columbus citizens were discussing a rail line from Montgomery to Savannah through Columbus. Calhoun worried that because Columbus lacked "energy and enterprise," rail projects would divert trade to other towns. "Will no one move in this matter?" he asked. He pleaded with citizens to forget party and personal differences and unite for their own common interests. The city council asked Calhoun, Robert Alexander, and five other men to meet with shareholders of the Central Railroad. "Something must be done, or the very fountains of our prosperity will be dried up," Calhoun said. Several manufacturers were then building factories in Columbus. "The elements of our prosperity are in a perfect ferment, and our prosperity would be without a parallel, if a few of our wealthy and intelligent citizens were a little more liberal and public spirited." Still hemorrhaging property to sheriffs' sales, Calhoun was clearly frustrated to no longer be one of those wealthy citizens. On October 30, Calhoun and others wrote to the president of the Central Railroad and Banking Company of Georgia that the people of Columbus desired a link with Savannah.[31]

Calhoun promoted the resort at Warm Springs, Georgia, operated by Colonel Seymour R. Bonner.[32] "The Lodges and Cottages, and the Hotel, are crowded with the gay and the happy. We are without Whigs or Democrats . . .

Soft, sedate, and smiling faces are found reposing in every shade. The laughter-loving give evidence of health and hearty dinners," he wrote. He lauded Bonner's cuisine and added, "There are about fifty of Georgia's fairest Lilies at this place . . . God bless them! And may they never be less happy than now."[33] Calhoun intended to play chess with two of those lilies, no doubt his daughters.

Women's Rights and Waterpower

Nominated by acclamation to run for Senate representing Harris and Muscogee Counties, Calhoun ran a dignified campaign, got appointed to the party's executive committee, and won his race. On November 1, 1845, Calhoun was lodged at the Harry Clay House in Milledgeville. "Our rooms are in a perfect state, and some of our friends who may or may not be candidates for official position before the Legislature now assembling are very happy to see us." The crowd of office seekers was "unusually large for so early a moment," he wrote, and outnumbered legislators. He was startled by their "reckless conduct."[34]

As a senator, Calhoun renewed his efforts to give married women property rights separate from their husbands. By law, married women in Georgia forfeited control over property to their husbands. Calhoun's concern was fitting for the father of two daughters and hearkened back to the hardships his Aunt Martha faced after the death of her husband. Several years earlier, he had introduced a similar measure, which the *Milledgeville Journal* called "a wise and salutary measure." His new bill would allow a married woman to keep and control property received by gift or bequest and even use it to purchase property. It was a measure "for the protection of our mothers, wives, daughters and sisters," he wrote.[35]

An amended bill passed the Senate, which provided that all "artificial increase" of the wife's sole property "over and above the necessary support and maintenance of the wife and family and the education of her children shall be the right and property of the husband." The House rejected the bill a few days before adjourning. "Many of the younger and unmarried members of both Branches of the General Assembly were its most violent assailants," Calhoun wrote.

These young members claim to be the especial guardians and protectors of female chastity. They boldly charged that wherever such a law is in force, there is a loose morality that held in contempt marital obligations—and in three days after a marriage solemnization, the paramour was preferred to the husband. From such views, it is inevitable that to woman's entire dependence and slavish obedience to man, her husband, is the sex indebted for whatever of virtue is accorded to them by their generous sons and brothers and husbands and fathers. If this be true, the greater the tyrant the more virtuous the wife.

It was not until the Married Woman's Act of 1866 that a wife had unqualified control of her property.[36]

Calhoun, who was on the Senate Finance Committee and the Internal Improvements Committee, also beat the drum for improving navigation on the Chattahoochee. For $300,000 the river could be navigable for two hundred miles above Columbus, which he claimed would open trade to the highlands, triple the population, quadruple commerce, increase agricultural production, and enhance real estate. He carried a bill authorizing the formation of the Chattahoochee Company to improve the river's navigation above Columbus to West Point by dams, canals, and/or locks and to command and appropriate the waterpower of the river. "The prospect of so legislating as to advance the interests of Columbus, is exceedingly remote," Calhoun wrote. The bill died. "The city of Columbus will yet see the effect of their shortsighted and unwise policy," he wrote, predicting that Macon, Savannah, Augusta, and Charleston would all fatten at the expense of Columbus. He decided not to stand in the way of applications for waterpower; if the people opposed improvement, the state might as well grant waterpower privileges, he reasoned.[37]

Calhoun got a bill passed to incorporate the Water Lot Company of Josephus Echols and John H. Howard. In 1840 he conceived of a canal to harness the Chattahoochee's waterpower for manufacturing, but Columbus city fathers, unsettled by their experience with railroad investment, refused to finance the project. In 1841 they authorized the lease or sale of water lots to Echols and Howard, who agreed to build and maintain a dam across the river, as well as a canal or raceway to deliver water along all the lots. Construction began in June 1842. "The beautiful Chattahoochee is to leave its 'winding way,' and be confined in the walls of a canal," the *Enquirer* reported. "They wish to straighten the river, and improve the water power for mills and factories." On completion in November 1847, the raceway measured 1,100 feet long, 75 feet wide, and 7 feet deep. The *Augusta Chronicle* reported that "the splendid granite Canal" was built with stone taken from the riverbed. When the fourteen gates were opened, the canal filled in fifty minutes. Industry grew along the banks. By the 1850s, five water-powered mills produced textiles, flour, and lumber, and smaller companies produced a variety of goods, making Columbus a manufacturing center. When steam power and electricity replaced waterpower, canal construction ended.[38]

Calhoun, diminished financially and discouraged in his diplomatic appointment, obviously hadn't given up and, in fact, hadn't even slowed down. He still had means enough to build a handsome house on the river and found new ways to make a living, but in this period he kept an eye to the future as an advocate for improved transportation—canals and railroads—and ownership rights for women. It mattered little whether they were popular causes or even widely opposed; he raised his voice in the legislature and in the press.

6

WAR WITH MEXICO

As 1846 opened, the United States and Mexico bickered over the border between the new state of Texas and Mexico. When President Polk sent General Zachary Taylor's army to the Rio Grande, the inevitable clash of troops gave Polk the excuse he needed. On May 12, 1846, he declared war, ordered up fifty thousand volunteers, and asked Congress for $10 million. "The president and the nation had a war now, and neither was up to it," writes historian Bernard DeVoto. The Mexican–American War would become one of the most divisive wars in American history.[1]

Georgia congressman Alexander H. Stephens blamed Polk for what he considered an unnecessary, unconstitutional, and costly war. Nothing good would come of it, he said. Senator John Berrien said on the Senate floor that the United States could have protected Texas at a small expense compared with the cost of the war. There is no doubt that Mexico, "comparatively feeble and distracted by internal dissensions," entered the war reluctantly, he said. Sending troops to the Rio Grande and occupying disputed territory were "open, undisguised acts of hostility."[2]

Georgians of both parties, caught up in the wave of patriotism enveloping the nation, rushed to enlist when Governor George W. Crawford called for volunteers. Columbus, with a long-standing and keen interest in Texas—former Texas president Mirabeau Lamar was from Columbus—was proud to be the rendezvous site for the Georgia regiment. But as Georgians began answering the call in May 1846, General Taylor wrote: "I much fear so many volunteers will come we will hardly find anything for them to do; the enemies' principal positions are so far off, with deserts intervening that it will be I fear impossible to reach them for want of transportation."[3]

Calhoun raised one of the first volunteer companies, the 140-man Georgia Light Infantry, which elected him captain, and was "ready to march at a mo-

VOLUNTEERS FOR MEXICO.

Now's the Day, and Now's the Hour.

FIGURE 22. An advertisement in the August 3, 1847, *Columbus Enquirer* urged men to sign up.

ment's warning," the *Enquirer* reported. "The war fever continues to rage at Columbus with unabated vigor." Captain Calhoun didn't know the first thing about soldiering, so, as he had in Cuba, he wrote to Congressman Thomas Butler King seeking information: "It is our purpose to do service <u>against</u> the Mexicans. We desire to know <u>how</u> <u>to do it</u>. We are unskilled in war matters—but we desire to know the <u>whole</u> <u>duty of officers and soldiers</u>. I am alike ignorant of the accomplishments, the etiquette and the duties of the soldier's life. I desire all the information that is necessary to enlighten and instruct a soldier." A week later, he wrote King that his company was awaiting orders. He believed he could raise a regiment, "<u>certainly a battalion</u>," and asked King "the moment you receive this note" to recommend him and his men to the proper authorities and urge their acceptance.[4]

Calhoun resigned from the *Enquirer* so abruptly that he caught his good friend and publisher, Samuel W. Flournoy, by surprise. His last issue was June 24, 1846. "We should be rejoiced if he [Calhoun] was here to make his own valedictory in separating from his numerous friends," Flournoy wrote, "but martial law admits of little ceremony, and when the word is given to march, a soldier cannot stop to parley with his kith and kin, much less the friends that have stood by and sustained him." Flournoy's annoyance is palpable, but he graciously wished "especial honor, fame and glory to our late associate."[5] Calhoun was taken with "war fever," but he also may have grown bored and restless at his newspaper job. Certainly, he was frustrated with the city's reluctance to embrace railroads and canals. And there was his uncharacteristic gushing about New Orleans widows followed by total silence, suggesting that the widower may have been disappointed in love. If so, he wouldn't be the first man to soothe a broken heart by joining the army. Altogether, military service was an acceptable escape as well as a path upward for an ambitious man like Calhoun.

As volunteer companies arrived in Columbus, Calhoun wrote that "the citizens may expect a gay and enlivening time." Soldiers "will have an opportunity to win laurels worthy to rest upon a soldier's brow." By early June, seventy-five of Calhoun's men were in uniforms, stitched by the city's women, and waiting restlessly for orders to march. When Governor Crawford arrived, he found Calhoun drilling his men. They had paraded through the streets "much to the gratification of our citizens who have been pleased to observe their soldier like deportment and their rapid improvement in military discipline." Other companies began to arrive in the camp a mile outside the city.[6]

Between May 22 and June 10, ten companies were mustered into service in the 910-man regiment: the Georgia Light Infantry, Richmond Blues, Jasper Greens, Macon Guards, Columbus Guards, Crawford Guards, Fannin Avengers,[7] Canton Volunteers, Kennesaw Rangers, and Sumpter Volunteers. On June 20 the volunteers elected Henry R. Jackson as colonel, with 310 votes; Calhoun drew 264 votes. The other officers were Lieutenant Colonel Thomas Y. Redd and Major Charles J. Williams. John Forsyth,[8] editor of the *Columbus Times*, would be an adjutant until he resigned in November; another adjutant, Charles P. Hervey, would resign in September, both for health reasons. Doctors John J. B. Hoxey and W. E. Beall, of Columbus, were the battalion surgeons. Beall would be dead in a month, one of many taken by disease. The Georgia Volunteers signed up for twelve months, from June 1846 through May 1847. As captain, Calhoun would earn eighty dollars a month; his privates would receive just eight dollars, the same pay as regulars. They furnished their own uniforms, but each man was reimbursed thirty-six dollars.[9]

The regiment marched on June 28, 1846, cheered on by a "large and imposing array of beauty, manhood and youth," said the *Enquirer*. As people caught a last glimpse of their loved ones, "it was a solemn and impressive separation." The regiment, with fifty baggage wagons, passed through crowds gathered on the bridge into Alabama to witness "the favored of Georgia's sons." They marched to Chehaw, Alabama, took the train to Montgomery, arriving July 5, and departed the next day on a steamer for Mobile. "They were in fine spirits, and anxious to arrive at the seat of war in time to take part in the next skirmish with the enemy." Calhoun lost his first man when the sound of venting steam jarred Peter F. Farrar awake. He and another volunteer jumped overboard and drowned. After spending their one-year allowance on supplies, the companies departed Mobile by boat from July 10 to 14. During the voyage south, so many were seasick, wrote Georgian John W. Fincher, that soldiers soon covered the decks and "nothing could be heared—but the bursting of the waves & the grones of the sick."[10]

As they traveled south, General Taylor wrote pessimistically: "I feel confident that our ambitious views of conquest and agrandisement at the expense of a weak power will only be restrained & circumscribed by our inability to carry out our view, & in six or eight months if the Mexicans hold out that long, we will be fully as anxious to make peace as they are; for by that time we will have expended with very little effect or purpose all the money in the treasury, when our govt. will have to resort to loans & taxation to carry on the war; a course never palatable to our people."[11]

Brazos Santiago

Their ships deposited the Georgians on Brazos Santiago, a barren island at the mouth of the Rio Grande in the Texas Gulf, where they and thousands of other volunteers waited until General Taylor needed them. The quartermaster couldn't provide transportation, by land or water, to move troops forward or get volunteers and baggage from the island to a place with wood and fresh water, and when the season of illness began, thousands sickened. "The whole country will be filled with sick volunteers & in many instances without suitable accommodations," Taylor wrote.[12]

The island hospital, packed with battle-wounded regulars, denied admission to sick volunteers. The Georgians occupied "a desolate sand bank about a mile square, with not a single tree or shrub to temper the fierceness of the tropical heat," reported the *Georgia Telegram*. The flies were so thick they could turn a white coat black, John Forsyth wrote. "At night the flies give way to mosquitos, who pursue their vocation of murdering sleep." The volunteers did enjoy fishing and swimming. With both Columbus newspaper editors—Calhoun and Forsyth—serving as officers, the city was guaranteed steady war coverage.[13]

Their move to Camp Belknap was no improvement. Located on a grassy ridge along the river about fifteen miles east of Brownsville, Texas, it became one of the largest volunteer camps of the war with eight thousand troops. Men stood in the mud because they had nothing to sit on and drew provisions by slogging through a swamp to reach the commissary. Calhoun's usual good cheer evaporated. At "this black prairie marsh," one of his young soldiers killed another when his musket accidentally discharged, and another

FIGURE 23. Zachary Taylor, shown here in a lithograph by Albert Newsam, became a hero of the Mexican war despite his poor management of it.
Library of Congress.

died of dysentery. "Not a sprig of straw is furnished to the well or sick, notwithstanding Dr. Hoxey's frequent requisitions," Calhoun wrote. "Here we lie in mud and water—with less regard paid to our comfort than is usually afforded by the farmers of Georgia to their mules." Hoxey reported the regiment had 162 sick. Within a three-mile square, Calhoun estimated ten thousand volunteers without organization. "This is a great country," he observed sullenly, expecting to languish there for the duration. On August 19, Dr. Beall, the regiment's assistant surgeon, died.[14]

Unwilling to lay blame where it belonged, with General Taylor, Calhoun instead blamed the government. Enduring death, disease, and discomfort through the next few months, he never wavered in his view of Taylor as a hero. History is less charitable. "Zachary Taylor was ignorant of generalship and culpably inattentive to the welfare of his troops," writes historian Henry B. Parkes, "but his physical courage, displayed by sitting on his horse and coolly writing despatches while bullets were flying past him, aroused the enthusiasm of the volunteers." Taylor wrote on August 19: "I fear there will be no end to this war in any reasonable time, & that it will be carried on with a view to conquest, with the expectation if successful it will secure Mr. Polk's reelection."[15]

Like most career officers, Taylor believed volunteers were unsuited to camp life. Many volunteers didn't know how to properly cook the pork and beans they received, and they avoided fresh fruit and vegetables, believing they would cause diarrhea. They drank too much and then lay on the wet ground with no blanket. Professional soldiers learned what Mexicans ate or avoided in summer months and generally took better care of themselves. One officer observed that volunteers might be well drilled and brave, but "the hospitals are crowded with them, they die like sheep; they waste their provisions." However, there was no protection or treatment for yellow fever, a mosquito-transmitted sickness the

Mexicans called *La Vomito*. Many would never return home, and if they did, their families would receive a sick, emaciated man who couldn't work.[16]

To get out of the mud, the Georgians moved three-quarters of a mile from Camp Belknap. The only sparkle of good news was the possibility of leaving for Camargo. "We are absolutely in as utter ignorance as though we occupied no spot on earth," Calhoun wrote. All of his men were upright, "but several are puny," and three were discharged because they were unfit for service. "My health was never better," Calhoun wrote.[17]

Relocated to Camargo, they hoped to be among troops Taylor chose for his march to Monterey, but they were disappointed. Taylor took only 3,000 volunteers out of 7,700 then on hand and left the Georgians behind. By September 6, only 370 of 795 Georgians were present for duty; other regiments were similarly reduced. In sweltering Camargo, sickness laid siege to the volunteers, whose numbers grew to 12,000 miserable men, living in squalor and neglected by the army's supply chain. Flooding contaminated the water, and volunteers died in such numbers that gun boxes were used as coffins. Forsyth expected measles to drill through the Georgia Regiment because they lacked medicine. In November his own health would force him to resign and return home. Of his regiment's losses, Jackson wrote:

> Where Rio Grande's turbid waves
> Roll with a current strongly fleet
> We placed them in their desert graves.[18]

Calhoun, too, succumbed, not rejoining his regiment in Camargo until September 17. Three days later, his and five other Georgia companies were ordered to ready themselves to march with only a knapsack, haversack, and tin cup, which "created some excitement, and much gratification," he wrote. On the march at a fast pace, "every man moved with an animation that gave evidence of decided pleasure." They joined Taylor's escort, which was carrying some $200,000 for the army's use.[19]

Monterey

As the escort made its way south, Taylor captured Monterey. It was the first battle with large numbers of volunteers, and they fought well. Taylor established his headquarters at Walnut Springs, and troops camped in and around the

FIGURE 24. Map of Mexico.

woods of San Domingo. Volunteers and regulars mingled, which improved conditions in the volunteer camps. Rations were still meager, but now locals brought bread, eggs, oranges, lemons, pomegranates, grapes, and bananas into camp, along with goats, milked on the spot. The Georgia Volunteers arrived October 2 and camped a mile from Taylor's headquarters. They were attached to General William O. Butler's division and General John A. Quitman's brigade. Calhoun had been talking with various informed sources, a practice he maintained throughout his war service. "Nothing has transpired, as yet, to weaken my confidence in Gen. Taylor's ability to manage the conduct of the war with decided credit to himself and the United States."[20]

On October 4 the four Georgia companies still in Camargo got orders to escort some 1,500 pack mules to Monterey. After a week of travel, they camped about six miles from Monterey. That night they learned that a party of Antonio Canales's guerillas were at a neighboring rancho. Lieutenant Orran C. Horne, of Captain Joseph A. S. Turner's company, found the guerillas and took ten prisoners and some of Canales's baggage. Canales himself had just left. The Georgians remained on duty the rest of the night. Horne was the first Georgia volunteer to cause Mexican blood to flow. "All honor to the gallant Lieutenant," Calhoun wrote.[21]

The Georgians hadn't enjoyed a full ration since the previous month, Calhoun wrote, and hadn't received a dollar in their five months of service. "Outrages, in the neighborhood, are frequently perpetrated. Men are stabbed, robbed, and occasionally killed—both Mexicans and Americans; yet the natives appear remarkably friendly, but charge exorbitantly for all that they sell us. Every Sunday night, a 'Fandango' is given, to which many of us are invited. They are said to be, by those who have attended, very pleasant affairs."[22]

Calhoun sifted rumors about Taylor's falling star in Washington and the direction of the war: "For myself, I greatly fear there are combinations formed, or being formed, to relieve Gen. Taylor of his command." Calhoun couldn't imagine how Taylor could advance any farther without more men, supplies, and weapons. "We are covering all the territory that should be attempted under present circumstances." For a winter campaign, the army needed another depot, and Tampico was the most practical, in Calhoun's opinion. "Veracruz should be the next point of attack. But these grave matters are to be settled at Washington, and we are, the soldiery of the country, merely entitled to think and speak in softened accents; and to obey is a duty we have pretty well learned."[23]

Tampico, the major city in the state of Tamaulipas and Mexico's second-most important port, fell without a fight on November 14. In early December, the troops in Monterey began to sicken and die. "Again there is much sickness in camp to chronicle, and it generally terminates mortally," Calhoun wrote. "Those who are at all incapacitated for duty by disease obtain their discharges very readily, and many who are convalescent, but debilitated, get a ready permission to go home." In a letter to the *Enquirer*, he asked whose duty it was "to care for the widows and orphans of those who die far removed from home," and concluded that if Washington didn't provide, Georgia should. Doctors Hoxey and Hill had cared for the sick as best they could "unaided by Hospital stores, tents and bedding . . . Strange, indeed, is it not strange, that proper medicines are not furnished to us by the Government. Many of our best men are dead and many others will die, for want of such."[24]

Victoria

The Georgia Regiment left on December 14, 1846, joining a volunteer brigade created by Taylor that also included the First Mississippi and First Tennessee Regiments. Their commander, General John A. Quitman, was one of the best of the six new brigadier generals appointed. Marching for Victoria, about two hundred miles southeast, they passed through orange groves, sugar cane, and cornfields. As the temperature rose, the column stretched out, marching grew difficult, and feet blistered. On December 17 they reached the flourishing city of Montemorelos.[25]

Trudging south through mountains, they were still on the move Christmas day, expecting Canales to attack them on the march. Near Hidalgo, they were told that Tennessee-educated General José de Urrea would attack in the next three days and spent the December 27 in close formation with arms loaded and bayonets fixed. For three days the enemy was on their flank, "designed to annoy us," Calhoun wrote, and he saw more to the rear. They could also see a force to the east, and the Mexicans let it be known they intended to attack. One night they made camp on grounds Urrea's men occupied two hours before. Sergeant W. T. Smith, of Calhoun's company, and other Georgians volunteered to scour the country ahead, "extremely dangerous duty," that occupied them night and day. The battalion reached Victoria at noon on December 29. Calhoun expected that with six thousand Mexican troops at Victoria, "the Georgians will, in all probability, have a chance to show their game." Instead, they saw their enemies retreating as they approached. Urrea followed them but Quitman never gave him an opportunity to attack. As Quitman took formal possession, the faces of citizens "showed they felt that their country was being humiliated, and I must say that I really felt for them," Calhoun wrote.[26]

On New Year's Day 1847, officers wandered the town. Victoria, a trade center, sat on an elevated plain, highly cultivated with corn and sugar. In camp a fierce norther blew in without warning, Calhoun wrote, leveling more than two-thirds of the tents, "and the dust made the night hideous." Wind filled the air with dust, sand burrs, and insects, and the men were defenseless against the storm. Overhead, clouds of parrots whirled and screamed. By midnight the wind calmed, the temperature dropped, and the men worked to get their tents back up.[27]

Major Williams, third in command of the Georgia Regiment, was acting governor of the town "and affairs go on quite smoothly." The Georgia companies of Dill, Davis, and Nelson, with two Mississippi companies, protected the town and guarded public stores. "The balance of us are immediately in front of the mountain pass to Tulu," Calhoun wrote. "We are in good health—dissatisfied with our position, and anxious to move forward." Of the Mexican government and its citizens, he wrote: "The truth is, there is no government here, but an absolute despotism, under the wild fanaticism of a religious garb. A more ignorant and servile race, so near a Christian world, the light of the sun has not reached elsewhere. The natives are sold to each other for trifling debts. Several have been bought by our officers, and liberated." Calhoun referred to peonage, a form of bondage he would encounter in New Mexico. But during a beautiful day on January 6, the men enjoyed abundant and excellent water, oranges, green corn, sweet potatoes, and beef. After weeks of rations, it was a feast.

Taylor, Twiggs, and Patterson arrived in Victoria on January 4. "Gen. Taylor commands the unqualified confidence of the entire army . . . and yet we learn with decided satisfaction that Gen. Scott is in the country," Calhoun wrote. "It is to us evidence that the Government has a distinct purpose to accomplish, which we are to pursue to its end. The want of a fixedness of purpose in army operations is exceedingly goading and harassing to the volunteer soldiery. Move us *forward* and give us something to do, and we are content."[28]

General Winfield Scott, chosen by the president to lead the attack on Mexico City, wasn't the beloved figure that Taylor was, but he was a better manager. "There is an awful tumbling of military officials," Calhoun wrote. Two major generals and three brigadier generals couldn't agree on the next step, but Scott would decide. "All men have a wonderful facility of appreciating truths when announced by military omnipotence," Calhoun wrote.[29]

On January 14, Taylor received orders from Scott to send most of his army— nearly all his regulars and the volunteer divisions of Worth and Patterson and the brigades of Quitman and Twiggs. Soldiers watched Taylor leave Victoria with profound sadness. Quitman's Second Brigade of the Volunteer Division now consisted of Georgia, the Fourth Illinois, and Maryland, all infantry, and one company of mounted Tennesseans. They marched before dawn on January 17. With the sun heating every stone in the dusty road, they hiked up and down spurs of the Sierra Madre and camped at the Santa Rosa River. Instead of bread, the men had three tin cups of flour to mix with water and fry with pork fat. Cattle, driven with the column, were slaughtered in the evening.[30]

They marched on, with wind whipping ankle-deep dust. They knew that "the enemy were hanging upon our flanks; and on the 18th Mr. Bigelow, a beef contractor, was shot by them and had his left leg badly shattered." Several weak soldiers fell behind and were killed. One of Calhoun's men, Private Lewis Chandler, escaped by running into the chaparral and climbing a tree; the Mexicans didn't see him. They tramped through chilly wilderness, thick chaparral, palmetto forests, and ended with a hard, cold, twenty-three-mile march through rough country. That night nearly all the Georgia Regiment gave out. As men threw themselves down, unable or unwilling to keep up, the column broke up. Some of the Georgians got their hands on some mescal, producing "a night of drunkenness which, once seen, is not desired again," an officer wrote. The next day a few were still so drunk they could hardly keep up.[31]

Tampico

Three miles from Tampico, on January 28, 1847, Calhoun wrote, "We have more to dread from the season and the climate than from the enemy. Our natural sympathies for the sick are surely blunted—since we left Camargo we have not had a hospital tent nor such medicines as our diseases required." Of the ninety-nine men Calhoun mustered in, twenty-three were discharged, ten died, two transferred, and five were sick, leaving fifty-seven. The regiment of 910 was down to 626, "a frightful falling off of 284." They sat for two weeks in silent gloom as daily rainstorms soaked the ground and invaded their dilapidated tents. Rations were short, the men ragged and nearly bootless. They hadn't been paid for six months. News was as scarce as a dry tent. "Gen. Scott has been looked for so long that our curiosity is worn out, and our anxiety has become threadbare," Calhoun wrote.[32]

Even after Scott arrived and ordered troop movements, Georgians sat out the Battle of Buena Vista on February 22 and 23 because they had no transportation. On March 1, Calhoun and his company boarded the brig *Pensacola* for Veracruz, Mexico's principal port, with the companies of Captains Bird, Shelton, and Turner. Colonel Redd and Dr. Lamar were with them. Colonel Jackson, Major Williams, Dr. Hill, and the other six companies would follow. "Our accommodations on this Brig are the most wretched we have had since we left Columbus," Calhoun complained. While they waited to sail, they tried to hold their tempers, eat the quantity of food allowed, "drink or waste the gallon of water allowed to us; fish occasionally, and some times go a birding, and kill a beef." But the *Pensacola*, held captive by northern winds or dead calm, took twenty days to reach Veracruz, instead of the expected eighteen hours. "We were most inhumanly crowded, not having the room said to be allotted to the victims of the slave-trade, to wit, six feet by eighteen inches to each," Calhoun wrote. The water shortage was acute.[33]

Veracruz

On March 6, Scott landed twelve thousand men at lovely Veracruz, with its walls and turrets facing the sea, all fronted by yellow dunes and sandhills. Captains Davis, Dill, and Corlett, along with Calhoun's lieutenants, arrived by steamer on March 9 and joined the second line of the battle. They camped at a ruin a mile and a-half from the beach, where they were joined by Major Williams, with Captains Jones, Nelson, and Sargent.[34] The invasion began that day. By 10 p.m. eleven thousand men were on shore. Brigades led by Generals Pillow, Quitman, and James Shields began to encircle Veracruz to bottle up the city's garrison and prevent reinforcements from reaching it. In three days Americans formed a seven-mile siege line in an arc around Veracruz and cut off the city's water supply. Scott decided on a duel of artillery, and on March 10 he attacked. Pillow pushed through the chaparral and reached position on a hilltop. The following day, Quitman and Shields formed their brigades on the left of the line.[35]

Quitman's command consisted of six companies of the Georgia Regiment and six of the Alabama and the South Carolina Regiments, all posted in trenches and told not to fire unless ordered. When Quitman's brigade relieved Pillow, the Mexicans could see Americans leaving the hill but not those coming up. From the top of the hill, Quitman's men and the enemy exchanged fire for

FIGURE 25. Veracruz during the bombardment, March 25, 1847,
by E. B. and E. C. Kellogg. Library of Congress.

about an hour. Quitman sent Captain Davis, of the Georgia Regiment, with
twenty riflemen to move around under the hill and engage them at close quarters. The Mexicans spotted Davis, and about two hundred men advanced on
him, but he and his skirmishers held them off until Colonel Jackson with the
remaining three companies and the South Carolina Regiment joined the fight
and forced a retreat. The Georgians counted five wounded.[36]

When the *Pensacola* finally reached its destination on March 17, they got
their artillery, ammunition, provisions, and horses on shore and found troops
preparing to storm the city. Scott had delayed the assault to avoid taking lives.
Calhoun found the lines extended in an arc "over mountains of sand, and over
which it requires immense labor to move." It took him five hours to cover the
five miles to his regiment. Cannons fired on and off all morning, began again
at noon, "and the explosions of shells are occurring above us." Hearing about
Davis's heroics, he wrote, "I must express my deep mortification, that it was
not my good fortune to be present when the first troops were landed opposite
Sacrificios. . . . If it were possible for us to harbor in our bosoms a feeling of
envy, we certainly would envy the proud position to which Capt. Davis and his
detachment were elevated."[37]

On the afternoon of March 22, batteries opened on the walled city. Firing was "somewhat wild, but from five until ten o'clock, it was most beautiful. Every shot seemed to take effect. We occupied the heights of a sand mountain . . . from whence we could see every shot, both from the enemy and our own batteries," Calhoun wrote. He expected the city to fall within forty-eight hours, and if there was no surrender, it would be "stormed by the infantry, the only chance we have of taking part in the stirring scenes around us." He described the enemy's shooting as admirable. On the night of the March 23 a large Mexican force approached their lines, and at 1 a.m., the companies of Calhoun, Shelton, and Sargent were ordered to occupy a gorge all night but again were denied the thrill of engaging the enemy. Two days later, Calhoun said, "the cannonading on both sides is tremendous." Finally, inevitably, the Americans breached the city's fifteen-foot walls. Calhoun, who had met General Scott when he quartered in Calhoun's hotel during the Creek War, visited his headquarters twice, each time finding him "in excellent spirits" but learning that four Georgians were killed and six wounded at one of the batteries. Late in the afternoon on March 25, the Mexicans asked for a cease-fire, which Scott granted. "We fear their women and children have suffered much. We would have had it otherwise. We are informed many of their dead are yet lying in the streets," Calhoun wrote. On March 28, the Mexicans accepted Scott's terms of surrender. The Mexican army would depart the next day. After seeing for himself what lay beyond the shattered walls, he reported, "Very near half the city is in ruins. The destruction is incredible."[38]

Alvarado

To avoid the yellow fever breaking out in Veracruz, one of Mexico's hottest and unhealthiest cities, Scott marched inland toward Jalapa, and ordered Quitman to coordinate with Commodore Perry in attacking Alvarado, a small coastal town thirty miles away, where Scott hoped they'd find cattle and horses. On March 30, Quitman left Veracruz with Georgia, South Carolina, and Alabama volunteers; two hundred dragoons under Major Robert G. Beale; and a section of Captain Edward J. Steptoe's battery under Lieutenant Henry B. Judd. Lieutenants Goulding and Anderson in Calhoun's company were too sick to march, but they would be glad they didn't. History records Quitman's brutal, unforgiving march in extreme heat with too little food and water, his troops stricken with dehydration, dysentery, and other illnesses. Calhoun wrote only that they endured a four-day march on the beach in deep, heavy sand, but "our hoisted flag floated over the most beautiful little city we have as yet seen in Mexico."[39]

Their hardship was for naught. One of Perry's lieutenants bombarded Alvarado instead of blockading the river's mouth as ordered. The town surrendered. When Perry and Quitman arrived on April 2, the gung-ho lieutenant had sailed farther upriver to capture other towns, effectively warning Mexicans to drive their cattle and horses away and burn supplies. Quitman came away from the lush ranching area with few animals. "In coming to this place, we have been much disappointed, for really, many of us had expected to see and feel a fight," Calhoun wrote. He was surprised the residents gave up so easily.[40]

The town's *alcalde* (mayor), ordered to furnish quarters, offered public buildings and vacated houses. Calhoun found this unsatisfactory "to gentlemen who had been in the woods for ten months." Using his Spanish, he asked for more comfortable lodging. The alcalde indicated some homes that were locked and told them they could force an entry. "I replied at once, sooner than do violence to the doors, or injure private property in the slightest particular, we would sleep in the streets. Whereupon a fine, manly and intelligent looking Mexican touched the Alcalde upon the shoulder, and authorized him to make a tender of his 'Casa'—and we are inhabiting a princely establishment, with all necessary conveniences attached, with bathing rooms, and beautiful Canaries and other birds . . . and we are preparing to dine today upon fish and fowl."[41]

After two days' rest and despite "excessive, exhausting and enfeebling" heat, Quitman hustled his troops back in three days. Several more men died. They arrived April 6, bringing four or five hundred horses, but the brigade was "suffering much from the fatigue of the march," Calhoun wrote. Quickly, the camps again rustled with preparations; Twiggs would leave the next day, Patterson would follow, and Quitman's brigade would bring up the rear with General Worth's division. "We are not pleased at this position," Calhoun wrote.[42]

When the forces of Antonio López de Santa Anna materialized suddenly near Jalapa, the prediction was the Mexican commander would fight another battle and then make terms with the Americans. "I give you this as the mere opinion of many intelligent Mexicans," Calhoun wrote. Mexicans were becoming less fearful of the American presence, but even though Americans had enriched the produce peddlers, "yet the artful misrepresentations of the Priesthood induced them to believe, if we subjugated them they were to be transported North, and sold as slaves."[43]

Quitman's brigade prepared to leave for Jalapa on April 17, and Calhoun wrote hopefully that "Santa Anna's position and the number of his troops will give us all something to do," but they dreaded the forced march more than encountering Santa Anna. Transportation was so limited they had to leave behind most of their baggage. The Americans had just begun to storm Cerro Gordo, a narrow pass between high mountains, and would destroy Santa Anna's force of nearly seventeen thousand men. Calhoun reported a victory, with four thousand prisoners taken and heavy American losses. He visited Santa Anna's hacienda April 19 and pronounced it "a magnificent retreat." The Americans also captured Santa Anna's carriage and even his cork leg.[44]

On April 23, they reached Jalapa, a handsome city set in a fertile, green country at 4,000 feet in altitude. The people were peaceful, and the wealthy were refined, well-educated, and hospitable. Sugar cane, coffee, grains, oranges, and pineapple grew "in luxuriant abundance," wrote an officer. Calhoun was exuberant with "the pure air we are permitted to inhale, the delightful scenery around us, the cool and refreshing waters of which we drink and that we rest upon a green sod instead of a burning sand . . . [I]t is difficult to conceive we are in the same country."[45]

Return home

On reaching Jalapa, their one-year term of service ended. Most volunteers were joyous, but not Calhoun and the Georgians. With six weeks left, they could have reached Mexico City before returning to Veracruz. General Scott offered inducements to reenlist, but only 10 percent accepted. Commanded by General Quitman, regiments from Georgia, Tennessee, Illinois, and Alabama, plus a Kentucky company, left May 6 for Veracruz. Calhoun believed that allowing seven regiments to leave meant the army had suspended its march on Mexico City "or our presence here was never necessary." It was unforgivable to ready troops for movement, "creating hopes and expectations never to be gratified or realized." He concluded that Scott didn't expect the volunteers to reenlist and expecting the volunteer officers to raise new companies "would be to suppose them devoid of all just personal pride and laudable ambition," because not one of the officers had been offered a promotion or a continuance. It was especially galling to be ordered home when they were only fifteen days from Mexico City and "anxious to take part in the finale of this war—to gather a few of its laurels, to deport ourselves as the faithful representatives of the chivalric soldiers of our beloved Georgia."[46]

Calhoun and his company sailed on the brig *Hemrico* from Veracruz to New Orleans. The voyage was pleasant, the vessel neat and clean, the passengers not terribly crowded. When they arrived in New Orleans on May 26, four thousand troops waited for their pay. The Georgians, with a few exceptions, were "in excellent health and spirits, and anxious to hasten to the embraces of their friends," wrote Calhoun. As the "gallant band of Georgia's representatives in the war with Mexico" returned home in early June, a reporter "read in their haggard looks, reduced frames, and bronzed countenances the story of their toils, their privations, and their hardships. Although it was not their good fortune, to have met the foe, and signalized themselves on the battlefield," they had served their state. The army mustered out just 450 men; 145 had died and another 315 were discharged early.

Historians remember the Georgia volunteers kindly but somewhat inaccurately. The regiment never once came within shooting distance of the Mexican Army, wrote Wilbur Kurtz. "It appears to be their luck to be always hard by, but never in a fight," said one newspaper. The *Cyclopedia of Georgia* concluded: "Although it did not take part in any of the engagements of the war, it rendered effective service and upon its return the legislature passed a resolution commending the men for their valor and patriotism." Let's give Calhoun the last word: "The Georgia Regiment has seen more unpleasant and severe service than any other volunteer regiment in the army: we have marched further and have been more exposed to the climate; we have visited a greater number of villages, towns and cities, where it was *supposed* the enemy would oppose us; and yet our term of service is near expiring and we have had no immediate participation in other of the brilliant achievements of the camps."[47]

From the outset, Calhoun's service was anything but the patriotic heroism of his imagination, and yet he harbored that expectation to the end. Despite his steady complaints, he did adjust to army life and the relentless march through Mexico and even enjoyed the experience of an exotic location—the parrots perched on women's hands in Linares, the mountain air of Jalapa. He conversed with Mexicans and Americans to stay informed and faithfully reported it all to Georgia's newspapers. He was critical of Mexico's government but expressed compassion for its people. Calhoun and most of the Georgians never engaged in battle heroics, and history records only the lopsided "victories" in an uneven fight, but their dreary slog was the experience of most who served.

7

DESIRE TO COMMAND

Calhoun came back to a Columbus he no longer knew. In October 1846, a disastrous fire had consumed block upon block of homes and businesses, injuring hundreds and displacing hundreds more. The following year another fire destroyed the *Columbus Enquirer*'s building and press room. Losses again were substantial. Still, the town was moving forward with a third massive mill, a new market house, telegraph service, and plans for the Mobile & Girard Railroad Company. However pleased he was to be home, his sense of dislocation must have been profound, and, despite his complaints, army life had agreed with him. When the governor asked again for volunteers, Calhoun quickly pledged to raise a regiment of a thousand mounted men in sixty days and to serve for a year. It would take twice as long to raise half the men.

While others dangled the promise of adventure in exotic places before would-be recruits, Calhoun said simply, "Those who desire to serve their country now have a fair opportunity to exhibit their qualities as soldiers and should come forward without delay." By June 15, 1847, only two companies had been accepted of the six required for a battalion. Georgia had seen too many of her sons come home sickened or not come home at all. "The service seems to have lost its charms for our people," observed a Milledgeville newspaper. Why would Calhoun, given the frustrations and boredom with his first stint, be so eager to return and to recruit men he was consigning to certain death from disease? His letters home make it clear he considered the war and his own part in it unfinished. He still believed it was his patriotic duty, and he'd become something of an adventurer. In July four companies were at the Columbus rendezvous. In mid-August the mounted battalion was still one company short. The *Enquirer* prodded potential volunteers: "We think it is time again to ask, where are the fire-side heroes who believe so strongly in the original necessity of this war . . . where are the fighters?" In September, Calhoun finally had his battalion.[1]

FIGURE 26 On the occasion of becoming a colonel in 1847, Calhoun sat for a small portrait. Courtesy of the Palace of the Governors Photo Archives (NMHM/DCA), Negative 050460

Calhoun made it clear to Governor Crawford that he wouldn't be satisfied with a captaincy: "I desire to command the Battalion—will you give me the necessary commission? If so there will be but little delay in raising the companies. Those who are willing to volunteer desire to know who are to command them, and until they know they will hesitate." After being recommended to Secretary of War William March as a man "of character, intelligence, influence and military zeal," March suggested that Crawford make him a lieutenant colonel. "No man in Georgia has done more to arouse and keep up the martial spirit of our people than Capt. Calhoun; and no man more deserves this tribute to his patriotism and worth," said the *Enquirer*. His political opponents said he "did not want to go unless he could be commander."

Crawford appointed Calhoun lieutenant colonel of the Battalion of Georgia Mounted Volunteers and Isaac G. Seymour lieutenant colonel of the Georgia Battalion of Infantry. Seymour's battalion left in July for its year of service. Crawford's enemies (and possibly a few of Calhoun's) later tried to pass a legislative resolution condemning Crawford for violating usage and "the rights of citizen soldiers" by appointing Calhoun and Seymour to command battalions. The resolution failed 73 to 43.[2] The next year would see Calhoun's transition from soldier to commander and cement his self-image as a military man.

Calhoun appointed Lieutenant John C. Hateley, adjutant; Lieutenant Thomas Berry, quartermaster; Allen Lee, sergeant major; and John E. Jones, quartermaster sergeant. His captains were Edwin R. Goulding,[3] Charles A. Hamilton,[4] Henry Kendall, William D. Fulton, William Tatum Wofford, and Charles H. Nelson. Goulding, who served as Calhoun's first lieutenant during the first tour, named his company the Calhoun Guards. (For a list of officers, see appendix 2.) Before they left, Daniel McDougald, Judge James M. Chambers, merchant Samuel A. Billing, Robert Alexander, and Hines Holt gave Calhoun a specially selected "gallant steed." Daniel Griffin, chief engineer of the Monroe Railroad Company, gave him a second excellent horse.[5]

The battalion reached Montgomery on September 13, 1847, gathered supplies, and left two days later. "Col. C. is an efficient officer, and has already, by remaining with his company in Mexico, suffering with disease, at imminent risk of his life, given indubitable evidence of his firmness in the discharge of duty, and his devotion to his country," wrote the *Alabama Journal*. "As a former member of the editorial fraternity—and as a whig good and true—we are proud of him." The battalion camped eight miles from Mobile on September 26 and 27. Troops were "subjected to constant drilling and to strict military discipline in every particular," JFB[6] wrote. "Too much praise cannot be said of the manly and efficient manner in which our commanding officer discharges the official duties of his station. His thorough acquaintance with the details of military duty, and his forethought and energy in providing for the welfare and comfort of his command, prove him eminently qualified for the responsible position which he occupies and have secured for him the utmost confidence from all his officers."[7]

More than forty men had measles, and others complained of chills and fever. Calhoun too succumbed and spent three days in bed but put in his orders for weaponry and transportation. "We have a pleasant location and the water is good. We drill at 8 in the morning and 4 in the evening—have but little sickness in Camp," wrote an officer. "The Colonel does not allow the men to go to the city, and it is well he does not, for I am told that the reason the yellow fever is not worse there 'tis for the want of subjects. Col. Calhoun is now in Camp, and I am glad to say has recovered his health. He has endeared himself to all the officers and men of the Battalion, and I doubt whether a better appointment could have been made."[8]

By late October fifty men were hospitalized with measles, but the rest sailed, divided among six ships. Calhoun departed on October 28 on the *Maria Burt*. The weather was good and promised fair winds. The men were "in good health and excellent spirits," Calhoun wrote. Their boat was crowded with 120 horses, but the men had "good berths, good fare and good weather," wrote JFB. The battalion received its arms and equipment, "which are of the best kind" and consisted of a carbine, sword, holsters, and one pistol. Officers had superior artillery sabers. Despite good weather, the voyage was slow, and their "dissatisfaction pent up." Four days out they learned the boilers weren't sound, and the boat was short of water and coal. Passengers wanted to cast anchor before Tampico. With time for idle chatter, one lieutenant declared that no females were as beautiful, fair, fragrant, or desirable as those of Georgia. "But a Mexican beauty he has not yet seen," Calhoun wrote.[9]

Tampico

Arriving at Tampico on November 3, 1847, they found their horses in worse condition than expected and learned that when the steamer transporting Goulding's company encountered rough weather, they had to throw their horses overboard and use their forage as fuel. Men wanted to visit the city, which JFB described as "quite a handsome, new built town" with an abundance of tropical fruit, but they were "busy as bees, washing and cleansing every thing, and doing the needful for our horses," Calhoun wrote. It was warm and the foliage luxuriant. "The market, adjacent to the plaza, presents an aspect so attractive this morning, it will be quite impossible to restrain the movements of those who love to look upon earth's beautiful daughters, and at the same moment indulge their appetites in the luxuries of Mexican viands and vegetables," Calhoun wrote. "No one who has once visited a Mexican market will refuse to go again." Lieutenant G. W. Anderson, despite his illness, roamed the market every morning, sometimes with Calhoun. "The market is always thronged with the most beautiful women, buying and selling coffee, chocolate, vegetables of every kind, rare flowers, jewelry, trinkets, and gew-gaws—but the languishing beauties, majestic and magnificent in their bearing, claim and enchain the admiration of every looker on in Venice," wrote the widower. "The market hour is the only one in the 24 in which the women seem to be free," meaning unchaperoned.[10]

The mounted battalion camped with 1,500 other troops, principally Illinois and Ohio volunteers, on the beach three miles northwest of the city. Captain Charles H. Nelson, who arrived on November 3, was sent on a short scout in search of Padre Jarauta, a guerilla leader and priest. Officers and men hoped for a battle, but Calhoun thought it unlikely. General Scott was sending no more troops beyond Puebla and instead trying to garrison the towns from there to Veracruz. On November 18 the mounted battalion and three other companies rode with a train to relieve the Georgia Battalion of Infantry, then garrisoned

FIGURE 27. This drawing of a vegetable vendor appeared in *The Mexican War and Its Warriors* by John Frost, 1848.

at San Juan, a small town on a lake thirteen miles from Veracruz. The mounted battalion, minus Captains Henry Kendall and William D. Fulton, marched on December 5 with General Thomas Marshall and his train toward Mexico City. Calhoun's 480 men were the only cavalry among Marshall's 1,780 troops.[11]

Jalapa

In mid-December they camped near Jalapa, where a storm dropped bone chilling rain, but they couldn't keep warm or dry because they had to leave their tents behind for lack of transportation. Captains Goulding, Hamilton, Kendall, and Fulton finally arrived with their companies, along with the rest of Nelson's company. Nelson was still in Veracruz, very sick. Calhoun was among the few who hadn't been sick a day since reaching Mexico. On Christmas Day 1847, JFB wrote that the battalion had been "lying idle in camp" with nothing to break the monotony except morning and evening drills. The country seemed peaceful, but it was dangerous for a lone traveler or small parties to travel the road, "which is infested throughout by petty bands of robbers" who operated in groups of fifty to a hundred. Calhoun wrote, "We are still without news from Mexico, and madam Rumor, that blessed old dame, seems to have exhausted her inventive powers, or she has become ill-natured and refuses to amuse us."[12]

The Georgia Battalion spent its second night at Perote, where Colonel Seymour, of the Georgia infantry, was military department governor and commandant. They reached Puebla, Mexico's second largest city, on January 16, 1848. As they approached, tolling bells from the cathedral's two bell towers "admonished us we were about to enter a city of no inconsiderable importance. It is one of the wealthiest cities in Mexico, and has a population of near 100,000 citizens," Calhoun wrote. Its plazas and public spaces "are beautiful, large and arranged with excellent taste" and he was told to expect a display of "beauty and fashion" every afternoon. Calhoun, Lieutenant Hately, and Dr. Bozeman were comfortably quartered with Colonel Willis A. Gorman, the civil military governor. But Puebla was as deadly as it was beautiful. Two-thirds of troops at the post were unfit for duty and three or four died every day. "We are alarmed at the dreadful mortality among them—but very few are cured." General Scott ordered them to remain in Puebla and garrison the city. "We are somewhat disappointed at being halted here, as all were anxious to proceed directly to the city of Mexico, the goal for which so many of us left our homes in the full expectation of reaching," wrote JFB. On January 23, Colonel N. S. Clarke of the Sixth Infantry left for Cuernavaca, taking with him the Georgia mounted men.[13]

Cuernavaca

Pretty Cuernavaca perched on a spur of land between two deep ravines, the whole surrounded by volcanoes. It was a tropical paradise even in February. Abundant flowers softened the outlines of houses, and orange or olive trees offered shade. And yet, soldiers died like flies. "The climate here is delightful, and every variety of tropical fruits are exceedingly abundant and cheap," Calhoun wrote. "A vast quantity of watermelons are brought to market every morning, and a more deadly poison in the shape of intoxicating fluids can not be fabricated elsewhere than is made here." Together with "the excessively severe duties necessarily required of the Mounted Battalion during the first ten days after our arrival," Calhoun wrote, left all but one of his men sick. Although he blamed the fruit, it was typhoid fever, malaria, and other unidentified fevers that felled his soldiers. In the temperate climate, wounds refused to heal, and most soldiers who lost limbs to amputations died.

On February 1, 1848, Calhoun deposited his sick officers, including Captains Goulding, Kendall, and Fulton, in Mexico City. A month later, only Kendall was still sick, and his friends advised him to go home. His response: He preferred death and understood that he would die. He breathed his last on March 9. Captain Nelson reached Mexico City "in greatly improved health," took charge of many of the battalion's sick from Veracruz, Jalapa, Perote, and Puebla, and brought them to Cuernavaca. "They are greatly needed at this time. We have 304 present, and our sick list today numbers 108," Calhoun wrote. He couldn't think of a single man who had not been sick since arriving at Cuernavaca, and twenty had died. "The fatal results have been, indeed, most alarming; and will cause many a heart, in Georgia, to bleed and wither."[14]

The whereabouts of Captain Wofford's company was simply unknown until Captain Nelson arrived with word that the steamer *Beaufort District* wrecked on the Texas coast, and forty horses drowned. When they reached Veracruz, Wofford and his men scoured the countryside for forty miles around for an enemy to fight, and on February 19, on the road to Orizaba, they learned that forty or fifty guerillas were on their left. They halted, and Colonel Briscoe of the Louisiana Volunteers, ordered twenty men of Wofford's company to chase them down. They raced over rough prairie about a quarter mile until the enemy was in view, drawn up to receive their charge and armed with lances, swords, and escopets. Wofford halted his men, formed a line, and ordered them to fire. The Mexican line quivered from end to end. On his order, they drew sabers and charged, breaking through the line and wheeling about and charging back toward the line that reformed behind them. Badly outnumbered, the Georgians became divided but continued fighting. They lost a number of men before Briscoe relieved them. After intense combat, Briscoe ordered a retreat. Wofford was "violently opposed" but overruled, and he retired to the wagons, taking his wounded with him. They continued the march to Orizaba. When Nelson left, Wofford[15] and his men were in Veracruz, resting their horses.[16]

Clarke rode to Mexico City on March 12, and Calhoun rode with him to ascertain orders for the rest of his command. "I am not pleased with the prospect before us," he wrote. Once there, Calhoun attended the court of inquiry proceedings resulting from disputes between General Winfield Scott and General

FIGURE 28. Gen. Scott's occupation of Mexico City is depicted
in this print by Carl Nebel. Library of Congress.

Gideon Pillow, appointed because he was President Polk's law partner. After
Pillow tried to take credit for successes in two battles, Scott court-martialed
him and took action against Generals Worth and Duncan for similar reasons.
Pillow wrote Polk accusing Scott of promising to pay Santa Anna $10,000 if he
would help secure a peace treaty; Polk relieved Scott of command and reduced
the proceedings against Pillow, Duncan, and Worth from a court-martial to a
court of inquiry, which began in March 1848 and ended on April 21.

Witnessing the conflicts between the war's leading generals, Calhoun re-
flected the vertigo many soldiers must have felt. Scott was "without a military
equal upon the earth," in Calhoun's opinion, and should be restored to his
command. "Military Commissions, and Courts Martial abound here," Calhoun
wrote on March 18. "But the great point of attraction is the room where the
great, yes, truly great accuser has become the chief criminal, and the chief
offender the pre-acquitted and rewarded." In court "Gen. Scott is always dignified, always sensible, and always self-poised. He knows what he is about, and
tyros cannot disconcert him. Gen. Pillow seems to be at home, crosses his legs,
throws himself back, and smokes his cigar in the court room, during its sit-

tings. I have not yet seen his example followed." Calhoun noted that "all ranks and conditions of Americans and Mexicans" were following the proceedings. Ultimately, Scott dropped charges against the three generals and was himself exonerated.[17]

As Calhoun left Mexico City on March 19, he heard that Nicholas Trist "would leave as a prisoner for the U.S. the next day . . . to answer for his treasonable doings with this people." Polk in 1847 sent Trist, a State Department clerk and Calhoun's predecessor as Havana consul, on a secret mission to Scott's headquarters in case Mexico was ready to negotiate a peace treaty. Scott initially resented Trist's presence; after Pillow criticized both Scott and Trist to the president, Polk recalled Trist, but Trist refused to return. With Scott's encouragement, he continued negotiating with the Mexicans and signed the Treaty of Guadalupe Hidalgo on February 2, 1848. Polk dismissed him when he returned in May.[18] The Senate ratified the treaty on March 10, 1848.

Calhoun settled in at Cuernavaca, where the Spanish conqueror Cortés had established himself three centuries earlier. With time on his hands, he explored caves and an old volcano in a group guided by the alcalde and village schoolmaster. He admired hailstorms and sunsets. He served on a court of inquiry after a camp sentinel shot a teamster; they concluded the sentinel was doing his duty. "To guard us against ourselves is a more vexatious job than watching for an enemy." The armistice, he wrote, had opened the door to a demoralizing indolence, and troops wished to be ordered forward or sent home. On May 17, the volunteers held an old-fashioned barbecue. When the Georgians began digging their barbecue pits, the alcalde and priests feared they were burying their dead. They later laughed at their error and "thought it a very beautiful affair."

Calhoun's time lobbying the brass in Mexico City didn't achieve the desired movement, but it may have raised his profile. Early in May, he became commander of the Cuernavaca Brigade, an honor darkened by the grim duty of presiding over a decimated force. Of the brigade's 1,838 men, 629 were sick, 331 present, and 298 left in hospitals in the rear. The rest were on detached service. "At this post every thing around us is exceedingly pleasant, and why we should be sick it would be difficult to image; and yet nearly every fourth man is sick," he wrote. The three Georgia companies there (two were posted elsewhere) numbered 197, with 64 on the sick list, 40 present, and 24 left behind sick.[19]

Back to Jalapa

General William O. Butler ordered the evacuation of Mexico City on May 29, 1848. The army pulled in troops from outlying posts, and detachments at Cuernavaca and Toluca marched to Mexico City and on to Jalapa, where vast numbers of troops awaited nonexistent transports. "Our march from Mexico was a terrible one, yet we were greatly favored by the weather," Calhoun wrote. Stragglers were "horribly butchered and mangled." He was thankful he'd lost no men in that way, but he had lost eleven to sickness.

In Jalapa, Calhoun was distressed to learn about the punishment of women who had aided Americans.

> Every woman who has shown the slightest kindness to the Americans, is under the ban of those who control the destiny of this people. It matters not whether we have met them in their drawing rooms, or as sisters of charity in our hospitals, it is said, they are condemned to have their heads shaved and the letters U.S. branded upon their cheeks; and many are incarcerated. Women are ever kind, and we have not found them less so here than elsewhere; and sorely it grieves us to hear of such maltreatment, such barbarity, to those who have soothed us in the hour of affliction.

Prostitutes in Mexico City were treated harshly after American troops departed, but the repercussions Calhoun described might have been faulty information.[20]

A final indignation was Patterson's order to abandon their horses at Vera-cruz. In 1849 Congress would provide payment up to $200 to any officer or soldier who lost a horse in battle or at sea or because the United States failed to supply transportation. The Georgia Mounted Battalion would be compensated for more than three hundred horses. "Some of the horses ordered abandoned by Gen. Patterson were very valuable," a newspaper reported.[21]

Home Again

Calhoun, his officers, and the 316 noncommissioned officers of the Georgia Mounted Battalion arrived on the *Alabama* at New Orleans on July 5, 1848. They carried the remains of Captain Kendall. Five other captains survived—Goulding, Hamilton, Fulton, Wofford, and Nelson—but Nelson would die at home in Cass County on October 30. In Mobile they were paid and discharged.

According to war statisticians, the battalion had six deaths in battle and 142 deaths from disease and accidents. "The Georgia boys have been kept, it is true, in the back ground; but they have always showed themselves ready and willing to do their part. Honor them as they deserve," wrote the *Enquirer*. The Milledgeville paper wrote that the volunteers were expected soon. "Col. Calhoun . . . has many warm friends here, and I should not be surprised if there be a little excitement upon his arrival. By the bye, Col. Calhoun has been spoken of as a candidate for Congress in this district." Because he was well known and quickly "rallied to the support of old Rough and Ready [Taylor]," Calhoun would make an excellent congressman, the paper asserted. Calhoun brought home with him "an intelligent Mexican youth," no doubt intending to provide him a home and education. The boy drowned a month later while swimming in the river.[22]

By mid-July, returning volunteers were on every stage and wagon. "The most of them that we have seen look rather the worse for wear, and some greatly enfeebled by disease and apparent exposure," wrote the *Enquirer* Newspapers began chronicling their deaths. "Many who are anxiously trying to get back to their homes, relations and friends are dropping into the grave on the road thither. Peace to their ashes. Curses loud and long upon the authors of a war which has brought about so much misery and sorrow, suffering and death!" The dying and misery didn't end with the Treaty of Guadalupe Hidalgo. Illness tormented thousands of veterans the rest of their days. In 1859 Congress debated whether to place David Watson, a private in Nelson's company, on the list of invalid pensioners to receive four dollars per month. Watson's diarrhea "has continued until the present time, disabling him," said his petition. A congressman argued that most soldiers in the Mexican War could make the same argument, "for I know, from my own observation, that this was a universal disease among the whole of them, from the commanding officer down to the last private."[23] Historian John S. D. Eisenhower wrote: "It was a dirty war, its costly nature due more to disease and hardship than to enemy action. The sufferings of the individual soldiers—American and Mexican alike—exceeded today's imagination."

For Calhoun, the war became more than a patriotic exercise and an escape from painful memories in Columbus. He had hardened, physically and mentally. He had become a leader of men and a garrison commander, with all the heartbreak and hardship that entailed, and earned the respect of his troops. He had embraced other settings and other cultures and employed his Spanish. His experiences would serve him in the next chapters of his life.

8

BOLD ADVENTURERS

Before he set foot again on Georgia soil, Calhoun was being talked up as a candidate for Congress. He was well known, and his service in Mexico endeared him to citizens. Whigs nominated Calhoun by acclamation as the Second District candidate, to applause from Whig papers. "Col. Calhoun is a strong man, a matter-of-fact man, a gentleman of strong practical mind and of proverbial persevering business habits," wrote the *Albany Courier*. "He does not claim to be of the 'upper ten.' He is not the silk-gloved, pastry-fed, carpet-knight but he is the man to defend his country's honor and his country's interests in the tented field, where death rides on whistling bullets and poisoned miasma." A Democratic newspaper sneered: "We have never heard that Col. Calhoun possessed any qualification for that office except that Governor Crawford once knocked him into a cocked hat and sent him to Mexico at the head of the Georgia battalion. The exploits of Col. Calhoun in Mexico have not yet come to light . . . It is enough however for our war loving Whigs that he has worn a pair of Epauletts, he has been to Mexico, and that is sufficient." Calhoun's opponent was Marshall J. Wellborn, a Columbus judge nine years his junior.[1]

Calhoun was in Washington, DC, then teeming with office seekers, trying to drum up business or a political appointment. He and two of his lieutenants, Goulding and Hamilton, had offered several times to raise a regiment of mounted volunteers to serve in New Mexico or California, but Secretary of War William L. Marcy saw no need. When Calhoun returned to Georgia on August 21, 1848, he accepted the nomination "with a profound sense of gratitude" and promised to meet people in their counties, "prepared to assault the enemies and traducers of that distinguished soldier" General Zachary Taylor. Since December 1846, Alexander Stephens and Robert Toombs had been agitating to make Taylor the Whig nominee for president, and on July 1, 1847, Stephens secured Taylor's nomination at the convention. Whigs, whose ranks included most of the landed gentry and professionals, believed they would find a sympathetic president in Taylor, a planter and slave owner.[2]

Calhoun and former governor George W. Crawford hit the campaign trail, meeting a blistering schedule of events around the district, accompanied at times by Toombs but not by the diminutive Stephens, who was badly injured in an altercation with a 200-pound, knife-wielding political opponent. The campaign quickly turned nasty. After Calhoun's opponents accused him of being "a Bankite and Tariffite," an old friend, probably Hines Holt Jr., rose to Calhoun's defense, writing that when the government called for volunteers, "Col. Calhoun was the first man in Georgia to enroll his name and to tender his services. He was the first man in Georgia to unfurl his country's flag and to plant it as a rallying point for Georgia's chivalric and patriotic sons" and then to serve again. He had known Calhoun since his youth and in every position he had "acted well and nobly his part." In times of good fortune, when he could help, no one was turned away. In business, "who made more effort and greater sacrifices to protect and advance the interests of the planters?" It was true that Calhoun "lives in 'the city of broken Banks'" and was once the president of a broken bank, but Farmers' Bank of Chattahoochee was the only troubled bank in Georgia that did "strict justice to its creditors." The bank honored every bill and liability, and when it was all over, Calhoun had plunged from affluence to poverty. "Col. Calhoun has served you in peace and in war ... faithfully, ably and honestly. He is worthy of your confidence. Give it to him. He has never abused it and never will."[3]

Calhoun's speeches, said Whig papers, were articulate, persuasive, and enthusiastically received. Democratic papers decried them as abominable and embarrassing to his supporters. He campaigned

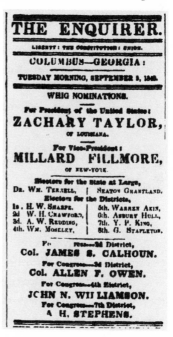

FIGURE 29. On September 5, 1848, the *Columbus Enquirer* ran this political endorsement of Taylor, Calhoun, and Stephens.

energetically for Taylor and convinced many a farmer to rely on a war veteran, himself, rather than Judge Wellborn. He told crowds he began as a farmer and had been a merchant and soldier but didn't mention being a banker. Democrats charged that he went to Mexico "to create a name and fame." Georgia that year was a hot election battleground, but Taylor prevailed. In Columbus, Calhoun outpolled Wellborn 840 to 515, but he lost the district by a scant twelve votes, 3,650 votes to 3,562. "Well, we are beaten, but such a beat as it is!" said the *Enquirer*.[4]

In the midst of the campaign, on September 14, 1848, Calhoun's younger daughter, Martha Ann, twenty-one, married twenty-two-year-old John H. Davis. He wasn't an up-and-coming businessman like William Love, the other son-in-law, but he was active in civic affairs and shared Calhoun's interests.[5]

In need of gainful employment again, Calhoun advertised his services as a general agent, "engaged in adjusting and settling accounts against the United States for Military and other services" and attending to business entrusted to his care. This allowed him to make a living and keep a presence in the nation's capital. In January 1849, he pestered Secretary of War Marcy about the position of inspector general: "It is an appointment I greatly desire if the novelty and excitement of an active life as a colonel commanding a mounted regiment in California cannot be assigned to me."[6]

Friends in High Places

Under the Treaty of Guadalupe Hidalgo, which ended the Mexican War, the United States claimed territory that would become New Mexico, Arizona, and California. It took responsibility for thousands of Indian people, many of them hostile, in the newly acquired region and promised to maintain the peace, protect citizens, and keep the tribes from raiding into Mexico. The government had just nine Indian agents. Because Congress had created no new Indian agencies, the president directed Interior Secretary Thomas Ewing to transfer the Indian agency at Council Bluffs to Santa Fe, and on March 29, 1849, Ewing appointed Calhoun, then in Washington, as Indian agent to New Mexico. That year, the Office of Indian Affairs had been transferred from the War Department to Interior, a sea change that infuriated the army and set the stage for years of conflict and competition between agents and officers.

Newspapers debated his qualifications. A Whig paper declared that his "knowledge of the Mexican and Indian character," and his energy and experience "eminently qualify him for the post." A Democratic sheet said he was a has-been who was once consul at Havana. "He cannot be supposed to be either qualified by knowledge or habit for an Indian agent."[7] In truth, the position of Indian agent was a function of political patronage. Agents were often former military men, and knowledge of Indian people wasn't a requirement. In light of his background, his honesty, and what today we call people skills, Calhoun was more qualified than most Indian agents for years to come.

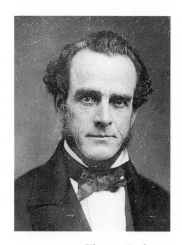

FIGURE 30. Thomas Butler King, a Georgia legislator and congressman, was well known to Calhoun before the two were chosen for posts in the West. Library of Congress.

Many a historian has written that Calhoun won the post because of his friendship with Taylor, but it was Georgia's powerful congressmen Stephens and Toombs who pulled the levers. Taylor relied on Kentucky Governor John J. Crittenden, a former United States senator and attorney general, for advice on appointments. (Crittenden chose his good friend Orlando Brown as Indian Commissioner.) As a senator, Crittenden had roomed with Stephens and Toombs; after he suggested that Taylor consult them, they delivered appointments to Calhoun and George W. Crawford, who became secretary of war. Separately, Georgia Congressman Thomas Butler King was named Taylor's special agent to California. Calhoun knew King well. They had served together in the Georgia legislature, mingled at Whig events, and corresponded.[8]

It was an ironic chain of events. Stephens opposed keeping New Mexico and California. Toombs declared earlier that he wanted no dismemberment of Mexico, that the United States had enough territory. Southern Whigs defended both the union and slavery but knew the new territories would spark contentious debate over their future as slave or free states. For the sake of the union, they wanted to avoid it. In the short, heated 1848–1849 congressional session, a compromise bill called for territorial governments for California, New Mexico, and Oregon, exclusion of slavery in Oregon, and a Supreme

Court vote to decide the matter for New Mexico and California. Toombs voted for the bill and Stephens against.

Taylor wanted New Mexico and California to enter the union as free states. He acknowledged that the statehood decision belonged to Congress, but in April 1849, he dispatched Calhoun and King with verbal instructions to move the statehood process. Beyond that, their duties were starkly different. King was the president's representative. Secretary of State John Clayton instructed King to assure Californians of the president's "desire to protect them in the formation of any government" they chose, but the plan must originate with them. Democrats accused King of being a special agent who would rob the South of its rights in the new territory. Calhoun was to serve as New Mexico's first Indian agent *and* to advance the cause of statehood. It was a tall order.[9]

A second, towering issue was the Texas claim to all of New Mexico east of the Rio Grande—the most populated portion of the region. From its beginnings as a republic in 1836, Texas insisted that the river formed its southwestern border, which gave it portions of three Mexican states and the eastern half of New Mexico. Texas had no valid claim over New Mexico, either by history, purchase, or conquest. Texas President Mirabeau Lamar sent an armed, 321-man trading expedition to New Mexico in 1841 with orders to consolidate New Mexico with Texas. The Mexican army arrested them at the border and imprisoned them in Mexico City. Lamar next sent Texas freebooters in 1843 to disrupt Mexican trade routes. They managed to whip a Mexican army patrol, but a few weeks later US troops protecting the Santa Fe Trail surrounded the Texans and sent them home.[10] New Mexicans adamantly opposed the Texas claim. The *Santa Fe Republican*, on August 31, 1848, advised Texas officials to bring a large force to serve as bodyguards on their way home.

Bold Adventurers

Calhoun received his commission on April 7, 1849, and with it a copy of the Treaty of Guadalupe Hidalgo. He would be paid in advance his year's salary of $1,500 ($50,633 in 2020 dollars), plus $500 for interpreters; $1,500 for contingencies, gifts, and statistical information; and $300 for the release of captives. The government knew so little about the tribes in New Mexico that Calhoun's first instructions were to report back their numbers, locations, territories, habits, and friendliness (or not) to the United States. Secretary Ewing told William

Medill,[11] the outgoing commissioner of Indian Affairs, that he wanted the agencies in California, Salt Lake City, and Santa Fe "to be well cared for, as the future action of the Department in our Indian Affairs depends upon its accuracy and extent." The newly appointed Secretary of War (and former Georgia governor) George Crawford, ordered transportation, subsistence, arms, and escorts for Calhoun and the other appointees.[12]

Columbus citizens gave Calhoun a public dinner at the Planters' Hotel, where his friends warmly toasted the new agent and wished him success. Almost as they spoke, the sheriff was selling sixteen adult slaves and their children belonging to Calhoun to satisfy debts of Charles Bass that Calhoun had guaranteed. After turning over his claims business to lawyer and postmaster J. A. L. Lee,[13] Calhoun left Columbus for the last time on April 15, 1849. With him were his daughters, Carolina and Martha, their husbands, William Love[14] and John Davis, and the Loves' three-year-old daughter Anna. (The four females Calhoun wrote were in the party probably included a servant or slave.) Ten friends accompanied them. They traveled to Chattanooga, Tennessee, and then St. Louis, Missouri, where another six people were to join them. "From Independence I shall have with me twenty bold & enterprising adventurers— several of whom served in the war against Mexico—as Volunteers under my command . . . I regard them as absolutely necessary to the entire success of my efforts to discharge my duties in New Mexico," he wrote.[15] Calhoun apparently had great, even grandiose, expectations for his mission.

The bold adventurers included Edwin R. Goulding, twenty-eight; John G. Jones,[16] thirty-four; and Dr. Brice Asa Hoxey,[17] twenty-four. All three served under Calhoun in the war. The others were Dr. Carroll C. Thomas; brothers Andrew and Benjamin Lee, of Charleston, South Carolina; William H. Mitchell, a fellow railroad investor[18]; former Columbus alderman and port warden George W. Martin,[19] thirty-one; Cyrus Choice; and Charles Jackson,[20] Calhoun's slave. General Cyrus Choice, like Calhoun, was fifty and widowed; a Georgia merchant, he served in the state's Indian wars.[21] Choice, Jones, and son-in-law Love would accompany Calhoun on all his trips into Indian country. Son-in-law Davis would run the office while Calhoun was away.[22]

Stepping off the steamboat at St. Louis, they found a noisy crossroads city where eastern goods and western produce entered the nation's market. The army quartermaster couldn't provide the two ambulances Calhoun requested for himself and his daughters, so he spent $849.29 on one ambulance to transport his bedding, supplies, and cooking utensils. Travelers on the Santa Fe Trail usually relied on freight wagons like the Conestoga; with his ambulance, Calhoun anticipated a trend of coming years. The weatherproof ambulance, which had a seat that made into a bed, became the choice of many a traveler.[23]

Even the agents' travel arrangements provoked debate in the press. Democrats questioned the transfer of Indian agencies and their new locations, insisted that Medill intended to hire more experienced agents, and sputtered over the cost of army escorts and transportation. A Whig newspaper countered: Was a new agent to go alone and "frown down the mounted warriors which infest the frontier settlements . . . with a single pair of eyebrows?" No one expected the agents to fit out their own expedition and spend their salaries "risking their throats" among the Indians, so it was necessary to have an escort and transportation.[24]

Santa Fe Trail

At Fort Leavenworth, immigrant trains assembled, and excited sojourners prepared for the trip west. Calhoun, impatient to reach Santa Fe "at the earliest practicable moment," sat for two weeks in a camp west of the Kaw (Kansas) River awaiting his military escort. He penned yet another offer to raise troops "and secure for New Mexico a desirable population." Finally, Brevet Lieutenant Colonel Edmund Brooke Alexander arrived with three companies of the Third Infantry and two companies of artillery, all weak and gaunt from a cholera epidemic. With whips cracking, cattle lowing, mules braying, and men whooping, Calhoun's party set out on the storied Santa Fe Trail, its wagon ruts stretching westward for 700 miles. They had the company of thousands of forty-niners headed to California. The Calhoun women, like the trader's wife Susan Magoffin three years earlier, were probably a novelty on the trail. Calhoun fussed about the plodding pace of the oxen, even though fellow travelers found the creatures' gentle, rhythmic gait allowed wagons to sway and not jolt. Because oxen fared poorly in the heat, bullwhackers started at dawn and drove until midday, then stopped and continued for a few hours in the late afternoon and evening.[25]

There was nothing luxurious about the journey, and it was often dangerous. The increased traffic of troops and settlers on the trail alarmed Plains tribes and offered new opportunities for plunder, and they struck regularly. Disease—malaria, dysentery, tuberculosis, yellow fever, diphtheria, cholera, and smallpox—were widespread. H. M. T. Powell, traveling at the same time, wrote that the trail "seemed like a lengthened cemetery. The mounds of graves of the emigrants thrown up at intervals on either side of the road and the bones and remains of cattle and mules strewn in all directions was but a dismal sight."[26] The forlorn spectacle made a lasting impression on Calhoun.

Leaving civilization behind, they entered a rolling prairie endless as the ocean, passing deep streams with near vertical sides and elm, black walnut, white ash, and oaks growing alongside. Deer and antelope bounded away from the trains. Nearly 150 miles from Independence, the two-year-old town of Council Grove welcomed travelers. The site of the treaty negotiation that made the Santa Fe Trail possible, it was a favorite stopping place. Beyond lay prairie as level as a billiard table without a tree in sight, and the dangers of Indian attack increased. "The eye wanders in vain over these immense wastes in search of trees. Not one is to be seen," wrote Lieutenant William H. Emory three years earlier. Calhoun's party was thankful for good grass along the trail and unusually abundant water.[27]

Friendly Indians visited the Georgians' camp in the evening to trade mules and buffalo robes. "I bought a very fine (buffalo robe) for about a tablespoon full of red vermillion," wrote George Martin. They learned to cook with buffalo chips when wood was scarce. "They make an excellent fire, but do not last long," Martin said. They thrilled to exciting hunts once they reached the buffalo plains. The first herd of fifteen thousand gave up one of its numbers to Andrew Lee, and they saw buffalo for another a week. "Thomas, Lee and Hoxey were the best hunters in the whole command," Martin wrote. "They had a decided advantage of most of our party, having fleet horses. My horse, Flummux, was not very fast in a chase, but was superior to any nag in the whole command to keep the road in a walk, he seemed to be conscious that there was value on his back, and did not care to be excited like most of horses at the report of guns, &c."

Calhoun relaxed and allowed himself to enjoy the hunting. "The buffalo, antelope, deer, rabbits (unreadable) together with birds and fishing gave us all the sport we could desire," he wrote. However, his daughter Martha had been sick several days, possibly, he speculated, from spending too much time on her horse. "The ladies generally rode 10 to 15 hours a day," he said. Goulding was also ill, and another man had wounded himself with his own knife.[28]

At the white sand hills of the Little Arkansas and the Arkansas Rivers, they reached the halfway point. There they were surprised by the presence of thousands of Indians, mostly Arapahos, Cheyennes, Kiowas, Comanches, and Utes, waiting for their agent, Thomas Fitzpatrick, to distribute gifts. The sight of genuine "wild" Indians, and not the settled, acculturated Creeks, rattled Calhoun profoundly as the looming reality of his duties invaded his well-laid plans. He wrote Commissioner Medill that the "obstacles to be overcome in adjusting our Indian relations in New Mexico, and its border, are of a much more formidable character than has been anticipated." The agitation of the waiting natives made the Georgians fearful for their safety, and they moved on.

Turning southwest at the Cimarron Crossing, they took the Desert Route of the Santa Fe Trail, which was shorter and drier than the Mountain Route. The Arkansas, a dividing line between the verdant prairies and the short-grass plains, became a shallow, muddy flow between treeless banks. This was the heart of buffalo country, dotted by dried buffalo chips, bleached bones, and trails leading to the river. At Pawnee Fork of the Arkansas, a clear, sparkling stream favored by the Kiowas and Comanches, a trading party met Alexander's troops and Calhoun's party and Major Howe of the second dragoons and reported them all well. Passing over a dry, thinly vegetated plain, they reached the Lower Spring of the Cimarron River, the only water for miles, followed by the Cimarron itself. Before long, the Mountain and Desert Routes joined.[29]

After seven hundred miles, they reached the New Mexico town of Las Vegas (The Meadows), established in 1823 on the western edge of the plains. Here travelers saw their first adobe houses constructed of mud and straw, the preferred building material of the Southwest. Las Vegas had about one hundred houses along streets laid out on a grid. Here the United States posted dragoons. Thirty miles farther west, the travelers entered San Miguel del Vado (Saint Michael of the Ford), larger and wealthier than Las Vegas and described by trader Josiah Gregg as "irregular clusters of mud-wall huts" with residents as brown as adobe bricks.[30]

In the distance the travelers could see the deep purple outline of the Sangre de Cristo (Blood of Christ) mountain range. They passed the ruins of Pecos Pueblo, once a sizable Indian community, and threaded Glorieta Pass through mountains of granite and sand with cedar, piñon, and pine growing wherever trees could get a perch. When they topped the last rise, they stared down at Santa Fe, another adobe town squatting at the foot of the mountains. George Martin wrote: "We were all astonished at the magnificence and grandeur of

FIGURE 31. Santa Fe appears as a farming community in a drawing from the "Report of Lt. J. W. Abert of his Examination of New Mexico in the Years 1846–1847."

the appearance of this place; when we came in view, about a mile off, there was a general exclamation of wonder, can this be Santa Fe? Imagine about 1,500 dirt houses, one story high, scattered without any regularity as to streets, surrounded by high and barren mountains."

Martin's first impression of Santa Fe was typical. "At first sight the town was not much to look at," wrote another traveler. "It was possible to be utterly disgusted with it at first sight, second sight, and last sight." If Santa Fe failed to impress travelers, at least its earthen walls signaled the end of an arduous, dangerous journey. The Georgians arrived on Sunday, July 22, 1849, after traveling forty-one days from Fort Leavenworth and sixty-eight days total.[31]

Ancient Capital

Santa Fe had been a trade and government center for Spain and Mexico since 1610 in a region claimed for the Spanish crown in 1598. Until the Mexican Revolution in 1821, New Mexico was a captive market for Chihuahua merchants. When the newly formed Mexican government allowed American traders to enter New Mexico, the Santa Fe Trail opened the region to the wonders of American commerce.

In August 1846, as Calhoun and the Georgia volunteers simmered in the muck of Fort Belknap, Brigadier General Stephen Watts Kearny rode into Santa Fe and completed a bloodless conquest of New Mexico. Troops marched to the Palace of the Governors, the seat of power through Spanish, Mexican, and now American control and "the living center of everything of historic importance in the Southwest," as historian Ralph Emerson Twitchell described the old structure. Kearny and his staff dismounted and met local dignitaries. He declared that he was annexing all of New Mexico to the United States. Acting Governor Juan Bautista Vigil y Alarid responded: "Do not be surprised that we have not manifested joy and enthusiasm in seeing our city occupied by your military forces. To us the political entity of the Republic of Mexico has died. She, regardless of her circumstances, was our mother. What son would not shed copious tears at the tomb of his parents?"[32]

New Mexicans had remained faithful to Mexico even as neighboring Texas fought for its independence and joined the United States. New Mexicans knew that Mexico and the United States had broken relations over the annexation of Texas in March 1845, but they didn't learn the two nations were at war until reports reached them of an American army marching toward them in the summer of 1846. New Mexico then had about sixty-five thousand people. Several hundred Americans, primarily traders, were living in Santa Fe and Taos.[33]

Kearny created a temporary civil government, promised to respect New Mexico's religious institutions, and vowed that the United States would protect citizens from Indian attack. In September, he issued the Organic Law of the Territory of New Mexico, later called the Kearny Code, which combined laws of Spain, Mexico, Missouri, and the Livingston Code, written for Louisiana when it was acquired from France. He appointed as governor Charles Bent,[34] a well-known trader who, with his brother William and Ceran St. Vrain, had built the famed Bent's Fort on the Santa Fe Trail. Kearny then departed for California and left Colonel Alexander W. Doniphan of the First Regiment of Missouri Volunteers in charge.

The following winter, seething resentment of the occupiers exploded. On January 19, 1847, Taos Pueblo Indian men and their Hispanic allies brutally murdered Governor Bent in his home; his family escaped through a hole chopped in the wall. American troops suppressed the rebellion a few days later and tried the leaders.[35] Lingering repercussions of the short-lived rebellion would shadow Calhoun's work in the territory.

Houses of Mud

When the Georgians entered Santa Fe, they found its heart at the plaza, an expanse of hard-packed clay unrelieved by greenery. On the north side was the Palace of the Governors,[36] a long, low building with some of the town's only glazed windows and fronted along its three-hundred-foot length by a *portal*, which is a covered walk. On the south side was a large military chapel with two low bell towers; on the east was the Catholic Church. Also fronting the plaza were an inn and shops of the American traders, all with *portales* to shield pedestrians from sun and weather. Unpaved, dirty streets radiated outward, connecting scattered houses surrounded by large fields of corn. Three days after Calhoun arrived, an army assistant surgeon, Lemise Edwards, reported the "filthy, unhealthy and unsightly condition of the public streets and alleys of the city." Standing pools of water should be filled, he said, and a slaughterhouse serving an American hotel should be moved outside the city.[37]

George Martin described residents to fellow Georgians as "mostly Mexican inhabitants of the lowest order, and about 500 emigrants for California, perfectly reckless, having gambled and lost all their money . . . (With) faro and monte tables in every corner and cross street," he wrote, "you can form some idea of the state of society." British traveler G. F. Ruxton observed dirty, rowdy, drunken soldiers filling the streets, to the disgust of the New Mexicans. And yet, everyone was welcome at the frequent fiestas, balls, and *fandangos* (dances). "New Mexicans of all social classes danced together, worshipped together and attended each other's family baptisms, weddings and funerals." W. W. H. Davis, who arrived in 1852, observed that New Mexicans were kind and considerate and their hospitality sincere. "They are naturally quiet and amiable, and their manners equal any people in the world," he wrote.[38]

Santa Fe and New Mexico were places the Americans could love and hate. Anna Maria Morris, who came to Santa Fe with her husband, an army major, in 1850, wrote, "It is the most miserable squalid looking place I ever beheld. The houses are mud, the fences are mud, the churches & courts are mud, in fact it is all mud." However, she admired the cozy corner fireplaces, praised local silverwork, and even took Spanish lessons.

Adobe houses, depending on the teller, were either comfortable and charming or wretched and dirty. The one-story house wrapped around a tree-shaded patio or enclosed courtyard; rooms opened into the patio. Floors were packed

FIGURE 32. "Morning on the Plaza" captures Santa Fe's lively social center
in an engraving from *Harper's Weekly* in the 1880s.

dirt, sometimes covered with a coarse rug called a *gerga*. Walls inside and out
were plastered with adobe and painted white with gypsum, which rubbed off;
to protect clothing, residents hung a shoulder-height, calico covering. Thick
walls kept rooms cooler in summer and warmer in winter. Mattresses covered
with Navajo rugs served as seats. In the better homes, beams supporting the
roof were planed and painted. By the time Calhoun arrived, Americans had
built a peaked-roof home or two.[39]

"Imagine the surprise of persons coming from places where houses are built
with every convenience and sanitary devices, suddenly to find themselves introduced into several oblong walls of adobes," wrote Sister Blandina Segale
years later. To enter, "instead of stepping up, you step down onto a mud floor."
Rafters made of tree trunks supported an earthen roof, which "had to be carefully attended, else the rain would pour in." Doors were covered with blankets,
and furniture consisted of "a few chairs, handmade and painted red [and] a
large quantity of wool which they were assured was clean and for their use" as
bedding. A corner fireplace provided heat and served as a stove.[40]

A market brought the plaza to life every day. Hispanic and Pueblo Indian
farmers sold their wares under the portales, stringing meat on lines and ar-

ranging their vegetables on mats. Shoppers could buy mutton, kid, pork, chile, beans, onions, milk, bread, cheese, and, in season, grapes, wild plums, berries, and melons. In winter there was game—venison, turkey, and, occasionally, bear.

New Mexicans ate a nutritious diet of tortillas made of blue corn, which Americans had never seen. Staples were tortillas, tamales, beans, and chile con carne (chile with meat). Another dish was *atole*, a kind of mush made of wheat or corn meal, with piñon nuts if available. Bread was made with unbolted flour that still contained both husk and germ of the grain. They dried fruits, vegetables, and strips of meat in the sun. Newcomer Louis Garrard described red chile sauce as "a hot mess at first," but after consuming a great many tortillas with the spicy sauce, he acquired a taste.[41] That Calhoun didn't embrace the native diet would be his personal tragedy, quite literally.

However unimpressive the earthen town of five thousand souls might have been, its surroundings were stunning. Santa Fe perched at 7,000 feet in altitude on the flanks of the Sangre de Cristo Mountains, named by Spaniards for their crimson sunsets. To the south, behind Albuquerque, rose the Sandia Mountains, and northwest were the Jemez Mountains. The Rio Grande coursed through the region from the Rocky Mountains in present-day Colorado to the Gulf of Mexico. "Such was the extreme purity of the atmosphere, any one peak seemed attainable by a few hours' ride. How simple, how imposingly great are these distant works of Nature!" wrote Louis Garrard.[42]

Americans often wrote home about the healthy climate. Santa Fe trader Francis X. Aubry would say in 1852: "This is called, 'the Land without Law.' But it is a land that has brought healing to the hearts of many. Many an invalid I have had in my caravans, but before they reached Santa Fe, they were eating buffalo meat raw and sleeping soundly under their blankets. There is something in the air of New Mexico that makes the blood red, the heart to beat high and the eyes to look upward. Folks don't come here to die—they come to live and they get what they come for."[43]

Settling In

Calhoun and his family camped a half-mile outside of town for several weeks while arranging for "a mud house at the enormous rent" of $100 a month ($3,375 in 2020), which he reduced to $70 by using only a portion of the building. It would need some modifications to Americanize it and make it comfortable.

"You are apprised that all the houses in this City are built up of adobes—with floors of dirt, and covered by spreading dirt three to six inches thick upon rough boards," Calhoun wrote the commissioner. "You will readily conclude, and correctly too, we have dirty, and leaky houses." Calhoun spent more than $200 of his $1,500 yearly salary on rough pine planks for the floor. They had to haul water by wagon.[44] It was a far cry from his brick mansion on the Chattahoochee.

William Mitchell and Benjamin Lee camped with Calhoun. Edwin Goulding, Asa Hoxey, and Carroll Thomas boarded at a hotel for twenty-eight dollars a month. George Martin, John Jones, and Andrew Lee rented two rooms for eight dollars a month and hired a free Black man as cook for twelve dollars a month. A grumpy Martin wrote home: "John Jones and Lee have gone to church, a Baptist preacher is stationed here. I am in this mud hole all alone, fighting flies with one hand, while I try to write with the other." The two physicians, Thomas and Hoxey, opened a practice. Their first patient was a "beautiful señorita with a dislocated knee," Calhoun wrote. Said Martin: "Asa Hoxey and Thomas are practicing medicine until Col. Calhoun wants them; we are all going to make expenses if we can. Col. Calhoun says he thinks he will have business for us in two months."[45]

Calhoun was allowed to buy supplies at the commissary at government prices, so his family had bacon, rice, coffee, and sugar. Everything else was expensive except flour, available from small local grist mills. Vegetables were scarce, but there were some onions, beans, radishes, peas, "and an abundance of pepper," meaning spicy chile pepper. The only fruit was apricots. Mutton was cheap; a whole sheep cost fifty cents, Martin wrote.

By October, Choice, Love, Jones, Davis, Mitchell, and the Lee brothers were providing services. Mitchell[46] involved himself in trade. Carroll Thomas by late November opened a practice with Dr. James. D. Robinson. The two would propose vaccinating the Pueblo Indians against smallpox.[47]

Carolina and Martha probably found female company rather sparse. The census in 1832 counted thirty-two Anglo women—wives of officers, merchants, or territorial officials—but they would have been warmly welcomed. American men were just beginning to bring their families with them, and they often didn't stay. American women were usually shocked by the low-cut blouses and short skirts of the local women, who smoked and gambled, although W. W. H. Davis found the New Mexican ladies healthy, graceful, and athletic. The town's most skillful monte dealer was Doña Gertrudes Barceló, an aging beauty who ran an elegant gambling hall. Because the Calhoun daughters had spent a year in Cuba and likely learned some Spanish, they might have been at ease with New Mexican women. Calhoun, who had fought for women's property rights in Georgia, would be fascinated to learn that under Spanish and Mexican law a woman could own, inherit, loan, convey, or pawn property, and she retained her property, legal rights, wages, and maiden name after marriage. This ended in 1846 under the United States.[48]

American occupation was quickly changing the ancient city. By 1848 Santa Fe had three hotels advertising choice liquors and meals "cooked in Mexican or American fashion." A Mrs. Jones operated the local theater and opened an even larger theater with a "fancy dress and masquerade ball." On October 1, 1849, a US Post Office was established, and regular mail service began the following year when stagecoaches began running, guarded by eight men armed with Colt's revolving rifles or pistols. Before long there was daily service at a fare of $250. And in 1851, Santa Fe would get a Masonic Lodge, which gave men like Calhoun, who were neither gamblers nor drinkers, a place to socialize.[49]

Santa Fe in the mid-1800s "was not merely the capital of a remote and thinly settled territory," wrtes historian Harvey Fergusson. "It was the capital of a racial frontier." After the Mexican War ended, some New Mexicans left and about five hundred Americans moved in. "The wagon trade across the plains was booming to the amount of nearly a million dollars a year. In Santa Fe men of the two great cultures that occupy the Western hemisphere were for the first time sitting down together in legislative assembly and in courts of law. They were doing business together, intermarrying, sometimes fighting and often looking down their noses at each other in mutual antipathy. This difficult process of adjustment was a dramatic thing, and one big with significance for the future."[50]

9

"NUMEROUS AND SAVAGE TRIBES"

Calhoun pored over a report sent by the commissioner that probably reinforced his alarm at the sight of wild tribes on the Arkansas. Governor Charles Bent, appointed governor of occupied New Mexico in 1846, estimated the number of Indians at forty thousand, and he probably underestimated. Fifty-year-old Calhoun was now responsible for all the Indians in a nearly 240,000-square mile area—most of present-day New Mexico and Arizona plus a bit of Colorado. Bent concluded that "it becomes a subject of serious import, how the numerous and savage tribes are to be controlled and managed."[1]

Bent, a long-time trader, summed up the region's tribes. In the north, the Jicarilla Apaches, numbering about 500, raided New Mexicans because game was scarce, and the plains tribes kept them from hunting buffalo. In the south, he said, about five thousand to six thousand Apaches were "warlike people . . . (who) live almost entirely by plundering the Mexican settlements." The Navajos to the northwest and west numbered between seven thousand and fourteen thousand. They were "an industrious, intelligent and warlike tribe of Indians who cultivate the soil and raise sufficient grain for their own consumption and a variety of fruits," Bent wrote. "They are the owners of large flocks and herds of cattle, sheep, horses and mules and asses." They also had many slaves and made excellent blankets and woolen goods. West of the Navajos were about 2,450 Moquis (Hopis), who lived in permanent villages, cultivated grain and fruit, and raised livestock. North of the Navajos were some four thousand to five thousand Utes, a "hardy, warlike people, subsisting on the chase." To the northeast were Cheyennes and Arapahos, buffalo hunters who traded with New Mexicans. Some twelve thousand Comanches living to the east were at peace in New Mexico but at war in the northern states of Mexico. Those were just the tribes Bent knew about. In the western deserts and canyons and on the eastern plains were more tribes that he didn't name. Bent said agents and subagents "are absolutely necessary" for regulation and control. Gifts were "indispensable in all friendly communications with Indians." He thought forts should be established in Ute and Navajo country "with sufficient troops to keep these in check."[2]

Bent didn't mention thousands of Pueblo people living peacefully in nineteen permanent villages, from the upper Rio Grande to the western mesas of present New Mexico. They were the original inhabitants of the Southwest, here for thousands of years—or the beginning of time, in their view. When the first Spaniards appeared in 1598, they found Pueblo people with well-organized governments, a system of law and order, and tidy farms. Spain recognized Pueblo land ownership but was also an oppressor. After a historic revolt in 1680 followed by reconquest twelve years later, the pueblos accepted priests but maintained their traditional practices. They furnished auxiliaries for military campaigns against common enemies.[3] Calhoun would spend the rest of 1849 learning about the tribes for himself and discovering there was no practical answer to Bent's question of how they could be "controlled and managed."

Navajo Expedition

Calhoun had barely settled in, when Colonel John M. Washington decided to make an expedition into Navajo country. Washington, a fifty-three-year-old Virginian and son of the first president's cousin, assumed command of the Ninth Military Department on October 11, 1848, becoming military governor of New Mexico. He was a West Pointer who won commendations for valor in the Mexican War. The day before leaving, on August 15, 1849, Calhoun wrote: "The Indians generally are in bad temper—the number of Troops are not sufficient here to keep upon them a proper check, and Infantry are useful only to protect posts—stations—and property. Mounted troops are the only military order of this country that can be effectively used against the Indian tribes of this remote region."[4]

The Navajos were "one of the most powerful and militarily adept tribes in North America," wrote historian Robert M. Utley. Their ancestors, the Athapascans, had probably arrived in the Southwest by the twelfth or thirteenth century; a distinctively Navajo culture began to emerge in the 1400s. The Navajo homeland, called *Dinetah*, stretched across the region from Taos to the Colorado River in present-day Arizona. Spanish farmers in the 1760s settled in Navajo country through a series of land grants, provoking decades of attacks and counterattacks. Navajos raided Spanish communities, but the raids were sometimes retaliation for Spanish attacks on Navajo camps to take captives for the slave trade. The Spanish introduced sheep and other livestock and taught Navajos to weave and make silver jewelry. By the 1840s, Navajos grew all the grains and vegetables to be found in New Mexico, and bred and raised livestock superior to that of New Mexicans. "These lords of the mountains may be said to live on horseback," wrote an officer in 1846. "They pay great attention to the breeding of their horses, and think scarcely less of them than do the Arabians."[5]

On August 16, 1849, Calhoun and his friends Cyrus Choice and John Jones and son-in-law William Love rode out with Washington's forces: 120 regular infantry, 55 regular artillery, 50 New Mexico volunteer infantry, 80 New Mexico mounted militia, and 55 men from the pueblos of Santo Domingo, Santa Ana, Zia, and Jemez. Troops carried with them one six pounder and three mountain howitzers. Their mission was to punish the Navajos for their raids on settlements and to explore and map Navajo territory, which was then unknown.[6]

James Hervey Simpson, a thirty-six-year-old lieutenant and engineer in the US Army Corps of Topographical Engineers, had orders to survey the country and keep a journal. With him were brothers Richard H. Kern, an artist, and Edward M. Kern, a topographer. On the forty-one-day, 590-mile journey, Edward Kern produced the first reliable map of Navajo country, and Richard painted portraits of chiefs and costumes, scenery, geological formations, ruins and ancient inscriptions.[7] Another in the expedition was trader and interpreter James L. Collins, who would become Calhoun's most ruthless adversary.

From Santa Fe, the expedition made its way to Santo Domingo Pueblo, where residents were harvesting their crops, and on through sand hills and dry arroyos to Jemez Pueblo in the foothills of the Jemez Mountains. They camped just north of Jemez Pueblo, where many of Washington's men watched the Jemez people's Green Corn Dance. Riding uphill toward the Continental Divide, they could see the massive reddish volcanic plug, Cabezon (Big Head) Peak,[8] and the 10,000-foot Sandia Mountains in the distance. Calhoun described it as "exceedingly rugged country, checkered, occasionally, by beautiful, fertile and extensive valleys."[9]

On August 26, they came to Chaco Wash and approached a prominent ruin that Simpson would call *Pueblo Pintado* (Painted Village), the easternmost of nine great houses of Chaco Canyon. Simpson and the Kerns would be the first Americans to describe and survey the thousand-year-old ruins of the Anasazi civilization. Calhoun marveled that the country was so devoid of cultivation that "trails and ancient ruins afford the only evidence that human beings have passed that way." Camping near Badger Springs, they found no grass or forage, so Washington ordered them to use the green corn from a nearby field— to the Navajos, a hostile act. Several Navajo men and women came into the army camp on August 30. American visitors had previously noted that Navajo women were good riders who saddled their own horses and did their own trading. The Navajos said they'd collected fifteen horses and mules and some sheep to deliver to the soldiers. They would observe the treaty made a few weeks earlier with Colonel Edward W. B. Newby, they said, and did not want to fight. Even so, Kern observed "multitudes of Indians around us" who were growing angry.[10]

The expedition continued northwest up the Tumecha (Chuska) valley in view of the Ojos Calientes (Hot Springs) peaks and camped at the Rio Tumecha, a tributary of the San Juan River. That afternoon, Calhoun got the first opportunity to act in his new role as Indian agent when he and Washington told several headmen that they must comply with the treaty and give up captives, stolen stock, and the murderers among them or expect troops to enforce it. The chiefs promised to send word to the other camps.

Narbona

On August 31, three chiefs came in for a council: Narbona, José Largo, and Archuleta. Through the translator, Washington said he wanted them to go to Canyon de Chelly to make a treaty. Narbona, then in his eighties, was one of the Navajos' most important leaders. In 1829 the towering warrior—he was six feet six—led his people in a successful battle against the Mexicans in the Chuska Mountains. When the Americans met Narbona in 1846, he was so crippled with arthritis that he could hardly ride a horse. He had to be helped from his horse and carried to the white men. With him was his son-in-law, Manuelito. The Navajos brought in about one hundred sheep and four horses and mules.

Calhoun said: "Tell them they are lawfully in the jurisdiction of the United States, and they must respect that jurisdiction . . . (A)fter the treaty is made, their friends will be the friends of the United States, and their enemies the en-

FIGURE 33. Edward Kern drew this portrait of Chief Narbona from a sketch by his brother, Richard Kern, on August 31, 1849.

emies of the United States ... (W)hen any difficulty occurs between them and any other nation, by appealing to the United States they may get redress ... (A)ll trade between themselves and other nations will be recognized as under regulations to be prescribed by the United States." Washington added, "And the object of this is to prevent their being imposed upon by bad men." Calhoun continued: "If any wrong is done them by a citizen of the United States, or by a Mexican, he or they shall be punished by the United States as if the wrong had been done by a citizen of the United States, and on a citizen of the United States ... (T)he people of the United States shall go in and out of their country without molestation." The government had the right to establish military posts in Navaho country and would fix and mark their boundaries to prevent mis-understandings. The government would also give them presents of axes, hoes, farming utensils, and blankets. The chiefs said they understood. Narbona and José Largo designated others to act for them at Canyon de Chelly. A fourth chief, Sandoval, whose people lived to the southeast near the old Spanish vil-lage of Cebolleta, had previously asked for peace.[11]

Then one of Washington's soldiers recognized a horse he owned among those of the Navajos, and the colonel demanded its return. The Navajos refused. Washington warned them to return the horse or his soldiers would shoot. Navajos said the man who owned the horse had fled. Washington told a lieutenant to take one of the Navajo horses. "The moment the guard was ordered forward," Calhoun wrote, "every Navajo Indian in the crowd, supposed to number from three to four hundred, all mounted and armed, and their arms in their hands wheeled, and put the spur to their horses; Chief Narbona was left lifeless upon the ground, and several others were found dead in the vicinity." Soldiers killed Narbona and mortally wounded six other people. Narbona was scalped.[12]

Navajos were appalled that the soldiers would kill their beloved chief and one of their greatest warriors and inflict so much injury over a horse. Washington, who had fought Seminoles in Florida and participated in the forced removal of the Cherokees from Georgia, had no regrets. Narbona, he said, had been "a scourge to the inhabitants of New Mexico for the last thirty years." That night they camped in Narbona's cornfields. Washington intended to teach the Navajos a lesson, and Calhoun didn't disagree. What they didn't understand was that any hope for peace died with Narbona. As angry young warriors like Manuelito gained influence, the Navajos would wage war for nearly two more decades.

Troops continued up the Tumecha, and Simpson described his first hogan, the Navajos' traditional rounded dwellings. They saw yellow pine (Ponderosa) eighty feet tall and twelve feet in circumference. In the valley of the Rio Negro, a place of towering pines and firs, they found oak, aspen, and willow. The stream bed was thick with shrubbery and a vine loaded with fruit. Simpson identified more than ninety varieties of flowers. Everywhere they went, troops helped themselves to Navajo gardens and melon patches and turned their animals into cornfields to graze. They were eating the Navajos' winter food supplies.[13]

Canyon de Chelly

On September 5, the expedition reached the red sandstone fortress of Canyon de Chelly (pronounced SHAY), the heart of the Navajo homeland. Navajos used its streams to grow corn and peach trees. Its walls protected them and provided a view of approaching friends and enemies. Washington, Calhoun,

FIGURE 34. *above*
Canyon de Chelly in 1904
by Edward Curtis. Library
of Congress.

FIGURE 35. *right*
Chief Mariano Martinez
was drawn by Edward
and Richard Kern on
September 8th, 1849.

Collins, the Kerns, Simpson, and two officers visited Canyon del Muerto (Canyon of Death). "We found it to more than meet our expectations—so deep did it appear, so precipitous its rocks, and so beautiful and regular the stratification," Simpson wrote. Calhoun described the canyon as "rich in its Valleys, rich in its fields of grain, and rich in its vegetables and peach orchards. Water at this season of the year may be had in any desirable quantity by digging a few feet, and wood in abundance, pine, juniper and cedar, a few miles off."[14]

Chief Sandoval brought in two Navajos on September 7. One was Chief Mariano Martínez. Both embraced Washington and Calhoun "with a great deal of good will," Simpson wrote. Martínez wore a blue American-made greatcoat, a tarpaulin hat with a narrow brim, and buckskin leggings and moccasins. He had a bow and quiver slung over his body and a pouch and knife at his side. Washington told Martínez he expected the Navajos to restore 1,070 sheep, 34 mules, 19 horses, and 78 cattle. Martínez responded that he knew nothing about cattle—the Apaches must have stolen them. If they entered into a treaty in good faith, Washington said, it would result in blessings upon him and his people; if they didn't it would mean their destruction. Martínez said his people would do all he has promised. He said they were the first Americans to visit Canyon de Chelly. The meeting ended, and the chief again embraced Washington and Calhoun.[15]

In the treaty made September 9, 1849, the United States claimed jurisdiction over the Navajos. The tribe agreed to cease hostilities, maintain peace, and return captives and stolen property; the government would return Indian captives and property stolen from the Navajos. Travelers would be guaranteed safe passage. The United States would establish military posts and agencies and authorize trading houses. And the government would "designate, settle, and adjust their territorial boundaries." Mariano Martínez, identified as "Head Chief," and Chapitone, "second chief," signed the treaty. This treaty, like many others to follow, offered little to the Navajos. Calhoun and the military didn't yet understand that each group of Navajos was autonomous; a treaty with two chiefs didn't mean all Navajos agreed.[16]

Simpson set out with sixty men to explore Canyon de Chelly and see the fort he heard was a retreat in times of danger. Riding deeper into the canyon, they marveled at walls that rose until they "begin to assume a stupendous appearance. Almost perfectly vertical, they look as if they had been chiseled by the hand of art." Several Navajos, high above, shouted at them and then

FIGURE 36. Richard Kern drew the Pueblo of Zuni on September 15, 1849.

descended as nimbly as goats, "one of the most wonderful feats" any of them had ever witnessed. Other Navajos simply watched from their elevated perch while friendly people on the canyon floor gave soldiers peaches from their orchards. Simpson's party found no fort and no towns. Navajos lived, then and now, scattered across the land.[17]

To Simpson, the treaty had merit, but penetrating the heart of Navajo country and gaining a geographical knowledge of the area was invaluable. He estimated the population at eight thousand to ten thousand. Their many horses were better than those of the New Mexicans and capable of long, rapid journeys, although they weren't as fine as Comanche or American horses. With the treaty concluded, the Navajos wanted to trade. They had blankets, dressed skins, and peaches. Simpson declared their woven blankets the best in the world.[18]

The expedition turned east. At Zuni Pueblo, they received a warm welcome and quantities of bread and fruit. Calhoun found the five hundred Zunis "a hardy, well fed and well clothed race" and their leaders intelligent. "But what is shockingly discreditable to the American name," Calhoun reported, "emigrants [forty-niners] commit the grossest wrongs against these excellent Indians by taking, in the name of the United States, such horses, mules, sheep and grain as they desire, carefully concealing their true name but assuming official authority and bearing." Such worthy people "ought to be immediately protected" against the Navajos and the emigrants, he said.[19]

Passing over a wild expanse of mountains and canyons between Zuni Pueblo and Laguna Pueblo, Calhoun noted on a map that "the valleys are more desirable and the water, which is abundant, is not surpassed in its excellent quality by any in the world." Calhoun learned that the Laguna people, too, were mistreated by American travelers, and Apaches and Navajos troubled both pueblos. They next passed through the towns of Albuquerque, Alameda, Bernalillo, and Algodones, as well as Sandia Pueblo. "Numerous bands of thieving Indians, principally Navajos, Apaches, and Comanches, are straggling in every direction, busily employed in gathering their winter supplies, where they have not sown," Calhoun wrote. "Not a day passes without hearing of some fresh outrage, and the utmost vigilance of the military force in this country is not sufficient to prevent murders and depredations and there are but few so bold as to travel alone ten miles from Santa Fe." The answer, he said was "compulsory enlightenment" imposed at the point of a bayonet.[20]

The expedition returned September 24, 1849. Within days, a man was found with sixteen arrows in his back. Navajos, Calhoun fumed, "were in every nook and corner of the country" and were "impudent, troublesome, and dangerous … The number of discontented Indians in this territory is not small and I regret to add, they are not the only evil people in it. The whole country requires a thorough purging." He offered yet again to raise a regiment. Calhoun returned to Jemez Pueblo on October 10 to meet with Navajos, but they didn't show. Chapitone had gathered stolen property and prepared to meet the terms of the treaty, but traders told him New Mexicans from nearby villages and American troops were marching to their country to exterminate them. The Navajos were afraid to come to Jemez Pueblo on the appointed day.

Calhoun railed against the traders and their unfettered access to the "wild and roving Indians." Always welcome in the camps, traders supplied arms and ammunition to the tribes and traveled without fear when no other citizen could venture out alone. They spread rumors that the Mexican government was sending troops to take back New Mexico and that Indians cooperating with the Americans would die. They told tribes the Americans wanted to take their lands. The traders' object was "to keep American settlers out of the country as long as possible" to protect certain powerful New Mexicans. Nearly every day, parties of Pueblos visited Calhoun bearing such tales.[21]

To gain some control, Calhoun announced in the first issue of the *New Mexican*, November 28, 1849, that he would issue licenses to trade with the Indians provided the applicants were approved by the army commander. They had to be US citizens, produce testimonials to their good character, and promise to observe the laws and not trade in arms and ammunition. Calhoun thought the licenses, which cost ten dollars, might curb illicit trade, but in practice, a dozen or more traders joined to do business under one license. Calhoun followed up with another notice that he had issued no licenses to sell to the Apaches, Navajos, and Utes. The second notice only made the traders more cautious. If anything, he lamented, there were now even more traders among the Indians. It would take months to undo the misdirected licenses.[22]

The new agent had glimpsed the dynamics of this complex and challenging region, and these themes would fill his future reports to the commissioner. Just a month into his new assignment, Calhoun became one of the first Americans to travel into unexplored Navajo country. He visited five Indian pueblos and spoke to all their leaders. And he cemented a friendship with Simpson[23] and the Kern brothers. The government sent three expeditions into Navajo country in 1846, 1849, and 1851. None accomplished much, and the government eventually gave up on treaties with them. It was not until January 1852, when Calhoun's agent John Greiner met with Navajo leaders, that anyone heard the Navajo side of the story.[24]

State of War

Reporting the expedition to the commissioner in early October, Calhoun penned a fairly accurate first report of the territory's tribes, although it was colored by American and New Mexican attitudes. Indian people didn't comprehend distance and numbers, he wrote. "Distance is measured by time, at their pace, which is never slow," and the governor of even the smallest pueblo couldn't accurately state its population. With the hostile tribes, "we are in a state of war."[25]

The Navajos, who possessed a wealth of crops, orchards, and sheep, "commit their wrongs from a pure love of rapine and plunder," Calhoun wrote. He could only guess at the extent of their territory because "they derive their title to the country over which they roam from mere possession" and their whereabouts depended on the season "and their apprehensions of danger." He recommended marking and limiting their territory. "These Indians are hardy and intelligent, and it is as natural for them to war against all men and to take the property of others as it is for the sun to give light by day." Calhoun estimated the Navajos at fewer than five thousand, while Colonel Washington weighed in at a more correct seven thousand to ten thousand, of whom two thousand to three thousand were warriors "who are almost invariably well mounted and generally well armed with guns, lances, and bows and arrows."[26]

The Apaches and Comanches lived primarily by depredation. "They look upon the cultivators of the soil with contempt, as inferior beings, the products of whose labor legitimately belong to power, the strongest arm." The hostile Indians had been even more aggressive since Kearny took possession of their country and "do not believe we have the power to chastise them." The Apaches and Comanches should be penned up, Calhoun said, and "made to cultivate the soil." He couldn't guess the extent of their territory. The Apaches seemed to be concentrated to the south and operated on both sides of the border. They held a majority of the captives. He predicted they would cost millions in reparations to Mexico, and yet Apaches from both sides of the border were raiding. "How are these people to live if you stop their depredations?" Calhoun asked. The solution would require a strong arm and "an enlightened patriotism." He advised, "Expend your million now, if necessary, that you may avoid the expenditure of millions hereafter."[27]

The Utahs (Utes), during the Navajo expedition, had met with Col. Benjamin Beall and agreed to his demands, but they too had been frightened away from subsequent meetings by the lies of traders, Calhoun said.

Calhoun devoted much of his report to the Pueblos. Mistakenly thought to be one tribe, they were in fact about twenty groups with several different, unrelated languages. They numbered 6,524, according to an 1847 census. They held their land through Spanish and Mexican grants, and they built pueblos (towns) one to six stories high with an eye to defense. They were Catholics with a mix of traditional ceremonials "all of which attaches them to the soil of their fathers." Their houses were better than those of Santa Fe, and in rich valleys they grew quantities of corn and wheat and raised horses, mules, sheep, and goats. Consolidating the Pueblos, Calhoun said, was out of the question. They were "as firmly fixed in their homes as anyone can be in the United States." Calhoun was so impressed with the Pueblo men who had accompanied them on the Navajo expedition that he recommended their regular engagement as auxiliaries. And yet, New Mexicans and Americans encroached on Pueblo boundaries, and "wicked men" told them the Americans would take their lands. "In New Mexico a better population than these Indians cannot be found, and they should be treated with great delicacy," Calhoun wrote. They would protest non-Indian encroachment time and time again. Calhoun sympathized but found himself powerless to help them.[28]

Calhoun recommended an additional mounted regiment. The infantry, he said, was only good for guarding public stores. Military posts should be established in Navajo country at Tumecha and Canyon de Chelly and at Jemez, Zuni, and Laguna Pueblos. Each Pueblo should have its own agent to protect them from the lawless behavior of Americans and New Mexicans and preserve their loyalty. They should also be furnished with blacksmiths, farm implements, firearms, and gifts. And he wanted to take parties to Washington. Later he refined his recommendations: an agency at Taos for the Utes and Taos Pueblo; an agency at Zuni Pueblo for Zunis and Navajos; an agency at Socorro for Apaches, Comanches, and Isleta Pueblo; sub-agencies at San Ildefonso, Jemez, and Laguna Pueblos; and a sub-agency at El Paso. With agents posted at the pueblos, he could monitor the movements of the hostile tribes, defuse rumors spread by troublemakers, and protect Pueblos from chicanery. "The powers here have neither the authority nor the means to reduce to order the chaotic mass in this territory—and the Government at Washington has not thoroughly comprehended the diversity and the magnitude of the difficulties to be overcome."[29]

Calhoun saw the Pueblos as a stabilizing presence in a region overrun by hostile nomads, but as he argued for their protection, he also questioned their status as citizens. Under Mexico, the Pueblos had the same right to vote as Mexican citizens. Calhoun thought they must sooner or later become American citizens, but he asked what rights the Treaty of Guadalupe Hidalgo intended to confer on them. Until a state or territory was created "on the western side of the Rio Grande," they should be subjected only to federal laws, he wrote. "It is a subject of great delicacy, yet, I apprehend it is easier to dispose of the tribes of roving Indians than the better, and more civilized Pueblo Indians."[30]

Long-established Spanish and Mexican Indian policy sought to make Indians good Catholics and good citizens. The Americans had no such mission. Their government dealt with tribes as separate nations and used treaties to acquire land for white settlement. When Calhoun received his appointment, the government was pushing tribes out of the way, trying to keep them away from settlements, or relocating them to Indian Territory. The notion of isolating them on reservations was just beginning to take hold.[31] The Navajo treaty contained no references to boundaries, but Calhoun and other agents would argue for containing the Navajos and other tribes within a defined territory. Americans assumed they possessed the entire territory, but as the Navajos would argue, they had fought no war with the Americans and had given up no land. Extermination was never an official policy, but it was a word tossed around in public and in the press, and it stained Calhoun's correspondence.

The Saga of Ann White

Point of Rocks, a narrow, rocky mesa with a spring at its base, was a stopping place for caravans and buffalo hunters along the Santa Fe Trail. On October 29, 1849, a merchant returning from the States thought he'd spend the night there. In the moonlight, he found the bodies of trader James M. White and five or six others who had traveled from St. Louis. A baggage wagon was overturned and smashed into pieces. The White party had been attacked by three groups: Jicarilla Apaches, "Apaches" (a reference to unnamed eastern Apache bands from the plains), and Utes. They carried away Ann White, her young daughter, Virginia, and a black female servant. When New Mexican buffalo hunters came upon the bloody scene, Jicarillas, led by Lobo Blanco,[32] killed them too. The Jicarillas weren't a large band, Calhoun wrote, "but they are bold, daring, and adventurous spirits . . . The liberation of Mrs. White and her daughter is, to me, a matter of deepest concern. But being entirely destitute of the means necessary to an efficient and prompt action in the premises I am left to lament the impotency of my aim, and if the two captives are not to be liberated, it is to be hoped they are dead."[33]

Colonel John Munroe,[34] New Mexico's new military governor, had taken command just six days before the slaughter at Point of Rocks came to light. A tall Scotsman and West Point graduate, he was described by Samuel Ellison, his secretary and interpreter, as "the ugliest looking man" and the best mathematician in the army.[35] Munroe was a seasoned officer with service in the War of 1812 and in the Florida and Mexican wars. He refused to act without more information. Calhoun was convinced they didn't have a moment to waste and that the military alone couldn't return the captives. He dispatched Encarnacion Garcia,[36] whom he described as a daring and fearless trader who knew the

Apaches and their haunts and trails. Calhoun promised Garcia a thousand dollars for the return of the captives. Garcia was off within the hour. The next day Calhoun sent three more men.

The Jicarilla Apaches lived and hunted across present-day northern New Mexico and southern Colorado and often camped along the streams descending from the Sangre de Cristo Mountains to the plains. Mexican and American settlement eclipsed their old territory and invaded their hunting grounds, but their enemies—Comanches, Kiowas, Cheyennes, and Arapahos—threatened them if they hunted on the plains. The Mexican government awarded thirteen land grants to citizens and towns—all on lands the Jicarillas considered theirs and without consulting them. The largest, at some 1.7 million acres, was awarded to Carlos Beaubien and Guadalupe Miranda. In 1847 Lucien B. Maxwell acquired the grant and two years later the legendary scout Kit Carson, who said he was "tired of the roving life," joined Maxwell at Rayado, where a mountain spur met the plains. It was an area frequented by Mouache Utes, Jicarillas, and plains tribes. Carson and Maxwell found it more practical to feed their Indian visitors than to lose livestock in raids. With traffic on the Santa Fe Trail, more interlopers poured into Jicarilla country.[37]

The Point of Rocks attack resulted from a series of tragic events. That summer, before the attack, forty Jicarillas had approached Las Vegas in peace to do some trading and acquire powder and lead, which wasn't unusual. Captain Henry M. Judd was suspicious and demanded that the chiefs come in to make a treaty, wrote John Greiner, who became an Indian agent in 1851. Judd's sharp tone alarmed the Jicarillas, who mounted their horses to return to their lodges. Judd ordered Lieutenant Ambrose Burnside[38] to arrest them, and the dragoons pursued. One soldier took an arrow, and Judd ordered his men to fire. "The Indians did not show fight but continued running in every direction, crying in Spanish, 'Why are the Americans killing us?' The reply was, 'Quien sabe?'" (Who knows?)[39]

The Jicarillas "delivered a flight of arrows and quickly fled over the rough hills and ravines around Las Vegas." Troops killed fourteen Apaches in a hand-to-hand fight and captured five men, a boy, and one woman, the daughter of Chief Lobo Blanco (White Wolf). "The Indians did not dream of being attacked by the troops, as they supposed they were at peace with the Americans, and they looked upon this affair as treachery deserving revenge," Greiner wrote, and so they attacked Americans near Wagon Mound and then the White party.

Chief Chacon told Greiner that they and the Utes had visited the Whites' camp, and the Americans chased them away. "We know such is the treatment the Indians usually receive from the [wagon] trains," Greiner wrote, because traders considered them a nuisance. Afterward, the fight began, Chacon said. They carried away Ann White and her daughter and kept them in camp on the Red River.[40]

That was the situation when Munroe ordered troops from Las Vegas and Taos. Sergeant Philip Swartout had with him Lobo Blanco's daughter to exchange for Ann White. The first night, the Jicarilla woman climbed a knoll, cried loudly all night, and the next day stabbed a teamster and killed a mule before being shot. Captain William Grier, with forty-two First Dragoons and forty New Mexico volunteers, rode to Apache gathering places on the plains, guided by Antoine Leroux, Kit Carson, Robert Fisher, Dick Wootton, Jesus Silva, and Tom Tobin—the most trusted mountain men in the region. When they caught up with the Jicarillas on November 17, Carson could see them breaking camp, and the guides prepared to charge, but Captain Grier called them back on Leroux's advice to parley first. Grier was shot so Carson ordered a charge.

Private James Bennett, of the First Dragoons, saw Ann White break away from a Jicarilla woman and run toward the troops. "The Indian woman very deliberately drew her bow and arrow, aimed, and Mrs. White with a shriek fell, pierced to the heart when we were within 15 paces of her." From an old Apache woman hiding in the rocks, they learned that the Jicarillas killed the servant girl because she couldn't keep up and that the Utes had the child. If the Americans had sent for them peaceably, Chief Chacon said later, the Jicarillas would have given them up. The child was never found.[41] Calhoun took the loss to heart and never gave up on finding Virginia White.

At War with Three Tribes

Within days of the White massacre and abduction, Apaches in the south attacked twenty-five German emigrants from Texas, killed seven or eight, captured the rest, and tried to exchange them with Mexicans for Apache prisoners. The Mexicans declined. Calhoun was just starting to learn about the fearsome Apaches called Chiricahuas, a group that included the Warm Springs and Nednhi bands along with the Chiricahuas proper. They targeted Mexico in their raids, but after gold seekers passed through their country in 1849, treating them with scorn, they began attacking Americans. That summer Warm Springs Chief Mangas Coloradas returned to his country near the Burro Mountains and renewed relations with New Mexican traders, who didn't like the Americans. Major Enoch Steen (Calhoun described him as "an excellent officer and a gentleman"), commanding the army's Doña Ana post in southern New Mexico, was well acquainted with Mangas Coloradas and other Apache leaders. On August 16, 1849, Steen, with a company of dragoons, drove Apaches into the hills during a hard fight near the Santa Rita del Cobre copper mine, where Steen was severely wounded. On August 22, the Warm Springs Apaches ambushed a party near the mine, killing a man and wounding two others; the Americans reportedly killed or wounded eight Apaches. "These impudent Indians are frequently near his post sending him words of defiance, and saying they desire to meet him again in the Canon from which he drove them," Calhoun wrote.[42]

In December Munroe appointed Calhoun's Georgia friend Cyrus Choice and Lieutenant Colonel Charles May,[43] commander of the small detachment at the Socorro post, to negotiate a treaty with the Apaches. Choice, like Calhoun, had been a merchant, bank director, and landowner, and he was also a widower. He had served in Georgia's Indian wars. Choice arrived in Socorro, in south-central New Mexico, on December 14, and waited. The Apaches didn't come in to parley, but on December 18, two chiefs and thirteen warriors "got into a drunken frolic" at nearby Lemitar, Choice reported. May had them arrested and brought to Socorro; he intended to force them to sign a treaty. As soon as soldiers took their horses and arms, thirteen of the Apaches fled, and the other two were allowed to go. Choice and May gave the Apaches more time to come in, and on the appointed day, twelve women, well mounted and armed with bows and arrows, came in. They said the principal chief was in council with other chiefs. The Apaches and Navajos had fought a few days earlier, the Navajos were victorious, and many Apaches had gone in pursuit of the Navajos. May angrily sent the women away, disappointing Choice who hoped to gain more information. Choice returned without a treaty.[44]

Navajos added to Calhoun's headaches. In November, they drove off a large number of horses, mules, sheep, and other livestock from Santa Ana Pueblo. A week later they raided Cebolleta, an old Spanish village sixty miles west of Albuquerque. "We are now at War with three tribes of Indians—the Apaches,

Navajos, and Utahs, and various spurious tribes," Calhoun wrote to his close friend, Congressman William Dawson of Georgia. The laws of the territory were "the most perfect jumble to be found in any country." New Mexicans and Pueblos asked why the Americans didn't permit them to retaliate as they did under Mexican rule. Calhoun was initially sympathetic because "they lose their women and children, and stock, and are remediless," but then wrote that the centuries of attacks and counterattacks "gave to many, a pleasurable excitement and afforded to all an opportunity of satisfying their own demands, whether founded in justice, or, in a mere desire to possess other people's property."[45]

The wild Indians were well mounted and better armed every day, Calhoun reported to Commissioner Orlando Brown, who had succeeded William Medill in November 1849. Regulating traders was one remedy, but Col. Munroe refused to extend the laws of trade and intercourse over the territory's tribes. He was, however, establishing posts at Jemez Pueblo and Cebolleta. "Every Indian difficulty, in this territory, should be settled, and fixed, during the ensuing twelve months, and I say, after due reflection, if the present course of policy, or management is to be continued, our troubles and difficulties with these Indians will not end in twelve years," Calhoun wrote. On learning of Ann White's murder, a disheartened Calhoun wrote the commissioner, "Matters in this territory are in a most deplorable condition—infinitely worse than you possibly can imagine them, and which, without being an eye witness, you can not realize."[46]

Brown,[47] the former Kentucky secretary of state, lacked Medill's experience, but he took Calhoun's complaints seriously. Brown approved Calhoun's actions and forwarded his comments about troop strength to the secretary of war. Brown said it was important to extend the laws regulating trade and intercourse with Indians to California and New Mexico. He considered his office "altogether inadequate" for its expanded duties. Some tribes had moved west of the Mississippi, enlarging Indian populations, while the war had added large numbers of Indians in Texas, Oregon, California, and New Mexico. Because of the distances between agents and Washington, DC, Brown, like Medill, recognized the need for superintendents to supervise agents. Brown wanted seven superintendencies, including one for New Mexico, and four agents per territory. It was of "utmost importance that we have an adequate number of active and efficient men ... especially in New Mexico and California," he wrote.[48]

Ute Peace

Calhoun ended 1849 by signing the first formal peace treaty with the Utes. In December 1849 several Utes told the prefect of Abiquiu, a century-old Spanish village about fifty miles northwest of Santa Fe, that they would like to discuss peace. Calhoun traveled up the Chama Valley to the old trading center and learned the Utes were camped nearby. They would have met with him that day or night, but meddling Navajos or traders dissuaded them. A Ute chief came to Calhoun in the middle of the night and told him to be patient, but Calhoun gave them until midday to come in. The chiefs appeared that morning. They were willing to sign the treaty but recoiled at the mandate to stop roaming and raiding, settle within defined boundaries, and farm. What would they do to sustain life? "I replied to them, the government of the United States had ever been just and humane and if they behaved well, would take care of them . . . I stated to them, I had no sword to frighten them into terms—that I brought no presents to seduce them—and that if they thought they ought not to agree to the terms of the treaty, that I would at the peril of my life secure them a transit to their own country unmolested and unharmed." At Calhoun's candid and forthright response, they brightened and decided the president would take care of them because he didn't authorize the agent to attempt force or bribery.

The peace treaty, signed December 30, 1849, wasn't ratified until September 9, 1860. It "forced the Utes to officially recognize the sovereignty of the United States and established boundaries between the U.S. and the Ute nation," Calhoun wrote. The Utes promised to submit to the government, cease hostilities, return captives and stolen property or make restitution for property that couldn't be returned, allow travelers to pass unharmed, remain within the boundaries of their territory, stop raiding, and "support themselves by their own industry." The government promised gifts and implements. Calhoun signed for the government. Chief Quiziachigiate, a Caputa Ute, made his mark as principal chief, along with twenty-seven subordinate chiefs. Georgians George Martin and William Mitchell were witnesses, as was Edward Kern. Antoine Leroux[49] and James Conklin were interpreters.[50]

These were the Southern Utes. The Ute tribe, by the late 1700s, comprised seven bands. The Caputa (also called Capote), Mouache, and Weeminuche Utes were the southernmost bands of a large tribe whose territory spanned the eastern Great Basin in present-day Utah, the Colorado Plateau in Utah and Colorado, and the Rocky Mountains and High Plains in Colorado and northern New Mexico. The Mouache band lived on the eastern slopes of the Rockies, from present-day Denver south to Las Vegas, New Mexico. The Caputa band lived south of the Conejos River and in the San Luis Valley near the headwaters of the Rio Grande and frequented the region near Chama and Tierra Amarilla, New Mexico. The Weeminuche occupied the valley of the San Juan River and its northern tributaries in Colorado and northwestern New Mexico.[51]

When trappers and traders entered the area in the 1820s, Utes exchanged buffalo robes and beaver pelts for flour, cloth, tobacco, trinkets, and whiskey. These white men posed no threat because they didn't stay. Utes, like their Jicarilla neighbors, grew hostile when the Mexican government awarded land grants in Ute territory and settlers invaded their country. They attacked ranches and farms in the Taos Valley and north of Española and were still at war when the United States claimed New Mexico. In 1846 about sixty Ute chiefs signed an informal treaty, but in the next two years relations soured, and Utes, Jicarillas, and Navajos stepped up their incursions. In July 1848, troops led by Major William W. Reynolds pursued Jicarillas into the San Juan Mountains, where their Ute friends joined them. In a fierce battle near Cumbres Pass, thirty-seven Indians and two soldiers died. Reynolds' guide was trapper Bill Williams,[52] who once lived with the Utes. Williams not only betrayed them by guiding soldiers to their camps, but he also cheated Utes who had trusted him to trade their furs in Taos by spending their money on a drunk. The Utes believed they were at war.[53]

On March 5, 1849, Lieutenant John H. Whittlesey of the First Dragoons left Taos in search of Utes, sending guides Leroux and Estes ahead to capture Chief Montoya. This they did and put the chief in jail, but he escaped. Captain Valdez, of the New Mexico volunteers, recaptured him; when he again attempted to escape, he was riddled with bullets. On March 13, Whittlesey with twenty-three men followed a small party across the Rio Grande. Following for about ten miles across the prairie, heavy with mud, snow, and rocks, they saw smoke rising from a village near El Cerro del Olla. A half mile from the village, five well-mounted men and some of their chiefs advanced and asked the soldiers what they wanted. "I replied, 'I came to fight,'" Whittlesey wrote. "They replied, 'It is well,' and turned and fled."[54]

Whittlesey gave them a head start and then charged. The large camp had one hundred well-armed warriors who advanced to fight. Soldiers took a position as Utes filled the woods above them without attacking. After about twenty minutes, they withdrew and fled, abandoning everything. Whittlesey lost two men; the Utes lost five men killed and seven or eight wounded. After taking the camp, the lieutenant saw warriors approaching from the north and chased them for miles through deep mud and snow, killing five and capturing five women and a boy, the son of a chief. Unaware of this clash, Bill Williams and Benjamin Kern, the physician brother of Edward and Richard Kern, rode to the Red River to retrieve a cache of drawings and instruments left by another party. Utes killed them to avenge Williams's betrayal.

About the same time, Captain John Chapman, commanding eighty American troops and New Mexican volunteers at Abiquiu, sent for Chief Quiziachigiate and told him to bring in the principal chiefs to make a treaty. After great effort, Quiziachigiate managed to bring the principal men as far as two days from Abiquiu. When they learned of Whittlsey's expedition against them, they refused to go farther. Quiziachigiate returned to the post without the chiefs. "Instead of being rewarded for the efforts he had made, Chapman ordered him to be thrown into prison." Overhearing a guard saying he would be hanged, he escaped. Late in the year, the Utes sent messages that they would make peace. The murders for which they were blamed occurred after the attack on them by Lieutenant Whittlesey, "and thus they balance that account current," Calhoun wrote.[55]

At the end of January 1850, Munroe posted a company of Second Dragoons at Abiquiu and asked Calhoun to make Cyrus Choice the Indian agent there. Choice became the Utes' first Indian agent and served without pay, having only Calhoun's promise to ask the commissioner to pay him. Abiquiu became a recognized meeting ground between the government and the Southern Utes.[56]

For Calhoun, his first half year as Indian agent was a period of on-the-job training, of reacting rather than acting. During the Navajo expedition, he gained an appreciation for the untamed lands the United States now claimed. He began gathering information about the tribes, as instructed, and quickly sized up the complexities of the region and its people. He bungled his attempt to control traders and trading, but he also signed two treaties, established a functioning Indian agency, and began to put his stamp on Indian relations. Maybe most important, he realized that the tribes weren't necessarily his biggest problem.

10

ALL IS NOT WELL

Calhoun rode through the icy Sangre de Cristo Mountains to Taos during a bitterly cold January when no reasonable person would travel unless forced by necessity. Alarming reports of unrest at Taos Pueblo sent Calhoun north to restore calm. The seventy-five mile trail wound through valleys and up steep, rugged mountains where the wind howled through pines and a slip in footing on the icy trail could lead to a deadly fall. Though roughing it on the trail to Taos, Calhoun had two servants.[1] When traveling, Calhoun told the commissioner, "you will suffer if you do not take with you a cook, cooking utensils, subsistence, forage, tents, and all necessary transportation." After several days' hard travel, the agent, his servants, and a military escort picked their way down a rocky slope and entered a valley about thirty miles across, framed by the spurs and peaks of the Rocky Mountains and crisscrossed by streams winding to the distant Rio Grande. At its eastern edge was Don Fernando de Taos, its lime-washed walls blending into the whiteness of the surrounding mountains. Calhoun's first order of business was to meet with Carlos Beaubien, one of Kearny's appointed judges, and Padre Martínez, who ministered to Taos and Taos Pueblo. The two men "have a controlling influence over the Indians," Calhoun wrote.[2]

Padre Antonio José Martínez, an intellectual and activist for his people, grew up in Abiquiu and Taos, studied for the priesthood in Mexico during its early years as an independent nation, and came to admire Father Hidalgo, the martyr of Mexican independence. Ordained in 1823, he became Mexican consul for the Americans drawn to New Mexico as well as the curate for Taos. In 1826, he opened the first school and after the first printing press arrived in 1834, he used it to publish textbooks.[3] Padre Martínez was so highly respected that he presided over the two political conventions in 1848 and 1849 and would help write the first territorial constitution.

Judge Beaubien and the priest were not friends. Padre Martínez took a dim view of Beaubien's massive land deals with Ceran St. Vrain and Charles Bent

because they threatened Taos Pueblo's communal lands. Kit Carson always suspected that the priest had a hand in the Taos Revolt, but trials afterward revealed no evidence of his involvement. Padre Martínez did criticize rulings against the rebels handed down by the two judges appointed by General Kearny, Beaubien and Joab Houghton.[4]

Accompanied by Padre Martínez and Beaubien, Calhoun visited Taos Pueblo, several miles away from the town. "I found the Indians moody and complaining, and, evidently in a feverish State of excitement," he wrote. "They complained of aggressions, encroachments upon their lands, and unjust and unusual interferences with their laws and customs, and the general administration of justice." They resented having to answer to a corrupt alcalde (chief magistrate) appointed by the government in Santa Fe instead of electing someone from the pueblo as they had before. Appointed officials demanded what they wanted for their personal use, and many Pueblo people obeyed, even though "there is not the shadow of a law," Calhoun told the commissioner. "Alcaldes go a step further and divorce a woman from her husband whenever it suits their pleasure." Troublemakers told the Pueblo people that American laws would be bad for them. He had been hearing these complaints for months.[5]

Calhoun explained to the people of Taos Pueblo that if federal laws were extended over them, they might vote for officers of a state or territory, but if the government secured their "separate and distinct community," they could only vote for officers of their pueblo. He discouraged voting in elections outside the pueblo. Then he asked Beaubien and Padre Martínez whether that advice was correct. They agreed. The people decided in council that they wanted the protection of the American laws, which Calhoun promised to provide. Beaubien and Padre Martínez assured Calhoun that from then on they would "act with General Taylor's real friends." With this, Calhoun settled months of unhap-

FIGURE 38. This photo of Taos Pueblo from the 1880s shows its multiple
stories and access by ladders. Library of Congress.

piness. He advised army officers posted in Taos that "mischievous individuals
are improperly interfering and meddling with the affairs of these Indians" and
asked them to convey his message to the Taos Indians with help from "my
excellent friends," Padre Martínez and Beaubien.[6] The man from Georgia still
had his gift for winning over potential adversaries. Beaubien was, for the moment, neutralized; Calhoun and Padre Martínez forged a lasting friendship.

Calhoun returned through a seven-day snowstorm to a volley of like complaints from other pueblos.[7] It was pointless to take their claims to court
because none of the three judges "ever studied the law for a moment." They
wanted to know what the president intended to do with them or for them. The
United States had promised protection, but Navajo raids and Hispanic encroachments troubled them daily. "The Pueblo Indians, all, are alike entitled to
the favorable and early consideration of the government of the United States,"
Calhoun wrote. "They claim that this whole territory originally belonged to
them ... but after the [Spanish] conquest, this place was taken from them and
their limits fixed by authority of the conquering government."

He believed each pueblo was about seventy-two square miles, although
many had bought additional land, and some were planting on unappropriated

lands. Some New Mexican villages occupied Pueblo lands, and pending lawsuits between the two groups threatened "bloody consequences." Because alcaldes had unjustly sued pueblos Calhoun provided a lawyer, Richard Weightman. Calhoun wanted a judicial commission to adjust Indian land titles. He said, "It would not do to agitate the subject of their removal at this time," a hint that removal was contemplated at some level.[8]

The agent now called for a superintendency of eight districts for the pueblos, each with an agent, interpreter, and horses. The superintendent should receive $2,000 a year and be required to visit every agency twice a year. Apaches, Comanches, Navajos, and Utes made frequent incursions into the territory, and "each of these tribes should be compelled to remain within certain fixed limits." He recommended tracts of land fifty miles long, at least one hundred miles from the border, and a suitable distance apart. All but the Navajos, who could feed themselves, should be supported for a time and taught agricultural pursuits. Each would need a military post. The only gifts should be food and implements. "To establish order in this territory, you must either submit to these heavy expenditures, or exterminate the mass of these Indians," he wrote to the commissioner. Calhoun, with his "districts," had essentially described reservations, although the reservation system was still years away. Calhoun's contemporaries, including Robert S. Neighbors in Texas, argued that this separation would protect the tribes and white people from each other. Calhoun penned this letter before meeting Neighbors later that year, but it's certain Neighbors made an impact.[9]

As the late Governor Charles Bent had foreseen, New Mexico needed agents and subagents. Calhoun himself expected to run a multi-employee enterprise. Considering the Native population in the region, the expensive and time-consuming daily visits of tribal officials, New Mexico's high costs, and the necessary travel, it wasn't an unreasonable expectation. Congress, however, was reluctant to spend more on the Indian Service or the military. The federal government never took steps to prevent encroachment on Indian lands, in New Mexico or anywhere else. Indian agents lacked the means, civil authorities had more pressing duties, and the frontier army was undermanned. And it was always the covert policy to allow non-Indian settlement to advance and Indian settlement to retreat.[10]

Together, Munroe and Calhoun tried to reassure pueblo leaders that they could regulate their own affairs: "We have learned that malicious representations have been made to you and in order that you may not be deceived by them nor in doubt, we have thought it best to say that you are neither abandoned nor lost. We say to you that yourselves as well as your people are in the same position and security which you occupied before the election." In July, Calhoun signed treaties with the pueblos of Santa Clara, Tesuque, Nambe, Santo Domingo, Jemez, San Felipe, Cochiti, San Ildefonso, Santa Ana, and Zia.[11]

As Calhoun reassured those ten pueblos, Navajos attacked distant Zuni Pueblo, killing the lieutenant governor and two others and driving off animals. Their war would last the rest of the year. Just 42 of 597 Zuni men had firearms. Calhoun wanted to station an agent there and furnish weapons. The Zuni governor asked Calhoun how it was that as the Navajos were making war on him, the soldiers were withdrawn from Cebolleta. "I suppose to give the Navajos a fair chance against us, who were promised protection," the Zuni leader said.[12]

Murders and Robberies

San Miguel del Vado, the last outpost of Spanish colonization, took root in 1794 with a land grant from the king to fifty-six families. Settlers chose a site at a natural ford on the Pecos River where the bottom was sandy but firm, and heavy wagons and carts could cross. Each house they built around a plaza shared a wall with neighbors. The authorities intended San Miguel to be a fortified village and a buffer against hostile plains tribes. When the Santa Fe Trail opened, the town became a port of entry and one of the busiest communities in New Mexico.[13]

Of the five hundred residents, a portion were *genízaros*, Indian captives acculturated and converted to Catholicism as servants. They were not people inclined to complain, but on February 23, 1850, an Apache band swept from the hills, killed a man, and wounded two more just eight miles from town on the broad trail from Santa Fe to Las Vegas. Days earlier, the same Apaches drove away twelve thousand sheep. "No one in this territory is safe in his person or property. Murders and robberies are of daily occurrence," wrote a large number of prominent citizens in a letter to the president. They believed the Apaches were trying to turn the Pueblo Indians against the United States and feared that Apaches, Navajos, and Comanches were conspiring to unite. The butchery of the White party might be their own fate "unless the Government of the United States shall promptly and efficiently come to our aid." The

FIGURE 39. San Miguel del Vado was sketched during the Abert expedition in 1847.

country should be explored and surveyed, military posts established, and the Pueblo Indians should be cared for."We beg for an adequate mounted force to accomplish these ends." The letter was signed by fifty-two men, including the territorial treasurer, the attorney general, Judge Joab Houghton, two sheriffs, merchants, and several lawyers.[14]

Since his arrival Colonel Munroe had pleaded for more men, more officers, more horses, and more equipment, and, like Calhoun, heard nothing from his superiors. Seven companies of dragoons operated in New Mexico, and not one was at full strength. Colonel May, commanding at Socorro, said his garrison, depleted by transfers and illness, couldn't mount more than twenty-five men. Lieutenant Colonel Benjamin L. Beall, in Taos, asked Munroe to strengthen his command. "I can undertake nothing with the force I have," he said. He complained that he was second in rank on duty in the territory but had only a lieutenant's command. Munroe wanted ten companies of cavalry properly officered and equipped and at least that number of infantry to occupy posts, he wrote on March 1, 1850. He wanted to mount a portion of the infantry then in New Mexico. His four companies of dragoons were inadequate for the service required of them, he said, and those companies were reduced in numbers and nearly without officers. Manpower was stretched so thin that when a dragoon captain went AWOL for more than a month and Munroe had him arrested, he had too few officers for a court martial and allowed the man to resign. Horses brought across the plains the previous summer were not yet acclimated and fit for service. He needed military doctors. But in mid-March Munroe pleaded to keep the forces he had, saying that "if we are reduced to the numbers contemplated, even the military posts will not be free from insult."[15]

The War Department concurred but was reluctant to mount portions of the infantry. "Footmen, in the saddle, constitute a mongrel force—inefficient, with great excess in the wear and tear of horses and equipment," wrote an assistant adjutant general. The bill before Congress "will not give one half the increase absolutely needed," and he didn't know how to reinforce the Ninth Military Department, nor could he offer any more officers or doctors.[16]

Congress was in no mood to expand the army after the war's expenditures. Although the Secretary of War wanted five thousand men for New Mexico and California alone, Whigs didn't value the new territory. On the Ways and Means Committee, Toombs wanted to keep the regular army small, believing that volunteers should make up the nation's defensive core. A large standing army was too expensive and a "source of corruption and great danger to the Republic," he said. In December 1850, he said "a standing army should not be maintained except at the lowest possible standard." Congress passed a bill reducing the army to a peace standing.[17]

Financial Strains

Early in the year, Calhoun wrote Indian Commissioner Orlando Brown: "All is not well. Murders and depredations are occurring daily, and they are of such frequent occurrence, we seem to await patiently, our fate." Unabated Apache and Navajo depredations moved him to write a few weeks later that "our Indian troubles are daily increasing and our efficiency as rapidly decreasing." He insisted that two additional mounted regiments were absolutely necessary. For a brief period, he seemed satisfied with his position. "The continuous and exciting character of the duties assigned to me here is agreeable," he told the commissioner, "and all I care for, independent of an honest and faithful discharge of my duties, is the means to sustain myself with usual respectability." Ten days after penning that statement, he decided to send his family back to Georgia because he couldn't support them in Santa Fe on his salary. On April

20, Carolina, Martha, their husbands, and little Anna departed for the States. Love and Davis "both gave me efficient aid up to the time of their departure," he told the commissioner.[18]

Accompanying them were troops commanded by the only officer Calhoun considered a friend, Captain Henry Judd, whom he met on the grueling march to Alvarado during the Mexican War. "There are but few Americans remaining that can get out of the country," he wrote forlornly. The party included Colonel Washington and Captain Robert T. Brent, who had been quartermaster in Santa Fe. Calhoun traveled with them as far as Las Vegas. Watching those he most loved disappear into the plains would have been disheartening enough for Calhoun, but by that time he had lost most of his Georgians. "The gentlemen who accompanied me to this territory have all left me, except Genl. Choice, John G. Jones, Dr. Thomas, and George W. Martin," he told Dawson. The departures, his eroding finances, his deepening despair over the state of the territory, and the resounding silence from Washington, DC, crushed Calhoun's customary cheerful outlook. "Our ignorance as to the purposes of the authorities at Washington has greatly distressed us."[19]

In late April 1850, Indian Commissioner Orlando Brown finally responded to Calhoun's many letters with praise: "I am satisfied you have done all in your power, and no doubt all that could be accomplished, under the embarrassing and trying circumstances in which you have been placed." He said it had been "a source of constant regret on the part of the department that it has been unable to place you in a more advantageous position." The Office of Indian Affairs was unable to act or even advise until Congress moved. Brown did favor a superintendency for New Mexico.[20]

Calhoun's financial situation was precarious. "I have exhausted my own means, and my own salary in the public service," he wrote in May. With steady arrivals of Indian delegations to the agency who had to be fed and sustained, "my means are exhausted, my necessary agents and assistants are unpaid" and yet they continued to work without complaint. He warned the commissioner that his accounts would be short by $1,302.94 the first quarter, $2,309.19 the second quarter, and $3,309.19 the third quarter. This didn't include compensation to his fellow Georgians: Cyrus Choice, his subagent in Abiquiu since December 9, 1849, and John G. Jones, secretary of the office for the previous four months, who accompanied Calhoun on the Navajo expedition and escorted thirteen freed captives back to Mexico on Calhoun's behalf. Calhoun wanted both men named agents and hoped Love and Davis could be paid. "It is of the utmost importance to my feeling, and to my usefulness as a public servant, that I should have immediate pecuniary relief," he pleaded in August. To Dawson, he wrote: "I now wish I had returned with my daughters to Georgia, there to have remained. I would leave today with Maj. Weightman and others, if I had the means."[21]

Commissioner Brown was helpless to relieve his agent, but he was at least sympathetic. "The ruinous condition of our Indian affairs in New Mexico demands the immediate attention of Congress," he wrote in his 1850 annual report. "In no section of the country are prompt and efficient measures for restraining the Indians more imperiously required than in this territory, where an extraordinary state of things exists, which, so long as it continues, will be a reproach to the government." Brown referenced atrocities committed upon citizens and on the Pueblo Indians, "an interesting semi-civilized people, living in towns or villages." Before American rule, they could retaliate against raids by their enemies; now they were forbidden. And they needed protection from "unprincipled white men." Brown believed the Pueblos would be fit for citizenship in a few years and said their lands should be surveyed. The wild Indians required agents and military posts to prevent cross-border raids. When Luke Lea[22] succeeded Brown, he too regretted that he lacked the means to support Calhoun's efforts more effectively and hoped Congress would make appropriations.[23]

Desperate Fight

Two of Calhoun's messengers returned from their travels with news of Ann White's daughter. Encarnacion Garcia returned on March 15, 1850, and said the child was killed on the same day as her mother. He visited an Apache camp of two thousand in the Guadalupe Mountains, on the present New Mexico–Texas border, with some Comanches present. They were all well mounted on fine mules and horses, and the grazing was good, he said, but they had few guns. They were also well supplied with food—horse and goat meat and the maguey root. Invited into a lodge to talk, Garcia learned that the captains were tired of war. They couldn't move in any direction without having to fight, and they had large numbers of captives, horses, and mules they couldn't sell because the traders didn't come to them as they had before. Calhoun doubted that there were fewer traders and figured the Apaches had been more successful than usual in their raids. Garcia estimated upward of fifty captives, all from Mexico and taken during the past year. The captains asked Garcia to find out if the governor was willing to make peace with them. Calhoun thought it would be an opportune time to inflict a decisive blow and seize horses and mules that were badly needed as well as rescuing captives and satisfying the nation's obligations to Mexico.[24]

The following day Auguste Lacome returned. Calhoun had sent the French trader to Ute country to ransom Ann White's daughter if possible and to gather intelligence about the Utes. He told Lacome he could take trade goods but no weapons. Lacome and his brother, Jean Baptiste Lacome, met with Utes near Red River and did some trading, but Beall had them arrested. This particular group of Utes hadn't made peace, so trading was unlawful, Beall said, and yet Beall himself knew they had asked for peace in January. The Lacomes said they had a license to trade and were authorized to make peace. Beall thought this was absurd; the brothers had been arrested previously for trading contraband items and were "utterly devoid of all character & principle," he said. Merchant Manuel Alvarez vouched for the traders, saying Auguste Lacome "is entitled to all respect & confidence & in our opinion no agent more fit or suitable could have been selected." Calhoun was indignant at Beall's interference. "It is enough to defer to the Chief of this Military Department—the right of a subordinate to control me or to be advised of my actings and doings, I can not, I will not recognize."[25]

Lacome met with the principal chiefs, who said they wanted peace with the United States, and promised never again to take up arms against Americans or Mexicans. They broke their old treaty because they were starving. They said only one chief made the treaty in Abiquiu, and he wasn't authorized to speak for all. That chief, Chico Velasquez, hated Americans and Mexicans so much he wore their fingernails on his leggings and boasted of his part in the White massacre. However, the Americans had also broken the treaty, the Utes said. They wanted to meet the agent at Costilla in distant northern New Mexico. "They are all very poor, & are entirely destitute of arms, powder & lead, but manifested a strong desire to be supplied with those articles," Lacome wrote. He too was told that Ann White's child was killed soon after her mother during Grier's attack.[26]

Once again, military interference would confound Calhoun's or the tribes' bids for peace. Apaches and Utes in May attacked eleven mail carriers and other men near Red River. Desperate fighting spanned twenty-five miles and raged until sundown, when the mail carriers reached Wagon Mound, a butte that was a stopping place on the Santa Fe Trail. There they all died, along with five Apaches and four Utes. Many Indians were wounded. The victors broke open and emptied trunks and tore apart mail sacks and scattered the mail along the road for two miles. They made off with forty revolvers. On May 18, 1850, about ten or twelve days later, a party of traders found the bodies.[27] Soldiers buried the dead behind Wagon Mound, near a lake, and collected the mail as best they could.

Agent John Greiner later explained that the Jicarilla Apaches were still at war because of the army's unprovoked attack on them the year before at Las Vegas. It was the reason for this attack and the one on the White party. Chief Chacon said there must have been many Indians in the fight or they couldn't have killed eight Americans. Greiner suspected that more Indians died than Chacon was willing to admit. Chico Velasquez was in both fights.[28]

Traders

Seven months after Calhoun urged Munroe to extend trade and intercourse laws over Indian tribes as a military measure, Munroe finally saw the light. Quoting Calhoun's letters, he said in June that he regretted not bringing the problem to the attention of the secretary of war earlier. He said five out of six mules in New Mexico were delivered by Indian raiders who traded them for arms and ammunition. Calhoun and agent Cyrus Choice then were trying to make peace with the Northern Utes. The chiefs told Choice that they had committed no acts of hostility, which Calhoun believed, but he also thought some of them rode with the Jicarillas in their raids.[29]

On July 17, a bit of information ignited a faint hope that the Whites' child might be alive. Calhoun sent Lacome out again, but this journey would be disastrous for the Frenchman. Traveling with only an interpreter and two peons, he found a Ute camp of twenty lodges at Valle Culebra, about two days north of the Rio Colorado. Forty warriors came out to meet him, snatched his rifle, filled his gun barrel with water, and helped themselves to his packs, loaded with $700 in trade items. An arrow fired at the trader missed only because the interpreter jarred the shooter, so the Utes severely beat the interpreter and a

FIGURE 40. An engraving
of Utes appeared in
*Harper's Encyclopedia
of United States History,*
vol. 9, in 1912.

peon. Lacome told them he was only looking for the Jicarillas to trade with
them, but they said it didn't matter to them. That country was theirs—the
grass, wood, water, winds, and sky above. They told him to tell Munroe they
would like to test him in battle and wanted no peace. These were the Mouache
Utes, led by Amparita, a bold and fearless chief. They said they got their arms
from Mormons at the Great Salt Lake. They had been with the Jicarillas.
When Lacome returned to Taos, citizens sent a petition to Munroe saying
that the Apaches were nearby and becoming more brazen in their raids. It was
signed by Lucien Maxwell, Carlos Beaubien, Lacome, Kit Carson, and others.[30]

    That summer, agent Choice allowed a few traders to visit the Utes so long as
they didn't take powder and lead. When the traders found their profits disappointing, they concocted a story that the Utes were holding thirty traders captive until they provided ammunition. Choice, Calhoun, and Munroe refused
to give in, and when Utes came in to see Choice, the chiefs were surprised to
hear the yarn. They assured Choice they were peaceful but begged for a little
powder and lead to hunt game, which Calhoun allowed.

During this episode, Choice died. "It is with extreme pain I announce the death of General Cyrus Choice, a well-known and excellent citizen of Georgia," Calhoun wrote to Lea. Choice died in Abiquiu on September 14 of erysipelas, an acute skin infection. He was Calhoun's age, fifty-one. To friends in Columbus, Calhoun wrote: "Gen. Choice died in a strange land, among strangers, but around his death bed true friends witnessed his ceasing to breathe. Such men will ever have friends—for he was always kind, generous and just." The general's earthly possessions sold for $227.37. Calhoun had advanced his sub-agent $388.78 but hadn't been reimbursed by the government. Calhoun credited Choice with the peaceful state of the Utes since the December 30 treaty and asked the commissioner for a salary paid to his estate.[31]

On September 20, 1850, Calhoun licensed Antonio J. M. Chavez to trade or send a party to trade with the Utes and others. In Abiquiu, Major L. P. Graham told Chavez he couldn't take arms or ammunition. The party set out on the September 27, but Graham was leery and sent a small detachment to overtake the traders and examine their packs. Their inventory included horses, mules, saddles, bridles, spurs, blankets, whips, 17 guns, bows and quivers, scarlet cloth, shirts, butcher knives, handkerchiefs, a sack of arrow points, 102 pounds of powder, and 151 pounds of lead. Graham imprisoned twenty-seven traders in the guardhouse.[32] Nicolas P. Valdes, the agent for Chavez, escaped. "These Mexican prisoners do not effect us in the way of rations, as I make them provision themselves," Graham wrote.[33]

Several weeks later, a large party of Utes came in asking for powder. Their families were suffering, and they lacked ammunition to hunt. Graham believed them and saw no harm in giving them a moderate supply, but he sent the chief to Munroe and asked the commander to not release the traders. Nicolas P. Valdes had been with the Utes since his escape and was doing his best to turn the Utes against the Americans. Calhoun complained that there were no suitable military posts in places where trading posts could be established for the Indians. Apaches, Comanches, Navajos, and Utes had no fixed homes, and trade was conducted by traveling dealers, which was "exceedingly pernicious—but until these Indians are confined within certain fixed limits, you may not expect the evils to be remedied."[34]

War and Peace

If the United States had a policy for the Indians of this territory, it was un-known, Calhoun told the commissioner in June 1850; he hoped his frequent blunders would be forgiven because "our charts and compasses are very incom-plete." He knew his letters had given the department no pleasure but "no human minds can appreciate, or understand, the character and extent of the disorder in this territory without being personally present, and I regret to add, there are but few present who seem to know, or care to know the true condition of affairs."[35]

In the summer of 1850, the pendulum swung wildly between conflict and reconciliation with different Apache groups. In early July some three hundred Apaches drove off livestock and killed a soldier and a civilian up north near Rayado. On July 23, Captain William N. Grier's dragoons, joined by ninety volunteers from Mora, marched northwest from Rayado, discerned an Indian trail, and made their way over mountains and through canyons until they found two small parties. They attacked them both and captured their animals. After marching all night, the soldiers and volunteers found the main village on the edge of a mountain on marshy ground in an almost impenetrable stand of aspens. Warriors had already removed their families; they abandoned camp and fled north pursued by soldiers, who killed or wounded more Apaches and captured a number of horses, mules, sheep, and cattle. Grier lost an officer. They returned the cattle to the owners at Rayado, Lucien Maxwell and Kit Carson, and gave the remaining stock to the volunteers.

On August 10, Apaches took captives and animals from Ojo Caliente, a northern village with a large hot spring in a farming valley with about a thou-sand residents. In October, fifteen or twenty Apaches riding to Abiquiu to ask permission to live nearby under the army's protection stopped at Ojo Caliente to eat. A resident encouraged them to walk around his property and then killed a man and three boys. He ordered his men to shoot the rest of the party, women and children, but they refused. Four people were missing. A man and woman who lost their son stayed at the agency with Calhoun. He gave them some supplies and hoped others might come in who would furnish more in-formation. The Ojo Caliente man was then in jail and eventually would be re-leased. Americans wanted to present a medal "to this cold-blooded murderer," Calhoun wrote with disgust.[36]

That summer, more groups asked for peace. Twenty Comanches made a treaty with Santo Domingo Pueblo and said they intended to make peace with the Navajos. Comanches joined Jicarilla and Mescalero Apaches to ask for peace and a treaty. They offered to return their captives if the United States would do the same.[37] The Mescaleros in September tried again to make peace. Three chiefs and eight warriors came into the posts at El Paso and San Elizario to see how they would be received. Treated well and given gifts, they promised to return and make a treaty.[38]

Reports from the Chiricahua Apaches were mostly discouraging. In early 1850, hostile Americans killed several Chiricahuas who were seeking peace. In retaliation, a Chiricahua war party, on February 2, 1850, raided Doña Ana and killed a man, wounded three, and drove off every head of stock. Steen's troops pursued, overtook them, and wounded several Apaches. In May, about fifty Apaches drove off stock and took captives from the Peralta area. And traders in the Gila area encountered Apaches with trade goods and fine mules, the result of raids in Mexico. Steen led a campaign to the headwaters of the Gila River in August. At Santa Rita del Cobre, the copper mine, he met with Chief Mangas Coloradas, who said they wanted peace with the Americans but would always be at war with the Mexicans. Subsequent conversations with Apaches convinced Steen that an agent with a "few thousand dollars worth of presents" could obtain "a lasting peace with this powerful band who have ... given us so much trouble."[39]

To help Calhoun discern one Apache band from another, Richard Kern supplied him with a list from Francisco Fletcher, interpreter at Doña Ana: Corrected for misspelling, they were Jicarillas, Mescaleros, Sacramentos, Aguas Nuevas, Norteños, Lipans, Garroteros, Tontos, Coyoteros, Mogollons, Copper Mines, Carlanas, Llaneros, Fronteranos, and Piñalenos.[40] These weren't even all of the Apache groups in the region, so it's understandable that Calhoun, the army, and the residents were often confused.

The Sacramentos were probably the people once called Faraons who lived in the Organ, Sacramento, and Sierra Blanca Mountains of southern New Mexico. The Aguas Nuevas and Norteños were Mescalero bands ranging from Presidio del Norte to San Elizario, Texas, on both sides of the border. The Lipans were on the lower Rio Grande and in Mexico. The Garroteros were not Apaches but Yavapais. Tontos referred to both Apaches and Yavapais. The Coyoteros and Piñalenos were western Apaches. The Mogollons and Copper Mine Apaches were bands of Chiricahua Apaches. The Carlanas were northern Apaches associated with the Jicarillas. The Llaneros were on the plains, associated with both the Jicarillas and Lipans. It's unclear who Fletcher meant by Fronteranos; it could refer to any number of border groups.[41]

Navajos

Cebolleta, fifty miles west of Albuquerque on the southern flank of Mount Taylor, was the earliest Spanish outpost in western New Mexico, begun in 1749 as a mission for Navajos. Abandoned a year later, Cebolleta (Little Onion, later called Seboyeta) was reoccupied by settlers fifty years later. Other people made their homes nearby on two Spanish land grants and in the Rio Puerco Valley. Angered at the intrusion into their country, Navajos raided the remote settlements, and Spanish colonists retaliated, beginning a century of attacks and counterattacks in which both sides took captives for slaves. In December 1849 Munroe stationed troops at Cebolleta,[42] but the new post made no difference to Navajos, who made war on Zuni Pueblo and raided area ranchers throughout 1850. In such isolated country, the Navajos could ride in force, strike, and disappear into familiar country before word reached the thinly manned posts.

New Mexicans chased Navajos on June 20 after they ran off all the livestock of four settlers on the Rio Puerco. Francisco Chaves went to the Cebolleta post to get help from troops, but soldiers returned to their post the next day, wrote Francisco Sarracino, the prefect at Pajarito and a former governor under Mexican rule. Addressing Calhoun as "Respected Sir and Friend," he said that Chaves with a few men from the village of Cebolleta pursued the Navajos and overtook them, but the raiders wounded five men, including Chaves, took their mules, and forced them to retreat. On October 21, a Navajo informer told the commander at Cebolleta that Navajos were running off stock about fifteen miles away. Troops left in pursuit and returned the next day, unsuccessful. Three days later, Navajos killed two shepherds and made off with 3,869 sheep.

Captain William H. Saunders, with twenty dragoons, followed their trail northwest over rugged terrain for five or six miles. He said that Indians and New Mexicans who promised to lead him abandoned him early in the day, and because of the poor condition of his horses, lack of grass and water, and no guides, they had to give up. At about 5 a.m. two New Mexicans came into camp from a small party that was ahead of him on the trail. They said the enemy couldn't be overtaken. Saunders complained that when he assumed command, he found broken-down troops and not even a dozen horses capable of active duty. He submitted his resignation ten days after arriving at Cebolleta but stayed on and died of chronic alcoholism on July 6, 1851.[43]

In early December Navajos ran off Sarracino's own stock along with 5,822 sheep of two others, passing within ten miles of Cebolleta. Stockmen again asked for help. Lieutenant Colonel Daniel T. Chandler said he received the report on a dark night with snow falling and couldn't send troops. Seven men left the next day, but found it impossible to follow the trail in drifted snow, and in below-zero temperatures several soldiers were severely frostbitten.[44]

The following month, Navajos stole 2,000 sheep at Valverde, and Ramón Luna, prefect of Valencia County, ordered the alcaldes to collect their best men and be ready at the village of Cubero the next day. Luna, too, went to Cebolleta for help, but the commander said his horses were "in a wild condition." Luna rode with fifty-six volunteers. At Colorado (Red) Lake, they recaptured five hundred stolen sheep. He continued to add men to his command, and the pursuit became a slave raid. Luna divided his forces at Mesa de la Vaca and sent them over various routes into Navajo country. They fought with the Navajos and took 5,000 sheep, 150 horses or mules, 11 oxen, and 28 captives. On the return trip, Luna lost 21 men who broke off from the main group and, assuming they were out of danger, let down their guard and were ambushed. Saunders said he heard rumors of missing New Mexicans, but the rumors were so conflicting, "it made prompt and decisive steps on my part impossible."[45] Sarracino's letters to Calhoun portray one side of a long conflict—the New Mexicans as victims. Luna's letter portrays the other side—the New Mexicans as raiders.

When Hopis visited Calhoun, they too complained bitterly about Navajo attacks. "I desired, and believed it to be important to visit these Indians," he wrote, but Munroe said he couldn't provide an escort. Late in 1850, Calhoun learned from newspapers that Congress approved Navajo and Ute treaties but not whether there was an appropriation to fulfill the treaties. The Navajos then had Zuni Pueblo under siege after months of warfare.[46]

Calhoun that year could only report on the dizzying attacks, counterattacks, pursuits, losses, and complaints from residents and tribes alike. He was realizing the federal government's great folly in assigning one lone agent to bring order to this cauldron of conflicts. The army was more often an instigator than a peacemaker and couldn't even provide an escort for him to conduct agency business. The federal Indian Office could offer no help and no more money. And yet, Calhoun successfully and repeatedly placated Pueblo people, made some influential friends like Padre Martínez, and identified resourceful men like Garcia and Lacome whom he could trust with agency business. Despite everything, he established a functioning Indian agency and mapped out a superintendency for the future.

11

STATEHOOD

A story often repeated is that Calhoun, on his arrival in Santa Fe, "declared that he had secret instructions from the government at Washington to induce the people to form a state government." The source is William W. H. Davis, who came to New Mexico in 1852 as the US District Attorney. It's doubtful that a man of Calhoun's political experience would simply blurt out his mission to strangers. He did, however, write the Indian commissioner within days of his arrival, "While en route, and during the few days I have been in camp here, I have omitted no opportunity that has offered to procure such information, as might enable me to execute discreetly, the important trusts confided to me by the President of the United States." On arrival, Calhoun made the rounds. "No one has ever come among us who has made a more favorable impression, both as a business man and an urbane gentleman," wrote Daniel L. Rood, publisher of *The New Mexican*.[1]

The statehood debate was a charged subject in New Mexico, and Calhoun soon met the key players. Judge Joab Houghton briefed him on Mexican laws. Calhoun was grateful "for valuable information, and for pointing out to me avenues through which I might glean more." A civil engineer from New York, Houghton moved to New Mexico in 1844 and was appointed US consul at Santa Fe in 1845. He and Eugene Leitensdorfer owned one of the leading mercantile houses. General Kearny named Houghton to the territory's Supreme Court, not because he possessed any legal expertise but because he was educated. Houghton would never be a competent judge.[2]

Another key player was Richard Hanson Weightman,[3] whom Calhoun called "a gentleman, and a very intelligent lawyer." Weightman, seventeen years younger than Calhoun, was a man of strong personality and stronger opinions. The oldest son of Washington, DC, Mayor Roger Weightman, Richard attended but didn't graduate from West Point. He and his father were political opposites. The father was a Whig, the son a Democrat; Roger favored abo-

FIGURE 41. *left* This undated photograph of Joab Houghton
appeared in Twitchell's *Leading Facts of New Mexico History*, vol. 2 in 1912.

FIGURE 42. *right* Richard Weightman, shown here as an artillery captain
in 1843, became an early ally of Calhoun in Santa Fe. Library of Congress.

lition, Richard would die fighting for the Confederacy. Richard Weightman
moved to St. Louis, probably to get out from under his father's thumb, and for
a time owned a small farm on the Missouri River thirteen miles from St. Louis.

When the Mexican War began, the dashing Weightman, then twenty-eight,
drew many young men to join his company of horse artillery in a regiment
of the Missouri Volunteers, but illness held him behind when the command
marched. Weightman and two other officers rode sixty miles in one night to
catch up and join the battle they expected with New Mexicans, and Weightman delivered Kearny's commission as brigadier general. When Kearny made
his speech at the Palace of Governors, and the flag was hoisted, Weightman's
battery fired the salute. In early 1847, when Colonel Alexander Doniphan led
troops into Chihuahua, Weightman fought bravely, commanded his howitzers
effectively, and was popular among the men. After the campaign, Weightman

briefly visited his family in Washington, DC, and returned to Missouri "ready for new enterprises."[4]

Calhoun also cultivated Manuel Alvarez, a successful trader and merchant with a store on the plaza and branches in four other towns. Five years older than Calhoun, Alvarez was born in Spain and formally educated. He came to the United States in 1823 and settled in Santa Fe in 1824. As a fur trapper, he led a forty-man party that in 1831 discovered the geysers and boiling pots of the future Yellowstone National Park. Appointed US consul in 1839, Alvarez diligently protected the rights of American citizens in what was then northern Mexico. When Texans invaded New Mexico in 1841, Alvarez was nearly killed by a mob enraged at the foreigners. The scar on his face was a badge of his near martyrdom, but Secretary of State Daniel Webster refused to compensate Alvarez for his losses. As merchants and former subordinates of Webster, Calhoun and Alvarez would have had much in common.[5]

Judge Houghton, Alvarez, and Weightman were already embroiled in the statehood question. Men like Houghton, whose bread was buttered by the military governor, preferred a territorial government. Houghton's allies included Hugh N. Smith, the military government's former attorney general; landowner and fur trader Ceran St. Vrain; Judge Carlos Beaubien; and Thomas S. J. Johnson, chief clerk of the army quartermaster. In the opposite corner were statehood supporters Alvarez and Weightman, who had the support of most Hispanic New Mexicans. (See appendix 3 for a list of faction members.) Houghton and Weightman despised one other.

Houghton had already shown ethical weakness. He and his business partner, Leitensdorfer, brought around $100,000 in goods to Santa Fe in June 1848 but ended their partnership a few months later. Leitensdorfer appointed Houghton his agent and left Santa Fe, but when he tried to settle with creditors, he found an unexplained deficit. Creditors couldn't sue because Houghton would decide their cases. In fact, many cases couldn't be heard because Houghton had personal interests in them. In July 1849, ten attorneys agreed that Houghton was incompetent, and eight signed a letter asking him to resign.[6]

In the months following, Weightman disparaged the judge in public, provoking Houghton to challenge Weightman to a duel. The two men met. At the command to fire, Weightman shot, the ball just missing Houghton's head. Slightly deaf, Houghton said he hadn't heard the command. Weightman raised his hands in the air and told Houghton to shoot, but their seconds intervened, and the duel ended. Soon after, Weightman wrote to Colonel Munroe with accusations that Houghton, as agent for several clients, received large sums of money on their behalf and kept it.[7]

As an attorney, Weightman saw directly the ruthless excesses of the military governor and the Houghton crowd. In November 1849, he represented young Simon Rosenstein, Albuquerque's first Jewish merchant. A noncommissioned officer and four soldiers arrested Rosenstein at his Albuquerque store on the south side of the plaza as he was engaged in business. Soldiers held him incommunicado in the guardhouse without food or bedding. The next day he was blindfolded, led to a room, stripped, bound, and "scourged," meaning he was whipped with a cat o' nine tails, an instrument of brutality consisting of leather strips knotted at the ends and attached to a handle. They flogged Rosenstein until he lost consciousness and never told him what he was accused of. Today we would say he was punished for being Jewish. The Albuquerque commander was Major Marshall Saxe Howe, whose "bad temper and impulsive conduct" Calhoun would note. Colonel Munroe did nothing.

A few months later, alcaldes in the Houghton camp replaced rightfully chosen priests in Valencia County with two suspended priests just to intimidate local residents into supporting the status quo on Election Day. In Sabinal, residents protested to Munroe in a petition. After the Belen constable demanded a list of petitioners, prominent rancher José Chaves sent Weightman south to advise residents and even paid $15,000 bail. They were indicted and jailed again.[8]

Calhoun threw in with Alvarez and Weightman, who became his good friends. "The State movement was set on foot by sixteen civilians, citizens of the United States—some of American and some of Mexican blood—some Democrats and some Whigs—some natives of southern and some of northern States," Weightman wrote. For the first time in Calhoun's adult life, political party didn't matter. An ardent Whig, Calhoun was now aligned with a Democrat, Weightman, and Alvarez, who never declared his political leanings. Many of their opponents were Whigs.

Historian Phillip B. Gonzáles sees in the two factions the seeds of political parties that held out valuable instruction to New Mexicans who had no previous exposure to a stable party system under Mexico. The Alvarez faction, which Gonzáles calls the "Mexican Party," gave Hispanos an avenue into political participation and more control of their future, while the Houghton faction, "the American party," sought to award power to the Americans. While some historians doubt the existence of political parties in the early Territory, Gonzáles roots them in the factions.[9] Calhoun, with years of political involvement in Georgia, saw them as parties, but very odd parties. He wrote:

> The most unimaginable incongruities have combined, and are divided into two parties, neither possessing the characteristics of a national party. It is a contest between those who have controlled, officially, since Genl. Kearny's organization of this territory, and a portion of the people who have not approved the civil administration of public affairs— because they thought it was arbitrary, partial and unjust in its operations, and all territorial legislation suppressed. The people never have been permitted a solitary voice in the selection of public functionaries. The contest is extremely violent.[10]

Historians usually assign leadership of the statehood faction to Weightman, but contemporary accounts and Weightman himself refer to "the Alvarez faction." Alvarez was, after all, Weightman's senior by twenty-four years and had considerable sway in the Hispanic community. Both men were ambitious and saw statehood as a stairway to higher office. Historians have been unfair to Weightman, calling him a political opportunist who was capable of chicanery and not particularly loyal to his friends, which is untrue.[11] Weightman stood up for the Catholic clergy and Hispanic New Mexicans and proved to be a devoted friend and advocate for Alvarez and Calhoun. If he was an opportunist, he was one among many in Santa Fe.

Statehood Movement

New Mexico's statehood was written into the Treaty of Guadalupe Hidalgo, although Congress was to decide when. In August 1848, Senator Thomas Hart Benton, of Missouri, encouraged New Mexicans to form a simple government. That fall, William Z. Angney, another lawyer who came to New Mexico as an infantry captain with Kearny, returned from Missouri fired up for statehood. On October 10, 1848, a group of influential citizens met in Santa Fe.[12] About half were members of the two factions. In their petition to the president, they asked for a territorial civil government, rejected slavery, and opposed the Texas claim. Congressman John C. Calhoun called the petition insolent; southerners, he said, should be able to visit New Mexico with their slaves. In November, Colonel Washington warned citizens against participating in "seditious meetings," and public meetings came to a halt. "The government of Colonel Washington is not at all liked. Americans and Mexicans have pronounced themselves against his laws," reported the *Augusta Chronicle*.[13]

While Washington was away on the Navajo expedition, Lieutenant Colonel Benjamin L. Beall permitted a convention to consider a civil government. On September 24, 1849, nineteen delegates, including Alvarez, voted to pursue territorial government, and if that wasn't feasible, state government. They sidestepped the issues of slavery and the boundary with Texas and chose Hugh N. Smith over Weightman as New Mexico's delegate in the nation's Capitol. (A delegate could sit with the House of Representatives and debate but not vote.)[14]

Calhoun wrote of the convention, "I understand this was a hurried affair, and manageable voters picked up at what ever place found and this arose from their extreme anxiety to secure the services of an exceedingly clever man, the Hon. Hugh N. Smith as the delegate of certain influential Citizens of this territory." When Calhoun used the word "clever," he meant "calculating." He sent Interior Secretary Thomas Ewing a copy of the convention's journal and advised him that Colonel Washington refused to recognize the convention's actions. Calhoun would subsequently keep his superiors posted on every political development related to statehood.[15]

The statehood question continued to burn. "The public mind in this territory is now agitated in reference to a civil government," Calhoun wrote on November 24, 1849, "and the controlling powers are opposed to a State organization, but their numbers are daily diminishing, and I think we shall have a Convention to frame a Constitution in January." On November 28, the first issue of *The New Mexican* exhorted citizens to vigorously pursue statehood. "We must form ourselves into a State Government, boldly asserting our rights, elect our Senators and Representatives, and demand of Congress an equal participation in the Legislative Councils of the country," wrote publisher Daniel L. Rood. "Our brethren all around us are acting for themselves."[16] California had written a constitution and would present it to Congress. The Mormons near the Salt Lake were forming a state government.

The newspaper carried warring commentary from the factions. In a message December 8 signed by fifteen men—Alvarez's name topped the list and

Calhoun's was last—they expressed their "desire to throw off the slavish man-acles" forced upon them by the military and opined that territorial govern-ment would mean a government run by outsiders who were chosen by out-siders. New Mexico could not sit back and permit Congress to allow others to make claims on its territory for the sake of preserving the Union. New Mexicans had no voice in governing and were taxed without their consent. "Taxes, when collected, are not applied to the public benefit but embezzled by officers irresponsible to the people . . . Judges unlearned in the laws de-cide upon life, liberty and property," and the military commander held none of them accountable. Other signers included Weightman, Angney, attorney Palmer Pillans, Santa Fe merchant William S. Messervy, and Calhoun's friend and fellow Georgian Cyrus Choice.[17] Two days later, sixty-two men—judges, prefects, sheriffs, alcaldes, and military officers—endorsed territorial govern-ment, saying they objected to the cost of a state government, meaning the implied taxation. Signers included Houghton, Beaubien, James L. Collins, Ceran St. Vrain, and William C. Skinner.[18]

In a second address, the Alvarez faction raised the prospect that New Mex-ico could be swallowed by California or the State of Deseret (Utah), as well as being "forced into an unnatural and repugnant association with Texas" that would mandate a tax greater than that for a state government "in order to pay the millions which Texas now owes." The newspaper, however, warned that any agitation on the subject would just cause Congress to postpone action.[19]

Rumors swept through Santa Fe that the War Department under two ad-ministrations ordered the military governor to not oppose Texas in taking half of New Mexico. The rumors were a barrier to state government, Calhoun wrote. Making matters worse were Indian attacks, which "are so blended with the civil disorders of this territory, you can not affect the one without the other, either for good or evil."[20]

In early February 1850, New Mexico's only printing press[21] fell into the hands of the Houghton faction through chicanery. The editors told Calhoun it would be sold either at the Exchange Hotel or at the quartermaster's door, and he sent his son-in-law, William Love, with instructions to bid up to $1,000. The press was sold in the printing room for $180 to the quartermaster's rep-resentative. Without the press, Calhoun said, "we are crippled; we cannot talk to the people." It was worse than that. From then on, the Houghton group could not only broadcast its own opinions and deny the Alvarez faction an audience, they could disseminate falsehoods and assault their enemies in print, which they did long after the statehood issue was settled.[22] In July, Alvarez and friends raised money through subscriptions for the purchase of a press, and in late August Weightman said he ordered one but never received it.[23]

Wicked Designs

Calhoun laid out New Mexico's political landscape and the obstacles to statehood in candid letters to his close friend, Georgia congressman William Dawson, and asked him to share them with the president, his cabinet, and the Georgia delegation. Munroe was "a soldier and a gentleman but, to use his own language, he is unwilling to be the 'cat's paw of any man' and therefore (I say) he will not aid us in the formation of a State Constitution." Munroe was a Whig but not a Taylor man and opposed any agitation for state government. "Americans, and some others, affecting to be Whigs, have united with Democrats of the most poisonous character, the first to perpetuate the present disreputable state of affairs in this territory, that they may, as contractors, sutlers, & Agents of every kind, together with their numerous train of employees, hold on to the pap they have been sucking since the American troops came into this country."

FIGURE 43. William C. Dawson was Calhoun's closest friend. Courtesy U. S. Senate Historical Office.

Nearly every military officer and every appointed office holder was a "Democrat of the deepest dye" who "ridicules the idea of a state organization."[24]

Next to Munroe, the second most powerful officer, Calhoun wrote, was the assistant quartermaster, Captain Alexander W. Reynolds,[25] whom Calhoun called a rabid Democrat and notorious gambler. The third was the chief assistant commissary of the department, Lieutenant Francis J. Thomas[26] who was "of the same school of politics, and of the same habits, as Capt. Reynolds, and the gentleman selected by Mr. Bedinger, of Virginia, to watch my movements." Isolated as he was, Calhoun didn't know that Congressman Henry Bedinger lost his election, and his term ended March 3, 1849. From Houghton, Reynolds, and Thomas "come all the ignorant scribbling against Genl. Taylor's friends in this territory." Unless these men and a few others were relieved from duty in the territory "the administration must consent to see their friends humbled, and sacrificed here." He asked Dawson to "let [Secretary of War] Crawford know the facts" about his officers in New Mexico." To this list Calhoun added Ceran St. Vrain, "a very clever man—the life and soul of the Sutlers and Contractors combination."[27]

Houghton was "an exceedingly clever gentleman, but an unaccountably strange political bird. He is a Whig—but prefers the advice, and is under the influence of" Senator Henry Foote, of Mississippi, a critic of Taylor's statehood policy. The day before, Houghton ally Hugh N. Smith told Calhoun that New Mexicans needed instruction before entering statehood. Calhoun was astonished. "There are other facts in the way of the formation of a State government—not generally understood at Washington, at least I heard nothing of them until I came here," he wrote. Calhoun described four special-interest groups in addition to the military: "a territorial party, fearful of taxation," that included frightened New Mexicans and the power brokers who held the contracts; "a Texas party" of speculators led by a man who served as Munroe's and Houghton's interpreter (probably James L. Collins); and a party led by Reynolds and William Skinner whose mission was to "break down Genl. Taylor."[28]

This was not what Calhoun signed up for. "I desire it to be understood, when I contracted for this service, I supposed there would be some potential voice in this territory that would have controlling influence in our favor," he wrote. "Instead of which, Governor Munroe will not reply to the most civil and polite notes from Genl. Taylor's friends, because he is apprehensive that his answers may reach the public eye through the public press. There are but few civil officers from their Master, Judge Houghton, down to the humblest Alcalde who do not inveigh against us. These men control absolutely, the personal liberty and property of every man in this territory. From Judge Houghton's decision there is no appeal." If Munroe could be persuaded to sympathize with the Alvarez group, "Mr. Justice Houghton's influence would be scattered to the winds, and the wicked designs of erring politicians would have to look elsewhere to sustain their wicked purposes."[29]

Calhoun begged Dawson for a new appointment. He was anxious to serve in the military and would settle for nothing less than senior colonel in the

Ninth Department, but he would also be satisfied to see the command given to Weightman. "He is a good man, a firm man, a true man, and an intelligent man, and a gentleman in every sense of the word." New Mexico needed two mounted regiments for its defense, and Calhoun proposed to lead them as a brigadier general. Five months into his agent appointment, Calhoun still aspired to military command. If that seems presumptuous, remember that in the Mexican War more than a few generals had no previous military experience. Calhoun at least had commanded men in the field and served as a military governor.[30]

"I am now fifty years old. I am pretty well acquainted with myself—have some experience, sufficient energy and physical powers, and I think, mind enough to guide me in the way I should go—and I repeat, my life upon it, in less than twelve months . . . every disorder and derangement in this territory should disappear. I am 'longing,' that is, I am hungry and thirsty for this service," Calhoun wrote to Dawson. But he wouldn't mind being a colonel of dragoons, inspector general, or consul in Liverpool or Havre. He was willing to stay in New Mexico provided he wasn't just an Indian agent and asked that his son-in-law John Davis be named postmaster. For marshal, he recommended Andrew Lee, who was known to Calhoun's old friends Robert Alexander and Hines Holt "and a more competent man cannot be found. Mr. Lee came out with me and has been active in his exertions to promote the objects I have had in charge and so far has received no compensation, nor has anyone of my party . . . For our support, the means of our party have been exhausted, and my own will soon fail." He concluded, "If None of these things can be accomplished for me, quietly inform, and quickly too, that I may decently retire, for I cannot play second fiddle to any one now in this territory. I am content to be Superintendent of Indian Affairs in this territory but not an Agent, to be subject to the control of a Territorial Governor."[31]

As he had in Mexico, Calhoun complained irritably that he had received no letters or newspapers, "and, as to the result of the fall elections of Georgia, I am as ignorant as a stone." He begged Dawson to send him news of the elections. Later, he said, "I should like to hear from Georgia." Santa Fe residents would finally start getting monthly mail that summer, after Waldo, Hall, and Company got a contract to carry the mail between Independence and Santa Fe.[32]

Calhoun and Dawson had been friends since they were young men; Calhoun's wife, Anna, died in Dawson's house in the arms of Dawson's wife,

Henrietta. In the depth of his disappointment in the new position, he appealed to his old friend. "This letter is to you—and upon you I rely most confidently— Not that others of the Georgia delegation would not willingly serve me, but I have not their affections and sympathies as I have yours," he told Dawson. "Not one friend, true and trusty, from this territory favorable to Genl Taylor's administration is at Washington or on his way to Washington—nor will there be, unless Maj. Weightman, or myself shall be able to reach there."

He invoked the war that everyone knew was coming, even in 1850. "Consult our Georgia friends and tell me the result," he wrote. By Georgia friends, he meant John M. Berrien, a prominent judge and US senator; congressmen Toombs and Stephens; George W. Owens, a former Savannah mayor and congressman; his fellow appointee Thomas Butler King; and Secretary of War Crawford. He added to that list "your excellent wife, should she be present. She will tell you what to do." Calhoun continued: "I want employment, and desire to be in the service of the Government of the United States, as it was, and should be." If the North and South should go to war he would get back to Georgia , but "if possible let us save the union." In another letter he wrote, "Let the worse come, I am with the South—with Georgia."[33]

Emissaries

Lieutenant Colonel George A. McCall, recovered from war-related illness, prepared to rejoin his regiment in Santa Fe, but the Taylor administration had a mission for him. On November 19, 1849, Secretary of War George Crawford instructed the forty-one-year-old McCall that the treaty with Mexico promised New Mexico admission to the union, with the approval of Congress, but Congress failed to provide a suitable government. Military rule was necessary, but it was outside the army's appropriate spheres of action, Crawford wrote, and so the people of New Mexico should have a government of their choosing. "Should the people of New Mexico wish to take any steps toward this object . . . it will be your duty and the duty of others with whom you are associated not to thwart but to advance their wishes."[34]

Historian Mark Stegmaier has written that because "Calhoun had not acted decisively enough in fostering a statehood movement," Taylor sent an army officer because "he had an abiding faith in his fellow military officers and in their ability to implement his wishes on policy in New Mexico." Ignoring for a moment that Calhoun's day job was inhumanly demanding, he faced impossible hurdles in Munroe and the Houghton faction, and he informed the president. Taylor responded by sending McCall, who could grapple with both. McCall arrived in Santa Fe on March 21, 1850. He "found politics the rage, engrossing the attention of all classes of people," but there were deep divisions. The territorial party was more influential, he wrote, while the statehood party had so little clout that asking for admission as a state seemed hopeless. McCall began pressuring Houghton. Congress wouldn't approve a territorial government, McCall told Houghton, and President Taylor "was determined that New Mexico should be erected into a state government, in order to settle the question of slavery, and also that of boundary with Texas." Houghton yielded. McCall reported these developments directly to Taylor through Colonel William W. S. Bliss, Taylor's son-in-law and private secretary.[35]

Both factions now supported statehood, but their enmity had a life of its own, and they refused to work together. Calhoun may have disagreed with McCall's approach, but the officer's involvement freed Calhoun to step back from the controversy at a time when he was preoccupied with Indian issues. "McCall thought it would be a bolder, and a much more advisable move to change the front of the Governor and the Houghton party, than to act with those who favored the views of the administration," he wrote. McCall's "violent anti-slavery prejudices" may have been a factor. Some of the original statehood proponents were willing to have New Mexico admitted to the union as a slave state. "But so soon as Col. McCall reached here, the Governor and Houghton changed their views, jumped ahead of all others in the formation of [a] state organization." Calhoun thought it unnecessary to advocate slavery. He recognized that the laws in New Mexico didn't allow slavery and that only a sovereign power, such as Texas, could introduce it. "The influential Mexican Landholders, when they perceive their system of Peonage is unsuited to a Republican Government, they will embrace Slavery as a great blessing," he wrote. Under New Mexico's peonage system, people pledged their labor to settle a debt. In reality, peonage meant harsh, life-long bondage. New Mexicans also held a great many Indian captives as slaves. Calhoun believed that Congress wouldn't debate New Mexico's admission to the union without settling the Texas boundary question and the slavery question "as we of the South desired."[36]

New Mexicans were anxiously watching Texas and Congress, Calhoun wrote, and if tensions triggered violence, the thinly stretched military would be powerless to control it. Hispanic New Mexicans originally favored statehood but shifted their allegiance to the territorial party after being told the statehood party championed Texas. Even the Pueblos feared that Texans would take their land. "A collision between the authorities of Texas and the people of Santa Fe would call forth the war hoop from every tribe of Indians in this territory," Calhoun wrote. Some members of the original statehood faction—namely Texas lawyer Palmer Pillans and possibly Weightman—sympathized with Texas, but Calhoun's thinking was more complicated.[37]

As a lawyer and Southern Whig, Calhoun argued for the respect due Texas as a sovereign state and the urgency of preserving the union. "I have suggested to these people that the Government of the United States might be compelled to yield to the claim of Texas, rather than endanger the integrity of the Union— to which they reply there is no danger of such a result" because the secretary of state and the president were both opposed "to the pretensions of Texas," he wrote. Personally, he believed "that it would be better for Texas, better for this people, and better for the United States, if an independent state government could be established here without disturbing the harmony of the Union, and to accomplish which, I would willingly see millions paid to Texas."[38] And that's exactly what would transpire.

Weeks after McCall's appearance, a second emissary approached Santa Fe. Robert S. Neighbors was on his way, sent by Texas Governor Peter H. Bell, to organize Santa Fe County, hold elections for county officers, and publish Bell's address claiming Texas "rights." Neighbors had been a quartermaster during the Texas war of independence and an early Indian agent, who started the practice of visiting the tribes where they lived instead of waiting for them to come to the agency. As a legislator he would introduce bills preparing the way for Indian reservations. Conscientious, hard working, and honest, he was the best Indian agent Texas ever had. The year before his assignment for Governor Bell, he helped open a road from Austin to El Paso. Like Calhoun, Neighbors was a Methodist and a Mason.[39]

Neighbors asked Munroe for his "friendly cooperation in organizing all the territory properly belonging to this state into counties." Calhoun, knowing Neighbors was on his way, had advised the Commissioner of Indian Affairs that New Mexicans were talking up resistance, egged on by the Houghton crowd and others who feared a Texas takeover. Munroe ordered his posts to "observe a rigid noninterference" with Neighbors and Texas judicial authorities. Neighbors received a copy of Munroe's noninterference orders, as well as "several letters from private individuals in Santa Fe" urging him to come.[40]

"Maj. Neighbors, the Commissioner from Texas is with us, and, as yet, has frightened no one to death," Calhoun wrote. "He is firm, resolute and courteous, and Texas could not have sent a more suitable agent." Neighbors said he "was well and courteously received by the inhabitants" when he arrived on April 8, but Munroe would do nothing for Texas and obviously preferred the status quo. "I have no right to abolish the present government," Munroe told him. In fact, Munroe and Washington before him refused to bend to Texas, a position that began with Kearny himself, who proclaimed the US intention of possessing all of New Mexico. Judge Houghton told Neighbors he intended to maintain the current government and even issued a proclamation in Spanish directing citizens to ignore the Texas commissioner and stay away from the polls; anyone attempting to exercise Texas authority over the region would be jailed. William C. Skinner, a Houghton ally, told the St. Louis newspaper during a trip east that opposition to the Texas claim was so staunch that New Mexicans would resist to the death "against the unjust usurpation of Texas to the soil of New Mexico."[41]

Weightman and friends warmly welcomed Neighbors. "A few evenings after my arrival in Santa Fe," Neighbors wrote, "I met a considerable party of gentlemen . . . and among them some of the most distinguished members of the bar for a consultation on the subject of organization . . . they were decidedly of the opinion that it would be necessary for the state to send a military force before she could exercise jurisdiction." They represented a minority, he said. McCall reported, not quite truthfully, that Weightman's group opposed forming a state government without the consent of Texas. He considered Weightman presumptuous and unscrupulous and wrote that Weightman had been dropped from the army, when in fact Weightman had performed gallantly and was well respected. McCall repeated an unsubstantiated rumor that Weightman agreed to support the Texas claims in return for support of his party. Neighbors wrote the Texas governor that the original statehood supporters hoped to escape the tyranny of the present government, which was accountable to no one, and which was corrupt and arbitrary in the extreme.[42] Alvarez is notably absent from this debate. His faction had the trust and support of native New Mexicans but not on this emotional subject. It was the one time when some members of the statehood group parted from the majority of New Mexicans and the one time the Houghton faction spoke for New Mexicans and not just themselves.

On April 20, 1850, the Houghton group restated their determination to resist Texas and enter the union as a state. They expected opposition from southern congressmen and understood that Texas had summoned an army for a bloody war on New Mexico. Munroe issued a proclamation calling electors to assemble on May 6 and choose delegates to a statehood convention, to be held in Santa Fe on May 15. The proclamation halted Neighbors' mission in Santa Fe, and he departed the next day, Calhoun wrote, "intending to return by July, with a sufficient force to establish the jurisdiction of his State over this territory—and he will do it, unless Congress shall adopt a plan to escape the crisis."[43]

Publicly, Neighbors was a good soldier. Privately, he harbored low expectations of success in Santa Fe. The state of Texas hadn't advanced him a dollar for contingencies, and New Mexico's high costs exhausted his salary. He was displeased that Texas offered no assurances to New Mexicans about land titles; Texas was even then surveying and granting lands in southern New Mexico. Major Steen, described by Neighbors as "a perfect Texan in principle and the strongest advocate of our claims I have found in this territory," had purchased a sixty-four-acre head-right claim that contained the entire village of Doña Ana. After receiving a petition from angry citizens, Munroe chastised the officer.[44]

Neighbors' entire report appeared in the *Columbus Enquirer* and included Munroe's proclamation. He said it was apparent "that the people of New Mexico are about to go into a separate State organization," which he traced to the president through McCall. He claimed to have copies of the president's orders to King and McCall to foment a state movement. Neighbors, obviously influenced by Calhoun, Weightman, and friends, described Houghton's party as "so void of principle that they would excite the Pueblo Indians to hostility or resort to any other measure whatever to prevent the extension of the jurisdiction of Texas." He said that "amongst the intelligent portion of the American Community" Houghton's group had a reputation for corruption and for that reason opposed change. Neighbors, a Democrat, called Houghton "a bitter, unprincipled and vindictive Whig." A Washington, DC, newspaper wrote that supporters of territorial government "were favorite contractors, appointed by the military governor, and used their positions to become rich … This clique of men, all of whom are recipients of pay from Washington" have used the press "to excite the prejudices of New Mexicans" and were only now supporting a state government because public opinion was against them.[45]

Statehood Quarrel

With the delegates chosen, the once reluctant Colonel Munroe enthused that "the different constituencies will have their sentiments fairly represented," and he anticipated no problems. On May 15, 1850, nineteen delegates, a majority from the Houghton faction, drafted a state constitution that was a marvel of compromise.[46] They endorsed Alvarez's stand against the military governor and described the military regime as "sinking, ineffective and abhorrent." The people had a right to organize a civil government, they said. On McCall's advice, they barred slavery, Calhoun wrote. They brazenly placed New Mexico's eastern boundary far inside territory claimed by Texas on the 100th parallel all the way to the Arkansas River, taking in the Texas panhandle and pieces of present Kansas, Oklahoma, and Colorado. "Slavery in New Mexico is naturally impracticable, and can never, in reality, exist here; wherever it has existed it has proved a curse and a blight to the State upon which it has been inflicted—a moral, social and political evil," they wrote. The Houghton faction wanted merchant Henry Connelly as governor, Ceran St. Vrain as lieutenant governor, and Hugh Smith for Congress. The Alvarez faction supported trader Tomás Cabeza de Baca[47] for governor, Manuel Alvarez for lieutenant governor, and merchant William Messervy for Congress.[48]

"The Pueblo Indians are excited, the Mexicans are excited, and a certain class of Americans are greatly excited," Calhoun wrote. He said Munroe's proclamation unsettled the Pueblo Indians. Partisan agitators visited them, and the Pueblos in turn sent representatives to seek Calhoun's counsel. He advised them against voting for delegates because it might undermine their status as a separate people under the direct authority of the federal government and bring them under state laws. From the Creek experience in Georgia, he knew the consequences of applying state law to tribes.[49]

On June 20, 1850, citizens approved the new state constitution by a lopsided 8,371 to 39. They elected Henry Connelly governor, Alvarez lieutenant governor, and Messervy congressman, and the Alvarez faction controlled the legislature. In choosing two senators, legislators considered Houghton, Reynolds, Weightman, Calhoun, Angney, Major Francis A. Cunningham and Dr. James

D. Robinson and chose Weightman and Cunningham. The people "approved with a voice, almost unanimous," Calhoun wrote, adding that the opposition "submitted to an overwhelming defeat" while his own party triumphed. "The wrath of the opposition—that is, Munroe, McCall and Houghton, is without bounds."[50]

Connelly was in the States on business, and so Alvarez, as acting governor, delivered his inaugural address on July 4. New Mexico's biggest problems, he said, were hostile Indians, loss of legitimately owned property to scoundrels, a prevalence of gambling, corruption and lack of professionalism in the judiciary, and disuse of the vagrant law, which allowed criminals to take advantage of innocents. Alvarez proposed to reorganize the judiciary, allow the Pueblos to decide if they wanted to participate in American government, and establish schools. He quickly clashed with Munroe, who insisted that civil government was "inoperative" until New Mexico was admitted as a state. There followed a furious exchange of letters, many of them published in outside newspapers. An anonymous writer in New York observed: "All seem to admire the letter of Lieut. Gov. Don Manuel Alvarez to Col. Munroe . . . An abler document has not lately appeared from the pen of the Executive of any of the old states. If Don Alvarez is a specimen of the educated New Mexican population there certainly is abundant cause to congratulate ourselves upon the acquisition of a body of useful, intelligent and respectable citizens." When Munroe threatened to use all the power at his command to sustain the military government and its officials, Alvarez backed down. Those officials, said legislators, were "detested and feared" by the people.[51]

New Mexicans knew California's new government was operating freely. In June 1849, the day before Calhoun's counterpart, Thomas Butler King, arrived in San Francisco, Lieutenant Colonel Bennet Riley, the military governor of California, called for a convention to organize a state government. King encouraged Californians to become a state: "The people of the old states ardently desire it. I speak knowingly when I say the administration desire it." On December 20, 1849, Riley relinquished all civil power to elected officials. Alvarez told Munroe that in California "the government went into immediate operation; the officer commanding the troops of the United States retired from the discharge of his civil functions and his conduct and the course of the people have met with general approbation in the United States."[52]

A Virginia newspaper blasted President Taylor for his "Machiavellian policy of secretly encouraging the squatters in California to form a State Constitution" and doing the same with New Mexico, "disregarding the rights of the South." The same paper wrote up the dispute between Alvarez and Munroe, "each denying the authority of the other." The writer believed New Mexico's small population of "mongrel people" were unfit for democracy. However, an Ohio newspaper found Munroe's actions "altogether unjustifiable" and said if population was the basis for statehood, Rhode Island and Delaware would be expelled from the union.[53]

In justifying his actions, Munroe blamed outsiders but let slip his own opinion of New Mexicans, referring to "the unstable elements of the Mexican character [and] the general ignorance of the people," as well as their "manifest dislike (although latent) to Americans and the strong sympathies a large number entertain for Mexican institutions and its government as opposed to that of the United States." He asked for congressional action "as soon as possible." Calhoun wrote: "These conflicting efforts have not created the slightest excitement except with the immediate actors in this triangular love of order and good government, and the old and time honored incumbents of misrule, as they are called by those who are not in office."[54]

The Ayes of Texas

In the heat of the Alvarez-Munroe squabble, on July 20, Spruce McCoy Baird reappeared. Baird, a thirty-three-year-old Kentuckian who had practiced law in Texas for five years, first came to New Mexico in 1848 as the appointed judge of Texas's newly created Santa Fe County. Governor George T. Wood wrote President Polk asking him to order troops in Santa Fe to support the new jurisdiction in the face of rumored movements toward statehood, and Polk obliged. Even though the War Department directed Colonel Washington to not interfere with Texas in taking possession of New Mexico lands and even to help, Baird got the same response from the army commander that Neighbors would a year later. Rebuffed, Baird left New Mexico.[55]

In his second act, Baird announced an August 1850 election to be held in Taos, Santa Fe, Algodones, Albuquerque, and San Miguel. Munroe ordered out troops, but Calhoun doubted there was even one man who "ever dreamed of seizing the reins of government by force." The *Santa Fe Republican* wrote: "We would inform our Texian friends that it is not necessary to send us a

FIGURE 44. A political cartoon from the *Missouri Republican*, August 29, 1850, calls attention to the inflammatory correspondence between Alvarez and Munroe.

Gunpowder Correspondence between 'Col. Monroe and Manuel Alverazx, acting Governor of New Mexico.

The telegraph yesterday fore-shadowed this correspondence, and we are happy in being able to lay it before our readers to-day in all its belligerent details.

Judge nor a District Attorney to settle our affairs or to put things to rights, for there is not a citizen, either American or Mexican, that will ever acknowledge themselves as citizens of Texas." The newspaper added, "Oh Texas, do show some little sense and drop this question, and not have it publicly announced that Texas smartest men were tarred and feathered by attempting to fill the office assigned them!!!"[56]

On August 5, the designated day for Texas elections, "not a solitary effort was made to proceed with the election," Calhoun wrote, "nor did it excite the talking qualities of our very inflammable fabricators of public sentiment." August 12, the date set for New Mexico elections, passed the same way. "The truth is, in my judgment, the much talked of insurrectionary designs, and certain movements and concentration of troops has so completely chilled" those who wanted a state organization, it would have taken a powerful effort to reanimate the movement silenced by Munroe, Calhoun wrote. "The thinking people were mortified that . . . the same authority that authorized them to confer on the subject is the same power that compels them to submit to the old order."[57]

Baird assured his governor that he "left nothing undone that could have been done," but without military cooperation, he couldn't enforce the laws. An anonymous letter writer pilloried Baird for not upholding Texas interests. "The Hon. Judge is a man who looks out for number one first. He has a flour mill . . . and when they refused to recognize him as judge he quickly (settled) down as a plain member of the bar and practicing lawyer . . . As he could not make decisions upon the bench for the people, he made them flour and meal." Baird admitted that he owned a farm with a mill and, taking aim at his critic, said it was more to his liking than the monte table. He still believed that Congress would confirm "the jurisdiction of Texas over the territory in question."[58]

In late August, Weightman arrived in Missouri on his way to Washington to "press the claims of the new State for admission into the Union," wrote the *Missouri Republican*. "If she should be admitted, there is no gentleman whom we would be more gratified to see her Representative in the U.S. Senate than Major Weightman. But we think her admission scarcely probable." From St. Louis, Weightman telegraphed the president that "the rights of the people of New Mexico are now being invaded by the commander of the 9th military department." The existing "civil authorities, in order to maintain their positions, have systematically poisoned the public mind of the United States, in representing the people of New Mexico as incapable of self-government," he said.[59] The New Mexico–Texas contest had been a regular topic of eastern newspapers for some time. "Between the nether and the upper millstones, viz: Texas on the one hand and the U.S. military government on the other," wrote a Richmond paper, "the new State of New Mexico is likely to be well pounded."[60]

12

THE COMPROMISERS

As New Mexicans squabbled over statehood, Congress was doing the same, at length. In the session that convened December 3, 1849, lawmakers also grappled with the questions of whether to permit slavery in the territories taken from Mexico and how to placate Texas in its demand for half of New Mexico. Feelings ran so high in Washington that men carried bowie knives and revolvers, and moderates feared violence over the border issue. Calhoun's Georgia friends William Dawson, Alexander Stephens, and Robert Toombs were front and center in the debates as champions of the union as well as southern rights. During a December caucus of Whigs, a dispute erupted over slavery in New Mexico, Utah, and Washington, DC, and Toombs, Stephens, and other Whig dissidents left the meeting. They resisted electing a northerner as House speaker and instead helped Georgia's Howell Cobb became speaker.[1]

President Zachary Taylor in December recommended statehood for California and predicted that New Mexico too would ask for statehood. Congressmen openly questioned whether Taylor was usurping their powers. On January 1, 1850, the House passed a resolution saying that "James S. Calhoun, the Indian Agent for Santa Fe, appointed by the President, instead of attending solely to his duties as such federal officer, is endeavoring to incite the people of Santa Fe and vicinity to form a State, in derogation of the claims of Texas to said territory" and that "the interference of said officer is improper." They asked Taylor if the interference was without executive approval. Taylor submitted his written orders and correspondence to King and Calhoun. He denied instigating statehood movements but said he expressed his desire for California to submit a constitution and ask for admission. If New Mexico had been admitted as a state, he said, the courts could resolve the boundary question, but no court had the authority to decide an issue between a state and the United States, so Congress would have to provide a solution. "New Mexico will at no

FIGURE 45. Alexander Stephens, shown here in 1859, would become vice president of the Confederate States of America. He was a friend and ally of Calhoun. Library of Congress

FIGURE 46. Robert Toombs campaigned with Calhoun in 1848 and remained a friend and advocate. Library of Congress.

very distant period ask for admission into the Union" as a state, Taylor said, and when they did "the residents of the region could settle questions of domestic policy to suit themselves."[2]

On January 29, 1850, Henry Clay, the venerable Kentucky Whig Calhoun had championed as president of the Clay Club, proposed a compromise he believed would save the union and resolve the statehood issue. California would be admitted as a free state, and New Mexico and Deseret (Utah) would be organized as territories without any restrictions on slavery. New Mexico would keep much of the disputed region, and Texas would be compensated for its "loss" in the border dispute. Clay said slavery, outlawed or not, wasn't likely to be introduced in New Mexico or Utah. Taylor, who opposed Clay's compromise, sent California's constitution to Congress on February 13 and strongly recommended its approval.

Stephens and Toombs said they didn't object to admitting California as a free state as long as citizens of New Mexico and Utah were allowed to decide the issue of slavery, and that's how the bill was written. Now they needed to make sure the president would support them and veto the Wilmot Proviso.

On February 23, Stephens, Toombs, and Thomas Clingman, of North Carolina, visited Taylor. During a heated discussion, Taylor made it clear he had no intention of vetoing the Wilmot Proviso. Stephens may have threatened secession. Taylor angrily told them he would take command of the army himself, and if the three were taken captive, he would hang them with less reluctance than he had hung deserters and spies in Mexico.[3]

During weeks of impassioned speeches by congressional giants in March, a scandal broke after Congress approved a measure to settle old claims of a prominent Indian trader in Georgia related to Cherokee and Creek land sessions. The government would pay the trader's heirs $235,000, of which Secretary of War George Crawford would receive $100,000 as their attorney. In the press, this became a "treasury raid." Other Cabinet members urged Taylor to dump Crawford. Stephens and Toombs defended the claim. Taylor was now under crushing pressure from the scandal and the controversy over California and New Mexico. He must have longed for the solid ground of war rather than the shifting sands of Washington politics. Friends thought the president looked fatigued, dejected, and haggard.[4]

That summer southern-rights radicals in Georgia tried to stoke opposition to the compromise and move their state to join South Carolina in seceding, but a new faction of moderates, intent on preserving the union, prevailed. Stephens, Toombs, and Cobb stood with the compromisers.[5]

Saber Rattling

When Robert Neighbors returned to Texas in June, his report to the governor set in motion plans to take eastern New Mexico by force. Houghton ally Hugh Smith, who was in Washington hoping to be seated as delegate, said several thousand Texans were already on their way. Taylor was determined to defend the federal government's rights in New Mexico. In June he told Lieutenant Alfred M. Pleasonton, who would soon depart for New Mexico, that if Munroe needed reinforcements, he would lead them, sword in hand. "I will be with you myself. I will be there before those people shall go into that country or have a foot of that territory. The whole business is infamous, and must be put down." Taylor revoked instructions to Munroe to avoid conflicts with Texas authorities over Secretary of War Crawford's objections.[6]

Senator Henry Foote of Mississippi declared, "If New Mexico continued to resist Texas, and Congress delayed to act, blood would be shed in July, and that the combined manhood of the South would rush to the conflict." Dawson submitted one of Calhoun's letters to the War Department stating that Neighbors, the commissioner of Texas, was involved in organizing a military expedition against New Mexico, reported a New York newspaper. "Mr. Calhoun belongs to Georgia, and probably expressed views in a private letter that he would have greatly modified in an official communication."[7]

Stephens expected Texas to send at least 2,500 men to New Mexico. Probably relying on information from Calhoun, he said that in Santa Fe were some two hundred Texan camp followers. Munroe's troops numbered five or six hundred, with another six hundred about to be added. Texans in Washington said their state would arrest US military officers and try them for obstructing Texas laws. If the United States interferes, "the cause of Texas in such a conflict will be the cause of the entire South," Stephens wrote on July 3.[8]

On July 9, Taylor died of cholera morbus (intestinal dysfunction). A northern newspaper called it "little less than murder" that Toombs and Stephens visited the ailing president days before and heartlessly "badgered him with the most unfeeling threats regarding Texas." Stephens said the reported threats were unfounded. Toombs described a "frank conversation" during which Taylor promised to hold New Mexico with all the power he commanded.[9]

On July 12 a courier arrived in Washington with letters from Texas Governor Peter H. Bell, protesting presidential interference in New Mexico and asserting his state's claim. The new president, Millard Fillmore, told Congress on August 6 that New Mexico was a territory of the United States, and its citizens were guaranteed protection by the federal government. The contested ground has been part of New Mexico "and actually governed and possessed by her people, until conquered and severed from the Republic of Mexico by the American arms," he said. If Texas forces invaded New Mexico, they would be nothing more than trespassers, and the president's duty was prescribed by law. He would utilize troops to protect New Mexico citizens. He reminded Congress that it had a responsibility to resolve the boundary dispute. "No Government can be established for New Mexico, either State or territorial, until it shall be first ascertained what New Mexico is, and what are her limits and boundaries." A Georgia newspaper intoned: "There is great excitement in Washington, many consider the sword of civil war already drawn unless the boundary between New Mexico and Texas is speedily settled."[10]

THE LONE STAR IN THE FIELD!

Santa Fe to be wallopped and Uncle Samuel chastised by Two Regiments of "Mounted Cavalry,"--The Enormous School Fund of Texas appropriated to defray Expenses.--$30,000 slap dab and who Keers!

FIGURE 47. A political cartoon in the *Minnesota Chronicle and Register*, September 23, 1850, lampoons Texas Governor Bell.

On the same day, Acting Secretary of War Winfield Scott informed Munroe that about 750 recruits were en route, to arrive in the next month, followed by the Seventh Regiment of Infantry and one or two troops of First Dragoons. These reinforcements would help protect against hostile Indians or forces from Texas. In the latter event, Munroe's position "will be one of much delicacy and difficulty," Scott warned. The president saw it as his duty to protect New Mexico and its inhabitants with all the means at his disposal. Munroe was to use his troops against any such act of violence.[11]

Governor Bell, on August 13, addressed the Texas legislature on "our relations with Santa Fe" and "the unwarrantable assumption of power" by the federal government." Duty and honor required them to meet it boldly with "manly and determined action." Legislators authorized him to raise and supply at least two regiments of mounted volunteers to occupy Santa Fe. Bell himself would lead the forces "and repair with all speed to the scene of federal outrage and rebellion." On August 31, Fillmore received news that Texas organized 1,500 volunteers to be sent against New Mexico, and he ordered Winfield Scott to "take all proper measures to protect the inhabitants of New Mexico according to the treaty of Guadalupe Hidalgo against the act of violence on the part of the invaders."[12]

In the midst of this saber rattling, a northern newspaper joked:

Oh! Governor Bell is come out of the south,
Thro' all the wide border he is noted for mouth,
His limbs they are dumpy, his body is fat,
But the spirit that fills him has no care for that,
In "embarrassing" questions, he sweats and he swells,
Till he's puffed to the size of two Governor Bells.[13]

The Compromise

The Senate debate on Clay's compromise dragged through a hot, humid July. On July 30, Calhoun's good friend William Dawson, in a concession to Texas, moved an amendment to allow commissioners to settle the boundary question. Without agreement on a boundary, he argued, the territorial government couldn't begin operating nor could a state be established. Compromise supporters countered that Dawson's amendment abandoned their goals of settling the boundary question, giving New Mexico a territorial government, maintaining New Mexico's rights until the boundary was settled, and protecting New Mexicans from Texas laws. It also "gave the whole country to Texas until such time as she agreed to surrender it." Clay supported the amendment in order to save the bill. Dawson's amendment passed by two votes. Lawmakers then split the package into separate pieces, and a new compromise emerged: the New Mexico–Texas boundary would fall along the 103rd meridian instead of the 100th meridian, and Texas would receive $10 million. The bill passed after four days of debate.[14]

The measure establishing a territorial government in New Mexico passed the Senate 27 to 10, with Georgians Berrien and Dawson voting in favor. Residents could decide the slavery issue for themselves. It was then known that New Mexico's senator-elect, Richard Weightman, was on his way to Washington with a copy of the proposed constitution. The administration feared abolitionists would rally for New Mexico statehood, which would undo their carefully crafted compromise, and they redoubled their efforts to move the package of bills later called the Compromise of 1850.[15]

In the House, Stephens appeared to soften his position, or at least clarify it. Texas was admitted as a state with boundaries belonging to her at the time, he said. Her rights were founded on the right of successful revolution. "I did not believe then nor do I now believe that she had established her jurisdiction

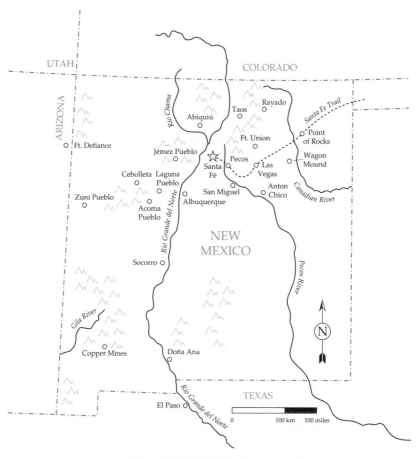

FIGURE 48. Map of New Mexico indicating key locations
during the territorial period.

to the extent of her claims." But the federal government settled her boundary
with Mexico, and President Polk said the boundary extended to the source of
the Rio Grande. On September 6, the House passed the Texas–New Mexico
border bill, amended to include territorial status for New Mexico. Toombs
voted in favor.

On September 9 President Fillmore signed the four bills establishing territorial governments for New Mexico and Utah, settling the Texas boundary,
and admitting California as a state. House Speaker Howell Cobb couldn't
vote but helped by giving the floor only to supporters. The Compromise of

1850 allowed California to enter the union as a free state; created two new territories, New Mexico and Utah; settled the boundary dispute and paid Texas $10 million; abolished the slave trade but not slavery in Washington, DC; and amended the fugitive slave law.[16]

Afterward, a calmer Stephens maintained that the compromise was not cause for the South to resist. He thought it was the duty of Congress to settle the boundary issue; if Congress hadn't acted, and the president tried to hold eastern New Mexico by force against Texas, it would be the duty of the South to help Texas. He knew this could spark civil war. Toombs said Texas "claimed a vast territory, much of which no Texan ever explored . . . Her title was purely technical. She had never conquered it nor bought it nor possessed it." In Washington, celebrations broke out with cannon fire, rockets, music from the Marine Band, and general revelry. The entire nation breathed a large sigh of relief. In November, Texas accepted the payment, which approximated its public debt. New Mexico Territory was official, its borders embracing present-day New Mexico, most of present Arizona, and chunks of what would become Colorado and Nevada.[17]

Stephens and Toombs returned home in October to campaign for the compromise and met stout opposition from secessionists and the press, but in the November 25 election, Georgians upheld the compromise and the union. While the radicals could talk disunion until they were hoarse, most Georgians weren't willing to leave the union and accepted the compromise as long as the union protected their rights. On December 11, Stephens, Toombs, and Howell Cobb, a Democrat, organized a new party, the Constitutional Union Party. The struggle over the Compromise of 1850 destroyed Georgia's traditional Whig and Democrat parties. Because the moderates had prevailed over southern extremists, the union was safe, at least for a few more years.[18]

Weightman

Weightman arrived for the drama just as the curtain came down. He hurried to present New Mexico's constitution to President Fillmore, but it was too late. Fillmore sent it along to Congress, but with the ink still wet on New Mexico's territorial bill, Fillmore thought it inappropriate to make a recommendation. Had the bill failed in the House, Fillmore told Weightman, he would have recommended New Mexico's admission as a state. In the opinions of both

Weightman and Hugh Smith, who was still in Washington after the House refused to seat him two months earlier,[19] New Mexico would have become a state but for Taylor's untimely death.[20]

On September 10, Secretary of War Charles M. Conrad sent a reprimand to Munroe. He informed Munroe of the new law and the boundary and said the president didn't plan to suppress the government New Mexicans had been trying to establish because it was consistent with the law and was not an attempt to rebel against the United States. "You are directed to abstain from all further interference in the civil or political affairs of that country," Conrad wrote. On September 13, Congress passed the Organic Act that declared New Mexico a territory and vested authority in a governor and a bicameral legislature. A council with thirteen members was to be elected for two years, and a house of representatives of twenty-six members for one year. The governor was also superintendent of Indian affairs under a 1787 law, and that gave him an additional $1,000 in salary, or $2,500. A messenger carrying copies of Conrad's message and the new law departed September 10 and arrived in Santa Fe on October 23.[21]

Weightman wasn't giving up on statehood. When the congressional session ended that month, he wrote to Alvarez, "I think New Mexico will be admitted," underlining the statement twice. He intended to keep the issue alive in Washington and to call attention to "the deplorable condition of New Mexico" and its need for "prompt and efficient protection against the Indians." His strategy was to keep New Mexico "aloof" from disputes over slavery. "I am still of the opinion that if New Mexico will stick to it she can get a state government."[22]

When Weightman's charges against Munroe appeared in a Washington newspaper, members of the Houghton faction wrote Munroe that the government "must continue until the constitution then framed should receive the sanction of Congress" and New Mexico was made a state. Signers were Ceran St. Vrain, Thomas S. J. Johnson, Francisco Ortiz y Delgado, and Joab Houghton. Weightman wrote Alvarez that Munroe would soon have Conrad's order to stop interfering in civil affairs. "Everybody repudiates the military government, and the opinion is that Munroe the Anglo American in his correspondence with you Sir has suffered a defeat at the hands of the Anglo-Mexican (yourself). This is the general opinion in high quarters." He was sure Calhoun would be governor and Alvarez secretary. "The appointment of Col. Calhoun as Gov. will I think be disposed of on this ground that as Indian Agent he had given great satisfaction and appointing any one else as Gov. would amount virtually to turning him out of office as the Gov. of the Territory and also Indian Agent."[23]

Historians have assumed that Weightman secured the appointment for Calhoun,[24] but Weightman makes it clear that Calhoun's friends were responsible. "Calhoun is <u>confirmed</u> Governor," he wrote Alvarez, and although Hugh N. Smith had been nominated as secretary, "Calhoun's friends are with you and against Smith." A cluster of Houghtonites, including Smith, were then in Washington circulating rumors that Alvarez was a Locofoco, a Whig who leaned Democratic, although Alvarez had never expressed a political preference. The Senate rejected Smith because he had once advised people in the territory to exclude slavery on economic grounds.[25]

In the end, the president appointed William S. Allen,[26] register of the Land Office in St. Louis, as territorial secretary. A New Englander transplanted to Missouri, he was an attorney and newspaper editor and had been a legislator in both Massachusetts and Missouri. Allen had never been to New Mexico. Secretary of State Daniel Webster was already familiar with Alvarez from his time as consul and probably remembered the outspoken Spaniard without warmth. Webster was also an unabashed admirer of anyone with New England roots.[27] Allen would prove to be a terrible choice.

At this point, William Messervy and Weightman had a falling out. Messervy, a member of the Alvarez faction, was previously nominated as delegate, but the House refused to seat him. He was still in Washington working alongside Weightman for statehood, when he abruptly changed his colors, decided territorial government was better suited to the needs of New Mexicans, and backed Hugh Smith. After that, Messervy was a member of the Houghton faction.[28] This break has never been explained, but it's possible that Messervy still hoped to be seated, but it became clear that Weightman intended to be seated and was accepted by the House.

Good Union Man

Daniel Webster,[29] Calhoun's old boss from his days as consul in Havana, famously said on the Senate floor in 1848 that New Mexico and California "are not worth a dollar," but he believed so strongly in the Compromise of 1850 that he risked his career and reputation in a single speech, and his Massachusetts constituents forced him to resign. Fillmore gave Webster a cabinet appointment. And so it was Secretary of State Webster who informed Calhoun on January 9, 1851, that he was now governor of the new Territory of New Mexico. President Fillmore forwarded the nomination to Congress on December 23, 1850, and after the Committee on Territories reported favorably, the Senate confirmed the nomination on January 7, 1851.[30] Word didn't reach New Mexico until late February.[31]

The *New York Daily Tribune* opined: "Mr. James S. Calhoun is a good Union man, a good Whig of the Southern stripe, and we presume will fill the office credibly, but the Governor of that Territory should not have been taken from Georgia. He ought to have been chosen from a Free State." The *Louisville Courier*, citing Calhoun's service in the war, weighed in: "He is a gentleman of great urbanity of manners, a sound lawyer, and a good scholar, and will, no doubt, make an excellent Governor. But as he was identified on one side of the issue in the contest held in the Territory for a State Government, it would . . . have given more satisfaction among those who inhabit the Territory, had some one been selected from the States who was in no way identified with their local struggles."[32] The Kentucky paper was prescient; the Houghton faction now turned its attentions from Alvarez to Calhoun.

13

HIS EXCELLENCY

News of its territorial status and fixed boundary with Texas didn't reach New Mexico until late November 1850, and an excited citizenry released their pent-up feelings about the military government. Calhoun learned of his appointment late in February 1851. "The appointments met with very general approbation here," wrote Reverend William G. Kephart. "Gov. Calhoun possesses many agreeable qualities, and though a Southern man and partaking, no doubt, of the Southern feeling (not the disunion feeling) on the subject of slavery, yet I think his first and great aim here, in his Gubernatorial capacity, will be to try to bring order out of the chaos into which we have been plunged."[1]

Well into February, Calhoun still fretted that the military governor "must correct errors, or they pass without correction." He wrote Commissioner Luke Lea, "There is no power in this Territory but what passes to the people through him or emanates from him." On February 28, Calhoun wrote his last letter as Indian agent. If he was pleased with his new station, he doesn't show it. As the new governor of New Mexico and superintendent of Indian affairs, he wrote, he was still without either funding or instructions and earnestly hoping to receive both.[2]

Inauguration

Calhoun informed Munroe on March 2 that he intended to begin his official duties the following day. Munroe detailed an artillery company, an escort, and the Third Infantry band. At 11:30 a.m. on March 3, a procession, "quite imposing in numbers and appearance," formed in front of Calhoun's home, wrote Kephart. William McGrorty, as parade marshal, led, followed by the musicians and honor escort. Next was Calhoun with four men who did not wish him well: Munroe, Houghton, Hugh Smith, and Donaciano Vigil. Territorial and county officers

FIGURE 49. Drawing by an unknown artist in 1851 or 1852 depicts an aging Calhoun. #000–742–0027, William A. Keleher Pictorial Collection, Center for Southwest Research, University of New Mexico Libraries.

followed, along with clergy, lawyers, army officers, citizens, and the remainder of the honor escort.[3]

Santa Fe Gazette editor Neville Stuart described the event:

> The Military all had their buttons chalked. The Committee of arrangements wore faultless kids. The Marshals had the due allowance of sash and horseflesh. The stage—Governor and Ex-Vicario, Army Chaplain, Interpreter, etc. etc.—all wore a distinguished look. Rev. Reed offered an eloquent, fervent, appropriate prayer. Chief Justice Houghton and His Excellency formed a graceful tableau, as the commission was displayed and the oath was administered. The Address—pungent and comprehensive—was read according to the rules of elocution on such occasions. The cheering was enthusiastic; the firing uproarious; and the evolutions in the mud—as the procession moved across the Plaza— truly magnificent.[4]

At the Palace, on a platform erected under the portal, Judge Houghton administered the oath of office: "I, James S. Calhoun, do solemnly swear that I will support the Constitution and laws of the United States and faithfully discharge the duties of Governor of the Territory of New Mexico, so help me,

God!" Houghton read the president's commission and proclaimed Calhoun governor of the territory. Calhoun made a speech "in a firm and dignified manner," Kephart wrote, which was also read in Spanish. The excerpted address appeared in the local newspaper and the *Columbus Enquirer*.[5]

"An era in the history of New Mexico commences this day," he said. "The problem as to the capacity of the people for self-government is to be solved, preparatory to the assuming of a higher and more glorious position as one of the sovereign and independent states of the Union. The fate of New Mexico, under Providence, is in the hands of her own sons, and if wise and patriotic counsels prevail, a brilliant destiny awaits her." He thanked the statesmen who risked their political careers for the compromise that saved the union. Promising impartiality and moderation, he called on every citizen to take an active role. (For more of the speech, see appendix 4.)

The guard fired a fifteen-gun salute, and the group proceeded to the church for a singing of *Te Deum*. Ceremonies closed with explosions of gunpowder and champagne corks. As Americans and New Mexicans happily mixed and mingled, Stuart predicted "the advent of better times" for New Mexico.[6] "It is generally believed the new incumbent will prove a competent and efficient officer—such a one as the administration of the affairs of the Territory, at this juncture, requires."[7]

Kephart wrote, "This has been a great day for Santa Fe and New Mexico." He added that "no individual, perhaps, in the Territory, (and certainly no one out of it) could have been appointed with more general approbation. He is gentlemanly, affable, dignified in his bearing, and commands general, perhaps I might say universal, respect and esteem." The pastor had been Calhoun's guest in November when he first arrived in Santa Fe and testified to his "personal excellence." He believed Calhoun had given satisfaction as Indian agent, and if he hadn't, it was the government's fault.[8]

William Kephart was a passionate abolitionist and a Free Presbyterian—a pastor who broke with the Presbyterian General Assembly over the issue of slavery. The American and Foreign Antislavery Society and the American Missionary Association paid his travel costs and living expenses in New Mexico. His duties were to distribute tracts, promote education, encourage the establishment of a free press, preach the gospel, and argue against slavery. He became a regular contributor to the *National Era*, a Washington, DC, newspaper. In his first letter, he blasted Santa Fe's "gambling hells and fandango rooms" for the thousands of dollars "swallowed up in these maelstroms of dissipation and ruin." He told eastern readers that drunkenness was prevalent among both sexes, "and among the Mexican women prostitution is almost universal." The local Catholic priest, he said, had five mistresses.

Kephart's distorted diatribes would influence the opinions of readers in the nation's capital and elsewhere, and in coming months he grew increasingly critical of Calhoun. For a time, Kephart shared a house with Reverend Enoch Nicholson, a Methodist missionary whose arrival in October must have pleased Calhoun.[9] On November 17, 1850, Nicholson and Kephart offered the first Protestant sacrament in New Mexico. However, neither could speak Spanish, both hated Catholics, and they distributed anti-Catholic tracts they'd brought from the States.[10]

New Government

With Calhoun's inauguration, New Mexico and its people entered the next stage of their transition. From being citizens of a Mexican territory to wards of a military occupation, they were now citizens—with rights—of a US Territory. Historian Calvin Horn wrote, "The citizens of New Mexico were totally unprepared for American democracy when James S. Calhoun became the first territorial governor of New Mexico."[11] They were actually better prepared than distant bureaucrats could have expected. Many prominent Hispanic men were educated in the States, and the Territory now boasted a handful of lawyers and judges.

Calhoun well understood the task ahead: He must guide the creation of a just and stable government in this remote outpost and see that New Mexicans were intimately involved in the process if the nation expected their allegiance. His experience as a judge and legislator prepared him well for the job, and he was well acquainted with the people. In his first month, he ordered a census and made dozens of appointments. (For a list of appointments, see appendix 6.)

The new executive was engulfed in a tide of citizen requests and petitions. (His successor would complain that his life was "one eternal round of appeals," with up to fifty visitors a day, each greeting him with an embrace.) Santa Fe residents wanted the military slaughterhouse moved. The military obliged. Various complainants wanted judges' or prefects' decisions overturned. Calhoun declined. Louis Dorrence in San Miguel County was holding a child because the parents owed him money. Calhoun quickly dispatched a message to the prefect saying no one had a right to possess children except their parents, relatives, and guardians. He granted licenses to trade with the Comanches and Utes. He tried to find out if the territory's accounts had ever been audited. Nobody knew. He asked treasurer Charles Blumner for an accounting of funds received and paid, approved by the auditor.[12] People from Isleta Pueblo complained the priest demanded too much money. Calhoun told them to pay what they thought was fair. And because appointees from the old regime were apparently still exercising authority, Calhoun instructed the prefects that only his own appointed public officers were legitimate; proceedings of all others were null and void.[13]

On March 18, Calhoun summoned every able-bodied man to form a volunteer corps made necessary by the "present condition of the Territory of New Mexico, surrounded as it is by hostile tribes of Indians, whose almost daily incursions and depredations are the source of the greatest evils which afflict the country." He named Ceran St. Vrain and Facundo Pino as his aides de camp and would authorize officers to pursue and attack any hostiles who entered the settlements to plunder and depredate, he said in his proclamation. Any property captured from hostile Indians "shall be disposed of in accordance with the laws and customs heretofore existing in this Territory" pending legislative action, but he warned volunteers against using their positions as a pretext for depredation on peaceable citizens. He sanctioned Pueblos to attack Navajos who approached their towns and ordered prefects and alcaldes to call out all available force "according to their old customs" in case of Indian attack. Volunteers would take orders from Calhoun as commander in chief, not Munroe.[14] Calhoun was attempt-

FIGURE 50. Manuel A. Chaves, soldier and rancher, was one of the most prominent New Mexicans of his time. Photographer, H. T. Fine. Courtesy of the Palace of the Governors Photo Archives (NMHM/DCA), Negative 009833.

ing to create the military command he wanted, but he slighted Munroe. From then on, the colonel lobbed any obstacle he could into Calhoun's path. Calhoun justified his actions to Lea, saying that Indian murders and depredations were almost a daily occurrence south and west of Santa Fe. Navajos and Jicarillas were everywhere driving off herds and killing stockmen, and troops failed to catch the attackers.[15]

The first man to step forward was the legendary Manuel Antonio Chaves, who responded the same day with a proposal to raise six companies of volunteers with a hundred men in each company, provided the government furnished one hundred mules, provisions, and six hundred rifles and ammunition. The thirty-two-year-old Chaves had been fighting Navajos for half his life, beginning in Cebolleta, a remote place even by New Mexico standards. He had lost a brother in a Navajo attack not long before. Chaves offered to hunt down Navajos "to their extermination or complete surrender."[16]

That year, Chaves began participating actively in military campaigns against Utes, Jicarillas, Navajos, and Apaches. Initially, he volunteered, but as his reputation grew, American army commanders and his fellow New Mexicans sought him out. "Manuel's deft coolness under fire, his familiarity with Indian ways and especially with their tactics of war, and his knowledge of terrain and trails preeminently qualified him as one of the finest New Mexico campaigners of this period," wrote historian Marc Simmons.[17] The new governor's proclamation appealed to New Mexicans like Chaves because it reestablished the old custom of volunteers making forays against Indians and keeping the spoils, namely slaves and livestock.

Calhoun had executive authority, political clout, a militia (on paper), and veto power over the legislature, but he had no funding.[18] Three weeks into the job, he told Commissioner Lea, "The people of this Territory are without the means of self protection, the Territorial Treasury is a blank," and protection depended on the government. He sent merchant Henry Connelly,[19] "one of the worthiest citizens of this Territory," to President Fillmore with a letter stating: "Until the Apaches and Navajos are completely subdued we can neither have quiet or prosperity in this Territory. You are aware that our Treasury is empty, and that we are without munitions of war. If we had the use of one thousand stand of arms at this time, we could effectually check depredations that are being daily committed in our very midst." Fillmore sent Connelly to speak to Secretary of War Conrad. Calhoun repeated the message to Interior Secretary

Alexander H. H. Stuart. "If I had the means at this moment I could, in a few months, secure a lasting peace with the Indians in this Territory."[20] Throughout his term as governor he would plead with Washington for financial relief, only to be told that Congress hadn't acted. Out of desperation, he wrote drafts on the government or absorbed costs personally and hoped for reimbursement, only to face excuses and obstacles from federal auditors.

Calhoun's challenges weren't unusual for the governors of new territories. Most made heroic efforts to shoulder their responsibilities, however impossible. The physical demands alone—the travel over vast distances, the danger, the ongoing crises—were daunting. Fiscal emergencies placed heavy demands on what few resources the new governors had. Like Calhoun, new governors wrote page after page to the Indian Office and the secretary of state (as superintendents they reported to the former and as governors they reported to the latter), but bureaucrats responded slowly or not at all. The objectives of the two offices were in conflict. "As governor he was responsible for advancing the interests of the white population; as Indian superintendent he was the guardian of the Indian's rights and welfare," wrote historian William Neil. In the West, most citizens saw the tribes as obstacles to progress.[21]

In March, the Senate confirmed more of President Fillmore's appointees: Calhoun's son-in-law, William E. Love, became postmaster of Santa Fe; William Allen, secretary of state; Elias West, US attorney, and John G. Jones, US marshal.[22]

In mid-April the census was complete.[23] There were 56,984 citizens in the new territory. The two most populous counties were Taos, at 11,038 people, and Rio Arriba, with 10,038. (Two months earlier, the US marshal counted 61,574, including soldiers, teamsters, and 7,867 Pueblo Indians in New Mexico. Calhoun estimated no more than 300 Americans in the Territory unconnected with the army.) The next step was to apportion thirteen senators, called councilors, and twenty-six representatives among the eight loosely organized districts. Calhoun delegated the task to his secretary, twenty-four-year-old David V. Whiting.[24] Born and educated in Venezuela, Whiting had worked for mercantile firms in the East before being sent to New Mexico to settle the estate of a company member. On April 25, Calhoun ordered an election for legislators to take place on May 19, 1851, and set the legislative session to begin the first Monday of June.[25]

Historian Howard Lamar has written that Calhoun "adopted the policy of turning local government over to the more conservative and anti-American New Mexicans in an effort to appease this group" and that "Calhoun soon had a political machine of sorts in operation."[26] That was certainly the view of the Houghton crowd, who owed their positions to the military, but it doesn't hold up under examination. Between March 3, 1851, and April 22, 1852, Calhoun made some seventy-eight (recorded) appointments, although his executive journal isn't always clear. For appointed positions, such as alcaldes, sheriffs, prefects, and justices of the peace, he named thirteen members of his own faction and one member of the Houghton faction, Albuquerque merchant Ambrosio Armijo. The lion's share, sixty-four, belonged to neither group. (See appendix 6.)

Calhoun was neither appeasing anyone nor building a machine. His choices were pragmatic. He favored people who were already local leaders. Calhoun had been part of Georgia's power structure and turned to the same kinds of people in New Mexico. For example, Pablo Melendres, a founder of the Doña Ana land grant in southern New Mexico, had already served as alcalde of the village of Doña Ana under the Mexican government.[27] It made sense to reappoint him alcalde of the village. Other appointees included Armijos, Chaveses, Oteros, and others of New Mexico's aristocracy. He appointed recognized leaders with militia commissions as well. His choices for brigadier generals and aides de camp were all well-known New Mexicans.[28]

Calhoun did reward his inner circle, naming Georgian John G. Jones as Santa Fe County sheriff,[29] and he undoubtedly had a hand in the president's appointment of Love as postmaster and Jones as first territorial marshal.[30] And even though Calhoun commenced his duties in 1849 complaining about the influence of the Catholic Church, he appointed several priests to civil positions. Clearly his friendship with Padre Martínez and the influence of Weightman, who was close to a number of priests, changed his mind. Donaciano Vigil, territorial secretary under the military governors, complained that "the miserable Colonel Calhoun" has "united with the vile clergy of the Territory" and was "able to quiet the people" through corrupt alcaldes and prefects.[31] Vigil and Padre Martínez had been at odds since the days of Mexican rule, when Padre Martínez urged the government to educate the tribes and make them self-sufficient; Vigil, the soldier, preferred to fight them.[32] Most important, Hispanic appointees outnumbered Anglo Americans by nearly three to one. While this might be expected, given that New Mexicans vastly outnumbered Americans in the territory, many newcomers considered the territory their goose to pluck. The political consequences of his choices would be staggering.[33]

On April 4, 1851, Kephart wrote in the *Santa Fe Weekly Gazette* that Calhoun's administration was hardly a month old, and "it is universally conceded that he has proved himself a most active and efficient officer." Kephart, who helped found the Gazette the year before, now served as its editor. The owners were Houghton cronies Hugh N. Smith and James L. Collins. After the *Gazette* nearly failed twice, Kephart took over, agreeing to make up a share of losses.[34] With that, Kephart joined Houghton's circle. Before April ended, Kephart wrote: "The Governor, with all his official patronage and influence, had formed an alliance with the Vicario, whose influence with the Catholic population is almost unbounded. To this add the influence of the minor priesthood, with that of several Mexican Ricos" (rich men). He declared that the governor, his appointees, and territorial officers, were "slaveholding, and in the slaveholding interest."[35] This heralded a change in rhetoric. The factions no longer argued over statehood; the Houghtonites, under Kephart's influence, now espoused abolition.

Collins, on the strength of his aggressive personality and control of the territory's only press, appears to have supplanted Joab Houghton as leader of the opposition faction. Born in Kentucky in 1800, Collins immigrated to Missouri in 1819, made his first trip to Santa Fe in 1826, and two years later established a trading business in Chihuahua. The Mexican War in 1846 forced him to abandon his business, and he resettled in Santa Fe. Kephart wrote that Collins "gambles, drinks his toddy, and sometimes keeps a woman," but was "socially much of a gentleman, honorable as a man of the world, and a man of good judgment and much influence in society."[36]

Making Laws

New Mexicans chose their legislators on May 19, 1851, in an election riddled with irregularities. Soldiers voted three or four times. Teamsters and other nonresidents, along with boys under age fourteen, were allowed to vote. Each side charged the other with fraud and corruption, and the *Gazette* thought they were both correct. That probably explains why Manuel Alvarez didn't win enough votes to join the Senate. The men chosen could be considered the fathers of New Mexico Territory, and most of them were Hispanic. (For a list

FIGURE 51. The Palace of the Governors was photographed by Nicholas Brown in 1868, seventeen years after Calhoun was a resident. Courtesy of the Palace of the Governors Photo Archives (NMHM/DCA), Negative 045819.

of legislators, see appendix 5.) Padre Martínez was elected president of the council (senate), and Taos lawyer Theodore D. Wheaton became speaker of the house. Both were Calhoun's friends. Calhoun asked Padre Martínez "as a learned and intelligent citizen of broad experience in regard to what is needed in this country" to work toward that end with George Gold of Taos and offered the priest his own house as headquarters during his stay in the capital.[37]

The high level of political participation by New Mexicans was unusual for a conquered people, according to historian Phillip Gonzáles. The American political process not only allowed New Mexicans to participate but was a way of rewarding them even as they submitted to the power of the United States. The leaders tended to be well-educated rich men whose families maintained their positions by riding the new wave of political power.[38]

Legislators assembled in two chambers on the east end of the ancient, rambling Palace. The council room, just large enough to accommodate its thirteen members and eight officers, had a wood floor. Members sat and smoked at pine desks arranged around the wall, facing inward. The House of Representatives occupied a larger room with a small gallery where visitors could sit. Each chamber had just two doors with hide panels tanned and painted to resemble wood.

Across the hall, Calhoun, the Palace's latest occupant in a line of governors stretching back three centuries, labored in an executive chamber with a few chairs, an old sofa and bureau, a pine table, and a crude rug. Bleached muslin covered the ceiling. His living quarters were adjacent. Because Munroe refused to release the large room used by the assistant adjutant general, Calhoun had to give up his living space and rent rooms for two months, which the territorial secretary would require Calhoun to pay from his contingency expenses.[39]

Calhoun's first address to legislators was a model of enlightened thinking, with two notable exceptions. The lengthy speech drew on his experience as judge, businessman, farmer, and legislator. Covering all the pressing issues of the Territory, it was an inventory of everything he considered important and had probably been the subjects of many conversations with Manuel Alvarez, whose earlier speeches sounded similar themes. He began by recalling the previous abuses of power. "It is at all times a delicate task to originate a government suited to the wants of the governed," he said, "but it is infinitely more difficult" when a new government must supersede one previously existing. "There is no effort more difficult than to unlearn early inculcations, strengthened by years of endurance of wrongs perpetrated upon our natural rights." He reminded new legislators of "the high responsibility of framing such laws as will secure the just ends of a representative government" after "military sway and dictation." Calhoun asked them to define the qualifications for voting and holding office so that "strangers temporarily residing in your midst" couldn't interfere in elections and suggested requiring voters to register before elections to prevent fraud. "It is our solemn duty, so to guard the rights of our citizens, that is, the people of the Territory, that their own votes shall reflect their own purposes."[40]

He proposed organizing three judicial districts and assigning the judges. He discussed judicial responsibilities. "Humanity shudders at the thought of capital punishments, but I am not prepared to recommend entire abolition at this time. The day is near at hand, I trust, when you will be prepared to substitute an effective remedy for such punishments." He recommended that legislators consider commuting punishments. Regarding taxation, it "should be borne alike, having a just regard to the means of each individual . . . Not one cent beyond the just wants of the government should be collected, and the most rigid economy should be practiced." On the subject of education, he thought it was as important to educate the daughters of New Mexico as her sons. Without wise and virtuous women, there could be no refinement in society, but provisions made by Congress "are utterly inadequate." He recommended asking Congress for an appropriation for schools. As for the poor, he said, "Let us, at the very commencement of our career in self-government, take special care of the weak and the innocent, and secure to them the means of an honest and virtuous independence."[41]

Relations between masters and peons should be defined, and each should understand their respective obligations and appropriate remedies for violations. Agricultural laws were needed to provide a just system of irrigation, proper disposal of animals, a record of marks and brands, and the sale of animals. Use of improper weights and measures should be penalized. Titles to some land in the territory were not affirmed. Even titles to the Palace and the adjacent grounds and other property in Santa Fe were in question. Church property seized by the military should be restored. The Territory needed to be explored and surveyed to realize its potential. Prohibition of gambling "would contribute immensely to the peace and happiness of society." People who retained their Mexican citizenship often did so because they were misled and "should be incorporated and regarded as a part and portion of the political community of New Mexico."[42]

The Palace, he said, "must be thoroughly repaired and remodeled. There is not a room in it that does not require repairs." The archives were exposed and in danger of destruction. (In 1853, on the night Governor David Meriwether took office, the roof caved in on the structure's west side.) Civil government should possess the Palace and adjacent grounds. The executive office, the secretary's office, and the residence of the civil governor had been in the Palace, and yet most of the grounds and part of the Palace were now in the possession of the military, which refused to give up rooms. "I have therefore been compelled, at a heavy expenditure, to remove to other quarters, in order to make room for the sitting of the Legislature."[43]

Then he ventured into two subjects so fraught that they eclipsed everything else he said.

There is not a more difficult problem arising in this Territory than that of a proper disposition of our Pueblo friends. What should we do with them? They are here in our midst, surrounded by our New Mexican population, and rightfully, in my opinion, without authority to mingle in our political affairs. These people, however, must necessarily have the same protection that is afforded to the most favored. It is a well known fact, that they own portions of the richest valley lands in this Territory, and why should they be exempt from paying a just proportion of the taxes which must be raised to support the territorial government.[44]

And if they are tax-paying citizens, he asked, are lawmakers ready to make them full citizens? He wouldn't recommend it, but it was inevitable that they should be dependents, equals, or removed to a better location. If they were willing to abandon their separate existence, the laws of the territory should be extended over them.[45]

The other troubling remark was this: "Free negroes are regarded as nuisances in every State and Territory in the Union, and where they are tolerated, society is most degraded." He asked the legislature to pass a law preventing the entrance of free Negroes into the territory. At that time, many Georgia towns imposed a tax on free people of color, designed to discourage the growth of this population. Milledgeville, where Calhoun once lived, had an ordinance forbidding free persons of color from living in town unless they lived with a white guardian and had a certificate of character and a bond for good behavior. Milledgeville wasn't Santa Fe, as he should have realized.[46]

The *Gazette* responded that Calhoun had "done an injustice to those sections of the Union where free negroes were tolerated." Most New Mexicans didn't understand slavery and cared nothing about it, the newspaper wrote. New Mexico had seventeen free black men and five free black women, according to the census, and fourteen lived in Santa Fe, including Jim Beckwourth, who ran the town's best saloon. With this remark, Calhoun brought down on himself the fury of the territory's abolitionists, particularly Kephart.[47]

His discussion of Pueblo people was surprisingly careless. From the beginning, Calhoun had advocated for their protection, but the former judge was also disturbed by their ambivalent legal status. He probably knew that while

Spain acknowledged pueblo land ownership, Mexico muddied the issue and looked the other way when New Mexicans appropriated pueblo land.[48] When the Americans took control, the two groups were still fighting over land, and Calhoun even hired Weightman to represent Pueblos in court. Calhoun told the commissioner the Pueblos shouldn't be relocated, but Indian policy then addressed only nomads at war with the government, not the highly organized Pueblos. In the blunt wording of the speech, he may have been thinking out loud or playing devil's advocate, airing what he heard from New Mexicans and Americans in order to provoke a discussion.

Calhoun's enemies were quick to capitalize on his remarks. A letter writer objected in the *Gazette* that neither the governor nor the legislature had any authority to take action on the Pueblos. They were citizens under terms of a treaty, and even the federal government couldn't "uncitizenize and disenfranchise the Pueblo Indians without the grossest breach of faith." The writer added that in "honesty, industry, and virtue, it is universally admitted that they are, to say the least, quite equal to the great mass of the other citizens."[49]

During the session, Navajos raided Isleta Pueblo, prompting a legislative memorial to President Fillmore signed by some of the territory's most important citizens. They charged that the attack occurred "while the officers and soldiers of the regular army were quietly reposing in quarters at Albuquerque and Socorro . . . [T]he masterly inactivity of the Government troops does not afford that protection from foray and rapine which the present unhappy and distracted state of this Territory imperatively demands." Legislators petitioned the president to arm a militia and volunteer force under the governor's direction because of the "utter inefficacy of the regular troops." They said they respected the officers and soldiers, but the territory would be better protected by "men who will fight for their altars and their firesides."[50]

They wrote Calhoun that they wanted to see an end "of the uninterrupted calamities which afflict the Territory." From 1830 to 1834 the country was prosperous. Millions of sheep and cattle and thousands of horses roamed the plains and sustained commerce with Mexico and the United States. Presently, "New Mexico does not possess one tenth of the property she owned in previous years, it has been swept away as by an impetuous torrent, our prosperity has been converted into misfortune, and the present miserable condition of New Mexico" has paralyzed every branch of industry, they wrote. They asked Calhoun to garrison frontier posts at the important entry and exit points for hostile Indians. They also asked him to consider volunteer companies and distribution of captives and other spoils among them.[51]

When the first territorial legislature adjourned after forty days on July 11, it had accomplished a great deal. Among other things, it declared and established the people's rights, provided for punishment of crime, regulated trade and intercourse with the tribes, attempted to raise revenues through taxes on licenses, established the territorial treasury, standardized master-servant contracts, and regulated water and *acequias* (ditches). It also declared mining laws in force, defined judicial districts and assigned judges, organized the militia of New Mexico, and regulated elections and the sale of animals. Legislators asked Congress to preserve certain tracts of wood and timber and not sell salt lakes, springs, and mines and recommended a geological survey.[52]

Insurrection

While the legislature was still in session on June 11, Charles Beaubien, one of the displaced judges, wrote Calhoun that he was convinced the lower classes in Taos County were again plotting a rebellion. Claiming to understand New Mexicans, he said, "Every effort has been made to excite the mass." Secret meetings were being held under various pretenses to organize an insurrection to exterminate the Americans and take their property. Beaubien believed any revolt would result in the massacre of Americans and foreigners in the area, followed by extermination of the insurgents. He said several hundred Jicarillas, emboldened by whiskey from the New Mexicans, assaulted Americans they found alone and defenseless and threatened St. Vrain at his mill. And the Utes, when visiting the settlements, were insolent and reportedly had killed a citizen. Because the infantry there was inadequate, Beaubien asked for reinforcements.[53]

Munroe sent Major H. L. Kendrick and a company of dragoons with two twelve-pound howitzers to Taos, but when they reached the town, Kendrick saw no sign of trouble and returned to Santa Fe. Major William H. Gordon, commanding the Taos post, said the excitement was purely political. Calhoun asked the prefect of Taos County to identify the instigators and, to be on the safe side, invited Taos Pueblo leaders to visit.[54]

He poured out letters to Secretary of State Daniel Webster, Indian Commissioner Luke Lea, and Interior Secretary Alexander Stuart. Such fabricated alarms demonstrated the obstacles he faced as governor, he said. Since April

FIGURE 52. This image of Don Fernando de Taos appeared in *El Gringo: New Mexico and Her People*, by W. W. H. Davis, 1857.

and May, "every element of discord has been called into requisition to disaffect the Pueblo Indians and others . . . [I]nsurrection and treason have been rife." Calhoun all but demanded instructions. "I say to you, it is important," he told Stuart. "There are dark secrets to be revealed, and there are persons of repute that may be implicated. That is my opinion. I hope I am wrong. But the truth must come out." He could remedy most of the territory's problems if he had authority, weapons and supplies, he said again.[55]

In June the representatives of twelve pueblos "visited me in a highly excited state of mind," Calhoun wrote. The Houghton faction exaggerated Calhoun's speech to the legislature to tell them "they were to be driven from their pueblos and their lands and property taken from them." Calhoun tried to calm them during a three-day council. "Not one of the Pueblos, at this time, desire to abandon their old customs and usages, and you may rely upon it, these people must be treated with the utmost delicacy, or bloody scenes will be witnessed in this Territory," he told Lea. "Treason is abroad and power is wanted in this Territory to catch the infamous who are administering to the disorders of the Territory."[56]

A tract titled "To the People of New Mexico," signed by Calhoun's political enemies, claimed that his goal was "to build up a political party that would secure the election of a certain individual as your delegate to Congress, and that the whole power and influence of his office has been prostituted from what was its proper end and aim, to the securing of this object." They complained that the best and most trustworthy officers had been removed to make way for political partisans, that Calhoun asked for the resignation of two circuit judges because they were political opponents of Calhoun's candidate for Congress (Weightman), and that he altered the Organic Law that created territorial government. Calhoun's comments about free negroes, they claimed, would "disenfranchise them of their rights" and "excite an angry discussion in the States of the Union that is calculated to raise a strong and influential party in the Congress against us."[57]

The authors recommended an equal and just system of taxation, a separation of the legislative, judicial, and administrative branches of government, modification of the governor's veto power, and election of county and district officers. They invited citizens to "go with us in opposition to the mal-administration and abuse of power by your present Executive." The signers were all Houghton partisans except for the surprising participation of Diego Archuleta, who had earlier congratulated Calhoun on his appointment. Another signer was Alexander W. Reynolds, an army captain and assistant quarter master then campaigning for Congress against Weightman.[58] Calhoun told Webster, "The minority damn everybody but themselves, and a few of them . . . are ripe for anything, and their motto, I apprehend, is 'rule or ruin.'"

In response, twenty-nine out of thirty-nine legislators wrote a tract on June 15, 1851. The law should protect all social classes, they said. They would value impartiality, experience, and knowledge based on the needs of the territory. Some men, who slandered the political body, would rather prey on ignorance to misinform citizens than guide them toward the path of progress. They pointed out that it was the Organic Law that denied Indians the right to vote, not the governor or the legislature. They objected to the invasion of Pueblo lands and said the accusations against them were made by the "enemies of truth."[59]

In just three months, Calhoun made an admirable start on creating a new order in the territory—making dozens of appointments, advising the new legislature, and with his inaugural speech and actions generally trying to quiet the fears of New Mexicans while encouraging them to engage in the democratic process, as he juggled his responsibilities as Indian agent. He still had to contend with the warring faction, which was now focused on displacing him as governor. It was exhausting and stressful. Six months into his governorship,

Calhoun asked Lea for some time off. "I have not been without pressing duties before me since I have been in this Territory. Night after night have I been compelled to be at my desk, or on watch—the entire night." He wanted to visit Washington and "my native state Georgia" in the fall and proposed to bring Indian people to Washington. He assured the commissioner that he didn't want to leave New Mexico and wouldn't go unless affairs in the territory were quiet.[60]

14

STEAL OR STARVE

As 1851 opened, Munroe reported peace on the frontier. The new posts "are already exercising a favorable influence in our Indian relations," he wrote. The Utes and Jicarillas were quiet. Navajos had shown no hostility since he and Calhoun met with them at their request on December 25. The Gila Apaches had committed no depredations since Fort Webster was established at the Santa Rita copper mines in southwestern New Mexico. "It is unquestionably true, that the most certain way to subdue Indians is to establish posts in the heart of their country," he wrote. "These posts confine them at home, they will never venture to make distant hostile expeditions, and leave their families and property within striking distance of vigilant garrisons."[1]

Calhoun and Munroe could have inhabited two different territories. Calhoun told his superiors that "the Indians have been active in every direction" and with greater success than in any month since the American occupancy. During 1850, Santa Ana and Bernalillo Counties alone lost more than 56,000 sheep, and travelers couldn't venture south of Albuquerque unless they rode in large, well-armed parties. "Such scenes will continue to occur, until the powers of Washington shall accord to the people of this Territory ample protection."[2]

In January the Gila Apaches were especially destructive. After they stole more than a hundred head of cattle from Isleta Pueblo, Prefect Francisco Sarracino ordered out forty New Mexicans who chased, overtook, and attacked them and recovered the stock. "The depredations they have committed on the lives and property of the inhabitants of this district are so numerous, and of so frequent occurrence, that it would take considerable time to collect the information of past injuries," Sarracino wrote. At the same time, Alcalde Juan Antonio Baca y Pino learned of Apache depredations and got help from the army post at Socorro. The march was fruitless because the soldiers insisted on a route with abundant water and demanded that Pino furnish them with everything necessary for their transportation. On April 7, Apaches attacked eight men at Dead Man's Spring in the Jornada del Muerto, an arid, ninety-mile stretch between Socorro and Doña Ana. One man died and two were wounded.[3]

Promises, Promises

Calhoun was still determined to find the White child. For that mission he chose the twenty-six-year-old Jewish trader Benjamin J. Latz, who came to New Mexico as a sergeant in the Missouri Volunteers.[4] After mustering out in 1847, instead of staying in St. Louis where his older brother was a successful merchant and attorney, young Benjamin returned to New Mexico. He made his home in La Cuesta, a village founded in the lush Pecos River Valley in 1808 as a buffer against Plains Indians that evolved into a trade center. By 1850, Latz had married Maria Baronia, a New Mexican, and was the only trader and only Anglo living in La Cuesta.[5]

Just eight days after his inauguration, on March 11, 1851, Calhoun licensed Latz to trade with the tribes between Santa Fe and Sierra Blanca in south-eastern New Mexico and recover the girl and any other American captives. If the tribes wanted to deliver captives and make treaties in Santa Fe, they could, Calhoun declared. It was a dangerous assignment, and few would have accepted it, but Latz had become friendly with the Eastern Apaches. Calhoun's olive branch paid off. On March 29 Latz and D. Salazar (probably Damasio Salazar, a stockman in San Miguel County) brought in six Jicarilla and Mes-calero Apaches. Among them were Josecito, a subchief of the Mescaleros, and Lobo, a subchief of the Jicarillas. Latz then rode back out to find the Jicarillas' Chief Chacon.[6]

In the Palace of the Governors, citizens and army officers packed into a large room to listen to "these wild birds of the forests," as Kephart described them. Their faces, painted with vermilion and streaked with black, were framed by black shoulder-length hair. "We are Apaches of the Jicarilla and Mescalero nations; our [Chief] Chacon is a ruler as our Father [Calhoun] is," they said. "All our people are south of the Rio Pecos. We are come to see our father to know if he is pleased with us." Calhoun told them that their father was glad to see them and not to fear but speak freely, that he would send them safe to their lodges. "We come to talk with our Father. We have no fear," they said. For hours, they answered questions.

FIGURE 53. Artist Antonio Zeno Shindler captured this likeness of an Apache warrior. Courtesy of the Miriam and Ira D. Wallach Division of Art, Prints and Photographs: Picture Collection, The New York Public Library.

Who attacked the Americans at Point of Rocks and Wagon Mound? Who took Henry Connelly's mules? "We don't know who killed our father's children or ran off the mules. The Jicarillas were at that time in the White Mountains (Sierra Blanca)." Do they have captives? Salazar said they had no American captives. "We don't lie to our father. We tell our story." Why did they come? "We want peace." Why didn't Chacon come? He was at Manzano, a village in the central mountains of the same name. "He went two moons ago. Three suns have gone down since we heard from Chacon. Had Chacon been at his lodge, he would have come with us to see the chiefs. He told us two moons ago to come in and make peace." They said the camp of Barranquito, the great chief of the Mescaleros, was on the Seven Rivers in southeastern New Mexico. How many warriors do they have? The Jicarillas had many lodges: Guero had thirty; Chacon, seventy; Barranquito, seventy. Do the chiefs here have the power to treat with the tribes? "We have power to speak for the Apaches, not for the other nations." Would the Apaches build lodges, sow seeds, and live within fixed boundaries? "If the rest of the tribes will make pueblos (villages), they will look handsome; we will go and talk with our old men and chiefs. The chiefs have power." Will they make a treaty now? Will they sign a paper? The question was met with twenty minutes of silence, followed by a long discussion among the chiefs. Finally, they said, "We will speak with our nations. We wanted to make a place at Las Vegas, but the people made war. We now come to our father. We come to know what he wants. If he says we must be killed, we die; if he tells us to kill for him, we will do it. We will sign the paper for the Apaches."[7]

At the same time, responding to reports of depredations, Munroe ordered Lt. Jonas P. Holliday, Second Dragoons, with forty-four men to search for Indians raiding near the Manzano Mountains, southeast of Albuquerque, and they learned that three days earlier Navajos stole six mules and a lot of sheep from Chilili. New Mexicans attacked them and took back the sheep, but one of their men was killed. A day later Apaches also stole a herd of sheep and drove them to their camp. Holliday found Chacon's camp of two hundred Apaches, sixty of them warriors, near the Smoky Mountains sixty miles east of Manzano. Chief Chacon asked Holliday why he had come. He said his people were peaceful, and he was on his way to see the governor. They brought in several hundred sheep they found wandering without a shepherd as evidence of their friendly intentions. Holliday escorted them to Santa Fe.[8]

On April 2, 1851, Calhoun and Munroe signed a treaty with Chacon, Lobo, Guero, and Josecito. It was the usual lopsided treaty favoring the United States. The Apaches declared their submission to the government and agreed to occupy lands assigned for their use, build towns, and cultivate the soil. They would refrain from killing and raiding, stay fifty miles from settlements or established highways, and deliver murderers, robbers, fugitives, and captives. The government agreed to establish military posts and trading posts and allow licensed traders to go to the Bosque Redondo and other places to trade with the Apaches.[9] Calhoun well knew he lacked the authority to specify such provisions. He complained again to Indian Commissioner Luke Lea that he had no instructions and was "groping my way in the dark."[10]

To the interior secretary he wrote: "This is an important move, and I commend it to the grave consideration of the President. The treaty *may* be observed—and, if I had the means to support a small Volunteer force, I could and would secure a reasonable compliance with the Treaty." Lacking instructions, Calhoun and Munroe believed that even a "temporary arrangement" would save lives.[11]

In mid-April, some Jicarillas camped uncomfortably close to Las Vegas and San Miguel. Calhoun sent Latz with Lieutenant Orren Chapman to investigate. They found a camp in violation of the treaty overlooking the Pecos Valley and several streams, and asked Chacón his intentions. "I and my family are starving to death," he said. "We have made peace. We do not want to do harm, as you see from our bringing women and children with us. We want to go to the clay bank at San José and make vessels to sell so as to procure an honest living. We can't steal and must do something to earn a living." Calhoun believed if they had an agent who could provide corn and other necessities, they would live peacefully. He would do it if he had the means, he said, but he didn't, and so he made them Munroe's responsibility. "It is perfectly evident that they must steal or starve unless some plan is devised to subsist them & without this subsistence it would be folly to suppose they could be subjected to proper restraint," he told Munroe. "If these Indians remain in their present localities we must anticipate bloodshed & depredations and their impoverished condition must become infinitely worse as they will sell every blanket and animal they possess and may be able to steal in order to procure ardent spirits." Chacon agreed to move two days from Anton Chico, a farming village at the edge of the buffalo plains, and Calhoun sent Latz to say they should be there by May 15 to receive corn and then move to an assigned location two days south. On the appointed day, Calhoun and Munroe found no Apaches at Anton Chico because they were frightened away by the sight of troops. Munroe reported that even though the Jicarillas had violated their treaty promise to stay away from the settlements, they had committed no depredations, and because they were hungry, Munroe thought it best to let them roam.[12]

Meanwhile, Comanches were gathering at the Bosque Redondo on the Pecos River, for a grand council with Jicarilla and Mescalero Apaches. Calhoun licensed Latz to trade with the Comanches and encourage them to meet with him in Santa Fe. On May 28, Latz brought in Chief Eagle Feathers, along with five men and five women, who visited Calhoun in the Palace. The chief said his people were friends with all the people north of Chihuahua and with the Apaches. The Utes hadn't been to see them for many months. They were at war with the Navajos. They brought in a captive Mexican boy from Durango, and Calhoun bought the boy to return him to his parents. Both sides declared friendship. Calhoun guaranteed their safety and had them quartered comfortably near the Palace, but on the second night, the Comanches ran away, leaving behind their mules, blankets, and other belongings. Apparently, someone told them that Calhoun intended to have them murdered. Munroe sent three officers to persuade them to return. Calhoun had the property inventoried and hired four men to deliver it to the Comanches. Everyone was satisfied, Calhoun said.[13]

When reports reached Santa Fe in July that Comanches killed livestock at Anton Chico and La Cuesta and some three hundred warriors were on their way to Navajo Country to make war, it was more rumor mongering. Troops found Anton Chico quiet, and the Comanche chiefs said again they were at peace but that a Comanche chief had killed cattle in anger at losing his captive. Calhoun recovered five captive boys from Mexico taken by the Comanches and would send them south to be returned to their families. He also liberated two New Mexico captives and restored them to their parents.[14]

Unsatisfactory Condition

Calhoun and Munroe were still squabbling. On April 8, the colonel abruptly cut off Calhoun's access to supplies from the quartermaster and commissary. Calhoun shot back that if the supplies "were proper for an Indian agent, they are not less so to a Superintendent of Indian Affairs, who is charged with all the duties of an Indian Agent." Withdrawing supplies "destroys my influence with the Indians by confining me to a locality where I can be but of little service." Munroe responded that he gave the authority because he knew no appropriations had been made for the agent, but things had changed. Congress made appropriations for Indian affairs, and in his opinion the Territory of New Mexico could supply stores and forage. But Congress had taken no action, and nothing had changed, Calhoun argued. Neither knew that Munroe, the butt of Weightman's letters to the War Department and Washington newspapers, was on his way out. The War Department had relieved him of command and sent a successor.[15]

Without access to military stores, he told the commissioner, he would have to rely on products available in the Territory because he didn't have time to send to the States for necessities. "The Indians (Pueblos) are moody when they come to the Agency, if you do not give them Sugar, Coffee and Whiskey." This was a stunning admission for a Methodist teetotaler. He gave them whiskey "with the greatest reluctance," he said, because if he didn't "they would roam through Santa Fe until they could find a small grocery that would indulge them. Thefts and bloody contests ensued, and I found it would be a matter of economy to give them a little at the agency and cause them to be watched until they were beyond the limits of town."[16]

As Calhoun jousted with Munroe over supplies, a Washington auditor disallowed a number of expenses. Trying to close out his accounts as Indian agent, he wrote: "What I have charged, I know to be just. But if you cannot allow them, discard them at once and allow me to know the result. I do not know when I am to die, and I would prefer absolute and unqualified injustice, while living, rather than to have suspended accounts against me in death." He mentioned death in a second letter to Lea, saying the auditor's decision "annoys me exceedingly. I desire the Government to be just and liberal with me, but I am infinitely more concerned that my accounts should be closed before I die, and God only knows when that event may happen." This is the first indication that Calhoun might have been experiencing the onset of illness that would worsen in the coming year. "To prevent terrible outbreaks by the Indians of the Territory has required all the ingenuity and means that I could command," Calhoun told Lea. He suggested that some auditor should "interfere to prevent the sacrifice of a faithful public officer," namely, himself.[17]

Calhoun's morale plunged to a new low. "My condition is a more unsatisfactory one, at this time, than at any former period since I have been in the Territory. I am without the slightest advice as to the purposes of the Government in reference to the Indians in this Territory, and I know nothing of the means provided by Congress for their management." He rallied upon learning that Congress appropriated $36,000 to fulfill the Ute and Navajo treaties and that the Indian Department appointed four Indian agents. With the proper laws and the means to locate and subsist the Indians for a time, he wrote, "We can lay the foundations of a quietude unknown to the people of New Mexico." Lea directed Calhoun and his agents to negotiate treaties, acting separately or together. If the military prosecuted hostilities against the Indians, one or more officers of the Indian service should accompany each detachment of troops. "The Government desires and expects that there shall be the utmost harmony and concert of action between the officers of the army and of this department," Lea advised. The secretary of war had given the New Mexico commander the same instructions.[18]

New Arrivals

John Greiner, the bard of Ohio Whigs, was on his way to New Mexico to become an Indian agent.[19] In May 1851, he excitedly reported seeing wolves, antelope, prairie dogs, and buffalo as he journeyed across the plains. Greiner could hardly believe his luck at finding 4,000 Indian people gathered to meet the agent, Major Fitzpatrick, and hold a council. A drought lingered. "The whole face of the country is dried up—many of the rivers even have run dry. For hundreds of miles not a single spear of grass had grown this season, and I suspect there will be no chance for any this year," he wrote.[20]

Born in Philadelphia in 1810, Greiner had been a paint dealer and state librarian. He began writing songs in 1840 as a stalwart of the temperance movement, and the same year tried his hand at political songs. From then on, Greiner jotted down, often at a moment's notice, doggerel and ditties, which he sang to whip up enthusiasm at political rallies. He penned the well-known "Wagon Boy Songs" and William Henry Harrison's presidential campaign song, "Tippecanoe and Tyler Too." His prominence among Ohio Whigs earned him an appointment as Indian agent, but it would mean long separations from his wife and six children.[21]

Greiner's fellow travelers were Richard and Susan Weightman and their three children, as well as the Baptist missionary, Louis Smith, and his wife. They joined Major Chilton's company and waited on the Arkansas for Munroe's replacement, Colonel Edwin Vose Sumner, who was bringing with him 342 recruits for the Third Infantry and 300 recruits for the nine companies of dragoons. Cholera hadn't yet sickened anyone west of the Arkansas and so the travelers believed they wouldn't be troubled by it, but cholera attacked Sumner's troops before they left Fort Leavenworth on May 20. By the time he reached the Arkansas, he'd lost one surgeon and about thirty-five men. Greiner wrote, "Sumner is the most business-like, energetic man in the army and has been appointed for the express purpose of teaching the Indians the difference between Americans and Mexicans."[22] The songster would soon change his tune about Sumner.

After fifty-three days of travel, they reached Santa Fe on July 19. With no rain in months, the wheat crop withered and corn would probably follow, Greiner wrote. Board cost thirty to sixty dollars a month "and living poor at that." He took up residence with the parsons Kephart and Nicholson. "The Mexicans are not well pleased with the American residents here, and the presence of the army has alone prevented their revolting before this time," he wrote after ten days. "The fact is they are treated little better than we treat our negroes, and it would not be strange at all if at some day they would rise and wipe out our whole American population." Living in New Mexico was "like living upon a volcano—not knowing how soon there may be an eruption."[23]

Two more agents—Abraham Woolley and Edward H. Wingfield—arrived on July 25, along with Calhoun's son-in-law, William E. Love, the newly appointed postmaster. For Calhoun it was a joyous day. He finally had help, as well as the company of a close family member and Weightman's family. Woolley, an officer in the War of 1812, was considered an "accomplished soldier and a gentleman."[24] Wingfield, once a temperance delegate from Greensboro, Georgia, was related to William Dawson's wife.[25] Weightman was also an agent. He intended to enjoy a brief stay in New Mexico while he campaigned for Congress, and he expected to win. Weightman applied himself to settling some problems between the Pueblo Indians and New Mexicans. Calhoun planned to station Woolley near Fort Union, Greiner near Taos, and Wingfield in Navajo country. Each agent received $1,000, half for presents to the Indians and half for traveling expenses.[26]

Greiner later wrote,

> The great difficulty in our Indian policy is in the election of Indian agents, who are generally appointed for political services. Mr. Wingfield comes here as an agent because he was the friend of Mr. Dawson of Georgia; Mr. Woolley, an old man of seventy years of age, because he was the friend of Mr. Clay; Mr. Weightman, because he wished to be returned as delegate; and myself because I could sing a good political song. Neither of us was by habit or education better fitted to be Indian agent than to follow any other business. The general policy of selecting men as agents for political service, rather than fitness for the position, and frequently changing them, is a great cause of all our Indian difficulties, in my opinion.[27]

Three territorial officials made their appearance on July 26: Judges Horace Mower and John Watts and Secretary of State William S. Allen. The judges' services were desperately needed. When Calhoun suspended county courts to end the influence of military appointees, the jails filled up in Santa Fe and

Albuquerque, but counties had no money to sustain them.[28] The judges and court clerk Caleb Sherman lodged with Calhoun because public houses had no available rooms. Sherman was surprised to find a political faction so hostile to Calhoun that they wouldn't even call to pay their respects to the judges. They wanted to enlist the judges in their cause but were told the judges wouldn't involve themselves in political matters.

Legislators cheered the new judges' arrival as a sign of better times; they had confidence in the governor and the judges and were law-abiding people, wrote Sherman. Calhoun is popular with the Mexican people, "and in my opinion, justly entitled to their confidence for the extreme care he has taken of their interests & his manifest desire to make them feel that they were American citizens" by appointing many prominent people to office. The only specific complaint Sherman heard was that Calhoun paid more attention to the (New) Mexicans than he did the Americans.[29]

On July 28, Calhoun bid a mental good riddance to the departing Colonel Munroe. The colonel would pull garrison duty for two years before the army trusted him with a command again.[30]

Severe Chastisement

Colonel Sumner assumed command the day he arrived. His orders, received that spring from Secretary of War Charles M. Conrad, were to evaluate the department's defense system and the suitability of its posts. Nearly 1,300 soldiers, scattered among eleven outposts at settlements throughout the territory, defended New Mexico. Conrad, dissatisfied with their cost and performance, ordered Sumner to "revise the whole system of defense," remove troops from the towns, and post them close to the frontier. He should strike the Navajos, Utes, and Apaches as soon as possible "and inflict upon them a severe chastisement." And he was to act in concert with Calhoun, allow him to ride along on the expeditions, and "afford him every facility for the discharge of his duties." Finally, he was to "reduce the enormous expenditures of the Army in New Mexico."[31]

Two years older than Calhoun, "Bull" Sumner was fifty-four and had been a professional soldier nearly half his life. A harsh, by-the-book officer with a booming voice, he'd served with Kearny in New Mexico and Winfield Scott in Mexico. In the Mexican War, a lieutenant wrote, "We are in perfect purgatory here, & Major Sumner would be chief devil anywhere." He kept troops marching,

FIGURE 54. Edwin V. Sumner is shown here between 1861 and 1863 during his Civil War service. Library of Congress.

running, and drilling in knee-deep sand until even men who never prayed begged the Almighty to get rid of him. That and the musket ball that glanced off his skull cemented his reputation and nickname.[32]

Sumner embraced Conrad's challenge. "My first step was to break up the post at Santa Fe, that sink of vice and of extravagance, and to remove the troops" to a new headquarters and general depot at Fort Union, twenty-one miles northeast of Las Vegas on the Mora River. He fired all of the 134 civilian employees except the few needed to move supplies to Fort Union and retained a few clerks and one carpenter. The commander was in such a hurry, he had supplies hauled to Fort Union before there were storehouses to protect them. Soldiers, who replaced skilled craftsmen building the fort, tacked up ramshackle buildings of green logs without foundations.

Sumner left only an artillery company in Santa Fe. He quickly broke up posts at Las Vegas and Rayado and by November would abandon posts at Abiquiu, Albuquerque, Taos, Cebolleta, Socorro, Doña Ana,[33] San Elizario, and El Paso. He founded four new posts in 1851: Fort Union, Fort Conrad on the west bank of the Rio Grande south of Belen, Fort Defiance in Navajo country, and Fort Fillmore about forty miles above El Paso near Mesilla. In 1852 he would reoccupy the abandoned Fort Webster at the Santa Rita copper mines and establish Fort Massachusetts near the San Luis Valley of present Colorado.[34]

Sumner "made quite a sensation in the military camps here," Kephart reported. "Trains were departing every day, and it seemed to be the determination of Col. Sumner to leave nothing behind. Santa Fe will be a mere country town in a few months, as all the business will be transferred to Las Vegas." Sumner upended the local economy. Without the army, merchants expected sales in Santa Fe to plunge by half. A horde of teamsters and mechanics were out of work and some joined a gang of robbers operating between Santa Fe and San Miguel. Citizens feared more crime, "as men will not starve," Calhoun wrote.[35]

Nervous residents petitioned both Calhoun and Sumner. Removing soldiers "would bring imminent peril to us, to the extent that our lives, our wives and families might be sacrificed and lose the little we have to live upon and will be exposed to the fury of the bloody bands of the Apaches just as we have been in past years," wrote citizens in southern New Mexico. From El Paso, citizens protested that removing all troops to Valverde except a small force at San Elizario "would be ruinous to this part of the country" because it would leave some two hundred miles of farmland without protection. Sumner dismissed them all. He believed most of the complainers had been living on "the extravagant expenditures of the Government" and that troops had become "in a high degree demoralized" by the "vicious associations in those towns."[36]

Calhoun was apprehensive about the new posts as well as Sumner's plans for a Navajo campaign. Navajos knew every corner of the Territory, he told the colonel. As soon as he marched, they would be in "our midst, and murder our people, and carry off captives and property." He asked if Sumner would provide transportation and supplies for an Indian agent to accompany troops to Navajo country. Sumner responded curtly that measures would be taken to prevent Indian incursions during his absence. And "no allowances, whatever, can be made to any person from army supplies, not provided for, by express law." This was contrary to his orders from the secretary of war and a blow to Calhoun. Calhoun queried Sumner's subordinates about providing escorts, and the answer was still no.[37]

Calhoun wrote the commissioner that Indian affairs would have to be conducted by the army or neglected. Woolley, Wingfield, and Greiner complained directly to Lea: "Traveling without an armed escort in this country is entirely unsafe." How were they to perform their duties as Indian agents when the military withheld cooperation? "We deeply sympathise with Govr. Calhoun." A month later, Wingfield, who had been an attorney in Dahlonega, Georgia, proposed going to Washington to explain the situation, and Calhoun approved.[38]

Sumner's terse responses telegraphed the man's starchy arrogance as well as his attitude toward civilians and agents. Like other officers, he was outraged when the government transferred the Indian Service from the War Department to the newly created Department of the Interior in 1849. Their belief that civilians and Indian agents were political hacks who could mistreat the

Indians and exploit their positions proved to be true in some cases but didn't apply to Calhoun. The result was Sumner's almost malevolent determination to undermine Calhoun and the Indian Service.[39]

Bishop Lamy

Three weeks after Sumner began to overhaul the army in New Mexico, Bishop Jean Baptiste Lamy came to Santa Fe to do the same to the church. As Lamy drew closer to Santa Fe, he expected to see "some of the faithful," but was astounded to find thousands waiting. "Most conspicuous in a magnificent carriage was the United States Territorial Governor James Calhoun. He greeted the bishop warmly," wrote historian Paul Horgan. The Very Reverend Monsignor Juan Felipe Ortiz advanced to pay his respects, and Calhoun took the two into his own carriage. Following Calhoun were the two Baptist ministers, Hiram Read and Louis Smith. The civil and military authorities were assembled as well as the leading citizens. Indian dancers in regalia performed. As they entered Santa Fe, the military fired a salute from its cannons at Fort Marcy. Cedars had been planted along the road the day before to create a beautiful tree-lined lane. That night they held a banquet attended by all the officials and leading citizens.[40]

Lamy's orders were to Americanize New Mexico's Catholic Church. "Rigid, puritanical, and zealous in his pursuit of his vision of Roman Catholicism, Lamy has been accused of displaying an incredible lack of sensitivity, much less empathy, for the New Mexicans among whom he came to live and work," wrote historian E. A. Mares. Lamy became so unpopular with New Mexicans that the legislature complained to the Pope. Some Protestants cheered the promised change. The new bishop "will make the cock fighting and gambling priests of New Mexico either move their boots or discard their evil practices," wrote agent Greiner. "He will not allow the priests to keep their women as they do now," and the priests would have to stay out of politics.[41]

Lamy established courteous relations with Calhoun and succeeding civil authorities. He was concerned about the poor repair of his churches and of his parishioners because of "the social and moral ignorance which flourished in Santa Fe's isolation from the world." Lamy chose the parish church of St. Francis as his cathedral. A few minutes' walk from the plaza, it was the largest building in the city. Lamy moved quickly to take possession of church buildings, chapels, and other properties and soon faced off with the newly arrived Chief Justice

Grafton Baker over use of the military church. Built in 1701 under Spanish rule, the Chapel of Our Lady of Light on the south side of the plaza, called the *Castrense*, became an army chapel under the Mexican government. The Americans turned it into an ordinance house.

Calhoun had already recommended its return to the church, but Judge Baker needed a place to hold criminal court and there was no other building available. The military said he could use the Castrense, and Baker reluctantly agreed and had it modified for use as a courthouse. Lamy wanted the church back immediately, but Judge Baker, after all his trouble, wasn't inclined to give it up. That led to a public spat repeated in national newspapers. Sherman wrote that the Houghton faction called the court's use of the church a desecration and tried to turn New Mexicans against Calhoun and the judges, hoping to defeat Weightman and send Alexander Reynolds to Congress. Citizens circulated a petition supporting the church, signed by Americans and New Mexicans. As angry crowds gathered around the church entrance, Baker held court. The military declined to keep the peace or to arm Marshal John G. Jones's posse. Baker backed down and decided to hold court in the Hall of Representatives. Calhoun gave the keys to Lamy, and the dispute ended.[42]

Navajo Campaign

On August 17, 1851, Sumner marched to Navajo country with four companies of cavalry, one of artillery, and two of infantry. They saw no Navajos until they passed Cañon Bonito. A single Navajo man came into camp, and Sumner sent a request through him to two chiefs to come in and talk. They refused and so Sumner ordered his men to shoot all Navajos on sight. "We killed and wounded a number of them but I cannot say how many," Sumner reported. "They never faced us or gave us an opportunity to inflict upon them any signal chastisement." They rode eleven miles into Canyon de Chelly intending to attack Navajos and destroy crops. From perches high on the canyon walls Navajos shot arrows and shouted insults at the troops below. Private James Bennett wrote that soldiers feasted on Navajo corn and melons. They filled their sacks with peaches at an orchard until the Navajos rained lead balls on them, and they had to take shelter under rocks. That night they could see a thousand small fires with dark forms moving around. "All concluded 'twas best for us to retrace our steps as no one knew the country and the Indians by far outnumbered us." They rode out in the dark. When they reached Fort Defiance, "we were minus over 200 animals which died from hardships and starvation." Sumner wrote to his superiors, "This expedition was not as decisive as I could wish."[43]

As Calhoun predicted, Navajos began raiding the unprotected settlements. Agitated and alarmed, he fired off letters to officialdom. "They have so successfully committed murders and depredations, and carried off captives, they do not fear the possibility of being caught by our troops. I will only add, until we can procure munitions of war, and the Executive is clothed with authority to call out the militia, there will be no quiet in this territory," Calhoun wrote to Secretary of War Conrad. "At present, we have not one dollar in the treasury, nor is there any probability of there being one in it at an early day because of a combination of tax payers who refuse to pay taxes." The same day, he again wrote Lea, "Without a dollar in our Territorial Treasury, without munitions of war, without authority to call out our Militia, and without the cooperation of the military authorities in this Territory, and with numberless complaints and calls for protection, do you not perceive, I must be sadly embarrassed and disquieted?"[44]

15

NO QUIET

From the moment Richard Weightman returned from Washington, DC, and began campaigning for Congress, his race against Alexander Reynolds increased the animosity between the two factions. As Reynolds canvassed across the territory, Calhoun worried that he was circulating lies and rumors and stirring up the tribes. Kephart disliked Reynolds, a slave owner, and considered him "morally and mentally" unqualified, but he supported Reynolds to "break down the Governor's faction." Colonel Sumner didn't think Reynolds could maintain his duties as quartermaster as he campaigned and ordered Reynolds to join him on the Navajo expedition "to secure his undivided attention to his military duties."[1]

On Election Day, September 1, 1851, Candido Ortiz and another Houghtonite, Rafael Armijo, entered the Albuquerque polling place along with a dozen Americans, each toting a bottle of liquor. Some of the Americans said they wanted to vote. The poll judges objected because the Santa Feans didn't live there and because Edward Burtinett was an enlisted man who wasn't entitled to vote. The rowdy group threatened election judges, who appeared intimidated, and attorney Spruce Baird, a Weightman friend, advised them to accept the ballots but note their objections in the poll book, which they did. Ortiz also voted. Then the group rode to Los Ranchos de Albuquerque, a village north of Albuquerque.[2]

Again, the group demanded ballots. When the election judges refused, they fired pistols, knocked an election judge unconscious, took over the polls, and ran off the New Mexicans. The local men then armed themselves and took back the polls. They imprisoned the Americans and shot Burtinett. Several Americans and New Mexicans were wounded. The day after the ruckus, rumors flew and Baird went to Los Ranchos. There he saw Atanacio Montoya, president of the election, who had a head wound, and confirmed that another New Mexican had been shot in the arm, several Americans were wounded, and Burtinett was dead. Baird was surprised because "the Mexican population, when left to themselves, are the most orderly people I have ever seen at any election," he wrote, but he'd heard that Reynolds' partisans intended to stir up trouble at precincts favoring Weightman.

The *Santa Fe Gazette* reported that the group's votes were refused and blamed the violence on "a spirit of enmity . . . between the Mexican and American population." It predicted more bloodshed. However, a writer to the *St. Louis Republican* said all of the unruly Americans "were men known for their determined hostility to Mexicans," and "their own indiscretion led to the lamentable result. The military . . . are bitterly opposed to the Governor, and have done all they could to annoy him."[3]

Weightman prevailed in the contest 4,200 to 3,458, to the surprise of nobody. Reynolds denounced the election as a fraud and sent a memorial to Congress charging intimidation, violence, and irregularities. Weightman's supporters also charged irregularities and intimidation. "The opposition party to the Governor, composed of Democrats, Free Soilers, and renegade Whigs, has been entirely beaten," wrote one newspaper correspondent. "The Governor's party have an overwhelming majority in both branches of the legislature and have succeeded in sending a Delegate to Congress. And now, our worthy people in despair, call for the removal of the Governor."[4]

The matter wasn't finished. On September 22, Houghtonite William C. Skinner[5] went to Juan Cristóbal Armijo's store in Los Ranchos and asked him to sign a statement saying that he, Armijo, was guilty of "numerous acts of tyranny and usurpation." Armijo refused to sign. The next day Skinner, who was drunk, said he was going to whip someone at Los Ranchos. At Armijo's store, Skinner got off his horse with one pistol in his belt and another cocked in his hand. He entered the store and assaulted Armijo. As the two grappled, Skinner died. Judge Grafton Baker described Armijo as a "quiet, well disposed man—very friendly towards Americans." At word Skinner's death, Calhoun's enemies held an emotional meeting in Santa Fe and blamed his policies for two murders. Led by Collins and T. S. J. Johnson, they stormed across the plaza to the Palace, interrupted Calhoun's fireside game of whist with friends, and demanded that he send two hundred armed men to Bernalillo County. Calhoun's card game, charged the *Gazette*, was "the fiddling of Nero over the burning of Rome." Collins and his cohorts were all monte players, Baker wrote, and their indignation at Calhoun's card game "was ridiculous in the extreme."

Baker put his finger on the real rub: "Since the removal of the troops business has been uncommonly dull in Santa Fe. Merchants doing nothing, gamblers doing nothing, and contractors doing nothing. This (is) the cause of the present discontent."[6]

The next day, Calhoun calmly rode south with interpreters, a few friends, and judges Watt and Baker. He spoke to Prefect Ambrosio Armijo, brother of Juan Cristóbal Armijo, despite warnings that Ambrosio intended to kill him. Calhoun then allowed the law to take its course. The accused merchant posted bail, appeared in district court, and the grand jury acquitted him. Collins claimed that District Attorney Elias P. West made a weak prosecution because his law partner, Spruce Baird, was the defense attorney, and more than half the members the grand jury, he claimed, were Armijo relations. The *Gazette* inflated the incident into a native insurrection made possible by Calhoun's ineffective policies.[7]

"That the Executive of the Territory should be charged with these murders for political purposes is at once absurd and ridiculous," wrote a man identified as Mack (Archibald McKinsie). "It seems that certain parties in New Mexico are disappointed and dissatisfied because certain men were not appointed to offices; and it seems also that they did not find James S. Calhoun as pliable as they expected, and consequently a strong disposition has been shown to annoy and thwart the Governor in his efforts for the amelioration of the people of the Territory." McKinsie wrote that he was not a party member but knew the Territory's affairs and spoke out "as an act of justice to the Executive of New Mexico.[8]

Desperation Is Abroad

In letter after letter to Secretary of State Daniel Webster, Calhoun set forth the territory's situation and his own sinking helplessness. "Agitators are hourly exciting the passions of the ignorant and those whom they control," he wrote on September 15, 1851. "The people are persuaded they are not properly cared for—they know that the wild Indians roam in every direction in this Territory, and commit depredations, without being chastised—that the Territorial Treasury is a mere void, that we are without munitions of war, or authority to call out the Militia."[9]

A week later he wrote that the Territory probably wouldn't collect taxes for

FIGURE 55. Navajos are depicted in a lithograph
by artist Balduin Möllhausen in 1855. Library of Congress.

months to come. It was no exaggeration. The military government left a deficit
of $31,562, and creditors were being paid with warrants; speculation over their
fluctuating value had become an industry. The territory's paltry treasury had
several causes. Kearny in 1846 ended the practice of requiring legal documents
to be written on stamped paper the government sold for eight dollars a sheet.
And as a territory, New Mexico could no longer collect tariffs on goods from
the States. Legislators passed a tax on licenses, but merchants refused to pay,
calling it "an unjust and unequal tax." The large landowners should pay their
fair share, they argued. If the treasury had a dollar, the territorial secretary
claimed he had no authority to spend it. "Nearly every appropriation made by
the Legislature, payable out of the appropriations of Congress for Territorial
purposes, are suspended," Calhoun wrote. "This is exceedingly disagreeable to
me." Calhoun retained Spruce Baird and Elias West to prosecute cases for
taxes and licenses and urged Webster to pay the salaries of territorial officers.[10]

Speaker of the House Theodore Wheaton wrote Calhoun in September
that five hundred citizens of Taos and Rio Arriba Counties wanted to campaign against the Navajos and asked Calhoun's approval. They knew the Navajos' mountain retreats and were willing to fight, armed only with bows and
arrows. With guns they could do more in a year to protect the frontier than

the regular army could in three, they said. Unless they could act, they predicted that New Mexico and northern Mexico would be scenes of robbery and bloodshed because the army was ignorant of the kind of warfare that would succeed.[11]

"Desperation is abroad in every direction in this Territory, and there are no effective means to check it," Calhoun wrote to Secretary of State Webster on October 1. "Rely upon it, there is no time for discussion. Action, action is demanded, and I doubt whether it can come soon enough to prevent foul deeds. For the last two years I have, faithfully, warned the proper officials of dangers to be apprehended—and now, they are immediately in front, and who can foretell the result." He called once again for two new mounted regiments and arms for the militia. He closed provocatively, "The military and civil authorities of the Territory, with but few exceptions are in hostile array and one, or both should be relieved from duty in this territory."[12]

The same day, Calhoun told Indian Commissioner Luke Lea that murders and depredations continued and he needed weapons and the authority to call out the militia. He had access to appropriations for the Navajos and Utes, but he couldn't get to Indian country safely for lack of military cooperation. He concluded darkly that "the Military officers and the executive can not harmonize, and I am not certain that the public interests would not be promoted by relieving us all from duty in this Territory."[13]

Failed Expedition

Colonel Sumner returned in the third week of October. "The Navajoe expedition has turned out a failure, as was anticipated by most persons here when it started," wrote Kephart, who now divided his caustic remarks between Sumner and Calhoun. "It was miserably conceived, and abortion was but a reasonable expectation." A great many horses died of starvation, even though corn and forage were plentiful on the route, because Sumner couldn't buy it at his price. He was sending several hundred skeletal mules to the States that would probably die on the trail, Kephart said. Some officers actively disliked Sumner, and others thought his judgment was poor. Calhoun told Webster, "Col. Sumner's expedition to the Navajo country has been productive of no good."[14]

The one accomplishment Sumner could claim was selecting the site for a fort to monitor the Navajos. It was a beautiful site, set between the Bonito and a steep cliff with a dependable supply of good water and wood and grazing in the surrounding meadows, but an army inspector would later describe it as wretchedly located from a military point of view. "Col. S. fixed upon a point, left five companies to garrison it and called it Fort Defiance," wrote Captain Isaac Bowen on his return to Fort Union. "I wish we were to accompany the train to the states, for if ever there was a country which our creator had deserted, forsaken and left to its own means of salvation, that country must be New Mexico." Bowen's wife Katie wrote her parents that Sumner "is not in very good standing among his officers in this country [who] call him hard names sometimes not even giving him credit for bravery."[15]

After losing too many horses, Sumner now argued for more infantry. To his convoluted thinking, horses worn down on long marches wouldn't be a match for Indian horses, and cavalry couldn't act decisively. It apparently didn't occur to him that foot soldiers would be even less of a match. He recommended withdrawing four companies of dragoons and dismounting the rifle regiment or sending a regiment of infantry. And yet, virtually every western commander before and after him maintained that infantry was useless in Indian warfare. Calhoun had insisted from the outset that they needed mounted regiments.[16]

Sumner did relent and offer to furnish Calhoun an escort to visit the Utes. Kiowas and Utes were at war, and Kiowas and Arapahoes twice attacked a Ute camp near the Red River, capturing two women and four children and driving off all their stock. Calhoun advised Sumner that no fewer than 250 well-mounted men were needed to keep the Utes quiet during the winter, "goaded as they are by our own people and at the moment by the Kiowas and other Indians. We ought if possible to act in concert." To make matters worse, New Mexicans planned to settle in the Conejos Valley, even though Utes had repeatedly driven settlers from the valley because it was their winter hunting ground and, as they said, held the bones of their fathers. "As our troops seem to be in winter quarters, our frontier disorders must increase," he told Webster. "If an effort I am now making fails, the people of the Territory, to some extent, will be forced to take care of themselves, or consent to lie down quietly, and be plundered and butchered."[17]

Trading Insults

Calhoun organized a militia with a proclamation on October 24, 1851. He ordered brigadier generals to assemble their men on the third Monday of November and have the men elect officers. He asked Sumner for seventy-five weapons on November 9, the same day Preston Beck, J. E. Sabine, Elias Brevourt, and David Whiting organized a volunteer company and needed only weapons. "The winter is at hand, and ruthless invaders are in our midst, and unless adequate protection is afforded, our firesides must be rendered desolate before the spring season," Calhoun told Sumner, setting off a three-day written spat.

Citizens had asked to protect themselves for a year, and Calhoun saw it as his duty to help them, unless he knew that troops could do the job, he told Sumner. "The small number of troops at your disposal, and the condition of your horses, I apprehend, renders such a result impracticable," he wrote. And if citizens did attempt to protect themselves against the Navajos, he wondered if troops would then point guns at the citizens. Calhoun said he wanted to harmonize but couldn't fold his arms and watch "scenes of desolation."[18]

Sumner asked what "scenes of desolation" had been witnessed. Calhoun referred him to his recent communications about murders and raids near Taos, Anton Chico, the Jornada, San Antonio, Cebolleta, and Laguna. Was this sufficient, Calhoun asked, to declare scenes of desolation? Sumner responded, "My policy is to keep them, for the present, beyond the line of our settlements; and yours . . . is to invite them to come into our settlements." He didn't want to interfere with the citizens' defense against Indians and even thought a militia should be organized for defense, but that wasn't the same as "organizing marauding parties to traverse the Indian Country." He would cooperate to protect the people provided the measures didn't violate the law and War Department orders.[19]

Sumner ordered a captain at Fort Union to turn over seventy-five flintlock muskets, cartridge boxes, and other supplies, but they were on loan, to be returned when the army needed them. And they were not to be used to make hostile incursions into Indian Country unless acting with regular troops. Beck and the others declined to accept arms on Sumner's terms because they could have their arms taken at a moment's notice. Besides, they didn't want Sumner to restrict their incursions and preferred to report only to Calhoun as the militia's commander in chief.

Calhoun sent along Beck's letter and asked Sumner if he intended to use federal troops to punish a militia ordered into Navajo country. Sumner said he wouldn't use troops to expel marauding parties that the governor might commission "as it will not be their fault," but he protested any such action as interfering with his duties and contrary to orders of the War Department. Calhoun responded, "I think you are discreet in your determination: but not wise in your application of the term 'marauding parties,'" which he considered a slur against citizens and himself. Sumner snapped that he had given Calhoun's communication "all the consideration that I think it is entitled to."[20]

Copies of their testy exchange made their way to Washington. Sumner apologized for troubling his superior "with voluminous correspondence with Governor Calhoun." He had "endeavored to avoid these differences as much as possible" but wanted to keep New Mexicans from marauding in Indian country. "This predatory war has been carried on for two hundred years, between the Mexicans & Indians, quite time enough to prove, that unless some change is made the war will be interminable. They steal women and children, and Cattle, from each other, and in fact carry on the war, in all respects, like two Indian nations." Hostilities would interfere with progress Sumner expected from establishing Fort Defiance. The Navajos had already said they would come to Santa Fe and make a treaty. He asked that the proper authorities order Calhoun to "abstain from sending any war parties of Mexicans into the Indian Country" and confine himself to defensive measures.[21]

Pompous as he was, Sumner accurately grasped the long antagonism between New Mexicans and Navajos. Their back-and-forth raids were so much a part of frontier life that it was hard to separate self-defense from the opportunity for plunder, but his own malignant conduct toward Calhoun guaranteed that the two couldn't hold a rational discussion.

War of Words

As Calhoun penned letter after letter to Washington, Greiner sat beside him writing a friend that "between the savage Indians, the treacherous Mexicans and the outlawed Americans" New Mexico was a dangerous place. "Three governors within twelve years have lost their heads and there are men here at present who talk as flippantly of taking Governor Calhoun's head as though it were of no consequence whatever." The civil and military authorities were at war, he wrote,

FIGURE 56. Artist Seth Eastman created "Near Fort Defiance, Navajo Country, New Mexico" from a sketch by Maj. Electus Backus, who built Fort Defiance in 1851. The image appeared in Schoolcraft's *Indian Tribes* in 1854.

and "the American residents are at war with the Governor, while the Mexican population side with him." The gulf between the two groups was so great that Americans "dared not leave without being armed to the teeth."Americans threatened to avenge Skinner's death on Calhoun. "Yet I have never known him to give any cause for such hostilities; cool, calm and deliberate, he is not easily thrown off his guard, and you may depend upon it, if he does fall, it will be with his face to the sky and his feet to the foe, and there will be men who will die with him." Greiner counted himself among Calhoun's supporters. He "has always treated me in the kindest possible manner… and has furnished me every information on subjects upon which I was ignorant."[22]

That fall a procession of officials journeyed to Washington. Weightman and his family returned, and he took his seat in Congress. Indian agent Wingfield left with them, intending to make the case for Calhoun and his fellow agents. Reynolds followed to contest the congressional seat. William Messervy, James Collins, Joab Houghton, and the Taos merchant James H. Quinn took their complaints to the nation's capital. Chief Justice Grafton Baker joined the exodus to seek improvements in the territory's Organic Law and to defend himself against accusations. Calhoun too wanted to travel but decided against it. "Anxious as I am to visit the States at an early day, I am constrained to say, the Governor of this Territory could not, with propriety, leave the Territory at this time," he wrote.[23]

Calhoun's critics had been carping to the St. Louis newspapers: "What do our agents do? They stay in Santa Fe or the neighborhood," they said. Wingfield was supposed to be assigned to the Navajos. Why didn't he accompany the expedition? They claimed Wingfield was traveling East to smooth over "some of Governor Calhoun's recent acts of imbecility and corruption." Messervy, who a year before recommended Calhoun for the governorship as a man of "high character and ability," wrote in November 1851 that Calhoun was "wholly unfit" for the office and predicted a civil war in the territory if Calhoun remained.[24]

When he reached St. Louis, Weightman found the newspapers riddled with misinformation and tried to set the record straight. "The Governor, a gentleman of high character, nominated by a Whig President and endorsed by a Democratic Senate, is charged with remissness in his duties and a culpable disregard of the lives of the native citizens of his own country," Weightman wrote. The "murders" blamed on the governor's policy and the declarations that Mexicans were hostile to Americans and unfit for self-government were "slanders and falsehoods, monstrous and deliberate." The great majority of Americans were Calhoun's supporters, but the Americans didn't number more than 600, while the New Mexicans exceed 65,000, he said. Weightman explained the power struggle between partisans of military rule and advocates of self-government, along with their opponents' control of the *Santa Fe Gazette*. He described Sumner's removal of troops from the towns, which their enemies blamed on Calhoun and himself.

"The Governor is well aware of the conspiracy which exists in New Mexico to bring about the belief in the United States that there is danger of the Mexican part of the population revolting against the Government of the United States." The American public had heard all about rumors of a revolt in Taos County and destruction of St. Vrain's mills, he said, but they hadn't heard that when troops arrived, they found farmers cultivating their fields and the mill making flour. Weightman referred to Collins as a monte dealer and said Thomas S. J. Johnson, chief clerk of the army quartermaster, was cashiered out of the army for embezzlement and speculation. (Collins was a merchant, and in 1849 he did receive a gaming license.)[25]

After Kephart wrote that New Mexicans "are deeply anti-slavery in their feelings" while the president's New Mexico appointees were "a set of slaveholders, slavery sympathizers and slavery indifferent," Weightman wrote a letter to Senator H. S. Foote, which Foote read on the Senate floor. New Mexicans were opposed to their country "being made the arena in which to decide political questions" like slavery when they had no interest in slavery. New Mexicans were opposed to the introduction of slave labor. He concluded, "Slave labor will not pay in New Mexico."[26]

Kephart maintained his drumbeat, but his rants were losing their punch. He feuded with Baptist ministers Hiram Read, Louis Smith, and James M. Shaw. The *St. Louis Republican*, which had indulgently published his every word, reported that Nicholson, the Methodist, and Kephart had become unpopular "by interfering in political matters and trying to stir up excitement about abolition." Neither had attracted even a dozen followers. *The Union* in Washington, DC, was inclined to give Calhoun the benefit of the doubt until someone spoke for him. "The office of governor of New Mexico is necessarily a very unpleasant one, because the mass of the population are so unlike our own citizens as to make it almost impossible that they should get along quietly together."[27]

Legislature

The legislature met for a second session in early December 1851 without two Houghton stalwarts—John R. Tullis and Candido Ortiz, who had resigned. The majority of legislators, wrote Kephart, were Calhoun's "pliant tools," and he had veto power. Legislation couldn't become law without the governor's signature, and legislators didn't yet have a veto override.[28] The larger concern was the treasury. Conflicting interpretations of the law creating the Territory entangled appropriations.

"The uncomfortable condition of the rooms in which you are assembled, has given me much concern, and I fear, will be a source of great annoyance to you," Calhoun said during his address on December 1, 1851. "The Palace is in a very dilapidated condition and I have been compelled to incur personal responsibilities to prevent the destruction of the building by fire, and to put it in a condition to enable the respective branches of the Territorial Government to discharge the duties with which they are charged." The legislature had appropriated $1,000 for Calhoun to repair the Palace and improve rooms for Secretary William Allen's office, a library, and archives, but when Calhoun asked Allen to approve the expenditure in September, Allen insisted that he had no authority. "I am not charged with the expenditure of so much as a single dollar of it," he wrote.[29]

In an eleven-page letter to Calhoun, Allen questioned the "legality of hold-ing a second session of the Legislature in the same year and by the same mem-bers." He said the legislature employed more clerks than the law allowed, al-though he understood their necessity because of two languages spoken. Allen spent $19,050 to settle existing debts. Calhoun told legislators they had the right, or should have, to appropriate, just as Oregon legislators did, but the Organic Act that created New Mexico Territory was not explicit about the use of congressional appropriations. Allen was painfully aware that if he erred in his disbursements, he could be held personally responsible for the debt.[30]

Calhoun set out further refinements in the laws passed that summer. He urged legislators to better define the duties of probate judges and justices of the peace. He found criminal laws and their enforcement efficient but not the jails. "Look at your jails and who can be surprised at the many escapes from them?" (In March, prisoners escaped from the local jail by digging through the adobe.) It was folly to spend money convicting criminals if they couldn't be punished. He asked the legislature to seek a penitentiary and jails from Congress. The estray laws needed to be changed to encourage people to restore lost livestock. "The subject of acequias [irrigation ditches] is a continual source of annoyance and some revision of the laws in reference to them may be advis-able." Calhoun also called for a well-regulated system of schools. Congress set aside land for schools, but it needed to be surveyed. He called their attention to his proclamation of August 2 regarding the terms of district courts. People awaiting trial added to the public cost of the trials; he recommended holding court frequently for criminal trials. Although the legislature directed him to organize a militia, the legislation failed to become law because of technical errors, he said.[31]

Calhoun was most agitated about the troublemakers attempting to stir up the Pueblos and upset the peace between Indians and non-Indians. Pueblo people were told that "covetous Mexicans are desirous to get possession of the fertile valleys of their Pueblo neighbors" and that Calhoun was treating them with great disrespect, that he had no right to interfere in their affairs and that he was degrading them, all to create doubt and dissatisfaction. "Ought not such people to be punished?" he asked. He maintained friendly relations with the Pueblos at great cost in time and money. He added that someone had fright-ened Comanches and Navajos away from planned meetings, telling them that Calhoun would have them killed. Without this interference, Calhoun said, he could have restored every captive held by the Navajos, along with stolen property.[32] Legislators passed a resolution asking Calhoun to reveal the identities of those stirring up the Pueblos. He responded that if they would pass an act to punish the agitators, he would disclose the names. He apparently had in mind a tribunal or official investigation, but legislators had no appetite for antagonizing Calhoun's powerful enemies or stirring up trouble. In his correspondence Calhoun named Reynolds and members of "the defeated faction" as his antagonists.[33]

In that session the legislature divided the Territory into nine counties— Taos, Rio Arriba, San Miguel, Santa Fe, Santa Ana, Bernalillo, Valencia, Socorro, and Doña Ana—and defined their boundaries. It established a territorial fair at Las Vegas and standard weights and measures and regulated gambling. Legislators spent much time on the court system, understandable among people who had never had impartial courts. They told Calhoun that any dealings with the Navajos must provide for restoration of captives and indemnity for injuries done in the last five years. The forty-day session ended on January 9, 1852.

On December 25, Sumner and Calhoun met Navajos at Jemez Pueblo. With some 2,500 Navajos present, leaders signed a treaty. Sumner said he spoke "very plainly" to a group of 200, telling them that troops at Fort Defiance would keep them from raising a single field of grain unless they kept the peace. Navajos agreed to give up New Mexican captives and turned over three. Calhoun distributed $2,500 in gifts, to Sumner's strident disapproval. "These Indians will undoubtedly feel that their submission has been purchased," he told his superiors. Had it been his decision, he would have put them all on probation "with a rod of iron over their heads."[34]

In his annual report that year, Indian Commissioner Luke Lea reported little change in New Mexico. The slow progress could be blamed on the wild country, the savage nature of most of its Indians, "the lawlessness of many of its other inhabitants, often more reckless than the Indians themselves," and the scattered, mixed character of the population "to produce a state of things so discreditable and deplorable, as to render its acquisition a misfortune, and its possession a reproach to the Government." He recommended money and "a more vigorous and untrammeled exercise of authority" by the Territory's civil officers. Lea recognized that the agents' usefulness was seriously impaired because the military hadn't provided transportation and escorts. Clearly, Calhoun had his ear and his sympathies, but it did little good. The policy Lea advocated differed little from the policy pursued in Georgia years before: Acquire tribal land for white settlement and relocate tribes "to save them." That wasn't going to work in New Mexico. The pueblos were too settled, too attached to their country to relocate, and the "wild tribes" held vast swaths of territory that they regarded as theirs.[35]

Lea articulated a growing sentiment in Washington that New Mexico wasn't worthy of becoming a state and was too uncivilized to even be a possession of the United States. Untruthful and bigoted reports from Kephart and other members of the faction made that point in the Eastern newspapers, and to some extent, Calhoun's correspondence helped cement that impression. Although he still believed strongly in New Mexicans' capacity for self-government, his repeated accounts of Indian depredations created the impression that New Mexico was under siege.

16

STATE OF MISERY

Five hundred people from six pueblos—Santo Domingo, San Felipe, Santa Ana, Nambe, Cochiti, and Zia—danced in Santa Fe's plaza on New Year's Day in 1852 to show their gratitude for Calhoun's actions toward the Navajos, Greiner told his boss.

Calhoun was ill, and news of his daughter Martha's death in November devastated him.[1] "The continuous and severe services to which I had been subjected for months and the overwhelming and mournful intelligence which I received from Georgia, announcing the death of my younger daughter rendered it necessary that the duties of the occasion should be confided to another," agent John Greiner, Calhoun informed Lea. "The news of the death of his daughter in Georgia has broke the old man down," Greiner wrote.[2] The "old man" was fifty-two.

Calhoun said he suffered attacks of catarrh (excessive accumulation of mucus) and jaundice but was able to work with Greiner's help. "The governor's health is so precarious that he will leave here for a trip towards El Paso as soon as the mail goes out," wrote Greiner on January 24. Calhoun's Georgia friend, Dr. Asa Hoxey, moved to El Paso in 1850 after finding the Santa Fe climate "too severe for his constitution."[3]

Calhoun yearned to visit Washington and then Georgia. "My physician has informed me that in my feeble exhausted condition I must leave the annoyances, vexations and duties of my post for the present," he wrote Lea after returning from El Paso. However, Calhoun wouldn't leave the superintendency in the hands of Secretary William S. Allen, Greiner said, because Allen "knows nothing about the Indians of this Territory." It was probably a relief to learn on March 29, that Allen would soon leave for the States. "Allen has played you all in New Mexico a pretty trick," Weightman wrote, by quietly resigning a month earlier, although Allen's intentions were known to Collins and Houghton, who tried again to have Hugh Smith appointed.

Calhoun set April 1 for his departure and appointed Manuel Alvarez, trusting his "integrity and ability," as acting governor during his absence. He revealed to Alvarez that he was "just recovering from a severe attack of scurvy which came near laying me in my grave." This was his first mention of the disease. Its symptoms were small hemorrhages around the hair follicles of the skin, bleeding gums, loose teeth, and, later on, large areas of hemorrhage in the skin, weakness, and pain.[4]

Scurvy was then the most common disease in the army, which marched on salt meat, bread, lard, coffee, and hardtack. It was also a scourge of travelers. Although a doctor discovered in 1747 that citrus fruits could prevent scurvy, it wouldn't be known until 1932 that a vitamin C deficiency was the cause. An army doctor in Santa Fe wrote in 1849 that scurvy was "especially due to the long privation of fresh succulent vegetables." He recommended potatoes, onions, and cabbages, but vegetables were scarce in Santa Fe that winter. Americans didn't seem to notice that locals, whose cuisine embraced vitamin C-rich chiles, didn't suffer from scurvy. Neither did their guests. The year before, McCall quartered with a local family and was eating "a good dose of chile" with each meal.[5]

Agent Greiner filled in for Calhoun and the absent agents. Now accustomed to New Mexico, Greiner was enjoying himself and becoming a good Indian agent. "I have about attained the summit of all human greatness in this country," he wrote. "I live in the Palace, board with the Governor, ride in his carriage, and sleep in the Post Office. Isn't that enough to satisfy earthly ambition?" Greiner visited the Odd Fellows Lodge, participated in Masons, and got on well with the army, the Catholic Church, and Indian leaders. He had even attended a few fandangos. His own health had improved "and the travel and excitement of Indian life agrees with me." He had met with Utes, Jicarilla Apaches, Navajos, and Pueblos and liked them all. Greiner said he had no enemies, counted some good friends, and was pleased that the Pueblos, Utes, and Jicarillas had "behaved admirably, are very kind and I get along with them first rate. But in this country a man's hair sits very loosely on his head."[6]

Yet Crying

Navajos came to the agency on January 27, 1852. Greiner met with Chiefs Armijo, Rafael Chavez, Luke Lea (it was not uncommon for Native people to take the names of important people), Black Eagle, Barbon, and José Miguel. Armijo, the principal chief and spokesman, said he had been a captain since he was a young man. His people wished to live in peace, cultivate the soil, and hunt, but too little rain fell and their crops failed. Mexicans killed his grandfather and two other family members.

"I have never sought revenge," he said. "We like the Americans. We have eaten their bread and meat, smoked their tobacco. The clothing they have given us has kept us warm in the cold winter and the snow. With the hoes they have given us we will cultivate our land. We are struck dead with gratitude. I am now before you. You can all see me. My name is well known everywhere. My people are better dressed than I am myself, and although I am ashamed to appear before you so poorly clad, I wished you to see me just as I am, to tell you I can plant corn and wheat and raise food for my people to eat." Greiner responded: "My brothers, let us talk plain so that we may understand each other. The people living in the Rio Abajo [Lower Rio Grande] complain that the Navajos have captured their children, stolen their stock, that their fields have to be idle for they cannot work them for fear of your people. Is this not so?"

"My people are all crying in the same way," Armijo said. "Three of our chiefs now sitting before you mourn for their children who have been taken from their homes by the Mexicans. More than 200 of our children have been carried off and we know not where they are. The Mexicans have lost but few children in comparison with what they have stolen from us. Three years ago they took from my people nearly all their [horse herds]. Two years ago my brother lost 700 animals. How shall we get them again? We leave our Great Father to decide. From the time of Col. Newby we have been trying to get our children back again. Eleven times have we given up our captives. Only once have they given us ours. My people are yet crying for the children they have lost. Is it American justice that we must give up everything and receive nothing?"

Greiner was astonished. "You have never told us this before," he said.

"The Great Father at Washington shall hear of it, and you shall hear what he says. Hereafter no more captives must be taken on either side. Depredations must no longer be committed by either party. Should our people injure you, instead of injuring them you must send one of your young men and let the governor or agent know. Justice will be done, and the offenders shall be punished. If any property is stolen on either side, it must be restored to the proper owners. The chiefs will be held responsible for the conduct of the young men."

The council ended with good feelings, and Greiner gave the Navajos blankets, flannel shirts, hoes, and other gifts. "There is too much truth in what these Indians complain of," Greiner wrote. "If the Indians must return all the captives and property taken from the Mexicans, is it anything but just that they should have what has been stolen from them? I think not," Greiner wrote. Calhoun agreed. "The truth . . . is boldly stated, and must make the just man pause," he wrote Lea. "Every suggestion made by them is true, and is worthy of consideration." He asked for blacksmiths, implements, and iron for the Navajos, Utes, and Eastern Apaches.[7]

On February 1, 1852, Calhoun appointed Spruce Baird as special agent to the Navajos. Baird, originally sent to make New Mexico a part of Texas in 1848, had remained in New Mexico after Texas dropped its claim, settling in Albuquerque. Calhoun posted him at Jemez Pueblo. Baird would serve as agent until 1853, working with Zia, Santa Ana, and San Felipe Pueblos.[8]

Constant Dangers

Sumner, on New Year's Day, painted a sunny picture of conditions in New Mexico. He founded four new posts in 1851: Fort Union, near the Mora River, on July 26; Fort Conrad, on the west bank of the Rio Grande near Valverde, on September 8; Fort Defiance, at the mouth of Bonita Canyon in Navajo country, on September 18; and Fort Fillmore, on the east bank of the Rio Grande near Mesilla, on September 23. (Fort Conrad's palisade of cottonwood timbers began to fail almost before the fort was completed. A new fort would be started the following winter.) On January 23, Sumner reestablished Fort Webster at the Santa Rita copper mines to curb the Apaches. His new posts were "exercising a favorable influence in our Indian relations," he wrote. He believed placing troops near the Indian homelands prevented them from making "distant hostile expeditions" out of fear that their families and property might be attacked by the troops located nearby. He predicted an era of unprecedented peace.[9]

In January, Gila Apaches attacked soldiers on the Jornada del Muerto, killing four, wounding three, and taking five mules and a horse and the contents of the wagon, Calhoun reported. From a second attack, all that was found of a mail wagon were human bones, wagon iron, and a bag of coffee. Calhoun claimed again that with weapons, his militia could "quiet the Apaches in ninety days," while the army's horses were so weak and starved that it couldn't mount one company. Greiner wrote that the Indians' "tough little ponies, carrying but little weight and knowing the country, have every advantage over our dragoon horses that have to carry about 225 pounds."[10]

After a spate of Apache raids in southern New Mexico, citizens of Socorro County petitioned Calhoun, saying that their "very towns are frequently insulted by the presence of the savages, that lives are sacrificed and property despoiled in their inmost squares and in the light of day." Troops at Forts Fillmore and Conrad couldn't even protect their own lives and property. Calhoun appointed Charles Overman as special agent in southern New Mexico. His pay would be $129.16 a month plus forage for one animal.[11]

The reports and petition brought Calhoun to a boil. "I cannot listen to the representations of their helpless and unarmed condition unmoved, nor disregard their petition for relief," he wrote Sumner. He asked again for arms and equipment so that he could make an expedition to Apache country with the militia. He was aware of their different views on troop strength but adamant that "the slaughter of our citizens and the spoliation of their property not only confirm my first impressions in the efficiency of your command but irresistibly appears to my most humane impulses as a man and patriotic exertions as an officer of the government." Sumner responded that he had just sent four companies from Fort Conrad into Apache country to punish them for recent depredations. Two companies would be left at Conrad and one at Los Lunas for protection. "Under these circumstances I do not feel at liberty to issue arms to the militia," Sumner said.[12]

Citizens protested that attacks were the predictable result of closing the post at El Paso, which Sumner considered "very expensive and useless." He dismissed citizen complaints with a racist slight common among officers. "If these Mexicans, when banded together in large numbers, have not the manliness to defend themselves from small parties of roving Indians, they deserve to suffer." The New Mexicans had an equally low opinion of soldiers. After the first attacks, the Apaches grew even bolder, openly attacking troops and forcing them to retreat. Escorts were little help, and mail was cut off in some areas. To Lea, he detailed a series of murders and depredations. "If Col. Sumner had furnished me with the arms and necessary accoutrements requested in my letter to him, it was my intention to have armed the Militia, take the field in person and see for myself that the hostile Indians were chastised into obedience or have them entirely exterminated." On March 21, Sumner agreed to issue Calhoun one hundred stands of arms with ammunition for the use of people in San Antonio in Socorro County, but the army delivered them to Santa Fe for lack of horses to transport them farther.[13]

Sumner blamed hostilities on "the remissness of the civil authority in this Territory." That fall, a New Mexican at San Antonio killed two Apaches and wounded a third as they gambled together. The Apaches demanded that the man be confined, but after they left, the murderer was released, and the Apaches were furious. Sumner brought this to Calhoun's attention. "I am convinced that the only way to subdue Indians effectually and permanently, is to improve their condition," and that meant establishing posts in their country where they could be instructed in agriculture and other skills, Sumner wrote to the secretary of war. The Navajos were peaceful, but it was unrealistic to expect an end to all depredations. "They are educated to believe that the stealing of horses is an act of prowess, and a few young men may occasionally band together for this purpose." Sumner couldn't spare troops to scout against the Gila Apaches, but he advised against using volunteers. It was important to communicate with the Apaches and get them to turn in the white men who reportedly rode with them. "These villains are at the bottom of all the mischief."[14]

In this exchange, Calhoun, a military man in his own mind, advocated military solutions. Sumner, in advocating improved conditions and agricultural instruction, seemed more the agent. Sumner sent Major John H. Carleton and a company on a reconnaissance and directed him to work with Indian agent Abraham Woolley in opening talks with the Mescaleros. It was a fateful journey. Reading Carleton's enthusiastic report about Bosque Redondo on the Pecos River, Sumner wrote, "I had no idea it was so fine a country down there. If I had troops to spare I should establish a post there immediately."[15]

The Bosque Redondo in another decade would become Carleton's choice for a reservation, later called a concentration camp, for Navajos and Mescaleros.

In February the Jicarilla Apaches, who kept the peace following their treaty, were restless, Calhoun said. "Mischievous persons have taunted them by saying that the Navajos and Eutaws had received large appropriations whereas the Apaches were considered as not deserving of any," Calhoun wrote. In addition, war parties of prairie Indians had driven the Jicarillas from their hunting grounds and stolen their horses. Many of their warriors were on foot, and they feared their families would be without food. Calhoun decided to call them together on March 15 and hand out provisions and presents. The Jicarillas could cut off all communications between New Mexico and the States if they chose, Greiner wrote, and they ranged through all the northern settlements. It was important that they remain at peace.[16]

On March 20, Greiner went to Pecos with Calhoun's secretary, David Whiting, and John Ward, an interpreter. Chacon, Lobo, Pablo, and San Antonio, captains of the four principal Jicarilla bands, were present with about one hundred warriors. They were pleased to see the three coming without arms or escort, as it showed confidence in them and indicated the government was well disposed toward them. They said Arapahos killed some of their people

FIGURE 58. Jicarilla Apache newlyweds, photographed in 1874
by Timothy O'Sullivan. Library of Congress.

and stole their horses, and they were unjustly imprisoned by the alcalde in Anton Chico. Greiner told them Calhoun would present their complaints to the president and gave them flour, meat, and blankets. In April Greiner learned the Jicarillas were moving to Pecos and intended to settle and make pottery and baskets to trade. Some, including Chacon, were starting to plant.

All was quiet during April, Greiner said, "a remarkable fact." Navajos complained that Laguna Pueblo was taking water they needed to irrigate, and their good crop of wheat died. "The question of right to water is one of the most difficult to settle that we meet with, especially with the Pueblos," Greiner wrote. Taos Pueblo had a school, and Greiner furnished books and promised to pay expenses for poor Indian children. He told Lea that it would help to have a mounted force at the command of the governor to enforce the agents' decisions.[17]

That month, Calhoun's son-in-law, William E. Love, returned from prospecting in Apache country. Love left Santa Fe on January 25 at the head of a sixty-man expedition to the Gila River in southwestern New Mexico, where gold had been found. After a month of digging, the prospectors learned that Mangas Coloradas and ninety Apache warriors were camped in the vicinity. Expecting an ambush, they split up and left. Some traveled on to California, some headed for the nearby copper mines, and twenty-eight returned to Santa Fe with Love. On April 24, Love reported favorably on his prospecting to the Georgia press.[18]

Determined to Ruin

By February 1852, Calhoun's political adversaries were beating their drums in Washington, DC. Weightman reported that James Collins, Alexander Reynolds, Joab Houghton, Thomas S. J. Johnson, John R. Tullis, William McGrorty, and James Quinn "do a great deal of business walking up and down the Avenue," and some of them were "doing what they can to thwart me in the performance of my duty." Referring to Collins as "Jemmy," Weightman told Alvarez, "He is very anxious to make a great man out of himself—but one could as easily make silk purse out of a sow's ear." Spruce Baird warned the Texas delegation that the faction was willing "to do all, any and everything to create any disorder, rebellion or revolution, or spread any falsehood to carry their point, and bring the present administration into disrepute." The group reminded Baird "of the cliques that used to infest the city of Austin . . . only tenfold worse; made up of worse material, and combined for fouler purposes."[19]

A February story unfairly accused Calhoun of licensing traders to buy Indian children as slaves for people in New Mexico. Weightman blamed Kephart, who repeated inaccurate and inflammatory information from a Utah newspaper that Pedro Leon, a trader Calhoun licensed on August 14, 1851, to trade with the Utes, had appeared at Manti, Utah, accompanied by about twenty Mexicans to trade horses for Indian children and firearms. He intended to supply guns and ammunition to the Navajos. There were two other companies of the same size, also carrying licenses from Calhoun. "Governor Calhoun, of New Mexico, is no better than an infamous kidnapper," editorialized the *Deseret News*. Greiner assured the Indian commissioner the report was false.[20]

Alexander Reynolds, meanwhile, wrote a memorial charging Calhoun with "corrupt interference in the election," fomenting disorder among the "mixed portion of the inhabitants, "pandering to the passions of the Mexican portion of the population and directing them against the American-born citizens," "gathering around him a corrupt Catholic Priesthood," and "protecting Mexicans in the perpetration of the murder of Americans." Collins and friends persuaded Representative John Phelps, of Missouri, to introduce the memorial in the House, and Phelps concluded that Reynolds was entitled to Weightman's seat in Congress.[21]

On March 15, 1852, Weightman took the floor to vindicate both Calhoun and the people of New Mexico. In a speech of twenty-nine printed pages that must have left him hoarse, the lawyer made his case. He desired to counter "promptly and at once, the gross charges which have been made against the honorable gentleman who is now Governor of New Mexico." Calhoun had "pursued a course calculated to make the Mexicans . . . feel that they are at least a part of this Government; that they have rights here that ought to be protected; and that the Government to which they belong was created by the people, and ought to be administered for their benefit."

He explained the "diverse and powerful influences" arrayed against the governor by describing the tumultuous history of the two political factions. Calhoun's opponents were "the legitimate successors of that old military party," but in the most recent elections Calhoun's state party prevailed in every county but one, and voters chose Weightman despite Colonel Munroe's partisan actions and the organized violence at polling places in Taos and Albuquerque. He assailed the *National Era*, the *Santa Fe Gazette*, and the *St. Louis Republican* for their "reckless and unscrupulous" statements against Calhoun. Regarding the allegations against the traders, Weightman explained that the licenses didn't authorize anyone to traffic in children. The source of the misinformation was the Santa Fe newspaper, edited by an agent of the American and Foreign Anti-Slavery Society (Kephart) "who does little else than malign the Governor, the gallant Sumner," and Weightman himself. He blasted the *St. Louis Republican* for taking up "the cudgels against Governor Calhoun" and obstructing anyone trying to balance the record.[22]

Weightman then introduced the Houghton group present in the chamber. "Here is the quartermaster, and his friends are here with him." The managers of civil and military spheres of influence were Houghton and Reynolds. As an attorney, Weightman said, in 1848 he charged Houghton with "putting other people's money in his pocket, of never paying over anything he got his fingers on, and of gross official misconduct." Calling Houghton "the fountain of justice in New Mexico," he provoked laughter on the chamber floor. He read into the record the list of charges against Houghton he made in a letter to Munroe, who did nothing. Thomas S. J. Johnson was cashiered for embezzlement, he said; he read documents from Johnson's 1845 court-martial in Florida. He said Collins was a monte dealer.[23]

Weightman quoted from a memorial sent to the president the year before by the Houghton group asking him to remove Calhoun because he protected the "Mexican" population in the murder of Skinner and Burtinett. They wrote, "We are fully convinced that there is no hope for the improvement of our Territory unless Americans rule it, and that the spirit of Mexican rule must be corrupt, ignorant, and disgraceful." Weightman informed lawmakers that of the 61,547 people in the territory, only 538 were born in the United States. The only way Americans could rule was for Congress to repeal the law organizing territorial government. The group also accused Calhoun of disenfranchising his enemies, advocating legislation unfriendly to Pueblo Indians, and creating racial hatred among the natives toward Anglo-American settlers. Collins wrote Fillmore that Calhoun was so indebted to New Mexicans that "he must protect them or fall." Drawing from his own legal experience in representing aggrieved New Mexicans against injustices inflicted by the military government, Weightman told House members about the military appointees' meddling in two churches to intimidate citizens into voting for them. The examples demonstrated the "character of the military government in New Mexico . . . upheld and maintained by the bayonets of the United States." Calhoun's administration was "supported by the people, because it in nowise resembles Munroe's."[24]

"Governor Calhoun thinks, as I do, that the people of New Mexico are capable of self-government. He thinks, as I do, that they are not the miserable, degraded, and vicious people they have been represented to be by the adherents of the immaculate military government now in this city . . . He thinks, as I do, that their right freely to exercise their religion is guaranteed as well by the treaty of Guadalupe Hidalgo as by the Constitution, and should not be infringed. . . . He thinks, as I do, that kindness and justice attract, and oppression and injustice repel . . . (T)he national character for sympathy with the oppressed will be illustrated by the administration of Governor Calhoun, in New Mexico." For himself, he held for Calhoun "the highest respect, admiration and affection; I esteem him one of the most worthy gentleman with whom it was ever my good fortune to become acquainted." On April 29, the Committee of Elections returned an adverse report on Reynolds' memorial.[25]

Newspapers all over the country carried excerpts of Weightman's speech. In Washington, the *Daily American Telegraph* wrote: "With Gov. Calhoun we were well acquainted in years gone by, and a more just, honorable, discreet and merciful man we have never known . . . Governor Calhoun was for many years regarded as one of the most intelligent, enterprising, and reliable commercial men of the South. In the vicissitudes of a few years anterior to 1840 he shared the common fate, and lost all but his chiefest treasure—an honest fame." Back in Georgia, the *Columbus Enquirer* observed: "Attempts we know have been made in New Mexico, to prejudice the government and poison the public mind against him . . . No man that knows him can or will for a moment believe, that he would use the powers of his office to effect unworthy purposes."[26]

Weightman wrote in Spanish to his friends Miguel Pino and Hilario Gonzáles that their mutual enemies "have published in various newspapers slanderous falsehoods stating that the inhabitants of New Mexico harbor hostility and ill-will toward the government and people of the United States, so much so, that it is unsafe for Americans to live among them . . . They have slandered our friend, Governor Calhoun, and myself and are saying of us that we are capable only of administering to the atrocious passions of a corrupt and brutal people." Weightman pledged to follow them step by step to "refute their slanderous falsehoods."[27]

President Fillmore sent for Weightman, handed him the twenty pages written by his opponents, and asked for a response. The letter had the effect, Weightman said, of prejudicing the president against New Mexicans as incapable of governing themselves and a danger to Americans so that a military government would appear necessary. When the president asked Weightman who he would recommend as territorial secretary, he named Alvarez, as he had before.[28] "You my dear Sir have always been my choice from the first and to the last," he wrote to Alvarez. Fillmore also asked Indian agent Edward H. Wingfield about Alvarez and Henry C. Johnson. Wingfield responded that most of the Americans living in New Mexico were "mere adventurers" who degraded the Mexican population. He said both men were qualified for the position. Alvarez had been a consul and was "a man of ability," but Johnson had stayed out of Santa Fe's dicey politics. Weightman kept Alvarez's name before the president, but Collins spouted false allegations, and so to spare his friend further "mortification," Weightman on June 16 withdrew the name. "I hope you will be pleased with the appointment of Greiner," he wrote. "I think him a nice person." So ended Alvarez's last bid for public office. He turned his attention back to business, and business was good. In addition to his store on the plaza, he served as business agent for others, joined the lucrative sheep drives to California, and rented out properties he owned on the plaza.[29]

That spring, the courts-martial of officers for profiteering took down Thomas and Reynolds. "Thomas is being tried. Reynolds will be tried," Weightman wrote.[30] Lieutenant Francis J. Thomas resigned June 30, 1852. Reynolds was accused of purchasing supplies for resale to the government and for buying three horses for himself. On October 8, 1855, the president ordered Reynolds' name dropped from the army for failure to render his accounts in a timely manner and for an unexplained deficit.[31]

Critical Condition

Greiner became acting superintendent of Indian affairs on April 1, 1852. "Do you know the responsibility I have to take with only a few months' experience in Indian affairs? There are 92,000 Indians (estimated) in this Territory. Many of them are at war. We have not 1,000 troops here under Colonel Sumner to manage them. Our troops are of no earthly account. They cannot catch a single Indian." Even though Sumner provided arms to the New Mexicans to defend themselves, the weapons were unfit for use. Many Americans were leaving, Greiner wrote. The attorney general resigned March 31. Chief Justice Grafton Baker had been gone all winter, and people lacked confidence in the other two judges. Reverend Nicholson lost most of his congregants when the army headquarters moved so he departed, and the Methodists abandoned their mission in New Mexico. "The Protestant Missionaries have a hard time in this portion of the Lord's moral Vineyard," Greiner wrote. New Mexico had just three Protestant ministers left: the Baptists' Smith and Shaw and Kephart, a Presbyterian. None spoke Spanish. Greiner hadn't met a single New Mexican who wanted to become a Protestant.[32]

Two days earlier, prefect Tomás Ortiz, clerk J. M. Giddings, US Marshall John G. Jones, and Sheriff R. M. Stephens asked Calhoun to intervene on behalf of prisoners who were starving for lack of funds to feed them. Calhoun made the humane decision to grant them a conditional pardon and ordered them to leave the Territory and not return for at least a year.[33] It must have been a distasteful decision for the former prison reformer. He decided to postpone his trip East "in consequence of physical inability."[34]

Indians raids were unrelieved, said a writer to the *St. Louis Republican* that spring, "We are in the most perfect state of misery and distress which you have ever seen." Sumner couldn't respond to attacks. "To carry out his fixed idea of economy, he has starved his horses; his men are all afoot, dragoons included, and he now finds himself and the country at the mercy of the Indians." The treasury held only enough money to feed prisoners for another day. "The merchants have all paid their licenses and taxes six months in advance; the money is expended, and nothing to pay for the support of the prisoners." Judge Baker had been gone for seven months. Major Wingfield, the Indian agent, had deserted his post. "I think there is great danger of a revolution."[35]

Wingfield, unhappily detained in Washington at Lea's request, knew of Calhoun's illness and that "he is entirely without the means essential to carry on the Government." He informed Lea that the law regulating trade and intercourse with the Indians assumed there was a "harmonious cooperation" between Indian agents and the military, but such harmony didn't exist. He wanted to return to New Mexico with the next mail.[36]

Calhoun believed the territory's situation was worse than ever. Colonel Sumner planned to withdraw troops from the settlements for a lengthy campaign against the Gila Apaches. And Calhoun had just learned from a trusted,

Comanche-speaking, Tesuque Pueblo man, Carlos Vigil, that Comanches and Mexicans were plotting to unite all the wild tribes and the New Mexicans against the Americans. The president of Mexico had sent for a Comanche chief, and a priest invited the Comanches in writing to join Mexico. Calhoun was so alarmed that he thought American women should leave. "If the Government of the United States intends doing anything for our protection, for Heaven's sake, let us know it or give us an opportunity for each one to look out for himself," he told Lea. He revealed that he had been "living at the point of death" and had to be propped up in bed to sign his name.[37]

Calhoun told Sumner on April 7 that he understood the need for a decisive strike against the Apaches, but he was more worried about the safety of citizens. "It is scarcely my privilege to speak to you of the defenses of this Territory, and that I know it to be your duty, and your duty alone." Then he leveled with Sumner: "You are perhaps advised of my weak, feeble, and almost hopeless condition, and I feel that I am speaking almost as a dying man, yet I feel desirous of doing all in my power to promote the public weal." He was unable to mount his horse to visit. "For the last four weeks I have been unable to stand alone without assistance, and for the same period have been constantly confined to my bed."[38]

Surprised by this revelation, Sumner promised to delay the Apache expedition and instead send two small columns to Gila country and Sierra Blanca and to concentrate a central force. "I regret very much to hear of your extreme illness," he wrote, and suggested that Calhoun set aside public matters until he was better. "Rest assured, Sir, that I will take such measures, that whoever expects to find me unprepared will find himself mistaken."[39] From this moment on, Calhoun's illness transformed relations between the two men from competitive rancor to a warm and solicitous friendship.

On April 8, Attorney General Henry C. Johnson informed Sumner that Calhoun "was at the point of death," and that Territorial Secretary William Allen would soon leave for the States. Although Charles Blumner agreed to be acting secretary, civil government would be essentially leaderless. Rumor had it that "insurrectionary movements" would begin with an April 11 attack on the Exchange Hotel. Sumner didn't believe that Mexico was stirring up unrest, but the constant rumors were troubling. "The Governor and I, although differing on many points, have agreed upon this, that there is nothing whatever to apprehend from the Mexicans if they are treated justly and properly."[40]

Sumner could see that New Mexico's most influential traders were doing business as usual, sending large trains East or traveling to California and leaving their families at home. "I believe that most of these stories originate with some unprincipled Americans, or if they do not create them, they distort and exaggerate them for the purpose of keeping up this excitement," Sumner wrote. "It is my deliberate opinion that there are some men in this Territory who would stick at nothing to increase the expenditures of the government." Certain merchants were known to conjure up a revolution and spread rumors only to bring back their military customers. If any difficulty arose, Sumner was prepared to assume the office of governor. "I have no desire to do this and shall never resort to it but from a sense of imperative necessity."[41]

At midnight, the night before Easter, a cry went up in Santa Fe that revolution was coming, and one man rallied the Americans. Awakened from a sound sleep, Greiner grabbed his pistols but found to his relief that there were "no Mexicans out that time of night wanting to shoot me." Calhoun believed "that evil disposed persons are hoping now to accomplish their fiendish purposes of Revolution which they have been attempting for more than twelve months past. We are not able to fight against the infamous Combination that has been so long & so stealthily at work to bathe this Territory in blood." He was relieved that Colonel Brooks quickly rallied to defend the Palace and protect Santa Fe, but still the rumors churned. Calhoun didn't believe for a moment that it was "a contest between races." He was recovering, he told Dawson, and with the return of his health, "I will strip this thing of all its mystery," he promised. Greiner wrote that "Gov. Calhoun wisely concluded he would neither die, resign, nor leave the territory until he was assured that the country was in perfect security."[42]

Calhoun told Sumner that he would appreciate some artillery because the "most imminent danger was from the savages surrounding us and who are now being excited against us by emissaries and traitorous persons." He thanked Sumner for his "commiseration" and signed off warmly, "hoping that you will make my family circle your home immediately upon your arrival here." Sumner diverted infantry then marching for Albuquerque to Santa Fe. "I have no doubt but there is some ill will towards us on the part of the Mexicans. This is perfectly natural with a conquered people but I think in this case, it has been considerably aggravated by our distrust of them," Sumner wrote. He cautioned Calhoun to not overexert himself. On April 15, Greiner issued an order directing all communications to himself because of Calhoun's condition. Calhoun asked Sumner to help law enforcement maintain peace, saying he lacked power to enforce the law and recently had to free criminals because he couldn't feed them.[43]

Sumner hurried north and found Santa Fe "in a state of anarchy," with prisoners released, general lawlessness, and "a constant dread of revolution." The colonel asked Calhoun if he wanted military aid. He did. Sumner established military police to act in concert with civil authorities, beefed up security at the Palace and on the plaza, and added infantry to the garrison. Calhoun and Sumner issued a joint proclamation, picked up by the nation's newspapers, that there would be no interruption in governance. If Calhoun had to leave before Secretary Allen returned, the military would take charge of the executive office to preserve law and order. Sumner thought that should quiet the disturbance and "crush the hopes of the intriguers." He worried about concentrating a force in Santa Fe when most of his men were widely dispersed in Indian country but felt he could do no less. Sumner returned to Albuquerque, satisfied that the schemers couldn't "force the people into an outbreak, especially when they see we are ready for them." He planned to establish a large camp in Albuquerque with four companies of dragoons and two of infantry. It annoyed him that he had thirty-four officers absent out of sixty-six and said that "it is utterly impossible for me to carry on the affairs of the department without more officers."[44]

Sheriff C. H. Merritt sent the joint proclamation to Interior Secretary Alexander H. H. Stuart and said: "We are or soon will be without a Governor, a Secretary, a Chief Justice, and two Indian agents . . . Can not the Govt. send men here who will at least live here until their successors arrive? The country is ripe for a revolution to overturn the Govt. here and they openly express their intention of putting a governor of their own upon the departure of Gov. Calhoun."[45] An unnamed writer reported the wretched state of Santa Fe to the world: "The great effort to make free American citizens of the Mexicans has exploded. The civil government is at an end, and but for the military force stationed here all would be anarchy . . . Disaffection and a determination to resist every thing American became apparent." The territorial scheme had failed and would continue to fail "until the Mexicans shall have become a more learned and civilized people." Greiner didn't disagree: "There is no use disguising the fact that many in this Territory have but little love for our people or our institutions, and they would at once throw off our Government if they had the power." Every man slept with a gun beneath his pillow. Violence was common, and there was no way to punish offenders.[46]

The same rumors circulated in Mora and Las Vegas. Major Carleton secretly sent weapons to Mora from Fort Union, but when he visited on April 30, he saw no sign of unfriendliness, much less insurrection. At Las Vegas the absence of the territorial secretary and the planned departure of Governor Calhoun alarmed the Hispanic population but only because they feared the administration of territorial affairs by the unpopular Sumner.[47]

By then, Calhoun was seriously ill. "Next week Governor Calhoun will leave for the States but I am in great doubt about his reaching there alive," Greiner wrote. "He is not able to stand alone today. I do trust he may live, for he is a man of whom this administration should be proud. No other man, I believe, could have kept this Territory from open rebellion. He will, if he lives, come back again in the fall." Calhoun's physicians, Dr. Bernard Byrne and Dr. Thomas E. Massey, strongly advised him to leave. Sumner wrote Calhoun, "I cordially reciprocate your kind feelings and trust that you will reach home in safety. I will be in Santa Fe on Wednesday night, as I wish much to see you before you leave. I would propose to you to go to Fort Union, and rest there for a few days. You will be very comfortable in my house, and it is entirely at your service."[48]

17

FINAL JOURNEY

Crowds of people from Tesuque, Santa Clara, and Nambe Pueblos saw Governor Calhoun off on May 5, 1852. "May God restore [his health] to him again and enable him to return to exercise his duties with his accustomed honesty," wrote an unnamed New Mexican. Calhoun gave Greiner $500 for contingent expenses and rolled out of Santa Fe accompanied by Judge Watts, son-in-law William Love, Attorney General Henry C. Johnson, his personal secretary David Whiting, Deputy US Marshall R. M. Stephens, and Dr. Bernard Byrne. They traveled with the train of well-known trader James Hubbel. "The governor's health was somewhat improved, though he was in quite a feeble condition, especially for such a trip," the *Santa Fe Gazette* reported. "It is hoped, however, that his health will be improved by the change and exercise. We wish them all a safe and pleasant journey." Kephart had ceased his attacks on Calhoun in print after learning he was ill and made peace with the ailing governor before he left. "We parted on excellent terms," Kephart wrote.[1]

Sumner ordered Major John Carleton to send twenty-five men to the Arkansas River and have them do everything they could to keep Calhoun comfortable. "I have advised the Governor to rest for some days at Fort Union, and have told him he had better take my house. I will thank you to do what you can for him while he is there." Carleton reported, "Gov. Calhoun arrived in a feeble state of health on the 11th. Doubtful if he is able to proceed further." They deposited the prostrate Calhoun at Sumner's newly completed log house in a row of officers' quarters. "He is a fine old gentleman," Katie Bowen wrote. "Last fall he got the scurvy and the yellow jaundice took hold of him reducing him so much that in traveling he has a bed in his ambulance and has to be lifted out and in like an infant."[2]

Calhoun had one final duty. When Carleton took command of Fort Union, he reminded Calhoun of his promise to the previous commander to remove the dram shops near the fort. Under Indian intercourse laws, it was forbidden

FIGURE 59. Captain Joseph H. Eaton sketched Fort Union in 1856.
It appeared in Davis's *El Gringo* in 1857.

to sell liquor in Indian country, and Carleton believed the civil authorities needed to act. Carleton proposed that Calhoun appoint as deputy marshal George W. Martin, "an intelligent gentleman resident at this post." Martin was one of the last Georgians remaining from Calhoun's original party. Calhoun asked another fellow Georgian, US Marshal John Jones, to proceed under Carleton's direction and arrest the liquor sellers and charge them with dispensing liquor in Indian country and purchasing and receiving stolen property.[3] Deputy Marshal Stephens arrested the men with the help of troops and burned down six houses.[4] Katie Bowen wrote:

> All the shanties and grogeries around this post kept by miserable Americans have by order of the chief of Santa Fe been burned down and the keepers put in irons and sent to that town for trial. A great deal of quartermaster and commissary property was found in the search and some gentlemen who were out on horseback when the places were set fire said that Mexican women scattered like sheep from all the places and hid in the rocks on the mountain. The Mexicans are very bitter toward Maj. Carleton for informing the Sheriff and requesting him to destroy those places.

Calhoun's last appointment, on May 21, was to commission George W. Martin as notary public.[5]

Sumner said he couldn't furnish Calhoun's party with subsistence stores but ordered Carleton to give them two wall tents, two water tanks, and a second-hand harness for eight mules. Sumner pestered Calhoun and Lea about $25,000 in Indian funds that Calhoun supposedly failed to turn over for the Navajos and Utes. He wanted to provide them with tools and fretted that he would have to use his own budget to feed visiting tribal members. Secretary William S. Allen left with $9,000 in public money, and Sumner had no money to carry on the government. Calhoun didn't have thousands in cash. Congress appropriated $36,000 for the Navajo and Ute treaties, and Calhoun had drawn and spent a portion of that amount, but more than $20,000 was still in Washington.[6]

As he convalesced at the post, Calhoun continued his downward spiral. Dr. Byrne, an assistant army surgeon, said "the probabilities are that he will die before he will be able to reach the States." Expecting Calhoun to not survive the trip, Carleton, probably in consultation with William Love, had a coffin made to be carried on the trail. Byrne didn't want to travel to the States and asked that a fellow assistant surgeon, Dr. Thomas A. McParlin, accompany Calhoun.[7] McParlin wrote to his family: "It is likely the Governor will die— but if he determines on going rather than that he should die unattended I will go some distance with him . . . It is not a duty, but a dictate of humanity" to do what he hoped someone else would do for his own father.[8]

On May 26, Calhoun resumed his journey for the States, hoping to reach home to die, wrote Katie Bowen. "His utmost endeavor is now to reach home. His only hope to meet his daughter, all the family he has . . . Mr. Love, his son-in-law, provided everything in case he should die on the plains, but we all hope to hear of his reaching Georgia.[9]

By that time Agent Abraham Woolley and five Tesuque Pueblo men caught up with the party. One purpose of the trip was to escort the Tesuque delegation (José María Vigil, Carlos Vigil, Juan Antonio Vigil, José Domingo Herrera, and José Abeyta) to meet with President Fillmore. The rest of the party turned back, but Attorney General Johnson continued on with Dr. McParlin and the soldier escort. Carleton sent a mountain howitzer with the dragoons, stating that it "adds the strength of fifty men to this party." Seven of the soldiers in the escort deserted, taking seven of the best horses, plus arms and equipment. "An expensive business," Carleton grumbled. When the party met Judge Grafton Baker on his return to New Mexico, he and the dying Calhoun chatted about conditions of governance in the territory. Along the Arkansas, they found large numbers of Comanches who were impatient for the arrival of Major Fitzpatrick and the promised gifts. This time Calhoun would have found them less frightening.[10]

On June 30, 1852, Calhoun died at Hickory Point, thirty-eight miles west of Westport. His body was placed in the coffin and on July 2 brought to Independence for burial with Masonic honors. A newspaper wrote of the Pueblo men: "The grief and lamentations of these poor fellows knew no limit, for they had learned to love the venerable old man intensely. On seeing the white men of their party fixing some pieces of crepe upon their hats, they eagerly inquired as to its use; and on being told it was the white man's mode of indicating his sorrow and showing respect for the dead, they earnestly begged for some of the strips, and at once bound them round their hats and arms."[11]

Weightman learned of his friend's death on July 3. "In him the people of New Mexico have lost a true and steadfast friend, whom they appreciated, and respected, and loved, and the country a faithful public servant. Peace be with his ashes!" Greiner didn't get word until July 31. "The melancholy intelligence of the death of Governor Calhoun reached here by this mail, and his loss is deeply felt by the citizens of New Mexico," he told Lea. To the Ohio press, Greiner wrote, "Governor Calhoun . . . worn down by the care and anxieties of his office, died on his way home to the States last summer."[12]

On July 13, 1852, the *Columbus Enquirer* outdid them all in its heartfelt obituary. Calhoun

was, in every sense of that comprehensive expression, a self made man. His patrimony was an orphanage of poverty, and his youth encumbered with every disadvantage . . . It was the peculiar good fortune of Gov. Calhoun to retain the confidence, esteem and friendship of his fellow citizens in every condition and amidst every vicissitude of his life. Candid, honorable, generous and charitable in all his dealings with men, the hour of adversity [spurned] the friends of prosperity but gathering the closer and standing the firmer by him. Raised in the humbler walks of life, when fortune smiled upon him the necessities and sufferings of the poor aroused his sympathies . . . From the door of his hospitable mansion, no helpless widow, no orphan child crying for bread ever turned away unaided. The young man of merit and industry found in him a friend and benefactor; the more advanced in life looked to him for counsel and help in the trying [moments] of their earthly struggles . . . Honor to the name and peace to the spirit of our departed friend.

The Great Father

From the beginning of his service as agent, Calhoun had wanted to take a group of Pueblo people to the United States, and Pueblo leaders had long sought an opportunity to talk directly to the Great Father in Washington. The five Tesuque Pueblo men, Love, and Whiting continued their journey. Carlos Vigil had been an emissary for Calhoun on several occasions, and his brother Juan Antonio had also represented the governor. "It was Governor Calhoun's wish that in case he should die they should be carried on," Whiting wrote Lea on July 5, 1852, but Whiting didn't have enough money to get them to Washington. Calhoun thought the visit was critical to strengthen Indian policy and "to secure more their confidence and esteem towards our people. Evil disposed Mexicans and others have been tampering with them and endeavouring to induce them to join in a scheme for the purpose of overthrowing the present government. If these Indians are turned back, the consequences will be injurious to the Government and the Territory alike." Whiting was still waiting for an answer two weeks later.[13]

Calhoun's loyal secretary went on ahead to St. Louis. Love and the rest of the party, including Johnson, spent the Fourth of July in Kansas City. The Pueblo men boarded a steamer with Love and arrived in St. Louis on July 13. There they were taken to the theater and so enjoyed the performance that they threw a pair of decorated moccasins to the actress. The Pueblos, wrote a reporter, "make a very respectable appearance, speak the Spanish fluently, and some of the present party can read and write that language correctly. They were surprised to see a steamboat and how easily it maneuvered, turning 'like a waltz,' they said. One man said he 'believed God almighty lived here and that he did not know New Mexico and Pueblo at all.'"[14]

They arrived in Washington on July 31 and checked into Maher's Hotel where they would spend six weeks. On August 5 they entered the East Room of the White House, marveling at its size and elegant furnishings, and met President Fillmore and Secretary of the Interior Alexander Stuart, shaking hands with both. With Whiting translating their Spanish, José María spoke first. He had traveled far to see the country and people of the United States, and what he saw astonished him. He lived in a poor country, he said, and his people suffered a great deal of trouble, but he looked upon the president as his Great Father. He and his people wished to live in peace. His New Mexican neighbors had taken several animals, and he wanted them restored. The New Mexicans cut more acequias (irrigation ditches) than they had agreed to and took too much water. He wanted the government to fulfill its treaty commitments. He would like to take home some tools and agricultural implements and some church ornaments. The president said this was the first time he'd met a Pueblo Indian. He was sorry there were bad men in their country, he said, but he had appointed Governor Lane to enforce the laws. Fillmore was gracious but cautiously referred problems to others and made no promises. They shook hands again and left. Whiting wrote that day that Calhoun's object in bringing the Pueblo men to Washington was to see the 1850 treaty fulfilled. "He has repeatedly informed the Department of the difficulties arising daily with said Indians on account of the nonfulfillment of said treaty, and the evident dissatisfaction which was spreading among them . . . As Governor Calhoun had received no answer to the various remonstrances and petitions made by him to the Government, he determined to bring, as many as he conveniently could, to this city." Love and Whiting next took the Pueblo men to the capitol. A newspaper reported, "José María is really a pleasant speaker, the Spanish sounding very softly and smoothly as it flowed from his lips." That evening, Weightman entertained the group at his home. The next day they saw the Navy Yard, the Smithsonian, and the Patent Office.[15]

On September 6 they met with Indian Commissioner Luke Lea, who gave each man a silver medal emblazoned with a portrait of President Fillmore, plus a set of clothing. The Pueblo men were wearing buckskin; the upper portion was painted yellow with yellow fringe and ornamented with bands of white and blue beads. Their woven hats still bore the black bands of mourning. "You have now become citizens of the American government, and I should be glad if you would adapt yourselves hereafter to the habits and customs of the whites, with whom you are associated," Lea said. José María Vigil said they would like to dress like the Americans, but they live in a poor country and the clothing would cost too much. The commissioner said he would also like them and their children to learn English. Whiting told a reporter the Pueblos elect a governor every year and have a council. They treat their women better than other Indians and were affectionate and sincere in their friendships. They could read and write in Spanish. The city's churches gave them many ornaments and promised more.[16]

Whiting carried with him a Tewa word list described as a "Pueblo of Tesuque vocabulary" that was presented to Henry Rowe Schoolcraft and subsequently published in his multivolume work on Indian tribes of the United States. The delegation left Washington on September 9. Whiting went to Philadelphia to get his family and rejoined the delegation in Westport, Missouri, during the third week of October. At Westport Love received $1,200 to buy an outfit for the party to cross the Plains and bought five brood mares for the men. Whiting and Michael Steck took charge of the party for the remainder of the journey. They left Westport on October 24. Love returned to Washington around November 1. Whiting, his family, and the Pueblo delegation arrived in Santa Fe late in the evening on December 7, 1852.[17]

The Understudy

Three days after Calhoun departed Santa Fe, Sumner began to seize control. He informed Secretary of State Daniel Webster that because civil government was without a head and "some designing Mexicans" were planning to overthrow the government, he felt it his duty—and Calhoun concurred—to assume the responsibilities of executive office. There were no funds to support civil government, and he was using army rations to feed prisoners. On May 25, Judge Mower wrote Weightman that the situation was critical because of the secretary's absence, the expected news of Calhoun's death, "and the assumption of the civil power by the military commander," but he saw no revolution brewing, and the pueblos were peaceful.[18]

Sumner wrote Secretary of War Conrad that civil government couldn't be sustained in New Mexico without a military force. "All the branches of this civil government have equally failed—the executive, for want of power, the judiciary, from the total incapacity and want of principle in the judges; and the legislative, from the want of knowledge—want of identity with our institutions, and an extreme reluctance to impose taxes."[19] Only in Sumner's mind was this true. In fact, the executive had functioned as well as it could without direction and funding from Washington. The legislature had produced a respectable body of laws, all the more remarkable because many of the legislators had no previous experience in American democratic institutions. The judges had delivered a level of learned and impartial decision making previously unavailable to citizens.

Greiner carried on as acting superintendent. Despite the absence of the governor, secretary, chief justice, attorney general, and a district judge, "we wouldn't miss anybody but the Governor much," he wrote. "He is a glorious old fellow and I only wish he may live and be able to attend to business at Washington." Two agents short, Greiner labored to keep up. In one month, he rode nearly six hundred miles—on some days, sixty-five to seventy-five miles. Like Calhoun, he was "without an inkling of advice from the Department on matters of vital importance, with no law to govern and no rule to guide—with wild Indians to rule and wilder ones to conciliate." The Pueblos routinely brought their problems to the agent and had to be fed and housed, as did groups of Navajos and Jicarillas. The Comanche conspiracy had amounted to nothing. "Not a single depredation has been committed by any of the Indians in New Mexico for three months." The oldest citizens couldn't recall that happening before.[20]

Soon after Calhoun left, the Mescaleros asked for peace, and after Greiner sent runners to their country, thirty leaders came in for a grand council at the end of June. Sumner and Greiner soon tangled because Sumner considered himself acting governor *and* Indian superintendent. "When Gov. Calhoun left for the States, it was with the understanding that Col. Sumner was not to interfere with the business of the Indian Department," Greiner told the commissioner. Greiner objected strongly. Sumner insisted. Greiner acquiesced, in the event Sumner was right. It helped that Sumner was providing bread, meat, and sugar to the Apaches. On July 1, they signed a treaty much like those with the Navajos and Utes. The Mescaleros reluctantly agreed to keep peace with Mexico. Greiner gave them coarse flour to keep them from starving until their corn was ripe and provided hatchets, tobacco, vermillion, shirts, and knives. For a change, Sumner approved of the gifts. Sumner then took the treaty with him to his office, "claiming to be the principal person by whom the treaty was to be made." He offered to instruct Overman, special Indian agent at the copper mines, in his duties, and Greiner again objected.[21]

The Gila Apaches led by Mangas Coloradas were afraid to visit Santa Fe, Greiner learned, but they would visit Acoma Pueblo on July 11 to make a treaty. Greiner planned to be there with agents Baird and Overman. When he asked Sumner for troops, the colonel said he would go himself to treat with the Apaches "in conjunction (if he chooses to accompany me) with the senior Indian agent" and "take such military force as I may deem necessary." Greiner and Baird responded that "the agents appointed by the president of the United States for the Indians in New Mexico will 'choose' (as suggested) to accompany Col. Sumner to treat with the Apaches at Acoma. No unwarrantable assumption of arbitrary power on the part of a military commander will for a moment cause them to swerve from their official duties." They also protested Sumner's assumption of power.[22]

Mangas Coloradas was pleased to meet the colonel, saying, "You are chief of the white men. I am chief of the red men. Now let us have a talk and treat." Greiner described the Apache leader as "a magnificent looking Indian" who was "undoubtedly the master spirit of his tribe." In his journal, Greiner wrote: "Made treaty with Mangas Coloradas yesterday Apaches wild as hawks, afraid to come in. Mangas is however their chief capt and councilor and can speak for all his people, he promises fair for them." Waiting for Greiner to return were more Apaches wanting to make peace. He learned there were five bands of Mescaleros: the Llaneros, Norteños, Agua Nuevas, Paseños, and Mescaleros. Their captains were Bigotes, Francisco, Mateo, Santos, and Hueltas. On July 16 he signed a treaty with these groups, gave them presents, and then rode with them for a distance. On July 31, Greiner wrote Lea, "We are now at peace with the Indians of New Mexico."[23]

Before negotiating with the Apaches, word reached Greiner that the president would appoint him secretary of state. He wasn't inclined to accept. "I prefer the Indian Department as I have the hang of the ropes and know what I am about, and have given general satisfaction to everybody," he wrote. That summer, Greiner had ridden hundreds of miles, from the Arkansas River to the Gila and Acoma to Anton Chico, and visited all the tribes and found them all at peace. But Greiner missed his wife and children. On August 30, the day he took his oath of office, he wrote, "I regret exceedingly that the Appointment of Secretary severs my connection with the Indian Department, but the complimentary manner in which this new post has been given me by the President does not give me the liberty to decline it."[24]

Love and Whiting planned to remove Calhoun's body, after sufficient decomposition, for burial alongside his wife and daughter, but he was instead buried in the old cemetery of the town of Kansas. On January 10, 1853, the New Mexico Legislature adopted a resolution expressing regret at Calhoun's death, appropriated $300 for a marble slab to be erected at his tomb, and directed legislators to "wear the accustomed badge of mourning for thirty days in honor of his memory." The mayor of Columbus, Georgia, recommended to the council in 1859 that Calhoun's remains be brought to Columbus "and interred with suitable testimonials of respect."[25] Kansas City continued to be his resting place.

In the 1870s Calhoun's remains were moved to the north end of Union Cemetery. W. L. Campbell, vice president of the Missouri Historical Society, visited Santa Fe in 1906 and said Calhoun was buried in a pauper's grave. When the body reached Kansas City it was badly decomposed, and the steamboat company refused to receive it for further transportation, so it was buried in the cholera cemetery. When this cemetery was transformed into Shelley Park,

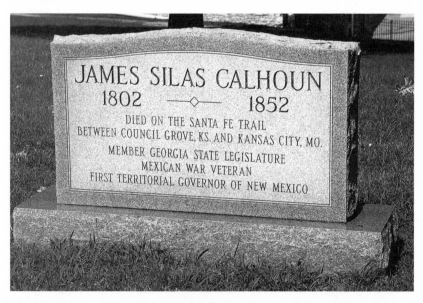

FIGURE 60 Calhoun's final resting place is in the far north end of Union Cemetery in Kansas City. The headstone incorrectly lists his birth year as 1802 instead of 1799. Sherry Robinson photo.

friends and relatives removed many bodies, but others, including Calhoun's, were removed to the pauper cemetery. However, L. Bradford Prince, governor from 1889 to 1892 and a founder of the Historical Society of New Mexico, wrote on the article "not true."[26]

Thanks to Ralph E. Twitchell, vice president of the historical society, we have an image of Calhoun. In 1911 he completed collecting portraits of all the governors since Calhoun when he secured a copy of the miniature of Calhoun and a photo of Governor Marsh Giddings. He donated the portraits to the Museum of New Mexico, along with a copy of *The Official Correspondence of James S. Calhoun*, edited by Dr. Annie Heloise Abel, professor of American history at Goucher College and an authority on Indian affairs. When the US Office of Indian Affairs published the book in 1915, the *Albuquerque Journal* described the period from 1849 to 1852 as "turbulent years in the history of New Mexico," and said "the graphic recital of Indian depredations, cruelties and troubles throws a lurid light on conditions in the then territory."[27] In 1994, historian Mary Jean Cook, of Santa Fe, raised enough money for a gravestone.[28]

Looking Back

As an officer of the occupying military during the Mexican War, Calhoun never missed an opportunity to chat up local Mexican men he considered intelligent and gentlemanly. He wanted to know their thoughts on the war and on their own leadership. He was not only better informed than his peers but often made friends in the process. He worried about the treatment of women who might have extended some kindness to the Americans, and he brought home a Mexican boy whom he would have raised and educated had the boy lived. A few years earlier in Cuba, Calhoun had so impressed Americans and Cubans during his short stint as consul that they passed a petition extolling his skills in settling differences. Earlier still, citizens in Columbus drafted him twice to serve as mayor, and he willingly served even though his many business entities were floundering in an economic crash. And we can't forget that Calhoun depleted his own fortune so that no one else would suffer when his bank failed. The people who knew him counted on that commitment. That's extraordinary. For all his adult life in Georgia, Calhoun was well liked and respected, as a Whig, a public servant, and a businessman.

In assessing Calhoun in New Mexico, it's as important to consider who he was as what he did. The man who rode into New Mexico in July 1849 wasn't the usual political appointee. He was an honest, energetic man eager for a new challenge. He had a knack for winning friends and a steely sense of right and wrong. He soon understood that President Zachary Taylor's statehood mission for New Mexico pitched him headlong into a political maelstrom that made Georgia's political duels and fistfights look benign. His chosen faction enjoyed the support of most New Mexicans, but the opposition had leverage with the military government and lost no sleep over scruples. As agent and governor, Calhoun would quarrel with two military commanders. Someone reading his letters for the first time might conclude that he was paranoid, but the military and his political enemies were, in fact, doing all they could to undermine him. Subsequent governors faced the same problems and some of the same antagonists.

"Calhoun must be numbered among the relatively few Americans who, in the public service of their country, met oppressive challenge with surprising capacities of wisdom, courage and integrity," wrote historian Frank McNitt. "His appearance in the Southwest coincided with a period of most virulent eruptions and sorest need . . . Calhoun's arrival was fortuitously happy; it was a man of his patient enduring fiber that this rough new territory demanded. Let him be numbered also among those men in public life whose services have been generally misunderstood or gone unrecognized."[29]

In the years after the American occupation, New Mexicans were expected to pivot away from more than two centuries as part of Mexico and pledge their allegiance to the United States, to them a foreign power. The military governors, with their arbitrary appointments of self-serving Americans to positions of power, sowed years of dissatisfaction. As Sister Mary Loyola wrote, "The history of the first years of American control of this former Mexican outpost are not of a nature to flatter the American sense of superiority."[30] It was the trusted leader Manuel Alvarez, in league with newcomers like Richard Weightman and Calhoun, who persuaded New Mexicans that they had a stake in the new government. In his inaugural address, Calhoun called upon every man "to take an active part in attaining the glorious objects to which, I trust, we justly aspire." Both Calhoun and Weightman worked hard to assure US citizenship, even to those who initially chose to be Mexican citizens. Calhoun understood his role; he promised in his inaugural address to discharge his duties so that in the transition from a military government "to one dependent upon your own wisdom . . . there may be no discordant jarrings." He would "observe, in all things, a proper moderation."

With personal persuasion and much hard work, Calhoun could count some accomplishments when he left New Mexico nearly on his death bed. As Indian agent, he signed treaties with Navajos, Utes, Eastern Apaches, and Pueblos. Agent John Greiner reported that New Mexico was at peace for the first time residents could remember, although the peace didn't last. Calhoun spent a great deal of time hearing out the Pueblos, tried to disabuse Washington officials of their misconceptions, and managed to take some Pueblo representatives to Washington, even though he couldn't complete the journey himself. He treated Apaches and Comanches fairly in negotiations. He restored a number of captives. As governor, he guided the first two legislative sessions in creating a fair judiciary and practical, equitable laws. On his watch, there were no further rebellions. One of Calhoun's first actions as Indian agent was to establish a rapport with Taos Pueblo, which helped birth the 1847 uprising, and he befriend the influential Padre Martínez. Agent John Greiner wrote, "No other man, I believe, could have kept this Territory from open rebellion."

His overarching contribution was his conviction that New Mexicans were capable of governing themselves and becoming good American citizens. He believed this so deeply that he was offended when anyone suggested otherwise. He appointed dozens of New Mexicans to public office. Predictably the appointments provoked loud complaints from his political enemies. Weightman argued on the House floor: "Governor Calhoun thinks, as I do, that the people of New Mexico are capable of self-government. He thinks, as I do, that they are not the miserable, degraded, and vicious people they have been represented to be by the adherents of the immaculate military government now in this city." However, the sentiments espoused by Kephart, Collins, and their crowd, intended to keep federal dollars flowing through the army to New Mexico, lingered in public memory and the press. That and the continued prejudice against New Mexico's Hispanic and Native American people kept statehood out of reach for more than six decades. It would take generations of Alvarezes, Weightmans, and Calhouns and fourteen more presidents to achieve statehood in 1912.

EPILOGUE

William Carr Lane, a physician and nine-time mayor of St. Louis, was Calhoun's successor. Lane was seriously ill when he reached Fort Union in August 1852. Carleton met him at Point of Rocks and hurried the new governor's arrival by a forced march so that he could receive medical attention. Lane relayed a message to Sumner that he was "anxious to come on and relieve you from all duties in relation to the civil government." He would soon learn that Sumner wasn't anxious to be relieved. When Lane reached Santa Fe on September 9, he found Sumner living in the Palace of the Governors. Sumner left Santa Fe and returned to Albuquerque, removing the American flag, which had flown in front of the Palace since Kearny had it raised. Lane asked Colonel Brooks to hoist the flag when the legislature met, and Sumner removed both Brooks and the flag. "Col. Sumner was a little chagrined that he did not receive the appointment of Governor, and finding it given to another he has thrown every obstacle in the way of pacifying and making smooth affairs in Santa Fe," reported a Missouri newspaper.[1]

Lane removed the sixty-eight-year-old agent Abraham Woolley. Edward Wingfield, Calhoun's emissary to Washington, finally returned on October 26, 1852, and three days later, Lane assigned him to Fort Webster, replacing Charles Overman. After seven months on the job, Wingfield was so dissatisfied that he informed Lane, "I can't think of holding office longer than the 30th of December." The job was draining. Resources were so meager that it appeared New Mexico was a "cancer on the body politic," he wrote. If the Apaches were treated kindly and provided food, there would be peace. Without rations, "hostilities will commence." Wingfield met with Mangas Coloradas and described the Apaches as proud, well mannered, and civilized. Although they were accused of robbing the Mexicans, the agent said he could describe a hundred examples of their good character and ability to determine right from wrong.

Wingfield returned to Greensboro, Georgia, became a judge, and participated in Democratic politics. He died in 1892.[2]

Lane visited six of New Mexico's nine counties before he addressed the legislature. The territory, he said in December 1852, "is over-run with Red and White thieves and robbers." Agriculture and stock raising were depressed, mines were nearly abandoned, and roads were in poor condition. Tax revenues were inadequate to provide basic services. A schoolmaster "is rarely seen amongst you." He objected to the use of two languages to conduct business. On the other hand, he said, "Your country is one of the very healthiest on the globe," and with irrigation, it had potential. He applauded the dignified manners and family life of native New Mexicans, and he encouraged them to continue using their "beautiful language" in daily matters.

Sumner, in contrast, recommended that the government return New Mexico to New Mexicans and Indians. He saw no future for the territory, and the cost of its defense, more than $3 million a year, was a burden on taxpayers, he wrote to Secretary of War Conrad in May. "The truth is, the only resource of this country is the government money. All classes depend upon it, from the professional man and trader down to the beggar." Conrad argued in December that "the struggle between the two races is destined, in all probability, to continue there long after it has ceased in every portion of the continent." The annual cost of maintaining a large military force to protect New Mexico equaled half the total value of real estate. Conrad famously proposed to reimburse residents and abandon the territory, "which seems hardly fit for inhabitation of the civilized."[3]

In the House, Weightman denounced the remarks as an "atrocious libel" and asked why lawmakers listened to the pronouncements of military officers and not the late governor. "I know he entertained the most kindly feelings toward the people and favorable opinions of their capacity and aptitude in appreciating the spirit and principles of our government." Weightman assailed Sumner for seizing control of civil government, saying the judges, Indian agents, and Sumner himself understood that he was to provide aid and support but not usurp executive, legislative, and judicial functions. Weightman characterized Sumner as gallant but stupid.[4]

Lane too crossed swords with Sumner, most notably over the possession of Mesilla, on New Mexico's southern boundary. Calhoun heard from Mesilla citizens that the US Boundary Commission misplaced the territory's southern border and reported the fact to his superiors.[5] Lane, on his own authority, declared jurisdiction over the Mesilla Valley on March 13, 1853, and ordered Sumner to take possession. Sumner refused. Mexican authorities learned of the plan and sent troops to occupy it before Lane could arrive. The president recalled Lane and replaced him with David Meriwether in August 1853.

Sumner was relieved of command and left Santa Fe on June 26, 1853. He went East and became a colonel in the First Cavalry. Sumner's successor, Brigadier General John Garland, wrote that Sumner "has left the Department in an impoverished and crippled condition." In his economizing, Sumner lost "a vast number of horses and mules," and his supplies, ordnance, and graineries were exhausted. Dragoons were mounted on country ponies instead of dragoon horses.[6]

Back and Forth

John Greiner turned over his responsibilities as Indian superintendent on September 30, 1852, and embraced his appointment as territorial secretary with his customary enthusiasm. He had the Palace and its attached structures cleaned, the first such overhaul under American rule. "In the course of two or three years we hope these antiquated models of a palace will give place to more modern structures better befitting the age and country," Kephart wrote in 1853.[7] The Palace, restored and stabilized over the years, is the longest continually used government building in the nation.

One of the secretary's duties was disbursing territorial funds and paying legislators, "and yet I have not a single dollar to do it with because my predecessor carried away with him to the States all the money," Greiner wrote. He had used his private credit and borrowed money to pay claims of the treasury. Kephart, at the Santa Fe Gazette, praised Greiner as an honest and faithful public servant and hoped he would return with his family. Greiner would spend the rest of his life in both New Mexico and Ohio, but he never returned with his family. In 1853 he acquired the Ortiz mine south of Santa Fe from the widow of the man who'd owned it since 1833 and sold it in 1854 to a group of investors led by Governor Abraham Rencher.[8]

In June 1861 Greiner was appointed the first US Receiver and Depositor (financial agent) for the Territory of New Mexico. He had a vault of native stone built in the Palace that drew praise, and he was generally considered honest and capable. He invested in the Kansas, New Mexico, Arizona, and California Railroad and Telegraph Company; its members were all prominent New Mexico officials and businesspeople.[9] In 1866 he turned over the receiver's office to James L. Collins and left on an expedition to gold fields near the headwaters of the Gila River.[10] Greiner's wife died while he was in New Mexico, and he returned to Ohio, settling in Zanesville as editor of the *City Times*. He joined the Republican Party, again championed temperance, and remarried. In January 1870, he moved to Columbus as editor of the *Columbus Gazette* and died on May 13, 1871.[11]

Calhoun's secretary David Whiting became Santa Fe's postmaster in 1854, translator for the newly established office of the Surveyor General, chief clerk of the New Mexico House of Representatives in 1855, and chief clerk of the Land Office in 1858. He was a charter member of the Historical Society of New Mexico at its founding in December 1859. Whiting left New Mexico in 1862 and involved himself in a variety of businesses in Kansas and later in Mexico. He died in Chicago in 1888.[12]

Fallen Heroes

Richard Weightman completed his term in Congress in March 1853 and was back in New Mexico by summer. He and Francis J. Thomas exchanged heated words at a public house; Thomas by then had been booted from the army. Thomas published a card insulting Weightman. Weightman struck Thomas. Thomas next sent a challenge, which Weightman refused to receive, and so the expected duel never occurred. Another story was that after an angry exchange, Weightman "used his cane over Thomas's head as long as it lasted, then picked up the pieces and would have used them, had the Sheriff not interfered and demanded order."[13]

Public discussion was then riveted on a railroad and its possible routes. Congress in 1853 funded expeditions to explore routes, and there were two that crossed New Mexico Territory—one from St. Louis through Albuquerque to San Francisco and another from El Paso through southern New Mexico to San Diego. Most movers and shakers hoped for the central route through Albuquerque, but Weightman championed the southern route, which doomed his chances for reelection.[14]

Former governor Lane ran for Congress, but New Mexicans wanted to send one of their own to Washington and nominated José Manuel Gallegos, the Albuquerque priest defrocked by Archbishop Lamy for refusing to give up his mistress or his business interests. Weightman was reportedly behind the nomination. While Lane was a Whig and Gallegos a Democrat, the election was really a referendum on Archbishop Lamy's church reforms. Gallegos represented traditional New Mexicans, and Lane drew support from the old Houghton crowd and other Americans. In the election on September 5, 1853, Gallegos won narrowly. Democrats also prevailed in the legislature and in the city and county of Santa Fe. Weightman declared it a "signal overthrow of the whig clique at Santa Fe." Gallegos went to Congress, but because he couldn't speak English his effectiveness was limited. Calhoun's old friend, Senator Alexander Stephens of Georgia, read a statement from Gallegos expressing his disappointment with his treatment in Congress.[15]

Weightman in 1853 finally acquired a press and realized his long ambition of becoming a newspaperman by publishing *El Amigo del Pais* in Albuquerque. It "bears evidence of considerable ability," wrote the *Daily Pennsylvanian*. Said Weightman: "The people of New Mexico are not properly known and understood by the people of the United States. Either ignorantly or mischievously, the people of New Mexico have been represented as wanting in capacity—unfit for self-government, ignorant, immoral and vicious" and the repetition of these lies had made an impression. *El Amigo del Pais*, a Democratic newspaper, would refute such disinformation.[16] The newspaper didn't thrive in Albuquerque, so Weightman moved it to Santa Fe, where James Collins made him a target of the *Gazette*.[17]

In late 1853, Weightman wrote about Francis X. Aubry's trip to California by the Albuquerque route. A trader, Aubry was legendary for setting and breaking speed records in journeys across the Santa Fe Trail. Aubry "reports the route practicable for a railroad, without other obstacles than Indians," wrote Weightman. "All hail! The Albuquerque Route!" When Aubry returned from a trip, the two met and discussed the route. Aubry gave his notes to Weightman and told him to make use of them. Weightman printed the journal and praised Aubry for his "enterprise and Public Spirit," but while Aubry was away on a second trip to California, Weightman withdrew his praise and suggested Aubry had deceived him. Aubry was livid.[18]

The trader arrived in Santa Fe on the afternoon of August 18, 1854, and went to the Mercure brothers' store and cantina on the south side of the plaza for a drink. Weightman stopped by, shook hands with Aubry, and sat on the counter while they talked. Aubry asked Weightman about the newspaper, which had stopped publishing, and Weightman said it died a natural death—it lacked subscribers. Aubry said he was glad because the stories about his trip to California were lies. "Last fall you asked me for information about my trip, which I gave you, and you afterwards abused me," Aubry said. Weightman denied it. Aubry slammed his fist on the counter and said, "I say it is so." Weightman stood, picked up a tumbler of water and liquor, and threw it in Aubry's face. Stepping back, he put his hand on his belt. Aubry reached for his Colt Belt Pistol, a five-shooter he carried on his left side. As he pulled it out, the pistol prematurely discharged into the ceiling. Weightman drew his bowie knife and stabbed Aubry in the abdomen. Henri Mercure jumped over the counter and grabbed Weightman while Joseph Mercure seized Aubry, but it was too late. Weightman's knife was covered with blood. Aubry collapsed into the arms of Henry Cuniffe, saying, "Let me bleed." He died ten minutes later.[19]

Weightman immediately surrendered to the marshal and was held on $2,000 bail. "Much censure is attached to each party by their respective friends. It is said that no one regrets it more than Weightman," reported a Boston newspaper. At the trial on September 20 and 21, 1854, in the US District Court in Santa Fe, Weightman was defended by his friend Spruce Baird and former judge John Watts. Although public sentiment tilted toward Aubry, the facts mandated acquittal. The many friends of each man knew both could be hotheaded. "A hero was killed, by another hero," wrote Aubry's biographer, Donald Chaput. Max Greene, who knew both men, wrote in the *New York Times* that Weightman had an "amiable wife, beautiful children, and many friends—is talented, a scholar and in his bearing a finished gentleman. But the ardent Southern blood in his veins, and living in a land of bowie knives, have made him quick to resent the shadow of an affront." Greene called Aubry "a man of forecast and alacrity . . . No one attempted competition with him. Danger could not appall him, unexplored districts were to him as familiar paths."[20]

Heavy-hearted, Weightman left Santa Fe a week after the trial, on October 1, and arrived in St. Louis on October 22. He opened a law practice. In 1859 he moved his wife Susan and their six children to the burgeoning, five-year-old town of Atchison, Kansas, where he again entered public life and Democratic Party politics, getting elected as city recorder and justice of the peace.[21] The following year, he was a founding director of the Atchison, Topeka, and Santa Fe Railroad, along with a Topeka newspaper editor named E. G. Ross, who would become a New Mexico governor.[22]

When the Civil War erupted, Weightman went to Independence and was elected colonel of a cavalry regiment of the Confederate Missouri State Guard. One member of Weightman's command was Thomas B. Catron, who would become New Mexico's largest landholder. Weightman died bravely in battle on August 10, 1861. General Sterling Price wrote: "Among those who fell mortally wounded upon the battle field, none deserve a dearer place in the memory of Missourians than Richard Hanson Weightman . . . He had already done distinguished service at Rock Creek . . . and at Carthage, where he won unfading laurels by the display of extraordinary coolness, courage, and skill. He fell at the head of his brigade, wounded in three places, and died just as the victorious shouts of our army began to rise upon the air." Weightman was forty-five.[23]

Had he lived, the frustrated publisher would have been proud that his son, Richard Coxe Weightman, succeeded in the newspaper business. The younger Weightman "became one of the most brilliant editorial writers in America" at the *Washington Post* and the *New York Sun*, reported the Atchison newspaper after Dick Weightman died in 1914. Local friends recalled, "The family was wretchedly poor in Atchison, but aristocratic, and held their heads high."[24]

Manuel Alvarez, although saddened by Calhoun's death, introduced Governor Lane to prominent Hispanic men and translated his inaugural speech. He paid to have 2,000 ballots printed for Rio Arriba, Santa Fe, and San Miguel county elections. His business flourished. Trusted and well known, he acted as legal representative for individuals and firms, and he participated in sheep drives to California by raising capital and acquiring sheep. He became a major landowner in Santa Fe, acquired properties on the plaza, and earned steady revenue from rents. He served on the Public Building Commission in 1853 and the Santa Fe County Board of Education in 1855. Alvarez died in Santa Fe on July 5, 1856, after a short illness, retaining the respect even of his adversaries until the end. He was sixty-two. He was interred in Santa Fe's Parroquia, which Lamy was transforming into a cathedral. The *St. Louis Republican* reported that he was "warmly attached to the institutions of his adopted country, was highly esteemed for his intelligence and integrity of character, as well as for his social qualities; he was a warm, a devoted friend."[25]

The Gazette

Newspapering ended abruptly for the man Weightman disparagingly called "Padre Kephart." By 1853 Kephart's share of the *Gazette*'s expenses reached $6,500. The Missionary Association refused to pay it and closed its Santa Fe mission. Kephart left Santa Fe with the mail in February 1853.[26] James L. Collins wasn't making money on the *Gazette*, but it was still politically worthwhile for him to control the territory's only press, and he found new partners in merchant Henry Connelly, who would be governor in 1861, and Charles P. Clever, who would be attorney general in 1862.[27]

In 1855 Collins was back in Washington, this time to demand Governor David Meriwether's removal. Collins wanted to be superintendent of Indian affairs and used the *Gazette* to criticize Meriwether's handling of Indian matters. President Buchanan appointed Collins to the post in 1857, even though Territorial Secretary William Davis, acting governor after Meriwether departed, wrote a long letter to Buchanan listing the reasons Collins was unsuited for the job.[28]

Collins was as unscrupulous as Davis predicted. Samuel M. Yost arrived on June 22, 1857, to be agent for the Navajos, Zunis, and Hopis, but in November he became editor of the *Gazette*, presumably on the government's dime. On August 10, 1858, Yost became agent to the Navajos, but that fall he was acting superintendent while Collins was in Washington. After Yost resigned in late 1859, John T. Russell, a former newspaper editor and former Indian agent removed by Lincoln, was appointed. In 1860 and 1861, the Navajos were still without an agent, and Russell, while collecting a salary as agent, worked in Santa Fe editing the superintendent's newspaper. When Connelly called for a war of extermination against the Navajos, Collins editorialized for a harsh policy toward the Navajos. While the tribe was at war that year, the *Gazette* distorted an already serious situation and exaggerated losses to Navajo raids. Chief Justice Kirby Benedict in 1861 wrote that Russell "is against the President, the North, the Government, and the Union. The paper's influence is pernicious."[29]

These conflicts of interest were dutifully reported by Collins' former employee and rival editor, Hezekiah S. Johnson, who blamed Collins for Navajo depredations resulting from "his willful neglect of his official duties." Johnson and his *Rio Abajo Weekly Press* gave Collins a taste of his own medicine. Johnson had followed his brother Henry to New Mexico in 1849; Henry, as a friend of Calhoun's, was regularly flogged in the *Gazette*. Hezekiah hired on at the *Gazette* in 1853 and rose from apprentice printer to editor. In 1863 he moved to Albuquerque and started the *Weekly Press*. The feisty Johnson wrote that Collins "holds as personal enemies those who differ with him on public affairs and if he, or any of his factional associates, think to terrorize us, they can apportion the work among them."[30]

A political chameleon, Collins was a Whig under Fillmore, a Democrat under Pierce and Buchanan, and a Unionist under Lincoln, wrote Samuel B. Watrous, an influential merchant in northern New Mexico who sent regular reports to the *Missouri Democrat* in St. Louis.[31] In a commentary that could have been written by Weightman or Calhoun, Watrous wrote: "Our public officers are leagued together to advance their own private interests, and they sustain a press to deceive the people, which is a very easy matter, since there is no other channel through which their false statements can be contradicted." He called the combination led by Collins an unholy alliance foisted on them by President Buchanan. "The *Gazette* does not express the sentiments of the people but simply those of the corrupt clique of which it is the mouthpiece."[32]

Collins hoped to be reappointed superintendent of Indian Affairs, but Washington favored Dr. Michael Steck. When Collins attempted to hold a public meeting to discuss the superintendency, the *Daily Press* skewered the idea, saying "the President did right in rotating him out." Collins was removed from office in May 1863 after the New Mexico House of Representatives investigated his conduct.[33] In September 1866, Collins, then sixty-five, withdrew from the *Gazette*.[34] He found himself another federal appointment, following Greiner into the job as US Receiver and Depositor in June 1866. A year later, during a robbery at the depository, Collins took a bullet to the heart.[35]

Joab Houghton practiced law after losing his judgeship. He drew the original plans for the territorial capitol, and Congress made its first appropriations in 1850. He supervised its construction as well as the building of a new penitentiary. When William Messervy became acting governor with the sudden departure of Lane, he named Houghton superintendent of public buildings. Houghton tried to milk the position for his own benefit, and the federal government cut off funding. In 1856 he married Caroline Shoemaker, daughter of a captain at Fort Union, and they had five children. Unhappily for New Mexicans, he returned to the bench as a Supreme Court justice from 1865 to 1869 with an appointment by President Andrew Johnson. The *New Mexican* wrote: "It is now clear that Judge Houghton is wanting in all the essentials necessary to a speedy and satisfactory administration of justice, and his appointment to the bench is but another evidence that those not bred in the law should not be entrusted with its administration." The legislature in 1868 passed a memorial asking Congress to withdraw him. Houghton moved to Las Vegas in 1874 and died in 1876.[36]

Georgians

Nearly all of Calhoun's traveling companions eventually returned to Georgia and probably regaled listeners for years with tales of life in the Wild West.

George W. Martin had one of the best stories. He worked successfully as a trader and survived a serious threat on the Santa Fe Trail, but not from Indians. He left Santa Fe on October 2, 1850, with a wagon train that included Samuel Wethered, a wealthy trader, attorney Murray F. Tuley, and dozens of government teamsters discharged by Sumner. Three days later, the travelers thought nothing of it when a man named Fox joined the train, but eleven days out, Kit Carson and a group of dragoons surrounded their camp and arrested Fox. He and the unemployed teamsters had planned to murder and rob their fellow travelers. Martin reached Columbus in time to be included in the 1850 census; he and his wife and three children were living with his parents. Martin returned to New Mexico. After Calhoun said his farewells in May 1852, Martin remained at Fort Union for at least the remainder of that year and used his notary public appointment from the dying governor in army disciplinary proceedings. After he returned to Columbus, he owned a livery stable. During the Civil War in 1862, as a volunteer in the Crawford Greys, he was wounded at the Battle of Sharpsburg, Maryland. After the war, he farmed. Martin was Muscogee County Sheriff in 1866 and 1867.[37]

The reliable John G. Jones became Calhoun's secretary after his son-in-law, John Davis, left. He accompanied Calhoun on the Navajo expedition in 1849 and escorted thirteen freed captives back to Mexico on Calhoun's behalf the following year. Calhoun appointed him as Santa Fe County sheriff on March 8, 1851. He resigned on August 15, 1851, to become the territory's first US Marshal. One of his duties was to open each session of federal court, which required riding hundreds of miles across the territory. Historian Durwood Ball writes that Jones and the early marshals played an important role in the transition from the Mexican to the United States judicial processes. "Among the servants of the courts, they and their deputies were most visible to the Hispanos and the sedentary Indians." Jones served until April 5, 1853, when he was removed by a new administration. He ran for sheriff of Santa Fe County and lost to R. M. Stephens, the incumbent.[38] During the Civil War, Jones was colonel of a Texas Regiment, attached to General John Magruder's command. After the war, he remained in Texas, got married, and settled in the Galveston area. He died in 1900.[39]

William H. Mitchell returned home in 1850 and joined his large family to grow cotton in Russell County, Alabama, across the river from Columbus. At a meeting of the Friends of the Union (he was later a member of the Constitutional Union Party) in July 1850, Mitchell proposed a motion, based on language from Congressman Robert Toombs, that the South had a right to participate equally in the US territories. Mitchell was a delegate to the Southern Commercial Convention in 1856, appointed by the Columbus mayor. By the 1860 census he was living in Wynton in Muscogee County. During the war, Captain William H. Mitchell fought in the Eleventh Georgia of Brigadier General George T. Anderson at Gettysburg in July 1863. After the war he involved himself in railroads and in 1867 was elected president of the Mobile and Girard Railroad.[40]

After treating Calhoun in El Paso in 1852, Dr. Brice Asa Hoxey remained in Texas for a time. He returned to Columbus in 1853 and joined the medical practice of his father, Thomas Hoxey, but he never recovered his health. He died at his father's home in Russell County, Alabama, on June 21, 1855, at age twenty-nine.[41] The other young physician, Carroll C. Thomas, was living in Santa Fe at the time of the 1850 census, but by the end of the year he returned to Augusta and opened a practice. During the Civil War he served in the Tenth Regiment of Georgia Infantry, which was mustered in June 1861. In 1863, for gallant and meritorious conduct in the field, he was promoted to the regiment's assistant surgeon.[42]

Edwin Goulding followed Calhoun to Mexico twice and then to New Mexico. Back in Columbus, on November 21, 1854, he got married, and in 1860 the family was living in Geneva in Talbot County. In 1861 he was a colonel in Company E, Georgia Ninth Infantry. On April 3, 1862, Goulding died of apoplexy (stroke) at Orange Court House in Virginia.[43]

Benjamin W. Lee and his brother Andrew returned to Charleston and the practice of law. Andrew moved to Columbia, South Carolina, where he led the Southern Express Company. In 1861 he entertained Thaddeus Lowe, a balloonist who had taken off from Cincinnati and landed in Columbia, frightening people. He was hauled before local authorities for an explanation, and Andrew Lee offered the balloonist his hospitality, possibly remembering his own days as an adventurer. The grateful Lowe gave Lee his anchor.[44]

Calhoun's daughters and their husbands left New Mexico in early 1850 and reached home in time to be counted in the 1850 census. Carolina, William, and Anna Love were living in the household of Isaac Mitchell, a Columbus lawyer and hotelier. The Loves had a second child in 1852, James Calhoun Love. After accompanying his dying father-in-law across the plains and helping lead the party of Pueblo men to Washington, DC, William was still with the party in Missouri, when he doubled back, returning to Washington, and checked into the National Hotel on February 22, 1853. He may have hoped for another federal appointment. He went on to Columbus. Love later opened a three-room office that caught fire that year, and he lost all his furniture. He was a port warden in 1855 and a health officer in 1856. Love died May 17, 1858, and Carolina remarried. (See appendix 1.)[45]

Martha and John Davis moved in with John's mother and the rest of the Davis family when they returned from New Mexico. The 1850 census lists John as a clerk. In late 1851, Martha died. Davis partnered with two other men as merchants and shipping agents in 1854. He was proprietor of the Warm Springs resort in Meriwether County when he died in July 1859.[46]

APPENDIX ONE

James S. Calhoun Family

Finding one particular Calhoun family in Georgia is like looking for one leaf on a very big tree. Working back from James S. Calhoun's first known residence in Milledgeville, I found an 1820 entry in a Baldwin County will book that became the Rosetta Stone of Calhoun's ancestry.

Phillip Calhoun

WIFE: Martha
BROTHERS: John Calhoun, Aquilla Calhoun, Michael Calhoun, Irwin Calhoun
SISTER: Patience Moss
NEPHEWS: Elbert Calhoun, Josiah and James Calhoun (sons of brother John), William and Cary Calhoun (sons of brother Aquilla), James Silas Calhoun and Phillip Calhoun (sons of brother Michael)
NIECE: Susannah V. M. Calhoun (daughter of brother Irwin)
WITNESSES: Charles Malone, Rigdon Norris, W. F. Peebles

This narrowed the hunt considerably. Following breadcrumbs from this entry, I found the earliest evidence of his family in Burke County and in Jefferson County, which was created from Burke County. They originally spelled their name Calhoon, although various clerks also spelled it Cohoon and Cahoon. In a day when few could read or write, it's not unusual. I have used here the spellings I found.

Another challenge is that parents then often named their children for a family member. In this family there were multiple Jameses, Elberts, Johns, Williams, Susans, and Marthas. I sorted them by location, when records allowed, but written records are not just spotty—they have serious gaps. Georgia censuses are missing for 1790, 1800, and 1810. In the famous "March to the Sea," Union troops burned county courthouses. Fires, hurricanes, and floods also destroyed material. So the paper trail becomes thinner—tax lists, land lottery drawings, marriage records and newspapers, along with some ambitious reconstructions by genealogists and historians.

We can probably assume this listing is by order of age, making John Calhoun the eldest. This is NOT the famous John C. Calhoun from South Carolina. Although a couple of James S. Calhoun's descendants claim ties to the famous public figure, I found no evidence to support that claim. As I once heard a genealogist tell beginning family historians: "I don't care what grandma or grandpa said, we rely on the written record." I've winnowed Cahoons, Cohoons, Calhoons, and Calhouns to the following, which I think is reliable.

John Calhoon

John Calhoon, his wife Mary, and their children, **Elbert, James,** and **Josiah,** lived in Jefferson County on Williamson's Swamp Creek, which heads in Washington County and flows southeast into the Ogeechee River. John Cohoon died in late 1796 or early 1797, and in 1799 Mary Calhoon was still trying to settle the estate. The following year, the Washington County sheriff sold two hundred acres to settle John's debts.

John and Mary's son **Elbert Calhoon,** who was living in Burke County in 1806, acquired eighty acres in Jefferson County. He served in the War of 1812 as a private in William Harvey's company. By 1813 he and his uncle Philip were landowners in Baldwin County, where Elbert was a lawyer and justice of the peace. By then they were spelling their names "Calhoun." In 1819 Elbert married **Susan Smith,** and their first child was **Aquilla Turner Calhoun.** Judge Calhoun's household in 1820 included seventeen slaves, according to the census for Baldwin County. In 1822 and 1823, he was a judge in Baldwin County Inferior Court. When he drew in the Bibb County lottery in March 1827 and won, the family relocated to Macon, where they remained. Elbert died on January 24, 1842, at about the age of sixty. In his will, he left slaves and/or land to his sons **Aquilla T., Seaborn Augustus,** and **Elbert,** and his daughters **Elizabeth Smith Bivens** (she married George Bivins on May 16, 1839), **Martha Victoria,** and **Susan Ella.** To his wife, he left his house, furnishings, and livestock and directed his heirs to "keep up the plantation."

Elbert and Susan's son **Aquilla Turner Calhoun** was one of four Georgians who received his medical degree from the University of Pennsylvania on April 6, 1838. On March 26, 1840, he married Lavinia C. Perry. He was named executor of his father's estate but by 1849 was no longer living in Georgia. He died in 1857 in Russell County, Alabama, leaving Lavinia with seven minor children. Their son **Elbert Calhoun** died in 1881.

John and Mary's son **James Cohoon** appears in a plat book on May 7, 1787, with 200 acres in the Hurricane District of Burke County; his uncle Aquilla was living nearby. The two men received headright grants there in 1790. In 1796, James Cohoon had 240 acres at Williamson's Swamp; this is probably the same property listed in 1799 on the Ogeechee River in Jefferson County, where he owned two slaves. At some point, James and his brother Josiah joined the state's westward movement. By 1820 they were living in Jones County, then Georgia's most densely populated county. James served in the militia. His farm was near Fortville, named for an old fort or trading post built at the crossing of two stage roads. When he died in 1828, his 200-acre property included horses, mules, cattle, oxen, hogs, corn, fodder, one gig (a two-wheeled carriage), and a crop of cotton. Eufema Calhoun, probably his wife, was the administrator. Euphema Hepzebah Calhoun died at thirty-seven on April 26, 1829, in Jones County, leaving three small children.

Josiah Calhoon was on the muster roll in 1793 in Captain Irwin's company in Washington County. He married Mary Goodwin, and their children were born in Jones County. Josiah died in 1825. Land he owned in Jones, Coweta, and Muscogee Counties was sold in the next few years. In 1832, four of the children, aged nine to fourteen, were educated by the Poor School Fund in Washington County.

Aquilla Calhoon

Aquilla (also listed as Equila and Aqualar) **Cahoon** was living on 100 acres on the Buckhead branch (later called David's branch) in Burke County as early as 1785. In 1787 Aquilla had 200 acres in the Hurricane District on an unnamed large pond, and nephew James was living nearby. Aquilla and James gained headright grants in Burke County in 1790. Aquilla received a commission from the governor as a member of B Company Militia. Between 1790 and 1795, Aquilla Calhoon served as a juror and grand juror in Burke County. In 1801 Aquilla acquired two triangular-shaped parcels totaling 103 acres in Burke County; one plot he shared with brother Irwin. When Aquilla died in 1803, the estate administrators were Sarah Calhoun, probably his wife, and their neighbor, John Raiford, who links the Calhouns to North Carolina and the Revolutionary War.

Born around 1750 in New Bern, North Carolina, Raiford was a lieutenant in the Second North Carolina Regiment during the Revolutionary War and received a 635-acre bounty grant of land in September 1784 for his service in Georgia. After settling in Jefferson County, he built Raiford's Bridge a mile from his home to connect the Old Savannah Road with Louisville. Aquilla Calhoon, his brother Philip, and his son William all had land adjoining Raiford, who died in Louisville in 1812. Although none of the Calhoons around John Raiford fought in the Revolutionary War, a **Jonathan Cahoon** in 1776 joined Captain Robert Raiford's company as a fifer. Captain Raiford's company was one of eight to make up the Eighth North Carolina Regiment, which in turn was part of the First North Carolina Brigade. They marched north to Pennsylvania and fought in the battles of Brandywine Creek and Germantown and then joined other wretched soldiers camped at Valley Forge that winter. Jonathan Cahoon's heirs received 1,000 acres in 1788 for his eighty-four months of service. Captain Raiford's brother was John Raiford.

Jonathan Cahoon was probably related to **Joseph Cahoon**. Both appear in the 1790 census for Edgecombe County, North Carolina. When Joseph Calhoun died in Dooly County on November 11, 1856, at one hundred years old, his obituary described him as a native of Edgecombe County, North Carolina, born on January 10, 1756. While serving in the Continental Army, he was severely wounded at the battle of Brandywine. He fought at Guilford and at the siege of Yorktown saw Lord Cornwallis surrender his sword to the victorious Americans. He moved to Georgia in 1792. For his eighty-four months' service, he received 640 acres. "He was a man of powerful muscular frame and retained the vigor and strength of his mind up to his death," said the account.

Aquilla's son **William Calhoon** appears in Jefferson County records in 1796 with 300 acres on the Ogeechee River. He owned three slaves. He later expanded his ownership to 691 acres and eleven slaves and held a separate parcel of 488 acres. He and his uncle Phillip Calhoon were Jefferson County grand jurors on July 3, 1797. William Calhoon was still living in Jefferson County in 1820 and 1830, according to the census. In 1834, William Calhoun Sr. had 440 acres on the Ogeechee River, along with 200 acres on Boggy Gut Creek and in Lowndes and Cherokee Counties.

William's son, **William Calhoon Jr.**, also appears in early tax records, which don't always distinguish between father and son. In 1805 William Sr. drew 202.5 acres in Wilkinson County, which he gave to William Jr. Wilkinson had been created from Creek lands two years earlier. In Wilkinson County, William Jr. was clerk of the inferior court from 1816 to 1819. By this time he was referring to himself as **William H. Calhoun** and was also a merchant in Irwinton. In 1831 he was living in neighboring Bibb County, where he was a merchant, lawyer, and judge. He married Martha Ann Smith in Bibb County on January 27, 1831, and they had two children, James and Martha. In the 1840 census, he was still living in Bibb County with three children and eighteen slaves. His property was adjacent to that of his father's cousin Elbert Calhoun. When Aquilla T. Calhoun was no longer in the state to oversee his father's estate, William H. Calhoun applied to be administrator.

Aquilla's son **Cary** doesn't appear in records for the period.

Philip Calhoon

Philip Cohoon had 700 acres at Bark Camp, 300 acres at Sleephill Bottom, and 200 acres on the Ogeechee River, all in Burke County in 1787. Philip Cahoon was commissioned by the governor as a member of the Burke County Militia in 1790 and received a headright grant in the 1790s. In 1796 Philip Cohoon, at Williamson's Swamp in Jefferson County, had eleven slaves. In 1799 Philip Cohoon had fourteen slaves and 250 acres near Williamson Swamp. In 1813 he moved to Baldwin County, where he and nephew Elbert Calhoun appeared on an 1813 tax list. When he died at age sixty on November 13, 1820, he and his wife Martha apparently had no surviving children. Administrators William Calhoun and Lewis Moss sold 506 acres that he owned with an improved well, six miles above Milledgeville, and Elbert Calhoun showed the land.

Michael Calhoon

Michael Calhoon appeared in the Jefferson County tax digest in 1799, the same year his son, **James Silas**, the subject of this book, was born, so it's safe to assume James was born in Jefferson County. This small fact would have disappointed his great-granddaughter, who believed James S. was related to the famous Calhouns from South Carolina, but James himself said repeatedly that he was a native Georgian. His father, Michael, appears in the tax digest again in 1804 with one slave and 250 acres on Boggy Gut Creek, a substantial stream that flowed south and southeast into Williamson's Swamp Creek where other Calhoons lived. His name was still on the tax list through 1805 and 1806. Then the name and the man disappear.

In 1805 James and his younger brother Philip were orphans. They were registered, along with their uncle Irwin, for the lottery in Washington County but didn't receive a draw. The following year, his aunt, Patience Calhoun, and James each drew in the 1806 land lottery of Hancock County. James married Caroline Ann Simmons of South Carolina on December 19, 1822. Their first child, Frances LaFayette, died at eighteen months in Hancock County in 1825. They had two more daughters—Carolina Louisa, born in 1826, and Martha Ann, born in 1827. Caroline died on July 13, 1828, in Milledgeville at age twenty-five and is buried in Memory Hill Cemetery. James married Anna V. Williamson, the widow of Dr. Charles Williamson of Greene County, on January 2, 1830, in Baldwin County with the Reverend Miles Green presiding. Anna died in Greensboro on July 16, 1841. In 1840, the Calhouns were living in Columbus, and the household also included a young man.

Michael's second son, **Philip T. Calhoun**, died at age twenty-one on March 2, 1825, in Milledgeville. The following year, James sold Philip's few possessions—a gold watch, clothing, books, and other belongings—to pay his brother's debts.

In 1843, James and Caroline's daughter **Carolina Louisa**, seventeen, married William E. Love, twenty-three, at the home of Colonel Van Leonard, a prominent businessman. They had two children: Anna Caroline Love, born in 1846, and James Calhoun Love, born in 1852. William died May 17, 1858, and in 1860 Carolina married thirty-four-year-old Dr. William W. Flewellen, of Columbus. In 1861, Flewellen applied to administer the estate of James S. Calhoun. In the 1870 census, the household included William, forty-four; Carolina, forty-three; Anna, twenty; and James, eighteen. Carolina died in 1875 at age forty-eight in Columbus. "This most excellent lady died ... after a lingering illness," the *Columbus Daily Enquirer* reported, describing Carolina as "one of our most distinguished former citizens." She was "a lady of rare accomplishments and sterling Christian virtues." She was a longtime member of the Methodist Episcopal Church "and died in the faith of a blissful reward of a well-spent life. Her death will cause general regret in Columbus." The *Columbus Times* called her "a greatly esteemed lady."

James and Caroline's younger daughter, **Martha Ann**, twenty-one, married twenty-two-year-old John H. Davis on September 14, 1848. She died in Columbus on November 7, 1851.

Carolina and William's daughter **Anna** "Annie" **C. Love** married James O. A. Simmons at 7:30 a.m. on December 18, 1877, at the home of Anna's aunt, Mary Jarrell, of White Plains, Georgia. Anna and James apparently knew each other for some time. In 1871 young Simmons entered a sailboat named *Anna* in a regatta in Savannah. He was a member of the Savannah Volunteer Guards. In 1880, according to the census, James, thirty-four and a bookkeeper, and Anna, twenty-eight, were living in Savannah.

Carolina and William's son **James** "Jimmie" **Calhoun Love** died of meningitis on January 22, 1871, in Montgomery, Alabama; he had been working in warehouses there and in Columbus. His body was returned to Columbus for burial. He was nineteen. "He was an honorable, industrious youth, generally respected by his associates, and his death is much lamented," said the *Enquirer*. Because he was a member of Fire Company No. 5, its members followed his remains to the grave.

Anna and James Simmons had two daughters: **Mary Calhoun Simmons**, born in 1880, and **Olive "Ollie" K. Simmons Arnold**, born in 1885. Mary was an inmate of the Georgia State Sanitarium at ages thirty and forty, according to the 1910 and 1920 census. She died March 13, 1962, in Baldwin County at eighty-two. Ollie and Thomas Joseph Arnold were married May 12, 1906, in Bartow County, Georgia, and were still living there in 1910, but in 1920 they were in Atlanta, where thirty-eight-year-old Thomas was an auditor with the phone company. Ollie applied for permission to sell her great-grandfather's land in spring 1912. Thomas J. Arnold died July 27, 1961, in Fulton County at age eighty-one. Ollie died September 15, 1969, in Winston-Salem, North Carolina, at eighty-nine.

Irwin Calhoon

Brother **Irwin Calhoon** owned forty acres in Burke County in 1801 and appeared on the Jefferson County tax list in 1802. Three years later, he and his orphaned nephews, young James and Philip, registered for the lottery in Washington County, but none received a draw. By 1808, Irwin was living in Baldwin County, where he married **Martha M. Lawrence** on May 16. Irwin died in 1810. James, then eleven, and Martha are listed as administrators for his estate of one horse, some cattle, and hogs, and household and kitchen furniture. In a sale on June 6, William Calhoun received a silver watch, Patsey Calhoun received several articles of stock, Philip received one lot of corn, and Irwin's widow, Martha, received one negro boy. In 1810, Martha, James, and Philip were listed among Baldwin County's first thousand taxpayers and slave owners. Irwin and Martha's daughter, **Susan V. M. Calhoun**, died at age thirteen on November 11, 1821. William H. Calhoun later sold a female slave belonging to Susan for the benefit of heirs and creditors. On July 5, 1821, Martha married the Reverend **Charles Malone**, who had been widowed twice. The clergyman died on February 13, 1836, at age sixty-seven. Records of Martha's death were not found.

Patience Calhoon

Unless and until more information comes to light, the sister named in Philip's will as Patience Moss will remain a mystery. **Patience Calhoon** and her nephew James S. Calhoon drew in the 1806 land lottery of Hancock County. Peter, William, and Lewis Moss were listed in the Jefferson County Tax Digest in 1802, along with William Calhoun. Several members of the Moss family relocated to Hancock County by 1804, but I was unable to find records of Patience being married to anyone by the name of Moss.

An Ancestry.com member family tree lists a Patience Calhoun as the daughter of William and Martha Calhoun and sister of William H. Calhoun. She married Henry Walden on November 12, 1809, in Jefferson County. From 1796, Henry Walden Sr. owned land adjoining Adam Cohoon on the Ogeechee River and was listed, along with Adam and Samuel Calhoon, in 1802 in Captain Prince's 79th District. Beginning in 1806, Henry Jr. had acreage adjoining his father, and from this point on, it's not always clear which Walden is in the records, but both steadily increased their acreage and ownership of slaves, adding land in Jefferson, Jones, and Wilkes Counties. Patience and Henry had a daughter, Quilla in 1816.

The Waldens' neighbor, **Adam Calhoon**, was probably related to the other Calhoons. In the 1790s, he received a headright grant. He was a member of the Burke County Militia and owned one slave and 200 acres on the Ogeechee in Jefferson County in 1796. He soon increased his acreage to 236 acres. Adam served as a petit juror in 1800 and died in 1802 or early 1803 in Jefferson County. The will names his wife, **Rosanna**, and his son, **William. Samuel Calhoon** was a witness. Rosanna was then listed as a property owner adjoining another Calhoon on the Ogeechee Swamp. In 1806 **Samuel Calhoon** owned 118 acres in Jefferson County, which also adjoined Henry Walden on Ogeechee Swamp.

Sources

Books: Allen and Andrews; Austin; Baldwin County, Georgia, Will Book A (1806–1829); Baldwin County Court of Ordinary, Book B, March 14, 1810; Brantley; Colonial and State Records of North Carolina; Crumpton, *Jefferson County* and *Burke County*; Davidson; Davis, Charles L.; de Lamar and Rothstein; *Early Marriages of Baldwin County*; Dodd; Gaissert; Gentry; Georgia Land Lottery Papers; Graham; Hardy and Lawrence; Houston; Huxford; *Index to Georgia Tax Digests*; Killbourne; Martin; Ports; Poss; Sherwood; G. B. Smith; Thomas; Williams, Carolyn White.

Newspapers: *Augusta Chronicle, Boston Evening Transcript, Charleston Courier, Columbus Daily Enquirer, Columbus Enquirer, Georgia Journal, Georgia Telegraph, The Louisville Gazette and Republican Trumpet, Macon Messenger, Macon Telegraph, Macon Weekly Telegraph, Reflector, Southern Recorder.*

Websites: The American Revolution in North Carolina; Ancestry.com, *Revolutionary War Bounty Land Grants*; New Georgia Encyclopedia; Georgia Archives, Headright and Lottery Loose Plat File; USGenWeb Archives, United States Census.

APPENDIX TWO

Battalion of Georgia Mounted Volunteers, September 1847–July 1848

Lieutenant Colonel James S. Calhoun

Companies

A. Captain E. R. Goulding, Muscogee County; 1st Lieutenant Bryce. A. Hoxey; 2d Lieutenants Jonathan O. Reeder and Lewis W. Chandler; 1st Sergeant William A. Yonge; 2nd Sergeant M. T. Bennett; 3rd Sergeant Jno. C. Goulding; 4th Sergeant N. P. Duke; 1st Corporal Charles E. Tooraine; 2nd Corporal William Robinson; 3rd Corporal William Logan; 4th Corporal John Logan; Musicians, Joseph T. Hodson and Leon Le Provost.

B. Captain Charles A. Hamilton, Cass County; 1st Lieutenant John C. Hately; 2d Lieutenants Seth Jenkins and Joseph Richardson; 1st Sergeant E. R. Forsyth; 2nd Sergeant Elisha Drummond; 3rd Sergeant Taliaferro Owens; 4th Sergeant William Jolly; 1st Corporal James Reagan; 2nd Corporal Nicholas Frost; 3rd Corporal Joseph Luke; 4th Corporal McArthur Frost.

C. Captain Henry Kendall, Muscogee County; 1st Lieutenant W. H. C. Renfroe; 2d Lieutenant Z. Boothe; 3rd Lieutenant C. B. Baker; 1st Sergeant B. P. Smith; 2nd Sergeant A. M. Collins; 3rd Sergeant J. L. Parker; 4th Sergeant Thomas C. Roquemore; 1st Corporal M. F. Shipp; 2nd Corporal C. A. Posey; 3rd Corporal William Moore; 4th Corporal Calvin Calhoun.

D. Captain William D. Fulton, Chattanooga County; 1st Lieutenant Thomas Berry; 2d Lieutenants William Cooper and James H. Hill; 1st Sergeant Austin; 2nd Sergeant William C. Boyle; 3rd Sergeant William C. Guinn; 4th Sergeant John H. Burnett; 1st Corporal S. M. Knox; 2nd Corporal Nathan Murray; 3rd Corporal James Cooper; 4th Corporal James Harlow.

E. Captain Charles H. Nelson, Cass County; 1st Lieutenant Isaac Wallen; 2d Lieutenants. J. C. Davis and G. W. Anderson; 1st Sergeant S. M. L. Allen; 2nd

Sergeant H. Gray; 3rd Sergeant T. J. A. Crombie; 4th Sergeant John Humphrey; 1st Corporal H. Miles; 2nd Corporal N. J. Fletcher; 3rd Corporal C. M. Chambers; 4th Corporal P. B. Nix.

F.   Captain William T. Wofford, Cass County; 1st Lieutenant William W. Rich; 2d Lieutenants William E. Curtis and Reuben C. Conner; 1st Sergeant Jacob Rhodes; 2nd Sergeant William H. Mann; 3rd Sergeant George W. Sarton; 4th Sergeant Henry Evans; 1st Corporal L. C. Goodwin; 2nd Corporal William Thompson; 3rd Corporal S. H. Sterling; 4th Corporal George C. Knowles.

Source: *Columbus Enquirer*, November 2, 1847.

Battalion of Georgia Mounted Volunteers, July 1848

Lieutenant Colonel James S. Calhoun
Adjutant G. W. Knight
Assistant Surgeon H. R. Rutledge
Acting Assistant Quartermaster Lieutenant Z. Boothe
Captains: Edwin K. Goulding, Charles A. Hamilton, W. H. C. Renfroe, William D. Fulton, William T. Wofford, Charles H. Nelson
First Lieutenants: C. B. Baker, Thomas Barry, W. W. Rich
Second Lieutenants: L. W. Chandler, T. A. Young, E. R. Forsyth, J. T. Parker, W. Cooper, W. Boyle, R. C. Connor, J. C. Davis, G. W. Anderson

Source: *Daily Chronicle & Sentinel*, July 6, 1848.

APPENDIX THREE

New Mexico Factions

Alvarez Faction

Leaders: Manuel Alvarez, Richard Weightman, and James Calhoun

John N. Abell: Trader[1]

William Z. Angney: Lawyer from Missouri; arrived with Kearny; commanded a battalion of infantry and accompanied Colonel Price on his march to put down the 1847 rebellion.[2]

Francisco Tomás Baca: Trader, delegate to the convention of September 24, 1849, Alvarez appointee as judge.

Román Antonio Baca: Born in Cebolleta, half-brother of Manuel Chaves.[3]

Juan Antonio Baca y Pino: Signer of the constitution in 1850.

Spruce Baird: Lawyer from Kentucky, named judge by Texas to organize Santa Fe County, lived in Albuquerque until the Civil War.

Tomás Cabeza de Baca: Son of the first settler of Upper Las Vegas, nominated for governor by the Alvarez faction in 1850; Santa Fe Trail trader.[4]

James Conklin: Merchant; came to St. Louis from Canada and settled in Santa Fe in 1821; married into the prominent Ortiz family; wife, Juana, was cousin of Vicar Juan Felipe Ortiz; died in 1882 at age ninety-one.[5]

Francis A. Cunningham: Paymaster elected as senator to Congress with Weightman in 1850.

Padre José Manuel Gallegos: Albuquerque priest; freighter and merchant in Albuquerque; signer of constitution in 1850; senator in 1851; territorial delegate to Congress in 1853; ex-communicated by Lamy in 1854.[6]

George Gold: Delegate to constitutional convention in 1850; census taker; territorial senator in 1851 and 1853 representing Taos County.

Hilario Gonzáles: Territorial representative from San Miguel County in 1851.

Samuel King: Trader[7]

General Elliott Lee: Survived the Taos Rebellion because of intervention by Padre Martínez; his brother, Sheriff Stephen Lee, was killed.[8]

Charles H. Merritt: Santa Fe County sheriff in 1849 and 1850.

William S. Messervy: Born in Massachusetts; trader on the Santa Fe Trail and in Mexico; relocated to Santa Fe after the Mexican War; elected territorial delegate in 1850; joined Houghton group in 1850; territorial secretary in 1853.[9]

Vicar Juan Felipe Ortiz: One of the leaders of the 1847 revolt; nominated by both factions to the Senate and served in 1851.

Palmer J. Pillans: Texas lawyer; nominated by both parties and served as representative in 1851; law partner of Ashurst and Skinner; represented Reynolds against Weightman.

Miguel Pino: One of the leaders of the 1847 rebellion and a good friend of Manuel Chaves; Santa Fe County Clerk in the 1860s.

James D. Robinson: Physician

Lewis D. Sheets: Merchant; secretary at meeting in August 1849 to discuss statehood; probate judge in Santa Fe County in 1851; commissioner of public buildings in 1851.[10]

Miguel Sena y Romero: Territorial representative for San Miguel County in 1851; alcalde of San Miguel County in 1851.

Murray F. Tuley: Attorney for the southern district in 1849; attorney general in 1850; delegate to constitutional convention in 1850; law partner of Weightman and Baird in 1853.[11]

Elias P. West: Kentucky lawyer who came to New Mexico in his twenties; delegate to the October 10, 1848, convention; attorney for the southern district in 1849; Alvarez appointee as judge; US district attorney; law partner of Spruce Baird; operated a grist mill in Albuquerque.[12]

Alvarez–Weightman–Calhoun Friends

Juan Archibeque: Records show several men by that name during the period in San Miguel, Bernalillo, and Santa Fe Counties.

Diego Archuleta: Born in 1814; from Rio Arriba County; educated in a seminary in Durango but decided not to be a priest; captain and second in command of military forces under Armijo; one of the leaders of the 1847 rebellion; appointed judge by Alvarez; served in the legislature for fourteen years; primary interest was education.[13]

Juan Cristóbal Armijo: Friend of Manuel Chaves; territorial representative in 1851 from Valencia County; wealthy merchant in Los Ranchos.

Florentino Castillo: Territorial senator in 1851 representing Valencia and Socorro Counties.

Juan Cristóbal Chaves: Territorial senator in 1851 representing Valencia and Socorro Counties; prefect of Valencia County in 1851.

José María Chaves: Brother of Manuel Chaves; took part in eleven campaigns against Indians, five as commander; appointed prefect of Rio Arriba County by Calhoun in 1851; died in Abiquiu at age 101.[14]

Manuel Chaves: Grew up in Cebolleta; sheep rancher; captain of the local militia; accompanied US troops as a volunteer in Indian campaigns.[15]

Cyrus Choice: Merchant in Georgia; fought in Creek Wars; accompanied Calhoun to New Mexico in 1849; appointed agent to Utes in 1850.

Henry Connelly: Physician and merchant, first in Chihuahua and then in New Mexico; governor during the Civil War.[16] Although the Houghton group nominated him for governor, he wasn't active in their cause and befriended Calhoun in 1851.

Raymundo Córdova: Territorial representative in 1851 from Taos County.

José Pablo Gallegos: Brother of Padre José Manuel Gallegos; delegate to constitutional convention in 1850; territorial senator in 1851 representing Taos and Rio Arriba Counties.

Dionicio Gonzáles: Territorial representative in 1851 from Taos County.

Gerónimo Jaramillo: Territorial representative in 1851 and 1853 representing Rio Arriba County.

Padre José Francisco Leyba: Arrived in New Mexico around 1820; concerned with poverty; parish priest at San Miguel and Abiquiu.[17]

Padre Antonio José Martínez: Ministered to Taos and Taos Pueblo; president of the October 10, 1848, and September 24, 1849, conventions; served in the Senate in 1851; friend of Calhoun.

Pascual Martínez: Territorial representative in 1851 and 1853 from Taos County.

Vicente Martínez: Territorial senator in 1851 and 1853 from Taos County.

Miguel Mascarenas: Territorial representative in 1851 from Taos County.

Dr. Thomas E. Massie: Born in Virginia; enlisted as a surgeon of volunteers in 1847; discharged in 1848 and remained in Santa Fe to practice medicine; private physician to Calhoun; returned to Virginia in 1854.[18]

Antonio J. Ortiz: Territorial senator in 1851 from Taos and Rio Arriba Counties.

Francisco Antonio Otero: From Peralta; territorial senator in 1851 from Valencia County; alcalde of Valencia County in 1851.

José Leandro Perea: Sheep baron of Bernalillo and the wealthiest man in the territory in the 1860s and 1870s; territorial representative in 1851 from Bernalillo County.[19]

Juan Perea: Trader from Bernalillo; stockman; brother of José Leandro Perea; delegate to the October 10, 1848, convention.[20]

Facundo Pino: Offered to lead Mexican regulars against Kearny's troops at Apache Canyon; participated in plan to attack American military in Santa Fe but after Governor Bent was murdered decided to help put down the rebellion; legislator in 1853.[21]

James W. Richardson: Auditor in 1851.

Diego Salazar: Territorial representative in 1851 from Rio Arriba County.

José Andres Sandoval: Territorial representative in 1851 from Santa Ana County.

Miguel Sena y Quintana: Territorial representative in 1851 from San Miguel County.

Juan Torres: Territorial representative from Socorro County in 1851; alcalde in El Sabino in 1851.

Theodore Wheaton: Came to New Mexico with Kearny; attorney for the northern district in 1847; territorial representative in 1851 from Taos County; territorial attorney general, 1854–58; US district attorney, 1861–1866; died at Ocate in 1875.[22]

Celedonio Valdez: Farmer and landowner in Rio Arriba County; member of the House in 1851.

Esquipuela Vigil: From La Parida; territorial representative in 1851 for Socorro County; sheriff of Socorro County in 1851.

José Ramón Vigil: Member of the House representing Rio Arriba County, 1847.

Members of Houghton Faction

Leaders: Joab Houghton, James Collins

Merrill Ashurst: From Alabama, attorney general in 1850; law partner of Hugh Smith; Speaker of the House in 1857.

Carlos Beaubien: Land grant cofounder; judge appointed by military commander; died February 10, 1864.

Robert T. Brent: Auditor appointed by military commander; assistant quartermaster; legislator from Santa Fe; killed by Apaches in 1851.[23]

James L. Collins: Merchant and trader; born in Kentucky in 1800; made his first trip to Santa Fe in 1826 and traveled from Santa Fe to Chihuahua in 1828; returned to Santa Fe when the Mexican War began and settled permanently in 1850; owner and editor of the *Santa Fe Weekly Gazette* in 1852; appointed Indian agent by President Buchanan and reappointed by President Lincoln; participated in the battles of Valverde and Glorietta during the Civil War.[24]

Jared "Jerry" W. Folger: Sutler at Fort Union; died at Fort Union; buried in the Odd Fellows cemetery in Santa Fe.[25]

Thomas S. J. Johnson: Chief clerk of the army quartermaster; signer of the constitution in 1850.

William G. Kephart: Presbyterian minister and abolitionist; editor of *Santa Fe Gazette*.

William McGrorty: Lumber supplier to the army.

Francisco Ortiz y Delgado: Prefect in 1848; delegate to constitutional convention in 1850.

Antonio José Otero: Wealthy trader and sheep rancher from Peralta; contractor supplying wheat to the army; superior court judge appointed by Kearny; delegate to convention on September 24, 1849; delegate to constitutional convention in 1850; died in 1871 at about sixty-one.[26]

James H. Quinn: Taos merchant; attorney for the southern district in 1846; Taos

County prefect in 1849; army contract for beef in 1849; president of the council (senate) in 1853.[27]

Captain Alexander W. Reynolds: Assistant quartermaster

William C. Skinner: Attorney; built a mill in Valencia County; involved in Santa Fe Trail trade; delegate to convention on September 24, 1849; territorial representative in 1851 for Valencia County.[28]

Hugh N. Smith: Territorial secretary appointed by military commander; served in St. Vrain's volunteer company to put down the 1847 rebellion; elected delegate to the US House in 1849; territorial senator in 1851 representing Santa Fe and San Miguel Counties; territorial attorney general, 1859–1860.[29]

Ceran St. Vrain: Fur trader; partner of Charles Bent; landowner.

Padre Nicolás Valencia: A "wayward priest" who ousted the appointed priest in Belen and Tomé and created a schism within the parishes; removed by Vicar Ortiz.[30]

Donaciano Vigil: Lieutenant governor under Mexican governor Armijo; appointed secretary by Kearny; acting governor after Bent was murdered; delegate to the October 10, 1848, convention; secretary of the constitutional convention in 1850.

Houghton Friends

Rafael Armijo: Wealthy Albuquerque merchant; Confederate sympathizer who lost his fortune after the war.

Santiago Armijo: One of the leaders of the 1847 rebellion; merchant.

Juan Cruz Baca: Territorial representative in 1851 and 1853 for Valencia County.

Alexander Duvall: Army beef contractor in 1851.[31]

James M. Giddings: Probate clerk in Santa Fe County, 1848–1852; delegate to the October 10, 1848, convention.

John Kelly: Member of the quartermaster's department in 1850.

Ramón Luna: From Sabinal; Valencia County prefect in 1850.

Thomas R. McCutcheon: Attorney, grand jury member in Santa Fe in 1850.

Candido Ortiz: Territorial representative in 1851 for Santa Fe County.

Tomás Ortiz: One of the leaders of the 1847 rebellion; chief alcalde under the military government; territorial representative in 1851 and 1853 for Santa Fe County; army contract for hay; probate judge in 1852.[32]

Serafin Ramirez: Teacher in 1841; territorial representative for Bernalillo County in 1853.[33]

Juan José Sánchez: Merchant and freighter; delegate to convention on September 24, 1849.

Antonio Sandoval: Major landowner, stockman, and politician in Albuquerque; owner of Las Lagunitas Land Grant; built the Barelas Acequia; died in 1862.[34]

Julian Tenorio: Confederate sympathizer whose property was confiscated during the Civil War.[35]

John R. Tullis: Territorial representative in 1851 from Santa Fe County.

Ennis J. Vaughn: Sheriff of Santa Fe County in 1847–1848.

Mariano Yrisarri: Los Ranchos de Albuquerque merchant who amassed real estate, sheep, and personal property; one of the wealthiest men in the territory.[36]

APPENDIX FOUR

Inaugural Speech, March 3, 1851

Fellow Citizens:

An era in the history of New Mexico commences this day. The problem as to the capacity of the people for self-government is to be solved, preparatory to the assuming of a higher and more glorious position as one of the sovereign and independent states of the Union. The fate of New Mexico, under Providence, is in the hands of her own sons, and if wise and patriotic counsels prevail, a brilliant destiny awaits her. Circumstances not anticipated in 1848, interposed a barrier to an early adjustment of questions associated with the well being of the people of New Mexico. Fortunately for the happiness of mankind, the threatening aspect of clouds, that lowered for a time, has vanished, and it is hoped, will never again appear above the political horizon. Thanks, thanks, to an illustrious conjunction of statesmen, many of whom periled their own political existence, that they might strangle discord and save the Union. Further, at this time, it is not my purpose to review the past; and I commend to the consideration of all the wise sentiment as recorded by the immortal Don Quixote: "Let the dead go to the bier, and the living to good cheer." Our business is with the future.

"In the great and unprecedented struggle to which I have adverted, New Mexico stood prominently conspicuous, and the law which accords to us a Territorial Government, is one of the most important results growing out of that contest. The Constitution, and all laws of the United States, which are not locally inapplicable, are extended over New Mexico. The Territorial Government is now to be put in operation. The distinguished Chief Magistrate of all the people of the sovereign States and Territories, Millard Fillmore, by and with the advice and consent of the Senate of the United States, has been pleased to confer upon the humble individual who stands before you the office of governor of New Mexico, and my duties are briefly defined in the third section of the territorial law in the following words:

> The governor shall reside within said Territory, shall be commander-in-chief of the militia thereof, shall perform the duties and receive the emoluments of Superintendent of Indian affairs, and shall approve all laws passed by the Legislative Assembly before they shall take effect; he may grant pardons for offences against the laws of

said Territory, and reprieves for offences against the laws of the United States, until the decision of the President can be made known thereon; he shall commission all officers who shall be appointed to office under the laws of the said Territory, and shall take care that the laws be faithfully executed.

I am also required to cause a census or enumeration of the inhabitants of the several counties to be taken, to district the Territory, and to give to each section representation in the ratio of its population, as near as may be (Indians excepted). Further it is my duty to order elections for thirteen members of council, twenty-six members for the House of Representatives, and a delegate to Congress. These and various other duties are imposed upon me by the law, such as appointing and commissioning certain officials previous to the meeting of the first Legislature for this Territory, and these duties I shall discharge with all prudent dispatch.

It is my purpose to discharge my every duty with the fidelity which an honest man observes, firmly and impartially, but soberly and discreetly, to the end that in your transition from a singularly constituted government, one hitherto unknown to the "manners of the times," to one dependent upon your own wisdom for such laws as may secure your happiness and prosperity, and upon your firmness and patriotism for their due enforcement, that there may be no discordant jarrings to disturb the minds or the passions of men. Removals must occur, and vacancies must be filled, and these shall be fearlessly accomplished, in the manner authorized by law. I trust, however, that I may have occasion to remove but few, and it is my unalterable purpose to hold the scales of justice with an impartial hand, and to observe, in all things, a proper moderation.

The protection of persons and property in this territory demands, and shall receive my earliest consideration. Agricultural and mercantile pursuits call loudly for protection. Our mineral resources must be accurately ascertained. Our sons and daughters must be fitted to take their position with the wisest of the age. A sound morality, in public and private life, must be established. To achieve for the people of New Mexico these important and essential points for the well being of individuals and communities, requires the hearty cooperation of every honest mind within her borders. The utmost of my powers shall be exercised at all times and in all places, to secure these grand purposes.

On a future occasion I shall, if permitted by that God who watches over us and orders all things aright, lay before the Legislative Assembly such further views and recommendations as I may think will advance and promote the general good.

In conclusion, my fellow citizens, I call upon every man in this Territory who loves his mother—every one who has an abiding affection for his wife, his daughter, his sister; each and every one who loves his country and desires its elevation in a Christian point of view, as well as in the grandeur and magnificence of its political destiny, to aid and to take an active part in attaining the glorious objects to which, I trust, we justly aspire. And may the God of all wisdom, of all truth, of all justice, and of all mercy, guide me in the way we should go.

Source: *Columbus Enquirer*, April 22, 1851.

APPENDIX FIVE

Members of the First Territorial Legislature

The twenty-six members of the House of Representatives were:

Taos County: Theodore Wheaton, Dionicio Gonzáles, Pascual Martínez, Raymundo Córdova, and Miguel Mascarenas

Rio Arriba County: Diego Salazar, Celedonio Valdez, Geronimo Jaramillo, José A. Manzanares, and Ramón Valdez

Santa Fe County: Tomás Ortiz, Palmer Pillans, Candido Ortiz, and John R. Tullis

San Miguel County: Miguel Sena y Quintana, M. Sena y Romero, and Hilario Gonzáles

Santa Ana County: José Andres Sandoval

Bernalillo County: J. Cristóbal Armijo, J. Leandro Perea, and Spruce Baird

Valencia County: Juan Cruz Baca, Juan José Chaves, and William C. Skinner

Socorro County: Juan Torres and Esquipuela Vigil

The thirteen council (senate) members were:

First district (Taos and Rio Arriba): Padre Antonio José Martínez, George Gold, Vicente Martínez, Jose Pablo Gallegos, and Antonio Ortiz

Second district (Santa Fe and San Miguel): Hugh N. Smith, Vicar Juan F. Ortiz, and Father José F. Leyba

Third district (Santa Ana and Bernalillo): Tomás Cabeza de Baca and Father José Manuel Gallegos

Fourth district (Valencia and Socorro): Juan Cristóbal Chaves, Francisco Antonio Otero, and Florentino Castillo

Source: *Daily Union*, July 10, 1851.

APPENDIX SIX

Appointments

Members of Alvarez faction in **boldface**.
Members of Houghton faction <u>underlined</u>.

1851

March 17: Horace S. Dickenson, coroner; Robert Perry and Nicolas Quintana y Rosas, constables for Santa Fe.

    Dickenson, a merchant from New York, came to Santa Fe around 1850. He was later territorial auditor and died at about age thirty in 1856.[1]

March 18: Miguel Sena y Romero, alcalde of San Miguel County, replacing Gregorio Valdez, resigned.

    Sena y Romero was a territorial representative in 1851.

March 20: Manuel (illegible), sheriff of Santa Ana County.

March 27: Ambrosio Armijo, prefect, Bernalillo County, replacing Francisco Sarracino; Ignacio Gallegos, sheriff of Bernalillo County, replacing Antonio Aragón; **Juan Cristóbal Armijo** and Henry Winslow, alcaldes of Bernalillo County in Albuquerque, replacing Manuel Armijo; and Pablo Melendres, alcalde of Doña Ana, Valencia County.

    Ambrosio Armijo was an alcalde of Albuquerque during the Mexican period, a prominent Albuquerque merchant and landowner, and a relative of the former Mexican governor.[2]

    Juan Cristóbal Armijo, brother of Ambrosio, was a close friend of Manuel Chaves and territorial representative in 1851.[3]

    Winslow was an Albuquerque merchant and army agent throughout the 1850s.[4]

    Melendres, one of the founders of the Doña Ana land grant, was the first alcalde of the village of Doña Ana, appointed by the Mexican governor.[5]

March 28: Herman Grolman, prefect and probate judge of San Miguel County.

    Grolman, one of the original grantees of the second Las Vegas land grant, was politically influential.[6]

March 31: Horace Long, prefect of Taos County, replacing Manuel Valdez.

April 2: Horace L. Dickenson, prefect and probate judge of Santa Fe County, replacing **Lewis D. Sheets**; Manuel Romero, alcalde and justice of the peace in Santa Fe County; **Dr. James D. Robinson**, coroner for Santa Fe county. Accepted resignation of Hugh N. Smith as secretary of territory.

April 7: David V. Whiting, acting secretary of the territory. Received resignation of Nicolas Quintana y Rosas as alcalde in Santa Fe.

April 8: Pedro José Peña, alcalde of Bernalillo; Vicente Chaves Padilla, alcalde of Padillas, Bernalillo County; and Miguel Antonio Labadie, alcalde for Alameda, Bernalillo County.

April 12: Ignacio Narvaez, alcalde and justice of the peace at Cienegilla in Santa Fe County. Revoked April 18 because Narvaez was appointed through false information.

April 19: Gabriel Vigil, alcalde in Taos County; Juan Ignacio Martín, alcalde of Ranchos de Taos; Rafael García, alcalde of Mora; and Antonio José Vigil, alcalde of Picuris.

April 21: Francisco Antonio Otero, alcalde of Peralta; Juan Cristóbal Chaves, prefect of Valencia (he later resigned to serve as territorial senator); Lorenzo Labadie of Tomé, sheriff of Valencia County; Francisco Saavedra, alcalde of the village of Luís López; Antonio José Castillo, alcalde of Belen; Antonio Lucero, alcalde of Cebolleta; Romualdo Baca, prefect of Lemitar; Salvador Armijo, alcalde of Albuquerque; **José María Chaves**, alcalde of Abiquiu; Antonio García, alcalde, Los Ranchos; Benito Larragoite, alcalde of Santa Fe; Francisco Antonio Otero, alcalde of Peralta; **Vicente Pino**, alcalde of La Parida; Esquipula Vigil, sheriff of Socorro County (resigned to be a territorial representative in 1851); Juan Torres, alcalde of El Sabino.

Antonio García was a prominent landowner in Bernalillo County.

Otero was a territorial senator in 1851.

Labadie, who would be sheriff from 1849 to 1853, was also a census taker. He was also Manuel Chaves's brother-in-law.[7]

Salvador Armijo was one of Albuquerque's most prominent businessmen and landowners.[8]

José María Chaves was the brother of Manuel Chaves. His great-great-great-grandfather was a captain under Don Diego de Vargas. José María Chaves took part in eleven campaigns against Indians, five as commander. He died in Abiquiu at age 101.[9]

Esquipuela Vigil and Juan Torres were territorial representatives in 1851.

Vicente Pino was a political leader in Socorro.[10]

Antonio García was a landowner in Bernalillo County.[11]

April 25: Jesús María Baca, probate judge of Santa Ana County; Miguel Sena y Quintana, prefect and probate judge of San Miguel County replacing H. Grolman, removed.

Sena y Quintana was a territorial representative in 1851.

May 1: Militon Vigil, alcalde of Algodones replacing Jesús María Miera, removed.

May 3: Manuel Valdez, alcalde of Rio Arriba County replacing Francisco Martínez, removed.

May 9: Jesús Lucero, sheriff of San Miguel County.

May 14: Joaquin Chaves, alcalde of Galisteo replacing Marcelino Ortiz, removed.

May 16: Carlos Romero, alcalde of Anton Chico.

May 28: Antonio Ruiz, sheriff of Socorro County replacing Esquipula Vigil, elected to legislature.

May 30: Received resignation of Robert Brent as auditor.

May 31: James W. Richardson, auditor.

June 4: Juan F. Castillo, prefect of Valencia County, replacing Juan José Chaves, elected to legislature.

June 6: Filomeno Sánchez and Manuel Sánchez, alcaldes of Valencia County.

June 7: José María Chaves, prefect in Rio Arriba County, replacing José Pablo Gallegos, elected to legislature; Pedro Salazar, alcalde in Rio Arriba County.

June 13: Francisco Martínez, alcalde in Rio Arriba County.

> Martinez was the son of Manuel Martínez, an early settler of the Tierra Amarilla area and land grant recipient.[12]

June 21: Joséph D. Ellis, acting secretary of territory in place of David Whiting, appointed translator.

> Joséph D. Ellis was a Santa Fe merchant.

July 14: Commissioned Charles Blumner treasurer; commissioned **James W. Richardson** auditor.

> Blumner was a trader in Santa Fe, 1837.[13]

July 21: Administered oath to Grafton Baker, chief justice of the Supreme Court.

August 11: Commissioned William M. Dalton, notary public for Santa Fe County.

> William M. Dalton was a merchant in Santa Fe.[14]

August 15: Commissioned Pinckney E. Tully, probate judge of Santa Fe County in place of Horace L. Dickinson, resigned. Commissioned Nicolas Quintana y Rosas sheriff of Santa Fe County, replacing John G. Jones, resigned.

August 29: Certified Caleb Sherman as district court clerk.

September 3: Commissioned Horace L. Dickinson coroner, Santa Fe County; appointed **Henry Connelly**, coroner in Santa Fe County.

September 19: Commissioned Jesús María Baca probate judge for Santa Ana County, elected. Commissioned José Antonio Mansanares probate judge of Rio Arriba County, elected.

September 20: Commissioned Ambrosio Armijo probate judge for Bernalillo County, elected; commissioned Salvador Armijo justice of the peace Bernalillo County.

> Ambrosio Armijo was an Albuquerque merchant, owner of Los Poblanos Ranch, and a member of one of Albuquerque's wealthiest families.[15]

September 23: Commissioned Manuel Herrera probate judge of San Miguel County.

October 1: Commissioned Fernando Aragón, sheriff of Bernalillo County. Granted certificate to James Stewart, justice of the peace in Santa Fe County.

October 2: Elias P. West took oath of office as US district attorney.

October 4: Commissioned **José María Martínez** probate judge in Taos County; Julian Soder, sheriff, Taos County; Pedro Salazar, sheriff, Rio Arriba County; Patricio Silva, sheriff, Santa Ana County; R. M. Stephens, sheriff, Santa Fe County; **José Felipe Castillo**, probate judge, Valencia County; Lorenzo Labadie, sheriff, Valencia County; Pedro Baca, probate judge in Socorro County; José Antonio Torres, sheriff, Socorro County (resigned December 1, 1851).

> Father José María Martínez was a member of Alvarez party and a delegate to the 1850 constitutional convention. He was also the first alcalde of Taos.[16]
>
> José Felipe Castillo was an officer during the Spanish period and a friend of Weightman.[17]
>
> Pedro Baca was a political leader in Socorro.[18]

December 1: Commissioned justices of the peace for Valencia County.

December 31: Commissioned G. A. Hayward notary public for Socorro County.

1852

January 10: Henry C. Johnson, attorney general

January 12: Certificate to Judge John S. Watts.

January 22: Commissioned José Apodaca sheriff of Socorro County.

January 31: Certificate to Francisco López, justice of the peace, San Miguel County.

> López, from Agua Fria near Santa Fe, was an original settler of the Las Vegas land grant who started a freighting business on the Santa Fe Trail. Francisco and Petra López, who owned large tracts of land south of the plaza, were among the most influential Hispanic families in Las Vegas.[19]

February 6: Lemuel J. Angney, justice of the peace for Santa Fe County, resigned.

March (no dates provided): Swore in and commissioned **Louis D. Sheets**, probate judge, also auditor in the absence of **James W. Richardson**; John G. Jones, sheriff of Santa Fe County; José Baca, justice of the peace; John D. Watts, justice of the second district; José Vigil, justice of the peace; Nicolas Quintana y Rosas and José M. Abreu, justices of the peace; **Manuel Alvarez** and **Lewis D. Sheets**, commissioners of public buildings; Charles Lucas, commissioner of deeds; William F. Dalton, notary public; José Baca, justice of the peace; **James W. Richardson**, auditor in place of Sheets who resigned; Lalo Schlesinger, inspector.

April 22: Commissioned José Estrada, justice of the peace.

Militia appointments

1851

March 19: Ceran St. Vrain and **Fecundo Pino**, aides de camp for the commander in chief.

      Pino offered to lead Mexican regulars against Kearny's troops at Apache Canyon in 1846. In 1848 he was involved in planning the insurrection but after Bent's murder decided to help put down the rebellion.[20]

March 28: **Tomás Cabesa de Baca** of Santa Ana and **Juan Cristóbal Armijo** of Bernalillo, aides de camp to the commander in chief.

May 1: Gen. Manuel Armijo of Lemitar, aide de camp to commander in chief.

July 14: Commissioned Tomás Cabeza de Baca, brigadier general, first brigade, southern division.

August 20: Pascual Martínez, brigadier general, northern district; **Vicente Pino**, brigadier general, second brigade, southern district; **Manuel Alvarez**, brigadier general, central district; Manuel Besserra (?), second brigade central; **José María Chaves**, brigadier general, second brigade, northern district. Commissioned **George Gold**, major general, northern division; **Richard Weightman**, major general for the central division; and **Spruce M. Baird**, southern division; Fecundo Pino, adjutant general.

      Martínez would be a legislator representing Taos County.[21]

September 10: **Henry Connelly**, aide de camp to commander in chief.

November 10: Commissioned José Andres Sandoval, brigadier general, first brigade, third division.

1852

March: Jesús Gil Abreu, brigadier quartermaster; Santiago Gonzales, colonel; Augustus D. Marley, aide de camp.

      Abreu clerked for John Calvin McCoy, who founded Kansas City. He returned to New Mexico with Kearny as sutler and interpreter. He was a mail contractor between 1847 and 1849. His wife Petra was the daughter of Charles Beaubien. He would be one of New Mexico's leading businessmen.[22]

NOTES

Introduction

1. *Columbus Daily Enquirer*, March 27, 1898.
2. *Columbus Enquirer*, July 13, 1852.
3. Calhoun to Marcy, January 13, 1849, Georgia Archives.
4. Keleher, *Turmoil in New Mexico*, 44.
5. Crane, *Desert Drums*, 15.
6. Crane, 12.
7. Abel, ed., *The Official Correspondence of James S. Calhoun*, xii–xiii.
8. Horn, *New Mexico's Troubled Years*, 15.
9. Lamar, *The Far Southwest, 1846–1912*, 84; Keleher, *Turmoil*, 130 fn65.
10. Rhodes, "God's Badgered Man," 12–13.
11. Rhodes, 12–13.
12. Keleher, *Turmoil*, 127 fn49.

Chapter One

1. "Ogeechee River," Georgia River Network.
2. Garstka, "The Scots-Irish in the Southern United States: An Overview"; Fischer, *Albion's Seed*, 613; Park, "The Georgia Scotch-Irish," 117.
3. Thomas, *History of Jefferson County, Georgia*, 23, 39, 40; G. G. Smith, *The Story of Georgia and the Georgia People, 1732 to 1760*, 59–61, 68, 116, 129, 217–20; Holmes, *Those Glorious Days*, 35.
4. G. G. Smith, 62, 68, 127, 133; de Lamar and Rothstein, *The Reconstructed 1790 Census of Georgia*, 10, 14, 16; Cooksey, "Burke County"; Crumpton, *Burke County*, 544, 555, 592, 738, 740; *Augusta Chronicle*, June 1, 1803.
5. Crumpton, *Burke County*, 557, 603, 660; Ebel, "Louisville"; Ports, *Jefferson County, Georgia Tax Lists*; de Lamar and Rothstein, *Reconstructed 1790 Census*, 13; Lucas, *Some Georgia County Records*, 1:180; Goff, *Place Names of Georgia*, 198; Cooksey; G. G. Smith, 68.
6. In 1754, a John Cahoon was a member of Captain Stephen Lee's militia company on Whiteoak River, belonging to Colonel John Stankey's regiment in Onslow County, North Carolina. And there was a John Calhoon listed as a prisoner on

board a British prison ship, the *Forbay*, on May 18, 1781. Colonial and State Records of North Carolina, Roster of Stephen Lee's company of the Onslow County Militia, 1754, 22:338, and List of North Carolina and South Carolina militia prisoners of war, May 18, 1781, 17:1044,.

7. Lucas, 1:19, 100–101, 171; *Louisville Gazette*, February, 19, 1799, and February 25, 1800; Crumpton, *Jefferson County*, 91; Ports, *Jefferson County*.

8. Crumpton, *Jefferson County*, 110, 113, 126, 146, 199, 229, 259, 347, 593; *Louisville Gazette*, January 4, 1803; Baldwin County, GA, Will Book A, 1806–1829; J. Kenneth Brantley, *Hancock County*, 347; Lucas, 1:119, 180; Coleman, Byrne, and King, eds., *Ireland and the Americas*, 105–6.

9. In 1942, historian Fletcher M. Green contacted Alexander S. Salley Jr., an authority on the John C. Calhoun genealogy, who said there was no evidence that James S. Calhoun was related to John C. or that he was born in Abbeville. Green, "James S. Calhoun," 311 fn10.

10. *An Index to Georgia Tax Digests*, 3:87; US Census, Santa Fe 1850; Baldwin County Will Book A, 1806–1829; Crumpton, *Jefferson County*, 171, 195; Sherwood, *A Gazetteer of the State of Georgia* , 132.

11. Hitz, "Georgia Bounty Land Grants," 339–40, 344; Coleman et al., 89–90, 106–7.

12. *An Index to Georgia Tax Digests*, vols. 3–4; de Lamar and Rothstein, *Records of Washington County*, 28; *Columbus Enquirer*, July 13, 1852.

13. Graham, *1805 Georgia Land Lottery Fortunate Drawers and Grantees*, i; Nichols, "Land, Republicanism, and Indians," 212–13.

14. Schwartzman and Barnard, "A Trail of Broken Promises," 697–98, 700; Burt and Ferguson, *Indians of the Southeast*, 128, 134.

15. Burt, 138, 173, 175; J. Cook, *The Governors of Georgia, 1754–2004*, 98.

16. Graham, i; Nichols, 212–13.

17. Ebel.

18. G. G. Smith, 257; Wilson, "Milledgeville"; Bonner, *Milledgeville*, 71; Abbott, "Memoirs of a Milledgeville Native," 435; Phillips, "Historical Notes of Milledgeville, Ga.," 1.

19. Houston, *Marriages and Land Lottery List of Hancock County*, 108; A. Cook, *History of Baldwin County, Georgia*, 258; *The Early Marriages of Baldwin County, Georgia*; Baldwin County Court of Ordinary; Bonner, *Milledgeville*, 84; Boatwright, *Status of Women in Georgia, 1783–1860*, 52; *Georgia Journal*, November 13, 1821; *Southern Recorder*, November 13,1821; Lucas.

20. Boatwright, 93.

21. Bonner, *Milledgeville*, 85–86; Mills, "Methodist Church: Overview."

22. G. G. Smith, 255, 257; G. B. Smith, *History of the Georgia Militia, 1783–1861*, 180.

23. Reed, *History of the University of Georgia*, 162–63, 166, 170–71; Hull, *A Historical Sketch of the University of Georgia*, 228; *Georgia Journal*, August 31 and December 7, 1819, July 18, 1820, November 27, 1821, and August 27, 1822.

24. E-mails to alumni offices of schools listed.

25. Calhoun was an officer; Hepburn was a member. *Georgia Journal*, November 21, 1820, and February 26,1822; Dawson, *A Compilation of the Laws of the State of Georgia*, 85, 279, 477; Bonner, *Milledgeville*, 75.

26. Born in 1798, Hepburn would marry Arabella Bostwick. He joined Thomas Bradford and William Danelly in business. His law firm was Rockwell & Hepburn. In 1820 he brought rice, cotton and dry goods from Savannah to New York on the brig *Hope*. By 1823 he was operating as Burton Hepburn & Co. Like Calhoun, he was a Mason. He was appointed aide-de-camp to the judge advocate of the 3rd Division, Georgia Militia in 1929. By 1830, he had a family of five and nine slaves, according to the census. *Sons of the American Revolution Membership Applications, 1889–1970*, Ancestry.com; *Georgia Journal*, February 22, 1820, and July 1, 1823; *National Advocate*, July 4, 1820; *American*, December 9, 1820; *Federal Union*, November 27, 1830; *Southern Recorder*, March 21, 1829.

27. His first wife, Mary, died in 1819 at age fifty-seven. "She had been an acceptable member of the Methodist Church for 32 years." A second wife, also named Mary, died at age forty-one. "For the last 20 years . . . she was an acceptable member of the Methodist Episcopal Church." The clergyman himself died on February 13, 1836, at age sixty-seven, leaving a wife and children. His funeral was preached in the Methodist Church in Milledgeville on March 27, 1836. *Georgia Journal*, July 13, 1819, December 12, 1820, and March 1 and 22, 1836.

28. *Georgia Journal*, November 13, 1821; *Southern Recorder*, November 13, 1821.

29. Caroline was the daughter of Benjamin A. Simmons and Sarah Stovall Simmons. Houston, 16; G. G. Smith, 207, 209–10.

30. *Georgia Journal*, December 9, 1823, and July 19 and December 27, 1825.

31. *Georgia Journal*, March 22 and April 26, 1825, April 25, 1826, January 14, 1828; *Southern Recorder*, July 1, 1823, April 30, 1827, March 3, 10, and 17, and April 21, 1828, October 10, 1829 and January 9, 1830; Bonner, 33–35; Phillips, 3; *Southern Banner*, September 15, 1829.

32. Dawson was also a Mason, elected Grand Master of the Grand Lodge of Free and Accepted Masons in Georgia in 1843. He served until his death in 1856. A. Cook, 230; *Southern Recorder*, December 21, 1826; Green, 317–18; *Macon Messenger*, December 11, 1830; Abbott, 434–35; Winn, *The Triumph of the Ecunnau-Nuxulgee,*, vii, 1–2, 16, 20, 23.

33. The Calhouns may have lived in Charleston for a time in 1825. *Charleston Courier*, May 4, 1825.

34. *Georgia Journal*, September 7, 1825.

35. Allen and Andrews, *Index of City of Milledgeville*, 20; Huxford, *Marriages and Obituaries*, 10.

36. Bonner, 52–53.

37. Burt and Ferguson, 138, 173, 175; J. Cook, 98, 102; Burnette; *Georgia Journal*, December, 21, 1824; Nichols, 199–200; Green, 312.

38. *Georgia Journal*, July 11, 1826; J. Cook, 102; *Hancock Advertiser*, December 22, 1828;, "The Georgia Penitentiary at Milledgeville 1817–1874," 304–7, 309.

39. *Georgia Messenger*, June 6, 1829.

40. Calhoun's efforts those two years were modest. One bill sought to add a piece of Hancock County to Baldwin County, another to incorporate the trustees of the Masonic Hall, a third to allow churches to rent or sell their parsonage lots. *Georgia Journal*, November 20, 1830, and November 24, 1831.

41. Bonner, *Milledgeville*, 59, 70; *Federal Union*, October, 30, 1830; *Georgia Journal*, August 4, 1831.

42. *Georgia Journal*, November 13 and 27 and December 25, 1830; Bonner, *Milledgeville*, 21.

43. Green, 314; *Georgia Journal*, July 14, 1828.

44. Coulter, "The Nullification Movement in Georgia," 3–7; *Federal Union*, February 25, 1851.

45. *Georgia Journal*, November 22, 1832; *Southern Recorder*, August 23, 1832; Coulter, "Nullification Movement," 14, 18, 36; Green, 317; Skelton, "The States Rights Movement in Georgia, 1825–1850," 399; J. Cook, 102.

46. *Southern Recorder*, July 19 and September 27, 1832; *Georgia Journal*, November 12, 1832; Green, 313–14, 318. Green said Calhoun was a director of the Cherokee Land Lottery, which is incorrect.

Chapter Two

1. Martin, *Columbus, Georgia, 1827–1865*, 6–7; Worsley, "Columbus," 366–67; White, *Historical Collections of Georgia*, 568; Debo, *The Road to Disappearance*, 96.

2. He would sell it in 1830. Lamar's wife died that year on August 20 at age twenty-one. He moved to Texas, where he became president of the republic in 1838. Gambrell, "Lamar, Mirabeau Buonaparte (1798–1859)."

3. Worsley, 369; White, 568.

4. *Columbus Enquirer*, August 4, 1832; Martin, 48.

5. Kilbourne, *Columbus, Georgia, Newspaper Clippings*, 1:189, 2:193. He was apparently living in neighboring Harris County in 1833. *Columbus Enquirer*, December 28, 1833.

6. Seaborn Jones was born in Augusta, Georgia, on February 1, 1788, to Abraham Jones and Sarah Bugg. Admitted to the bar in 1808, he was an aide to governors Peter Early and George Troup and practiced law in Milledgeville and Columbus. In 1810 he married Mary Howard, daughter of John and Jane Howard. Jones started a grist mill, City Mills, in 1828. A Democrat, he served two terms in Congress, from 1833 to 1835 and 1845 to 1847. He died on March 18, 1864. Northern, *Men of Mark in Georgia*, 2:236–42.

7. Martin, 41; *Columbus Enquirer*, October 19, 1833.

8. Martin, 17, 31, 39, 43, 88; *Letter from the Secretary of the Treasury*, 204; G. G. Smith, 418.

9. Edward G. Cary was born May 10, 1789. He married Lucinda Clayton on September 4, 1811. Following her death, he married Elizabeth Jane Howard on April 29, 1826. Elizabeth's sister Mary was married to Seaborn Jones. Cary died on June 24, 1860. The Tabb Family in the United States, 110.

10. *Federal Union*, May 2, 1833; *Georgian*, December 20, 1831, and May 16, 1832; *Georgia Telegraph*, June 18, 1831; *Columbus Enquirer*, November 23, 1833.

11. *Columbus Enquirer*, August 20, 1869; Mahan, *Columbus*, 32–33; Martin, 47, 168–69; Lamar, "Reminiscences of Columbus," *Columbus Daily Enquirer*, October 11, 1891), 12; *Federal Union*, November 27, 1830; *Savannah Republican*, February 3, 1826.

12. Hepburn was listed in the Baldwin County census in 1830, and he drew in the 1832 Baldwin County lottery. He was cashier in the Insurance Bank of Columbus; Daniel McDougald was a director. *Columbus Enquirer*, May 19, 1832.

13. Charles L. Bass was born January 5, 1812, to Sterling and Elizabeth Bass. He married Rebecca Mary Fluker on May 9, 1837, in Bibb County. Their daughter Helen Campbell Bass was born April 9, 1838. He died June 26, 1852, and is buried in Russell County, Alabama. Ancestry.com.

14. *Columbus Enquirer*, December 28, 1833, and January 9 and July 10, 1835; *Georgia Journal*, December 16, 1823, and May 4, 1824; Martin, 167; Mahan, 22, 32.

15. *Columbus Enquirer*, October 19, 1835, and February 19 and April 15, 1836.

16. *Columbus Enquirer*, July 17 and 31, August 7, October 9, November 20 and 27, 1835, and January 5, 1837; *Federal Union*, September 12, 1833; *Georgia Journal*, July 17, 1830; Green, 319; Martin, 48; Galer, *Columbus, Georgia*, 1, 3–6, 8–9.

17. Mueller, 35; *Columbus Enquirer*, March 4, 1836.

18. *Columbus Enquirer*, January 27, 1833; *St. Joseph Times*, September 17, 1839; *Southern Recorder*, September 27, 1836; Martin, 77, 81, 88, 101.

19. Scott, "The Troubled World of Antebellum Banking in Georgia"; Acts of the General Assembly of the State of Georgia, 143–45.

20. *Macon Weekly Telegraph*, June 30, 1836; *Georgia Journal* and *Southern Recorder*, March 1, 1836; *Columbus Enquirer*, March 4, 1836.

21. Ware, "Cotton Money," 215–33; *Columbus Enquirer*, August 4, 1832; Scott, "Banking Lessons from the Antebellum South", and "Troubled World."

22. Winn, 315, 317–18; *Macon Weekly Telegraph*, December 24, 1835.

23. *Columbus Enquirer*, July 3 and 10, 1835; Martin, 51; Lamar, 10–11.

24. *Georgia Journal*, December 1, 1835; *Southern Recorder*, November 10, 13, 17, 27–30; *Macon Weekly Telegraph*, November 19, 1835; *Augusta Chronicle*, November 28, 1835.

25. *Columbus Enquirer*, December 29, 1836.

Chapter Three

1. Winn, 10; Causes of Hostilities of the Creek and Seminole Indians in Florida, 6:14; Ellisor, *The Second Creek War*, 51.

2. Wright Jr., *Creeks and Seminoles*, xi, 21–22; Winn, 11; Causes of Hostilities, 14; Ellisor, 51; Debo, 1; Tyler, *A History of Indian Policy*, 11.

3. Ellisor, 3; Winn, 9–10; Foreman, *Indian Removal*, 108; Martin, 19, 23, 28–29.

4. Young, "The Creek Frauds," 411–12, 414; Young, *Redskins, Ruffleshirts and Rednecks*, 74; Ellisor, 47; Martin, 35–36; G. G. Smith, 418.

5. Other investors were merchant Jonathan A. Hudson, James Wadsworth, merchant G. W. Dillingham, Anderson and Charles Abercrombie, Dr. Stephen M. Ingersoll, merchant Hampton S. Smith, Henry and Joel Branham, Farish Carter, Charles D. Stewart, merchant John Fontaine, and Seaton Grantland.

6. Young, "Creek Frauds," 414, 419; Winn, 321; Ellisor, 63; Foreman, 112.

7. Young, "Creek Frauds," 419; Young, *Redskins*, 79; Ellisor, 91–92; Foreman, 124.

8. T. Hartley Crawford to J. R. Poinsett, Secretary of War, May 11, 1838, in *Alleged Frauds on Creek Indians*, 9, 10; Winn, 372–73.

9. Alfred Balch, Report on the Sales of Indian Reservations, 28–29; Winn, 376; Young, "Creek Frauds," 424.

10. Others on the list were G. W. Dillingham & Co.; Eli S. Shorter and John S. Scott; M. W. Perry & Co.; John H. Howard; Shorter, Tarver, and Shorter; John J. Owens; John Fontaine; James Boykin; and Elliott & Hargraves. Jones to Cass, April 17, 1834, Message from the President of the United States, in compliance with a resolution of the Senate, 123.

11. Winn, 374–76; Young, *Redskins*, 84; Balch, 123.

12. *Columbus Enquirer*, October 25 and December 20, 1834.

13. *Georgia Constitutionalist*, December 13, 1833; *Federal Union*, December 11, 1833, and July 19, 1836; *Southern Recorder*, November 13, 1833; Winn, 420.

14. Shorter to John S. Scott and M. M. and N. H. Craven, January 28, 1835, in Alleged Frauds, 63; Shorter to Scott, Corley, and Craven, March 1, 1835, in Alleged Frauds, 64–65; Tarver to Craven, March 1, 1835, in Alleged Frauds, 63.

15. *Columbus Enquirer*, March 13 and September 18, 1835; Winn, 384, 389; McDougald to Lumpkin, February 4 and 21, 1835, F2McDougaldDaniel0105, Georgia Archives.

16. Other members of the company were Luther Blake, Dr. Mills, William Walker, Thomas S. Woodward, and John D. Howell. Sanford to Cass, June 22, 1835, in *Daily Constitution*, July 17, 1835; Young, "Creek Frauds," 427.

17. Winn, 393; *Columbus Enquirer*, June 19, 1835.

18. Foreman, 133; Alleged Frauds, 10–11; Hogan to Herring, October 15, 1835, in Causes of Hostilities, 667; *Federal Union*, July 19, 1836; Young, "Creek Frauds," 426.

19. Shorter et al. to Cass, October 16, 1835, Causes of Hostilities, 667–69. Others on the list were Eli S. Shorter; Shorter & Scott; Shorter, Tarver & Co.; J. A. Hudson; Hudson & Fontaine; Huson & McDougal; Alex J. Robeson & Co.; Wellborn & Robison; Luther Blake; Blake & Carr; G. W. Dellingham & Co.; J. J. Fannin & Co.; Jno. D. Howell & Co.; McDougald, Howell & Co.; J. W. Woodland; Peabody &

Woodland; Powell & Watson; Daniel McDougald; McDougald & Mills; N. B. Powell & Co.; T. J. Worsham; Worsham & Calhoon [sic]; William Ellis.

20. Shorter, Tarver & Co. et al. to the President, November 18, 1835, in Causes of Hostilities, 676. On the list were Shorter, Tarver & Co.; Shorter & Scott; Seli S. Shorter; G. W. Dillingham & Co.; Luther Blake & Co.; Powell & Watson; McDougald & Co.; McDougald & Hudson; J. A. Hudson; Peabody & Woodland; Hudson & Fontaine; J. W. Woodland & Co.; Columbus Mills; J. G. Worsham and J. S. Calhoun; McDougald & Mills; Shorter, Tarver & Shorter; Eli S. Shorter & Co.; William C. Hill & Co.; E. Corby & Co.; and E. E. Bissell & Co.

21. Shorter et al. to Cass, November 23, 1835, Causes of Hostilities, 677–79. On the list were Shorter, Tarver & Co.; Shorter & Scott; Eli S. Shorter; G. W. Dillingham & Co.; Luther Blake & Co.; Powell & Watson; McDougald & Co.; McDougald & Hudson; J. S. Hudson; Peabody & Woodland; Hudson & Fontaine; J. W. Woodland & Co.; Columbus Mills; J. G. Worsham; J. C. [sic] Calhoun; McDougald & Mills; Shorter, Tarver & Shorter; E. E. Bissell & Co.; Eli S. Shorter & Co.; E. Corby & Co; and William C. Hill & Co.

22. Martin, 51, 53–55, 58–59, 66, 77; Causes of Hostilities, 15; *Federal Union*, December 13, 1832; McDougald to Towns, January 23, 1849, Georgia Archives. Burton Hepburn was first lieutenant, Hines Holt was second lieutenant, and Charles Bass was a private.

23. McDougald to Schley, January 20, 1836, FM2McDougaldDaniel0109, Georgia Archives.

24. *New York Evening Post*, February 8, 1836; Martin, 58–59.

25. McDougald to Schley, January 20, 27, and 30, and February 1 and 2, 1836, Vertical files, Muscogee County—Military, Georgia Archives; Calhoun to Schley, January 27, 1836, F2CalhounJamesS, Georgia Archives; *Patriot and Democrat*, February 20, 1836; Winn, 413.

26. Winn, 414, 428; McDougald to Schley, March 18, 1836, F2McDougaldDaniel0118, Georgia Archives.

27. Martin, 66; Ehle, *Trail of Tears*, 286; Winn, 434–35.

28. Winn, 437; *National Banner* and *Nashville Whig*, May 23, 1836.

29. Wright, 267–68; Winn, 438–40, 448.

30. Wright, 266; Winn, 429; Foreman, 153 fn4; Ellisor, 302–3; Martin, 67.

31. Winn, 443–44, 455–57; Martin, 61.

32. Wright, 267–68; Winn, 410, 450, 452–53, 459; *Macon Messenger*, May 19, 1836; Martin, 63–64, 72–73; Burt and Ferguson, 178–79; Ehle, 286; Foreman, 152, 154, 166.

33. Young, "Creek Frauds," 428; Ellisor, 324; Causes of Hostilities, 14, 17; Deposition of Captain John Page, Creek Superintendent, December 5, 1836, in *Contract: General Jesup*, 76–79; Alleged Frauds, 12–14, 16, 56–61; Letter from the Secretary of War; Young, *Redskins*, 90; Ellisor, 327–28; Message from the President of the United States, 137.

34. Young, *Redskins*, 91–93, 107; Young, "Creek Frauds," 431, 433; Ellisor, 328; *Columbus Enquirer*, December 13, 1836; *Georgia Constitutionalist*, December 20, 1836. Watson would die in 1843 in Alabama at fifty-six years old (Martin, 144).

35. Indian Depredations.

36. Winn, 457–58, 462; Ellisor, 49, 310; Young, "Creek Frauds," 436.

Chapter Four

1. Bancroft, "The Financial Panic of 1837"; "The Panic of 1837"; Sobel, "Panic of 1837."

2. Ware, 223, 225, 229.

3. *Macon Weekly Telegraph*, June 30, 1836; *Columbus Enquirer*, October 20 and 27, November 3, 17, and 24, December 13 and 29, 1836, and October 5, 1837.

4. *Columbus Enquirer*, January 5, March 9, and April 1 and 27, 1837; *Federal Union and Georgia Journal*, May 2, 1837; *Southern Recorder*, May 23, 1837.

5. *Columbus Enquirer*, May 18, 1837.

6. *Spectator*, May 11, 1837; *Georgia Journal*, June 2, 1840; *Columbus Enquirer*, August 10, 1837, and August 29, 1848; *Georgia Constitutionalist*, October 10, 1840.

7. *Columbus Enquirer*, December 29, 1836, January 12 and 26, 1837, February 16, 1837, April 6, 1837, March 8, 1838, and December 19, 1838.

8. *Columbus Enquirer*, December 1, 1836, June 1, 1837, May 3, 1838, April 24, 1839; *Columbus Daily Enquirer*, May 26, 1982; Hayward, *Gazetteer of the United States of America*, 336; Historic Markers Across Georgia.

9. E. Whittlesey, Report by Committee of Claims; Green, 319–20; Abel, *Official Correspondence*, xii. In June Calhoun arrived in New York after a sixteen-day journey aboard ship to deliver sixty-seven bales of cotton to E. D. Hurlburt. *Evening Post* (New York), June 28, 1837.

10. *Columbus Enquirer*, October 26, 1837; Martin, 91.

11. Adolphus Cary, also known as Adolphus Rutherford, was born in Milledgeville in 1810. He was a sheriff and court clerk of Baldwin County. He lived in Columbus and Russell County, Alabama. He died in Montgomery, Alabama, in 1861. *Commercial Advertiser* (New York), October 6, 1840; Ellis, *Norwich University, 1819–1911*, 335, 342.

12. US General Land Office records show repeated acquisitions in 1837, 1838, and 1841.

13. Martin, 85–86, 99; Wood, "The Georgia Railroad and Banking Company," 545, 549; G. G. Smith, 419; Mahan, 34–36, 38.

14. *Columbus Enquirer*, January 26 and December 19, 1838; Green, 322; Martin, 91; Indian Depredations.

15. Martin, 97; *Southern Recorder*, December 4, 1838; *Columbus Enquirer*, September 20 and 27, 1838, and March 17, 1841; *Macon Weekly Telegraph*, December 18, 1838; *Augusta Chronicle*, November 5, 1847; Gates, "Canals"; Lupold, "Columbus";

Acts Passed by the General Assembly of Georgia, 143–46. Calhoun also carried a bill to incorporate Muscogee Insurance Company; when it opened for business in 1841, Calhoun's friend Hampton S. Smith was a director.

16. In the lottery that year Calhoun drew a ninety-acre lot in Talbot County and a lot bordering the Ocmulgee River in Houston County. Campbell and Henry, *Land Records of Houston County*, 3:108, 5:66.

17. *Columbus Enquirer*, September 11, 1839; Galer, 9, 10, 12; Luckett, "Charles McDonald (1793–1860)"; *Georgia Telegraph*, June 30, 1840.

18. *Columbus Enquirer*, October 7 and 14, 1840; *Federal Union*, September 12, 1843; *Southern Banner*, December 11, 1840; Green, 325, 327; Skelton, 401–2.

19. Hines Holt Jr. was born in 1805 in LaGrange, Hancock County, where his father practiced law. He ran for state treasurer in 1827, was elected to the State House of Representatives in 1841, served briefly in Congress to fill the vacancy caused by the resignation of his cousin, Walter T. Colquitt, and returned to his law practice. He was treasurer of Georgia in 1859, and in 1859 and 1860 he was a state senator. He became a member of the House of Representatives of the First Confederate Congress in 1862 and resigned March 1, 1863, after the third session. He died November 4, 1865. *Biographical Directory of the United States Congress*; *Augusta Chronicle*, April 9, 1796; *Georgia Journal*, September 17, 1827.

20. Hines Holt Sr. was born in 1770, married Mary Dixon Seward, and in 1842 died at age seventy-two in Russell County, Alabama, where he'd moved shortly before his death at the urging of his children because of its milder climate. He was a native of Virginia who moved to Georgia in 1797. *Columbus Enquirer*, May 12, 1842.

21. Robert B. Alexander was born in Putnam County, educated at the University of Georgia, and read law with William H. Torrance. He married Ann Maria Harris in Athens on April 4, 1837. He would become a judge on the Chattahoochee Circuit in 1846 and in Superior Court in 1849. When he died in 1851 at age thirty-nine, he was described as "one of our best, most useful, and most estimable citizens." *Columbus Enquirer*, February 18, 1851; *Southern Recorder*, February, 25, 1851.

22. *Columbus Enquirer*, July 15, October 14, November 18, and December 2, 1840, and June 19, 1849; Green, 328–29; *Southern Recorder*, November 3 and 17, 1840.

23. On December 8, 1840, Calhoun presented a letter to the state legislature asking for banks to resume specie payments. Although legislators passed a bill compelling several banks to resume payments of their liabilities in specie, it wasn't possible unless the legislature provided the means for the Central Bank and the Bank of Darien, owned by the state of Georgia, to aid the banks. *Columbus Enquirer*, December 16, 1840.

24. *Columbus Enquirer*, October 21, November 25, and December 9, 16, and 30, 1840; *Southern Recorder*, November 24, and December 8, 1840; *Federal Union*, November 24, 1840.

25. *Federal Union*, December 22, 1840; *Columbus Enquirer*, December 23, 1840; Skelton, 403.

26. *Columbus Enquirer*, March 4, 1840, and May 12 and July 28, 1841; Ware, 220; *Macon Weekly Telegraph*, June 22, 1841.

27. In 1849, before leaving for New Mexico, Calhoun sold the house to Daniel Griffin, who had its grounds landscaped to the river with camellias, azaleas, daffodils, dogwoods, crepe myrtles, and shade trees. In 1856 Griffin sold the house to Colonel Randolph Lawler Mott, who saved it from destruction during the Civil War. It became the headquarters of Union General James H. Wilson in 1865 when his army torched most of the riverfront structures during the last land battle of the Civil War. In 1867 the Muscogee Manufacturing Company rose on the site of the burned Coweta Factory, and the house was used as offices. Mott owned the home until his death in 1881. The cotton factory eventually surrounded and encapsulated the house, which remained hidden for nearly a century. It was again used for administrative offices of Fieldcrest Mills in 1986. In 1997 a technology company, TSYS, bought the property and in 2014 was beginning to renovate the home as a conference center and board room when it burned to the ground. It was the last remaining Chattahoochee riverfront mansion between Columbus and the Gulf of Mexico. *Ledger-Enquirer*, September 7, 2014; *Columbus, Georgia and the Counties of Marion, Muscogee*, 98; Mahan, 47.

28. Boatwright, 17, 46, 78, 114–15; *Columbus Enquirer*, January 22 and September 30, 1840. James Calhoun was a reference for the high school, and so was the more famous Calhoun, John C.

29. *Columbus Enquirer*, October 18, 1834; Boatwright, 56.

30. Boatwright, 91–92.

31. *Stryker's American Register and Magazine*, 3:427; *Columbus Enquirer*, October 9, 1849, and June 17, 1851. Dawson studied law with Thomas W. Cobb and in the Litchfield Law School. In 1836 he was captain of volunteers under General Winfield Scott in the Creek and Seminole Indian War in Florida. As a senator Dawson supported the Compromise of 1850.

32. Wyly-Jones, "Dawson, William Crosby" /; Mellichamp, "William Dawson," 127–30. Dawson County and the town of Dawson were named for him.

33. *Columbus Enquirer*, August 4, 1841.

34. *Columbus Enquirer*, May 12, July 28, and August 4, 1841.

Chapter Five

1. *Columbus Enquirer*, March 31 and April 14, 1841; *Weekly Advertiser*, May 11, 1841.

2. *Columbus Enquirer*, November 10 and December 8, 1841; Whittlesey, 5; *Georgia Journal*, November 16, 1841; *Baltimore Sun*, December 20, 1841.

3. Gott, *Cuba*, 46–48, 61, 141; Paquette, "The Everett-Del Monte Connection," 1–2; Shewmaker, ed., *The Papers of Daniel Webster*, 1:326; *Augusta Chronicle*, December 3, 1842.

4. Paquette, *Sugar Is Made with Blood*, 138–41.

5. Trist married Virginia Jefferson Randolph, a granddaughter of Thomas Jefferson, whom Trist served as private secretary and executor of his estate. He was later Andrew Jackson's private secretary. In 1847 he was chief negotiator on the peace treaty to end the Mexican War. "Nicholas Philip Trist."

6. Paquette, "Everett-Del Monte," 1, 4, 8; Paquette, *Sugar*, 188–89.

7. Tyler to Webster, December 16, 1841, in Shewmaker, 367; Waddy Thompson to William Butler, November 24, 1841, in Shewmaker, 367–68.

8. Calhoun reported to Daniel Webster on February 2, 1842, that the schooner *Liberty*, of New York, was lost on the Great Stirrup Key on January 21. The *Woodbury* saw a signal of distress, hove to, and was boarded by Captain W. A. Howard of the *Liberty*, who asked for help. The *Woodbury* took onboard ten people. A Baltimore brig took on the rest of the crew. No lives were lost but a large amount of money and baggage were lost. *Charleston Courant*, February 14, 1842.

9. Paquette, *Sugar*, 194–96.

10. He also asked King to support a Captain Morris who wanted to establish steamer service to Havana. Calhoun to Thomas Butler King, March 4 and 13, 1842, Thomas Butler King Papers, Roll 2.

11. Paquette, *Sugar*, 196–97; Gott, 60; *Georgia Telegraph*, May 24, 1842; *Columbus Enquirer*, April 7, 1842; *Civilian and Galveston Gazette*, December 28, 1842.

12. Webster to Campbell, January 14, 1843, in Shewmaker, 369–70; *Columbus Enquirer*, October 19, 1842; Webster to Washington Irving, March 14, 1843, in Shewmaker, 372; *Augusta Chronicle*, December 3, 1842.

13. Gott, 61–64; Paquette, "Everett-Del Monte," 11–14; Paquette, *Sugar*, 197, 198, 200, 202; *Columbus Enquirer*, October 19 and December 21, 1842; *Georgia Journal*, December 27, 1842. Webster was secretary of state under Harrison and Tyler from March 6, 1841, to May 8, 1843. Duniway, "Daniel Webster and the West," 3.

14. *Columbus Enquirer*, December 21, 1842, and September 3, 1845.

15. Keleher, *Turmoil*, 130–31 fn65

16. *Columbus Enquirer*, January 11, 1843; *Georgia Journal*, January 16 and 31, 1843; *New York Herald*, January 13, 1843; Martin, 135.

17. *Evening Post*, January 14, 1843.

18. *Columbus Enquirer*, March 13, 1849, February 19, 26, and July 23, 1850; Martin, 109, 129; "Personal Recollections of the Late General Daniel McDougald," *Columbus Enquirer*, August 20, 1869.

19. Martin, 225; *Columbus Enquirer*, June 30, 1842; Skelton, 404; *Southern Banner*, August 19, 1842; *Georgia Journal*, November 7, 1843.

20. *Columbus Enquirer*, April 19, June 7, and 28, 1843; *Weekly National Intelligencer*, July 1, 1843.

21. *Columbus Enquirer*, August 9 and October 4, 1843.

22. *Columbus Enquirer*, March 11 and April 8, 1846; Martin, 142–44; Kilbourne, 4:404; Boatwright, 27. In June Love represented Lumpkin County at a State Rights convention to choose a candidate for governor (*Augusta Chronicle*, June 10, 1843).

23. *Federal Union*, September 12, 1843; Martin, 149–50; *Columbus Enquirer*, January 17, 1844; "Martin Van Buren—The Independent Treasury."

24. *Columbus Enquirer*, May 7, 1845; *Macon Weekly Telegraph*, May 27, 1845.

25. *Columbus Enquirer*, May 14, 1845.

26. *Columbus Enquirer*, May 14, July 2, and October 30, 1845.

27. *Columbus Enquirer*, May 14 and 21, 1845.

28. *Columbus Enquirer*, July 16 and August 27, 1845.

29. *Columbus Enquirer*, August 20, 1845.

30. *Columbus Enquirer*, December 3, 1845.

31. *Columbus Enquirer*, May 7 and 14 and October 29, 1845; Finlay, "Central of Georgia Railway"

32. Seymour R. Bonner was born in 1809 in Hancock County. He was sheriff of Muscogee County for four years and served a term as state representative. He died suddenly in Columbus in 1856 at age forty-seven, leaving a widow and six children. *Columbus Enquirer*, December 2, 1856.

33. *Columbus Enquirer*, August 20, 1845.

34. *Columbus Enquirer*, November 1, 1856.

35. *Columbus Enquirer*, November 26 and December 3, 1845.

36. *Columbus Enquirer*, December 3, 1845.

37. *Columbus Enquirer*, November 19 and 26, and December 3 and 17, 1845, and January 7, 1846; Boatwright, 25, 51.

38. Martin, 119; *Augusta Chronicle*, November 13, 1845, and November 5, 1847; *Savannah Daily Republican*, November 1, 1846; *Columbus Enquirer*, August 5, 1846; Gates, "Canals"; Lupold, "Columbus."

Chapter Six

1. McCrary, "Georgia Politics and the Mexican War," 211; DeVoto, *The Year of Decision*, 189, 203.

2. Berrien, *Speech of Mr. Berrien of Georgia*; McCrary, 215.

3. Telfair, *A History of Columbus, Georgia*, 74; Kurtz, "The First Regiment of Georgia Volunteers in the Mexican War," 306; Taylor to Dr. R. C. Wood, May 19, 1846, in Taylor, *Letters of Zachary Taylor*, 4.

4. *Columbus Enquirer*, May 13; *Southern Recorder*, May 19, 1846; Calhoun to King, May 9 and 16, 1846, Thomas Butler King Papers, Roll 3.

5. *Columbus Enquirer*, July 8, 1846.

6. *Columbus Enquirer*, June 3 and 10, and July 8, 1846.

7. One member of the Fannin Avengers was Henry Burroughs Holliday, father of Doc Holliday. The Fannin Avengers were sent to Monterrey, Veracruz, and Jalapa, where Henry was discharged on June 30, 1847. He returned home to Georgia with a ten-year-old orphan named Francisco Hidalgo, whom he raised as his son. Pendleton and Thomas, 194–195.

8. John Forsyth Jr. was born in 1812 and graduated from Princeton in 1832. He was US minister to Mexico in 1856; mayor of Mobile, Alabama, in 1860; chief of staff of the Confederate Army of Tennessee in 1863, with a commission as colonel; and editor of the *Mobile Register*. He died in 1878. Burnett, "John Forsyth, Jr."

9. *Federal Union*, June 16 and 23, 1846; *Columbus Enquirer*, July 1, 1846; Kurtz, 307.

10. *Georgia Telegraph*, July 1, 7, and 14, 1846; *Federal Union*, July 7, 1846; *Columbus Enquirer*, July 1 and 15, 1846; Butler, "Alfred Butler in the Mexican War"; *Southern Recorder*, July 21, 1846; McCaffrey, *Surrounded by Dangers of All Kinds*, 15; Kurtz, 309.

11. Smith and Judah, eds., *Chronicles of the Gringos*, 74.

12. *Georgia Telegraph*, July 28, 1846; *Federal Union*, August 4, 1846; Taylor to James Buchanan, August 29, 1847, in Taylor, 173, 177; Jenkins, *History of the War*, 154; Taylor, 42.

13. *Georgia Telegraph*, July 28, 1846; *Federal Union*, August 4, 1846.

14. *Columbus Enquirer*, August 3, 12, and 26, 1846; *Southern Recorder*, August 25, 1846; Eisenhower, *So Far from God*, 107–8; Historic Sites of the U.S.–Mexican War; Butler.

15. Parkes, *A History of Mexico*, 214; Smith and Judah, 283.

16. Smith and Judah, 320–25; Taylor to Wood, August 19, 1846, in *Letters of Zachary Taylor*, 43; DeVoto, 236; Tschanz, "Yellow Fever and the Strategy of the Mexican–American War."

17. *Columbus Enquirer*, August 26, 1846.

18. DeVoto, 288; Smith and Judah, 27; Kurtz, 310; Eisenhower, *So Far from God*, 109; *Southern Recorder*, August 25, 1846; *Columbus Enquirer*, November 24, 1846; *Federal Union*, October 6, 1846.

19. *Columbus Enquirer*, September 9, 1846.

20. Chance, ed., *The Mexican War Journal of Captain Franklin Smith*, 22–23, 31, 33; *Columbus Enquirer*, November 11, 1846; McCaffrey, 135; Kenly, *Memoirs of a Maryland Volunteer*, 151, 153.

21. *Columbus Enquirer*, November 11 and 18, 1846.

22. *Columbus Enquirer*, November 24 and December 29, 1846.

23. *Columbus Enquirer*, November 18, 1846.

24. Bauer, *The Mexican War 1846–1848*, 119; *Columbus Enquirer*, February 2, 1847.

25. Chance, 299–300; Bauer, 75; Kenly, 174–80.

26. *Columbus Enquirer*, December 29, 1846, January 5 and 12, and February 2, 1847; Kenly, 186–93.

27. Kenly, 195–97; *Columbus Enquirer*, February 2, 1847.

28. *Columbus Enquirer*, February 2, 1847.

29. *Columbus Enquirer*, February 2, 1847; Taylor, 41; Bauer, 75; Kenly, 174–80, 193; *Southern Recorder*, February 2, 1847.

30. Brooks, *A Complete History of the Mexican War*, 202; Kenly, 209–11; *Columbus Enquirer*, February 23, 1847.

31. Kenly, 211–34; Livingston-Little, ed., *The Mexican War Diary of Thomas D. Tennery*, 60.

32. *Columbus Enquirer*, March 2 and 9, 1847.

33. *Columbus Enquirer*, March 23 and April 13, 1847.

34. Like Calhoun, Captain Harrison J. Sargent would be a Whig candidate for office when he returned, in his case for the state senate. *Georgia Telegraph*, July 20, 1847.

35. Eisenhower, *So Far from God*, 257 fn; Jenkins, 251–55; Ober, *Travels in Mexico*, 174.

36. Sergeant Joseph King, Henry Lanbeck, and John G. Eubank were wounded slightly; Private T. J. Scott and quartermaster sergeant B. F. McDonald were wounded severely. Furber, *The Twelve Months Volunteer*, 556; *Southern Recorder*, April 6, 1847.

37. *Columbus Enquirer*, April 13, 1847.

38. *Columbus Enquirer*, April 13 and 20, 1847.

39. Jenkins, 265–66; J. Oswandel, *Notes of the Mexican War, 1846–1848*, 51; Johnson, *A Gallant Little Army*, 60.

40. Jenkins, 265–66.

41. *Columbus Enquirer*, April 20, 1847.

42. Columbus Enquirer, May 4, 1847.

43. Oswandel, 54; *Columbus Enquirer*, May 4, 1847.

44. *Columbus Enquirer*, May 11, 1847; Oswandel, 39, 41, 51, 54; Jenkins, 265–66, 285; Johnson, 60; Ober, 12.

45. *Columbus Enquirer*, May 18, 1847; Oswandel, 75; Kenly, 367; Ober, 186.

46. Jenkins, 287–88; Eisenhower, *Agent of Destiny*, 296; Oswandel, 81, 82; *Columbus Enquirer*, May 18 and 25, 1847; *Federal Union* June 1, 1847.

47. *Columbus Enquirer*, May 18 and June 1, 1847; *Southern Recorder*, July 20, 1847; *Federal Union*, June 1 and 15, 1847; Kurtz, 312; Candler and Evans, *Cyclopedia of Georgia*, 2:578.

Chapter Seven

1. Martin, 9–12, 19, 21, 23; *Columbus Times*, June 23, 1847; *Southern Recorder*, June 15, 1847; *Columbus Enquirer*, June 1, 22, and 30, July 27, and August 3 and 17, 1847; *Augusta Chronicle*, June 5, 1848.

2. *Columbus Enquirer*, September 7 and 14, 1847; *Albany Patriot*, September 23, 1848; Candler and Evans, 2:578; *Southern Whig*, November 11 and December 9 and 23, 1847.

3. Edwin Ross Goulding was born July 26, 1821, in Oglethorpe County. He was the son of Reverend Thomas Goulding, a prominent Presbyterian minister in Columbus and in Georgia. Ancestry.com.

4. Captain Charles A. Hamilton became a prominent leader during the Kansas

troubles. He died at home in Jones County on July 7, 1879; G. B. Smith, *History of the Georgia Militia, 1783–1861*, 1:247, fn38.

5. *Columbus Enquirer*, December 30, 1840, July 9, 1843, August 17 and September 7 and 14, 1847; Green, 330; *Augusta Chronicle*, January 14, 1848.

6. The initials JFB don't correspond with anyone in the command. The closest possibility is John H. Burnett, a fourth sergeant in Captain Fulton's company.

7. *Columbus Enquirer*, September 21 and October 12, 1847.

8. *Columbus Enquirer*, October 12, 1847; *Federal Union*, October 19, 1847.

9. *Columbus Enquirer*, October 26 and November 23, 1847; *Southern Recorder*, November 9, 1847.

10. *Columbus Enquirer*, November 23, 1847; *Southern Recorder*, November 23 and 26, 1847.

11. *Columbus Enquirer*, December 7, 21, and 23, 1847; *Federal Union*, December 10, 1847; *Southern Recorder*, February 1, 1848; *Albany Patriot*, December 29, 1847.

12. *Southern Recorder*, February 1, 48; *Augusta Chronicle*, January 27, 1848.

13. *Daily Chronicle and Sentinel*, February 22, 24, and 26, 1848; Ober, 501; *Southern Recorder*, February 22, 1848.

14. Smith and Judah, 403–4; Robarts, *Mexican War Veterans*, 43; *Daily Constitutionalist*, February 26, 1848; *Columbus Enquirer*, April 18, 1848; Ober, 402; *Federal Union*, April 25, 1848; *Southern Recorder*, April 25, 1848.

15. William Tatum Wofford was born June 28, 1824, in Habersham County, Georgia. He was a lawyer when he volunteered for the Mexican War. After returning home to Cassville in 1848, he served in the state legislature, edited a newspaper, and ran his plantation. In the Civil War, he was colonel of the Eighteenth Georgia Infantry and fought in the battles of Yorktown and Second Bull Run in Virginia and in Maryland at South Mountain, Sharpsburg, and Antietam. At the Battle of Fredericksburg, when Thomas R. R. Cobb fell, Wofford assumed command and was promoted to brigadier general. He led the Georgia Brigade at Chancellorsville, Virginia, and Gettysburg, Pennsylvania. Wofford was wounded in Virginia at the Battle of the Wilderness and in Spotsylvania. He defended Georgians from rogue forces and guerilla attacks until the end of the war. After the war, he was active in Democratic politics and the law. Wofford died on May 22, 1884, in Bartow County. Horney, "W. T. Wofford (1824–1884)."

16. *Columbus Enquirer*, November 23, 1847; *Southern Whig*, March 23, 1848.

17. *Columbus Enquirer*, April 18 and 25, and August 1, 1848; Johnson, *Winfield Scott*, 210–12; Eisenhower, *Agent of Destiny*, 313–14.

18. Tucker, *The Encyclopedia of the Mexican-American War*, 666; *Columbus Enquirer*, May 2, 1848.

19. *Columbus Enquirer*, April 4 and 18 and May 30, 1848; *Augusta Chronicle*, June 15, 1848.

20. Wilcox, *History of the Mexican War*, 550; Bauer, 387–88; *Columbus Enquirer*, July 4, 1848; Tucker, 734.

21. *Columbus Enquirer*, July 11, 1848; *Augusta Chronicle*, April 2, 1849.

22. *Southern Whig*, November 16, 1848; *Daily Chronicle and Sentinel*, July 6, 1848; *Southern Recorder*, July 18, 1848; Winders, *Mr. Polk's Army*, 147; *Columbus Enquirer*, July 4 and August 29, 1848.

23. *Augusta Chronicle*, July 20, 1848; *Columbus Enquirer*, August 1, 1848; *Congressional Globe*, February 18, 1859, 1,111.

Chapter Eight

1. *Southern Recorder*, July 18, 1848; *Albany Courier*, August 8, 1848; *Albany Patriot*, August 5, 1848.

2. *Daily National Intelligencer*, July 29, 1848; Abel, *Official Correspondence*, 11–12; Calhoun to Marcy, November 25, 1848, and March to Calhoun, December 7, 1848, in Abel, *Official Correspondence*, 13; *Daily Union*, July 11, 1849; *Columbus Enquirer*, August 22, 1848; Von Abele, *Alexander H. Stephens*, 117; W. Y. Thompson, *Robert Toombs of Georgia*, 45–47, 50.

3. *Savannah Daily Republican*, August 26, 1848; *Albany Patriot*, September 16, 1848; *Columbus Enquirer*, August 29, 1848.

4. *Columbus Enquirer*, September 12, October 3 and 10, and November 14, 1848; *Albany Patriot*, September 23 and 30, 1848.

5. Martin, 32; *Columbus Enquirer*, June 27, 1875. Davis enlisted in the Crawford Guards in July 1846. In 1848 Davis was secretary of the newly organized Vigilant Fire Company No. 2 and dutifully voted to pay a special tax for the railroad. *Columbus Enquirer*, July 1, 1846, and March 7, 1848; Martin, 27.

6. *Columbus Enquirer*, November 21 and December 12, 1848; Calhoun to Marcy, January 13, 1849, Georgia Archives.

7. Abel, *Official Correspondence*, 1 fn2, 2; Adams, *Indian Policies in the Americas*, 179; Annual Report of the Commissioner of Indian Affairs, for the year 1849; *Savannah Daily Republican*, April 10, 1849; *Daily Union*, July 6, 1849.

8. Green wrote, "Calhoun saw service under General Zachary Taylor, and the two became firm friends." Calhoun never met Taylor until after the war. Green, 330; Steel Jr., *T. Butler King of Georgia*, 60, 69–70; *Daily Union*, November 29, 1849; *Biographical Directory*; Coulter, "John Jordan Crittenden"; Von Abele, 113, 119; *Georgia Telegraph*, September 4, 1849; Calhoun to King, December 14, 1837, King Papers.

9. Larson, *New Mexico's Quest for Statehood*, 27; *Georgia Telegraph*, September 4, 1849; Thompson, 42, 44; Von Abele, 118; Hubbell, "Three Georgia Unionists and the Compromise of 1850," 307; Richardson, *A Compilation of the Messages and Papers of the Presidents*, 5:27–28; Steel, 73.

10. On February 16, 1843, Texas President Sam Houston made Jacob Snively a colonel with instructions to lead his 176-man "Battalion of Invincibles" on raids against Mexican merchants on the Santa Fe Trail to retaliate for injuries to Texas citizens. Their payment would be in seized trade goods. Colonel Stephen W. Ke-

arny sent dragoons to guard the traders and, if necessary, capture the Texian land pirates. In late May, Captain Philip St. George Cooke began patrolling the trail and accompanying caravans. In June, Snively and his Invincibles intercepted and released the wagon train of veteran trader Ceran St. Vrain, who then informed Cooke of Snively's location, and on June 30 Cooke disarmed Snively's men and sent them home. Texas diplomats protested and the United States ignored them; the Invincibles had been inside the United States. Gorenfeld, "The Snively Affair," 28, 30, 31, 40–42, 45–47.

11. William Medill was born in New Jersey and moved to Ohio as a young man. A Democrat, he served in the Legislature and in Congress. President Polk appointed him commissioner of Indian Affairs, and he served from 1845 to 1849. In 1853 he was elected governor of Ohio. He died in 1865. *Plain Dealer*, September 6, 1865.

12. Abel, *Official Correspondence*, 2–3; Records of US Army Commands, Crawford, War Department, April 3, 1849, DNM LSR, RG 98, 92, 192, roll 1, NA.

13. J. A. L. Lee, born in 1813 in South Carolina, was a delegate to the Whig Convention from Muscogee in 1844 and an alderman in Columbus in 1848. He was appointed postmaster in 1849. That year he was representing claims against the government for property lost or destroyed in military service. He was still in Columbus in 1873. *Southern Recorder*, July 2, 1844; *Columbus Enquirer*, February 29, 1848, and August 14, 1849; *Columbus Daily Enquirer*, June 1, 1873.

14. The sheriff was selling an additional eight slaves and their children belonging to William E. Love to satisfy debts to Seaborn Jones. *Columbus Enquirer*, February 27, 1849.

15. *Columbus Enquirer*, February 27 and April 29, 1849; *Southern Recorder*, April 24, 1849; Calhoun to Ewing, April 17, 1849, in Abel, *Official Correspondence*, 9–10; *Daily Chronicle and Sentinel*, April 23, 1849.

16. John G. Jones was born around 1815 in Laurens County, Georgia. He was a first sergeant in the Columbus Guards, a volunteer company mustered into service for the Creek War. He was regarded as one of the Guard's best soldiers. *Columbus Daily Enquirer*, November 15, 1903; *Commercial Appeal*, April 26, 1864.

17. Brice Asa Hoxey was born October 22, 1825, the son of Thomas and Mary Reid Gaither Hoxey. Ancestry.com.

18. Mitchell, born in 1811 in Georgia, served as a private in the Columbus Guards and was a member of the Columbus bridge committee in 1847. *Southern Recorder*, June 30, 1846, and *Columbus Enquirer*, February 23, 1847.

19. Martin was born in 1818 or 1819 in Georgia. He was a second corporal in the Columbus Guards, a volunteer company mustered into service for the Creek War. *Columbus Daily Enquirer*, November 15, 1903.

20. According to the 1850 Census, Jackson, age twenty-five, was from Washington, DC.

21. Born in South Carolina in 1799, Choice participated in the land lottery in Carroll County and won acreage in DeKalb County in the 1827 lottery. He was first

lieutenant in the DeKalb Independent Guards, a militia unit, in 1836, starting as a first lieutenant. All of DeKalb's militia companies were attached to the Fifty-fourth Regiment of the Georgia Militia. His wife Aviline died at age thirty-three in Decatur after a "long and protracted illness of several years." He served as a director of Merchants and Planters Bank of Florida in Tallahassee in 1842. He was a candidate for state representative on the Nullification ticket in DeKalb County. Cyrus Choice owned two lots in Columbus and lost them to satisfy debts. He applied for service in Calhoun's regiment of mounted volunteers during the Mexican War but by then the regiment had enough men. *Columbus Enquirer*, July 17, 1839, May 28, and July 2, 1845; *DeKalb County, Georgia, Military Indian Wars*, USGenWeb Archives; *Star of Florida*, March 31, 1842; *Federal Union*, September 26, 1833; Price, *The History of DeKalb County Georgia, 1822–1900*, 210.

22. Calhoun to Medill, October 15, 1849, in Abel, *Official Correspondence*, 48; *Federal Union*, October 26, 1841; *Southern Recorder*, September 26, 1848; *Columbus Enquirer*, May 29, 1844; *Charleston Courier*, August 18, 1849.

23. Barbour, *Reluctant Frontiersman*, 32–33; Calhoun to Clayton, April 27, 1851, in Abel, *Official Correspondence*, 332; Gardner, "Wagons on the Santa Fe Trail: 1822–1880," 53–55.

24. *Daily Union*, July 6, 1849; *Republic*, July 26, 1849.

25. Russell, *Land of Enchantment*, 12, 18; Calhoun to Crawford, May 22, 1849, and Calhoun to Medill, May 24, 1849, in Abel, *Official Correspondence*, 14–15; *Boston Courier*, June 14, 1849; M. Simmons, *The Old Trail to Santa Fe*, 36, 144; *Columbus Enquirer*, September 11, 1849.

26. Calhoun to Clayton, April 27, 1851, in Abel, *Official Correspondence*, 334; M. Simmons, *The Old Trail to Santa Fe*, 25; Barbour, 46, 49–50, 83; Dary, *The Santa Fe Trail*, 212–14; Magoffin, *Down the Santa Fe Trail and into Mexico*, 2.

27. Russell, 14; Emory et al., *Notes of a Military Reconnaissance*, 11, 13; Gregg, *The Commerce of the Prairies*, 30;. Myers, "The Journal of Captain Philip St. George Cooke," 44–7; Twitchell, *Leading Facts of New Mexican History*, 2:111; Dickerman, "Mid-Nineteenth-Century Botanical Exploration in New Mexico," 167–68; *St. Louis Republican*, May 17, 1849.

28. *Columbus Enquirer*, September 11, 1849.

29. Myers, 50–51; Kattell, *At the Confluence of Two Cultures*, 102–3; Calhoun to Medill, July 29, 1849, in Abel, *Official Correspondence*, 7–18; J. Robinson, *Journal of the Santa Fe Expedition*, 75–76, 121; *Boston Courier*, August 9, 1849.

30. Emory, 48; Rathbun and Alexander, *New Mexico Frontier Military Place Names*, 105; Gottschalk, *Pioneer Merchants of Las Vegas*, 1; Laumbach, "Las Vegas Before 1850," 251; Weber, *The Taos Trappers*, 158; Gregg, 100.

31. Emory, 31; Twitchell, *Leading Facts*, 2:121; Duffus, *The Santa Fe Trail*, 156–57; Russell, 26; *Columbus Enquirer*, September 11, 1849; Davis, *El Gringo*, 101.

32. The Palace of the Governors is the nation's longest continuously used government building. Twitchell, *Leading Facts*, 2:147.

33. Tórrez, "Mexican Patriotism in New Mexico, 1821–1846," 139; Weber, *The Mexican Frontier, 1821–1846*, 19, 180–81, 272.

34. Bent, a Virginia native, graduated from West Point, resigned from the army, and went into business in St. Louis. In 1828, he set out on the Santa Fe Trail to find a location for a trading post and, with his brother William and Ceran St. Vrain, built the famous Bent's Fort. Loyola, "The American Occupation of New Mexico, 1821–1852," 65.

35. Larson, 4–7; Loyola, 65; *Alexandria Gazette*, October 3, 1846.

36. Settlers were already living along the south bank of the Santa Fe River in 1608, when Governor Pedro de Peralta established the villa on the north bank. The Palace was built around 1610. Lera, "The Palace of the Governors Stamp Designs," 461–63; "Palace of the Governors," historicsantafe.org.

37. Twitchell, *Leading Facts*, 2:147; Duffus, 158–61; Edwards, *A Campaign in New Mexico with Colonel Doniphan*, 24; Gregg, 137; Records of US Army Commands, Edwards to AAG, July 25, 1849, DNM LSR, RG 98, 92, 192, roll 1, NA.

38. *Columbus Enquirer*, September 11, 1849; Lecompte, "The Independent Women of Hispanic New Mexico," 73, 75; Duffus, 168–69; Twitchell, *Leading Facts*, 2:229 fn165; Davis, 13–14.

39. Foote, *Women of the New Mexico Frontier, 1846–1912* , 33–34, 47; Duffus, 160–62; Edwards, 26–27; Davis, 40; *Columbus Enquirer*, April 24, 1849; Horgan, *Lamy of Santa Fe*, 122; Twitchell, *Leading Facts*, 2:155.

40. Segale, *At the End of the Santa Fe Trail*, 97.

41. Twitchell, *Leading Facts*, 2:154; Edwards, 29–30; Duffus, 172; Lecompte, 73–74; Garrard, *Wah-to-yah & The Taos Trail*, 166.

42. Weber, *Taos Trappers*, 210; Horgan, 116; Garrard, 123; "Notes on the Population of New Mexico, 1846–1849," 200.

43. Russell, 26–27; M. Simmons, "Hygiene, Sanitation, and Public Health," 208. Cordelia Jackson, whose husband was chief justice, wrote in 1858, "I think this is one of the healthiest places I ever lived in." She commented on health and the "delightful climate" in every letter and noted the number of elderly men and women at the market who said they had never been sick in their lives. But, surrounded by Catholics, she pined for a Protestant preacher or missionary. Jackson, "Mrs. Alexander M. Jackson Letters," 340–43.

44. Calhoun to Medill, July 29, 1849, in Abel, *Official Correspondence*, 17; Calhoun to Brown, November 17, 1849, in Abel, 81–82.

45. *Columbus Enquirer*, September 11, 1849.

46. There were two William Mitchells in Santa Fe. Kingsbury mentions a Bill Mitchell accompanying his wagon trains to St. Louis, and a Bill Mitchell clerked for Ceran St. Vrain. Elder and Weber, eds., *Trading in Santa Fe: John M. Kingsbury's Correspondence with James Josiah Webb*, 83, 85; Calhoun to Clayton, April 27, 1851, in Abel, *Official Correspondence*, 335.

47. *Columbus Enquirer*, September 11, 1849; Robinson to Calhoun, November 30,

1849, in Abel, *Official Correspondence*, 89–90; Wetherington, *Ceran St. Vrain*, 42; Calhoun to Medill, October 15, 1849, in Abel, 48–49; *New Mexican*, November 28, 1849.

48. Foote, "American Ladies," 128–29; Duffus, 167; Lecompte, 73–74, 78–80.

49. Montezuma Lodge No. 109 was chartered on May 8, 1851. Most of Santa Fe's prominent Americans were members. Elder, 106 fn27; Dary, 219; *Weekly Arkansas Gazette*, August 23, 1850; Twitchell, *Leading Facts*, 2:140; *New Mexican*, November 28, 1848.

50. Davis, introduction, i.

Chapter Nine

1. Bent to Medill, November 10, 1846, in Abel, *Official Correspondence*, 6–8.

2. Bent to Medill, November 10, 1846, in Abel, *Official Correspondence*, 6–8.

3. Sando, *Pueblo Nations*, 21; M. Simmons, "History of the Pueblos, 209.

4. Hamilton, 180; Sides, *Blood and Thunder*, 200; Calhoun to Medill, August 15, 1849, in Abel, *Official Correspondence*, 20.

5. McNitt, *Navajo Wars*, viii, 6, 9–10; Iverson, *Diné*, 16, 25–26, 32–33; Sides, 140.

6. Abel, *Official Correspondence*, 25.

7. Weber, *Richard Kern*, 68, 72–75; Keleher, *Turmoil*, 46; McNitt, *Navajo Wars*, 138; Schubert, *Vanguard of Expansion*, 75; Sides, 202–4.

8. Cabezon Peak, at 7,785 feet, is the largest of a number of volcanic plugs ringing Mount Taylor, larger even than the better known Devil's Tower in Wyoming. It's sacred to Pueblos and Navajos. S. Robinson, *El Malpais*, 148.

9. McNitt, ed., *Journal of a Military Reconnaissance*, 8, 32 fn29; Weber, *Richard Kern*, 75; Rathbun and Alexander, 92; Sides, 210, 229; Calhoun to Medill, October 1, 1849, in Abel, *Official Correspondence*, 26.

10. McNitt, *Journal*, 35 fn34, 61–62; Sides, 217.

11. McNitt, *Journal*, 64–65, 69; Sides, 135–36.

12. McNitt, *Journal*, 67–68, 68–69 fn77; Calhoun to Medill, October 1, 1849, Abel, *Official Correspondence*, 28.

13. McNitt, *Journal*, 71, 73, 78.

14. McNitt, *Journal*, 82–83; Iverson, 28–29; Calhoun to Medill, October 1, 1849, in Abel, *Official Correspondence*, 28.

15. McNitt, *Journal*, 87–89, 103.

16. McNitt, *Journal*, 99; Calhoun to Medill, September 25, 1849, in Abel, *Official Correspondence*, 21–25; Weber, *Richard Kern*, 99.

17. McNitt, *Journal*, 90–95.

18. McNitt, *Journal*, 99–100, 103–8.

19. Calhoun to Medill, October 1 and 4, 1849, in Abel, *Official Correspondence*, 30, 39.

20. Calhoun to Medill, October 1 and 4, 1849, in Abel, *Official Correspondence*, 39.

21. Calhoun to Medill, October 5, 13, and 15, 1849, in Abel, *Official Correspondence*, 41–42, 44, 49, 51–52; McNitt, *Navajo Wars*, 156.

22. Calhoun to Brown, January 25, 1850, in Abel, *Official Correspondence*, 105–6.

23. Calhoun had such respect for Simpson that he would write to his old friend, Secretary of War George Crawford, seconding Simpson's request for two brevet commissions. Calhoun praised "Lt. Simpson's unflagging zeal" and said, "His high moral qualities are equaled but by few and excelled by no man in the army." President Fillmore also wrote that he considered Simpson a man of high character, but Crawford had to wait for Congress to act. Calhoun to Crawford, May 11, 1850, and Fillmore to Crawford, July 1, 1850, in Abel, *Official Correspondence*, 203–4.

24. Keleher, *Turmoil*, 59; Spicer, *Cycles of Conquest*, 216.

25. Calhoun to Medill, October 1, 1849, in Abel, *Official Correspondence*, 32.

26. Calhoun to Medill, October 1, 1849, in Abel, *Official Correspondence*, 32–33; McNitt, 172–173.

27. Calhoun to Medill, October 1, 1849, in Abel, *Official Correspondence*, 32, 34–35.

28. Calhoun to Medill, October 1, 1849, in Abel, *Official Correspondence*, 33–36.

29. Calhoun to Medill, October 1 and 4, 1849, in Abel, *Official Correspondence*, 35–36 and 40 and October 15, 1849, in Abel, 52–58.

30. Calhoun to Medill, October 15, 1849, in Abel, *Official Correspondence*, 54.

31. Spicer, 343–46; Adams, xi, 152–53; M. Simmons, "History of the Pueblos," 9:209.

32. Lobo Blanco was leader of the Llaneros (plains) Jicarillas. Michno, *Depredation and Deceit*, 22.

33. Greiner, "Overawing the Indians," 5; Twitchell, *Leading Facts*, 2:128; Calhoun to Medill, October 29, 1849, in Abel, *Official Correspondence*, 63–64.

34. Munroe assumed command on October 23, 1849. After his graduation from West Point in 1814, he was involved in operations against the Creeks, Seminoles, and Cherokees. *George W. Cullum's Biographical Register of the Officers and Graduates of the United States Military Academy at West Point*.

35. Ellison described Calhoun as "very popular and very intemperate." If by "intemperate" he referred to liquor, he was mistaken. Ellison was writing three decades after the events. Espinosa, "Memoir of a Kentuckian in New Mexico, 1848–1884," 7–8.

36. The 1850 census for Santa Fe shows an Encarnacion Garcia, son of Pablo and Juana Garcia, who was twenty-five.

37. Bennett, *Forts and Forays*, 17; V. Simmons, *The Ute Indians*, 86; Bullock, *Mountain Villages*, 98.

38. Burnside, a future Civil War general, was a cousin of Calhoun's son-in-law, John Davis.

39. Greiner, "Overawing the Indians," 4–5.

40. Greiner, 4–5; *Daily National Intelligencer*, January 24, 1853.

41. Bennett, 24–26; Tiller, *The Jicarilla Apache Tribe*, 9–10, 13–14, 30, 34–35; *Sandusky Register*, September 28, 1849; Dunlay, *Kit Carson and the Indians*, 135–37; Hutton, "Kit Carson's Ride," 33–37.

42. Sweeney, *Mangas Coloradas*, 159–60, 168, 176–78; Kiser, *Dragoons in Apacheland*, 64; Calhoun to Brown, November 7, 1849, in Abel, *Official Correspondence*, 73.

43. Calhoun wrote that May was "a gallant officer, originally a thorough going democrat, then a Taylorite, and now a bitter denunciator of the President." Calhoun to Dawson, February 4, 1850, James S. Calhoun Letters.

44. Munroe Orders, December 9, 1849, in Abel, *Official Correspondence*, 90–91; Choice to Calhoun, December 24, 1849, and January 29, 1850, in Abel, 93, 121; Kiser, 68.

45. Calhoun to Brown, November 7 and 15, 1849, in Abel, *Official Correspondence*, 73, 76; Calhoun to Dawson, October 31, 1849, Keleher Papers, Box 5, Folder 7.

46. Calhoun to Brown, November 7, 15, and 30, 1849, in Abel, *Official Correspondence*, 74, 77, 88.

47. Orlando Brown was so unknown that an Ohio newspaper devoted an article to his background. He succeeded Colonel Medill, "removed for being a democrat or a good officer." Brown, Kentucky's secretary of state, had run the *Franklin Commonwealth*, a Kentucky newspaper. He served for a year before resigning, "tired of the cares and annoyances of his desk and anxious to return to Kentucky." *Ohio Statesman*, June 4, 1849; *Boston Evening Transcript*, August 8, 1850.

48. Brown to Calhoun, December 28, 1849, in Abel, *Official Correspondence*, 94–95; Annual Report of the Commissioner of Indian Affairs, 1849, 17–19.

49. Antoine Leroux was born around 1801 in St. Louis to a French Canadian father and Hispanic mother. He was a trapper and guide who arrived in New Mexico around 1822, married Juana Catarina Vigil, whose family was prominent in the Taos valley and settled there. Leroux was rich, literate, and always traveled with a personal servant, a Crow Indian. He was a guide for a number of government expeditions before his death in Taos in 1861. Gordon, ed., *Through Indian Country to California*, 258.

50. Calhoun to Brown, January 1, 1850, in Abel, *Official Correspondence*, 96–97; "Treaty between the United States of America and the Utah Indians," *New Hampshire Sentinel*, December 12, 1850; P. Smith, *Ouray*, 38–39; Delaney, *The Southern Ute People*, 38; G. Thompson, "Southern Ute Lands, 1848–1899," 3.

51. P. D. Smith, 19; V. Simmons, *The Ute Indians*, 1. Today, the Mouache and Caputa bands make up the Southern Ute Tribe, headquartered at Ignacio, Colorado. The Weenuchiu, now known as the Ute Mountain Utes are headquartered at Towaoc, Colorado. "History of the Southern Utes."

52. Old Bill Williams was translator in negotiations between the United States and the Kaw and Osage tribes on August 10, 1825, to allow the Santa Fe Trail to pass through their lands. Commissioner George Sibley named the site Council Grove. Historic Markers Across Georgia, Council Grove.

53. Delaney, 36; P. D. Smith, 37; V. Simmons, 84–85.

54. *St. Louis Republican*, May 17, 1849; Greiner, 1–4, 8–9.

55. *St. Louis Republican*, May 17, 1849; Greiner, 1–4, 8–9; Calhoun to Brown, November 15, 1849, in Abel, *Official Correspondence*, 77.

56. McLaws to May, January 13, 1850, in Abel, *Official Correspondence*, 102; Munroe Orders, January 29, 1850, in Abel, 122–23; Calhoun to Brown, January 31, 1850, in Abel, 124–26; Gregory Thompson, 3.

Chapter Ten

1. The 1850 census lists Calhoun, then fifty-one years old, and his household: Joseph Collins, twenty-eight, a teamster from Kentucky; Charles Jackson, twenty-five, a slave or servant from Washington, DC; José Trujillo, a sixteen-year-old servant from New Mexico; and William Kephart, twenty-four, a Presbyterian missionary. Because Kephart didn't arrive until November and was a guest of Calhoun's temporarily, the census enumerator (Charles Blumner) must have taken the information in November or early December.

2. Bennett, 49; Garrard, 156; Calhoun to Brown, February 2, 1850, in Abel, *Official Correspondence*, 133; Calhoun to Brown, March 30, 1850, Annual Report of the Commissioner of Indian Affairs, 1846-1850, 32nd Congress, 100.

3. Creider, "The Publications of Padre Antonio José Martínez," 161–62; Boyd, "The First New Mexico Imprint," 33, 35.

4. Weber, *Mexican Frontier*, 193; Mares, "The Many Faces of Padre Antonio José Martínez," 23, 26–30; Mares, "Padre Martínez, Defender of the People," 57–59; F. Chavez, 82–83.

5. Calhoun to Brown, January 25 and February 2, 1850, in Abel, *Official Correspondence*, 103, 134.

6. Calhoun to Brown, February 2, 1850, in Abel, *Official Correspondence*, 134–135; Calhoun to Beall, Grier, and Whittlesey, February 2, in Abel, 136–37.

7. He spent $14.37 on provisions for his guide, servants, and Taos Indians who came to visit. Abel, *Official Correspondence*, 335.

8. Calhoun to Brown, January 25 and April 15, 1850, in Abel, *Official Correspondence*, 103, 187; Calhoun to Brown, March 29, 1850, Annual Report of the Commissioner of Indian Affairs, 1846–1850, 32nd Congress, 97, 99.

9. S. Robinson, *I Fought a Good Fight*, 213; Dunlay, 152; Calhoun to Brown, March 30, 1850, Annual Report, 1846–1850, 100–101.

10. Dunlay, 156; Tyler, 49–50.

11. Munroe and Calhoun, June 25, 1850, Letters received by Office of Adjutant General, RG 94, roll 432, NMSA; Calhoun to Brown, July 16, 1850, in Abel, *Official Correspondence*, 227.

12. Calhoun to Brown, August 12 and October 12, 1850, in Abel, *Official Correspondence*, 249–50, 263–64; Calhoun to Lea, November 30, 1850, in Abel, 274.

13. Weber, *Taos Trappers*, 158; Gregg, 100; McCall, *New Mexico*, 143; Baca, 90–91; Bullock, 59–62.

14. Gregg, 100; Baca, 90–91, 94; Citizens to President, February 27, 1850, in Abel, *Official Correspondence*, 157–59; "Notes on the Population of New Mexico, 1846–1849," 200.

15. Beall to McLaws, January 27, 1850, Records of US Army Commands, DNM, LSR, RG 98, 92, 192, roll 1, NMSA; Munroe to AAG, March 1 and 15, 1850, Records of the Office of Adjutant General, DNM, RG 94, roll 432, NMSA; Munroe to

Howell, May 26, 1850, Letters received by Office of Adjutant General, RG 94, roll 432; Kiser, 74.

16. AAG to Munroe, May 27, 1850, Records of US Army Commands, DNM, Selected Documents Related to the Navajo Indians, 1846–1868, RG 98, roll 1.

17. W. Thompson, 45, 77; Rippy, 370–71.

18. Calhoun to Brown, January 3, March 1 and August 5, 1850, in Abel, *Official Correspondence*, 99, 157, 249.

19. Calhoun to Dawson, February 4, March 10, and April 20, 1850, Calhoun, Letters; *Plain Dealer*, May 25, 1850.

20. Brown to Calhoun, April 24 and July 15, 1850, in Abel, *Official Correspondence*, 190–92, 222.

21. Calhoun to Brown, May 20, July 15 and 30, and August 5, 1850, in Abel, *Official Correspondence*, 205, 227–31, 248–49; Calhoun to Dawson, July 16, 1850, Calhoun, Letters.

22. Luke Lea, of Mississippi, was appointed commissioner in July 1850. Lea, a Whig in the Mississippi legislature, had voted against the Texas annexation in 1844. He ran unsuccessfully for governor of Mississippi in 1849. *Times-Picayune*, July 14, 1850; *Mississippi Free Trader*, Natchez, October 3, 1849.

23. Commission of Indian Affairs Annual Report, November 27, 1850, 10–11; Lea to Calhoun, December 5, 1850, in Abel, *Official Correspondence*, 275.

24. Calhoun to Brown, March 15, 1850, in Abel, *Official Correspondence*, 160–62.

25. Calhoun to Lacome, February 26, 1850, in Abel, *Official Correspondence*, 168–69; Beall to McLaws, January 27, 1850, Records of US Army Commands, DNM, LSR, RG 98, 92, 192, roll 1; Beall to McLaws, March 13, 1850, in Abel, 167; Alvarez to McLaws, March 16, 1850, in Abel, 168; Calhoun to Brown, March 16, 1850, in Abel, 166.

26. Lacome to Calhoun, March 16, 1850, in Abel, *Official Correspondence*, 169–70.

27. Munroe to AAG, May 23, 1850, in Abel, *Official Correspondence*, 207; Burnside to Ward, May 23, 1850, in Abel, 198–99.

28. Greiner, 7–8; "Confessions of an Apache Chief."

29. Calhoun to Brown, May 20, June 12, and November 2, 1850, in Abel, *Official Correspondence*, 70–71, 205, 209–9; Munroe to Major General R. Jones, Adjutant General, June 11, 1850, in Abel, 108–9; Choice to Calhoun, May 8, 1850, in Abel, 195.

30. Calhoun to Brown, July 30, 1850, in Abel, *Official Correspondence*, 229–30.

31. Calhoun to Brown, August 12, September 30, 1850, in Abel, *Official Correspondence*, 251–52, 259; Calhoun to Lea, February 28, 1852, in Abel, 484; *Columbus Enquirer*, October 1, 1850.

32. They were Miguel Velasquez, Antonio María Vigil, Francisco Espinosa, Luciano Archuleta, Francisco Lopez, José Angelo Saucedo, Nicolas Archuleta, Juan Santos Giron, Antonio Rafael Trujillo, Antonio José Archuleta, Tomas Chacon, Baltasar Morphi, José Gabriel Velasquez, José María Valdez, Fernando Montaño, Ignacio Archuleta, Andreas Trujillo, Desiderio Valdez, Antonio María Martínez,

Francisco Montoya, Martín Martínez, Pedro Velasquez, Bernardo Sanchez, Juan de Dios Revilla, José Antonio Garcia, Fernando Montoya, and Mariano Griego.

33. Graham to McLaws, September 29, 1850, Records of US Army Commands, DNM, Selected Documents, RG 98, roll 1, NMSA.

34. Graham to McLaws, October 13, 1850, DNM, Selected Documents, RG 98, Roll 1; Calhoun to Lea, January 6, 1851, in Abel, *Official Correspondence*, 282.

35. Calhoun to Brown, June 19, 1850, in *Official Correspondence*, Abel, 212–13.

36. Calhoun to Brown, July 15, August 12, and October 12, 1850, in Abel, *Official Correspondence*, 217, 252, 262–63; McLaws to Grier, June 28, 1850, in Abel, 215; Grier to McLaws, July 31, 1850, Letters received by Office of Adjutant General, RG 94, roll 432; Bennett, 42.

37. McLaws to Grier, June 28, 1850, in Abel, *Official Correspondence*, 215; Calhoun to Brown, June 19, 1850, in Abel, 212–13.

38. Van Horne to McLaws, September 19, 1850, in Abel, *Official Correspondence*, 260–61.

39. Sweeney, 190, 206; Calhoun to Brown, May 10, 1850, in Abel, *Official Correspondence*, 196; Kiser, 79–80.

40. Kern to Calhoun, October 12, 1850, in Abel, *Official Correspondence*, 266.

41. S. Robinson, *I Fought a Good Fight*, 33, 227–28, 305; Opler, "Apachean Culture Patterns," 10:386; Opler, "Chiricahua Apache," 10:417–18; Chaput, *Francois X. Aubry*, 131.

42. S. Robinson, *I Fought a Good Fight*, 18–20.

43. Saunders to Whittlesey, October 25, 1850, Records of US Army Command, DNM, Selected Documents, RG 98, roll 1; Tyler, 72; McNitt, *Navajo Wars*, 165 fn18.

44. Chandler to McLaws, December 6, 1850, Records of US Army Commands, DNM, Selected Documents, RG 98, roll 1.

45. Luna to Calhoun, January 20, 1851, in Abel, *Official Correspondence*, 284–86; Sarracino to Calhoun, January 29, 1851, CIAAR, 187–88; McNitt, *Navajo Wars*, 166–67; Saunders to McLaws, February 2, 1851, DNM, Selected Documents.

46. Calhoun to Brown, October 12, 1850, in Abel, *Official Correspondence*, 264–65; Calhoun to Lea, November 30, 1850, in Abel, 274.

Chapter Eleven

1. Davis, 305; Calhoun to Medill, July 29 and October 14, 1849, in Abel, *Official Correspondence*, 17–19, 49; *The New Mexican*, November 28, 1949.

2. Loyola, 69–70; Twitchell, *The Bench and Bar of New Mexico*, 10.

3. Richard Hanson Weightman was born in Washington, DC, December 28, 1816, and attended private schools there and in Alexandria, Virginia. He graduated from the University of Virginia at Charlottesville in 1834 and attended the United States Military Academy (West Point) from 1835 to 1837. *Appleton's Cyclopedia of American*

Biography says Weightman was expelled from West Point "for cutting a comrade in the face in a personal encounter," but West Point archives don't confirm that account. He studied law and was admitted to the bar in 1841 in the District of Columbia and moved to St. Louis. On March 29, 1842, he married Susan Bradford Coxe, oldest daughter of Richard S. Coxe, of Washington, DC. *Alexandria Gazette*, April 1, 1842; Alicia Mauldin, West Point archives curator, to author, personal e-mail, July 29, 2015; *Biographical Directory of the American Congress*.

4. Edwards, xv–xvi, 78; Calhoun to Medill, October 15, 1849, in Abel, *Official Correspondence*, 53; *Daily National Intelligencer*, December 6, 1844; *Daily Union*, June 12, 1846, and July 29, 1847; Emory, 27; *Alexandria Gazette*, October 3, 1846.

5. T. Chávez, *Manuel Alvarez*, 6–7, 31, 81–83, 141; T, Chávez, "The Trouble with Texans," 136; Boyle, *Los Capitalistas*, 69.

6. The eight signers were Pinckney E. Tully, William Z. Angney, Theodore Wheaton, Elias P. West, Palmer J. Pillans, Merrill Ashurst, (?) Beach, and Weightman. Hugh N. Smith and Willard P. Hall didn't sign for personal reasons. Speech of Honorable Richard H. Weightman of New Mexico, delivered in the House, March 15, 1852, in reply to the Honorable Mr. Phelps, of Missouri, Benjamin M. Read Collection, #1959–179, Box 6, Folder 310, NMSA.

7. Larson, 29; Ball, *Army Regulars on the Western Frontier*, 7; Twitchell, *Leading Facts*, 2:399 fn324; Twitchell, *The History of the Military Occupation* , 392; Chávez, *Manual Alvarez*, 135.

8. Weightman, Speech of Hon. Richard H. Weightman of New Mexico; Calhoun to Dawson, February 4, 1850, Calhoun, Letters.

9. Gonzáles, "Mexican Party, American Party, Democratic Party," , 254–56.

10. Calhoun to Brown, June 19, 1850, in Abel, *Official Correspondence*, 213.

11. Lamar, 74; Ganaway, "New Mexico and the Sectional Controversy," 215; Chávez, *Manual Alvarez*, 130.

12. Members of the convention were Francisco Sarracino, Donaciano Vigil, Padre Martínez, Santiago Archuleta, Elias P. West, James H. Quinn, Charles Beaubien, Gregorio Vigil, Manuel A. Otero, Ramón Luna, Jose Pley, Antonio Saenz, and Juan Perea. Padre Martínez was president, and J. M. Giddings was clerk. Larson, 14–15.

13. Larson, 13–15; Keleher, *Turmoil in New Mexico*, 4; *Augusta Chronicle*, November 28, 1849.

14. Larson, 18–19; Calhoun to Brown, August 30, 1850, in Abel, *Official Correspondence*, 257; Caffey, *Chasing the Santa Fe Ring*, 35. Alvarez, Tuley, and Angney were appointed to publish the proceedings of the meeting. *Albany Courier*, November 12, 1849.

15. Calhoun to Medill, October 15, 1849 in Abel, *Official Correspondence*, 53; Calhoun to Ewing, October 16, 1849, in Abel, 58–59.

16. *Schenectady Reflector*, March 8, 1850; *New Mexican*, November 28, 1849; Calhoun to Brown, November 30, 1849, in Abel, *Official Correspondence*, 89.

17. The signers of the December 8, 1849, letter were Alvarez, J. D. Robinson, El-

liott Lee, Weightman, John N. Abell, Miguel E. Pino, Cyrus Choice, James Conklin, W. T. Angney, J. J. Pillans, Murray F. Tuley, William S. Messervy, C. H. Merritt, Samuel King, Vicar Juan Felipe Ortiz, and Calhoun. *The Republic*, March 2, 1850.

18. Elder and Weber, xxiii and fn33; Chávez, *Manual Alvarez*, 133–34; *Times-Picayune*, February 23, 1850; *Daily Union*, October 10, 1850; Lamar, 75.

19. *Times-Picayne*, February 23, 1850.

20. Calhoun to Brown, November 2, 1849, in Abel, *Official Correspondence*, 70–71.

21. The small Ramage press was initially used in a political campaign. Padre Martínez bought it in 1837, and General Kearny appropriated it to print governmental decrees and military orders. Creider, 162.

22. *Daily Union*, October 10, 1850; Weightman speech; Calhoun to Dawson, March 3, 1850, Calhoun, Letters. Secretary of War Conrad told Calhoun that claims must be sustained by evidence other than the claimant's own statement, such as reports by army officers, and an examination officer's reports found no mention of the purchase or use of the press. Conrad to Calhoun, September 4, 1851, in Abel, *Official Correspondence*, 420–24.

23. The other subscribers, for $100 each, were Juan Perea, W. Z. Angney, Juan C. Armijo, J. Manuel Gallegos, J. Chávez, Messervy & Webb, William S. McKnight & Co., Juan F. Otero, and Benito A. Larragoite. La Farge, 7–8; Weightman to Alvarez, August 26, 1850, Alvarez, Papers.

24. Calhoun to Dawson, February 4, 1850, Calhoun, Letters.

25. Reynolds was dismissed October 4, 1861. He became a confederate brigadier general and died May 26, 1876. McCall, *New Mexico*, 195.

26. Thomas resigned June 30, 1852. A confederate colonel, he was killed July 21, 1861, in the Battle of Bull Run. McCall, *New Mexico*, 196.

27. Calhoun to Dawson, February 4, 1850, Calhoun, Letters; *Biographical Directory of the United States Congress*.

28. Calhoun to Dawson, October 31, 1849, Keleher Papers; Calhoun to Dawson, March 3, 1850, Calhoun Letters.

29. Calhoun to Dawson, March 3, 1850, Calhoun Letters.

30. Calhoun to Dawson, March 3, 1850, Keleher Papers.

31. Calhoun to Dawson, February 4 and March 10, 1850, Calhoun Letters.

32. Calhoun to Dawson, March 16, 1850, Calhoun Letters; Duffus, 224.

33. Calhoun to Dawson, March 3, 1850, Keleher Papers; Calhoun to Dawson, February 4, March 3, Calhoun, Letters.

34. Stegmaier, *Texas, New Mexico, and the Compromise of 1850*, 68; Ganaway, 216.

35. Stegmaier, 75-76; McCall, *New Mexico*, 68; Larson, 28–31; Davis, 305–6.

36. Hays, "The Curious Case," 251–52; Calhoun to Dawson, March 31 and July 16, 1850, Calhoun, Letters.

37. Stegmaier cites a document bearing Calhoun's initials in the papers of Senator Thomas J. Rusk of Texas as evidence that Calhoun was keeping him informed. Rusk, like Calhoun, was a lawyer, a Georgian, and a Mason, but he could have provided

information as a courtesy. Stegmaier, 66, 366 fn7; Benham, "Rusk, Thomas Jefferson (1803–1857)."

38. Calhoun to Dawson, October 31, 1849, Keleher Papers; Calhoun to Dawson, March 10 and 31, and April 20 and 24, 1850,Calhoun, Letters.

39. Robinson, *I Fought a Good Fight*, 213; R. Richardson, "Neighbors, Robert Simpson (1815–1859)"; Van Horne to McLaws, February 23, 1850, in Abel, *Official Correspondence*, 163.

40. *Daily Missouri Republican*, June 18, 1850; Calhoun to Dawson, March 10, 1850, Calhoun, Letters; Munroe to Beall et al., March 12, 1850, in Abel, *Official Correspondence*, 164; Neighbors, report, *Columbus Enquirer*, July 9, 1850; Hamilton, *Zachary Taylor*, 374–75.

41. Larson, 47; Neighbours, "The Taylor-Neighbors Struggle," 447–48; *Daily Missouri Republican*, April 24, 1850; Bancroft, *History of Arizona and New Mexico*, 426; Edrington, "Military Influence," 379; Calhoun to Dawson, April 20, 1850, Calhoun, Letters.

42. *Columbus Enquirer*, July 9, 1950; Larson, 47–48; Neighbours, 450.

43. *Trenton State Gazette*, July 1, 1850; Larson, 31, 37; McCall, *New Mexico*, 68; Munroe Proclamation, April 23, 1850, Letters Received by Office of Adjutant General, RG 94, roll 432; Calhoun to Brown, April 24, 1850, in Abel, *Official Correspondence*, 189; Calhoun to Dawson, April 24, 1850, Calhoun, Letters.

44. Neighbours, 446; *Daily National Intelligencer*, March 1, 1850; Kiser, 76, 304 n62. Steen claimed that he purchased the land; Munroe didn't believe it and scolded Steen for making unfounded claims. Steen to McLaws, April 29, 1850, Neighbors to Munroe, May 3, 1850, Munroe to Jones, May 20, 1850, Letters received by Office of Adjutant General, RG 94, roll 432.

45. Neighbours, 447–50; *Weekly Union*, July 13, 1850.

46. From the Houghton party were Houghton, St. Vrain, James Quinn, Judge Antonio José Otero, Thomas S. J. Johnson, Robert Carey, Donaciano Vigil, Charles Overman, Francisco Ortiz y Delgado, and Levi J. Keithly. From the Alvarez party were Padre José Manuel Gallegos, Padre José María Martínez, José Pablo Gallegos, Ramón Luna, Juan Antonio Baca y Pino, and Juan Perea. Others were George Gold, José Antonio Mansanares, and Murray F. Tuley.

47. Tomás Cabeza de Baca, son of the first settler of Upper Las Vegas, was a Santa Fe Trail trader. Gottschalk, 27.

48. Munroe to Jones, May 13, 1850, Letters received by Office of Adjutant General, RG 94, roll 432; Calhoun to Dawson, July 16, 1850,Calhoun, Letters; Larson, 32; *Weekly Union*, July 27, 1850; Stegmaier, 51.

49. Calhoun to Brown, June 19, 1850, in Abel, *Official Correspondence*, 213–14; Calhoun to Dawson, April 20, 1850,Calhoun, Letters.

50. Larson, 38; Calhoun to Brown, July 15, 1850, in Abel, *Official Correspondence*, 217–18; Calhoun to Dawson, July 16, 1850,Calhoun, Letters.

51. Chávez, *Manuel Alvarez*, 142; Calhoun to Brown, July 15, 1850, in Abel, *Official*

Correspondence, 217–18; Munroe to Alvarez, July 12, 1850, Alvarez to Munroe, July 12, 1850, Letters received by Office of Adjutant General, RG 94, roll 432; *Cleveland Plain Dealer*, August 29, 1850; *Spectator*, September 5, 1850.

52. *Georgia Telegraph*, September 4, 1849; Steel, 74; Ball, *Army Regulars*, 10; Alvarez to Munroe, July 13, 1850, Letters received by Office of Adjutant General, RG 94, roll 432.

53. *Richmond Enquirer*, September 6, 1850; *Daily Ohio Statesman*, August 29, 1850.

54. Munroe to AG, July 16 and 31, 1850, Letters received by Office of Adjutant General, RG 94, roll 432; Calhoun to Brown, July 31, 1850, in Abel, *Official Correspondence*, 233.

55. Binkley, "The Question of Texan Jurisdiction," 7–10; Edrington, 379–81.

56. S. M. Baird, Election Notice, July 20, 1850, in Abel, *Official Correspondence*, 233; Calhoun to Brown, July 31, 1850, in Abel, 232; Edrington, 378. Oliver P. Hovey and Edward T. Davies, privates in the First Missouri, published *The Santa Fe Republican* until about November 1849. It then became the *Santa Fe New Mexican*. The *Republican* was the first English-language newspaper in New Mexico. Its first issue was September 10, 1847. Michno, 35; Boyd, "The First New Mexico Imprint," 36.

57. Calhoun to Brown, August 13, 1850, in Abel, *Official Correspondence*, 252–53.

58. Baird to Bell, December 4, 1849, and February 20, 1850, Bell, General Correspondence, 1849–1853.

59. *Missouri Republican*, August 23, 1850; *Richmond Enquirer*, September 6, 1850.

60. Weightman to Alvarez, August 26, 1850, Alvarez Papers; *Richmond Enquirer*, September 6, 1850.

Chapter Twelve

1. Von Abele, 121, 123; W. Thompson, 56; Hubbell, 307–9; *Augusta Chronicle*, October 9, 1850.

2. Larson, 25–27; *Journal of the House of Representatives*, January 1, 1850, 759; Hamilton, 264–65; J. Richardson, 28–29.

3. Hamilton, 278–79, 283, 331; Hubbell, 310–14; Von Abele, 124–25.

4. Hamilton, 345–47, 352.

5. Boney, "The Politics of Expansion and Secession, 1820–1861," 140–41.

6. E. Smith, *The Presidencies of Zachary Taylor & Millard Fillmore*, 56, 60, 151–53; Ball, *Army Regulars*, 8; Hubbell, 315; Von Abele, 127–28.

7. *Commercial Advertiser*, June 28, 1850.

8. *Daily National Intelligencer*, July 3, 1850; *Spectator*, July 8, 1850.

9. *Boston Evening Transcript*, July 9, 1850; *New London Weekly Chronicle*, July 18, 1850; *Commercial Advertiser*, July 17, 1850.

10. *Macon Weekly Telegraph*, August 13, 1850; Hubbell, 317; Von Abele, 127; Thompson, 68–69; Stegmaier, 169–71; *Federal Union*, August 20, 1850.

11. Scott to Munroe, August 6, 1850, in Abel, *Official Correspondence*, 164–65.

12. *Georgia Telegraph*, September 3, 1850; Munroe to AG, August 31, 1850, Letters received by the Office of Adjutant General, RG 94, roll 432.

13. *Minnesota Chronicle and Register*, September 23, 1850.

14. Larson, 54–55; Thompson, 69; *Augusta Chronicle*, August 20, 1850.

15. Larson, 56; Stegmaier, 278.

16. *Daily National Intelligencer*, August 26, 1850; *Alexandria Gazette*, September 10, 1850; W. Thompson, 71.

17. *Daily National Intelligencer*, September 14, 1850; *Macon Weekly Telegraph*, September 17, 1850; Larson, 55.

18. Von Abele, 130–31; Hubbell, 318; W. Thompson, 76.

19. Smith had alienated southerners by writing and circulating a pamphlet condemning slavery and the slave states. On July 18, 1850, the House refused to seat him. Larson, 23.

20. Richardson, 75; Stegmaier, 124–25, 296; Larson, 57; Davis, 306–7.

21. Conrad to Munroe, September 10, 1850, in Abel, *Official Correspondence*, 20–21; Loyola, 274; Stegmaier, 298; Neil, "The Territorial Governor as Indian Superintendent," 213.

22. He asked Alvarez to show the letter to Pillans and Calhoun. Weightman to Alvarez, October 18, 1850, Alvarez Papers.

23. He asked Alvarez to share his letters with Father José Manuel Gallegos, Diego Archuleta, Father José Francisco Leyba, Calhoun, Pillans, and others. Weightman to Alvarez, September 14 and 18, 1850, Alvarez Papers; Petition to Munroe, October 26, 1850, Letters received by Office of Adjutant General, RG 94, roll 432.

24. Larson, 60; Stegmaier, 315.

25. Weightman also wrote to Archuleta, Padre Leyba, Ramon Baca, Miguel Sena y Romero, and José Maria Cháves. *National Era*, January 1, 1852.

26. William Stickney Allen was born in Massachusetts on April 30, 1805, the son of Ephraim W. and Dorothy Stickney. He graduated Dartmouth College in 1825, read law for Stephen W. Marston, and was admitted to the bar. He had a large law practice, was editor of the *Newburyport Herald*, and served several terms in the Massachusetts House of Representatives. In 1837 he moved to Missouri and became editor of the *St. Louis Gazette* and also practiced law. For twelve years he was an editor of the *St. Louis Republican*, represented the city in the legislature, and was a county judge. A prominent Whig, he was appointed Register of the Land Office in St. Louis and territorial secretary of New Mexico. He died at home in 1868 at age sixty-three. *Boston Traveler*, June 27, 1868.

27. Chávez, 148–49, 152.

28. Weightman to Alvarez, December 16, 1850, and January 15, 1851, Alvarez Papers; Chávez, 150–51, 155; *Daily Union*, February 7 and 15, 1851.

29. Webster would be secretary of state under Fillmore from 1850 to 1852. He died in office in October 1852. Duniway, 3.

30. Webster also asked to know the name of the state or county where Calhoun

was born. Abel wrote that Calhoun's response, if he wrote one, has not been found. Abel, *Official Correspondence*, 296 fn4.

31. Stegmaier, 109, 112; W. Thompson, 63; Holtby, *Forty-Seventh Star*, 4; Webster to Calhoun, January 9, 1851, in Abel, *Official Correspondence*, 296.

32. *Albany Patriot*, January 17, 1851; *New York Daily Tribune*, December 25, 1850; *Daily Missouri Republican*, January 21, 1851.

Chapter Thirteen

1. *National Era*, April 17, 1851; *Daily Missouri Republican*, January 10, 1851.

2. Calhoun to Lea, February 16 and 28, 1851, in Abel, *Official Correspondence*, 292–95.

3. Munroe, Special Orders, March 2, 1851, in Abel, *Official Correspondence*, 296; *National Era*, Washington, DC, April 17, 1851.

4. *Daily Illinois State Journal*, April 11, 1851.

5. *Columbus Enquirer*, April 22, 1851; *National Era*, Washington, DC, April 17, 1851.

6. When the *Santa Fe Gazette* started in 1851, Neville Stuart was editor. James L. Collins was publisher. Stuart left Santa Fe on May 1, 1851. *Daily Illinois State Journal*, April 11, 1851.

7. *National Era*, Washington, DC, April 17, 1851; *Columbus Enquirer*, April 22, 1851.

8. *National Era*, Washington, DC, April 17, 1851.

9. Nicholson was appointed from South Pittsburgh by the Pittsburgh Conference of Methodist Episcopal Church for 1850 and sent west when the Baptists and Presbyterians ordered men to New Mexico. On the family's journey from Pittsburgh, one of his children died. He preached the first Methodist sermon in Santa Fe in October 1850 from 2 Corinthians 1:2 to a small number of parishioners, mostly connected with the army. "The mission at Santa Fe is in a prosperous condition," reported a newspaper. "The Rev. Mr. Nicholson speaks in high terms of Mr. Kepheart, the missionary from the Presbyterian church. They work together in great harmony." *Washington Reporter*, July 17, 1850; Annual Report of the Missionary Society of the Methodist, 73–74, 300; Twitchell, *Leading Facts*, 350; Harwood, *History of New Mexico Spanish and English Missions*, 371; *Daily Missouri Republican*, October 11, 1850; *Spectator*, February 24, 1851.

10. Murphy, *Antislavery in the Southwest*, 4–5, 7, 15, 18–19, 21; *National Era*, January 23, 1851.

11. Horn, 14.

12. Charles Blumner, a German immigrant, arrived in Santa Fe in 1846. He worked for Manuel Alvarez collecting debts and handled Alvarez's business affairs. Kearny appointed him territorial treasurer, and he was reappointed in 1851. Alvarez and Ceran St. Vrain posted his security bond. Jaehn, "The Unpolitical German in New Mexico, 1848–1914," 7–8.

13. Calhoun, Executive Journal, March 3–April 26, 1851, roll 21, TANM; Lamar, 84.

14. Proclamation, March 18, 1851, Read Collection, Territorial Archives, roll 21, NMSA.

15. Calhoun to Lea, March 22, 1851, in Abel, *Official Correspondence*, 300–301.

16. Born near Albuquerque, he grew up in Cebolleta, about thirty miles west. He was a sheep rancher, sometime slave raider, and captain of the local militia. His bravery in battle had earned him the nickname the "Little Lion." Chaves had also fought as a volunteer alongside US troops in the 1847 action against the Taos rebels. In the years after 1851, Manuel was absent for long periods, attending to his ranch in the Pecos valley and participating in an increasing number of Indian campaigns. Sides, 271–72; M. Simmons, *The Little Lion of the Southwest*, 114.

17. Proposal, Manuel Chaves, March 18, 1851, in Abel, *Official Correspondence*, 302–3; M. Simmons, *Little Lion*, 121; McNitt, *Navajo Wars*, 174; Calhoun, Executive Journal, March 22, 1851, roll 21, TANM.

18. Not until 1868 was the Organic Act amended to allow the legislature to override a veto with a two-thirds vote.

19. Henry Connelly went to Chihuahua in 1828 and became a merchant and a naturalized Mexican citizen and married a Mexican woman. In 1848 he moved to New Mexico and continued in business. After his first wife died, he married the widow of José Mariano Chávez, of Peralta. Connelly was elected governor in 1850, but Munroe didn't allow him to take office. He was appointed territorial governor in 1861 and reappointed in 1864. He died in Santa Fe in 1866. McCall, *New Mexico*, 69 fn36.

20. Calhoun to Lea, March 22, 1851, in Abel, *Official Correspondence*, 299; Calhoun to Fillmore, March 29, 1851, in Abel, 305; Calhoun to Stuart, March 31, 1851, in Abel, 306.

21. Neil, 217–19, 234, 236.

22. Post Office Department Appointments, Records of US Army Commands, February 12, 1851, 1849–77, RG 28, roll 1, NMSA; *Palmyra Weekly Whig*, March 27, 1851.

23. Census takers were George Gold, Taos County; Celedon Valdez, Rio Arriba County; Mauricio Duran, Santa Fe County; Turner Donaldson, San Miguel County; Pablo Gutierrez, Bernalillo County. South of Bernalillo County, census takers were Lorenzo Labadie, Charles Overman, and C. H. Hoppin. Calhoun Proclamation, March 12, 1851, State Department Territorial Papers, New Mexico 1851–1872, RG 59, roll 1, NMSA.

24. David Virdin Whiting was born on April 1, 1827, in Caracas, Venezuela, and educated there. He moved to Baltimore in 1844 and worked for a large mercantile house in Philadelphia. He married his wife, Anna Teresa, a Venezuelan, in 1847, and they had two children. In 1849 he was sent to New Mexico to settle the estate of a junior member of the Philadelphia firm who had been slain near Wagon Mound; that may have been James M. White. He wrote to Manuel Alvarez to say he intended to open a school, but he clerked for merchant Joseph D. Ellis and became Calhoun's interpreter and secretary. Hendricks, "David V. Whiting."

25. Calhoun to Lea, February 16, 1851, in Abel, *Official Correspondence*, 292–94;

Annual Report of the Commissioner of Indian Affairs, 1851, 191–92; Calhoun, Executive Journal, April 11–25, 1851, roll 21, TANM.

26. Lamar, 85–86.

27. Owen, *Las Cruces, New Mexico 1849–1999*, 20–21.

28. Calhoun, Executive Journal; Calhoun to Lea, March 31, 1851, in Abel, *Official Correspondence*, 307–8.

29. Jones would spend $786 to feed prisoners between March 10 and September 15 and be reimbursed by the legislature. *Laws of the Territory of New Mexico*, 348.

30. Jones chose Lafayette Head, a merchant in Abiquiu, as his subordinate in the northern district. Head was a veteran of the Mexican War and later served as agent to the Jicarilla Apaches and Utes. His wife was Martina Martínez, whose family was prominent in the area. He also was a member of the legislature. Ball, *The United States Marshals*, 25.

31. Donaciano Vigil, born in 1802 in New Mexico, became a protégé of the Mexican governor, Manuel Armijo, serving as territorial secretary. Educated and bilingual, he was openly pro-American. When Governor Bent was assassinated, Vigil became acting governor until Colonel Washington arrived. He was elected to the territorial legislature from San Miguel County. He died in 1877. Kraemer, "Donaciano Vigil, 'The Gifted Giant,'" 1–3.

32. Calhoun, Executive Journal; Vigil, *Arms, Indians, and the Mismanagement of New Mexico*, xi–xii.

33. Calhoun reversed two of his appointments. After naming German immigrant and land-grant founder Herman Grolman as prefect of San Miguel County on March 28, he replaced Grolman with a reliable ally, Miguel Sena y Quintana. Calhoun doesn't say why, but Grolman apparently caused problems with Jicarillas and Utes several times and even wrote to Calhoun saying soldiers should "drive the Indians out of the settlement." He also revoked the appointment of Ignacio Narvaez as alcalde of Cieneguilla, saying he was "appointed through false information." Calhoun, Executive Journal; Gottschalk, 6, 11; Michno, 89, 101; Espinosa, 6.

34. *St. Louis Republican*, May 19, 1851; *Columbus Enquirer*, April 22, 1851; *National Era*, July 17, 1851; Murphy, 31–32, 47.

35. *National Era*, June 12, 1851.

36. Keleher, *Turmoil*, 484 fn10; Murphy, 41; *Spectator*, March 20, 1851.

37. *Daily Missouri Republican*, May 28 and June 30, 1851; *Daily Union*, July 10, 1851; Calhoun, Executive Journal, May 19–23, 1851, roll 21, TANM; Vaughan, *History and Government of New Mexico*, 186; Chávez, *But Time and Change*, 89–90.

38. Gonzáles, "La Politica: Stories of Politics and Nuevomexicanos."

39. Davis, 170, 255; Nusbaum, *The City Different and the Palace*, 16; Shishkin, *The Palace of Governors*, 26–29; McCall, *New Mexico*, 63 fn12; Munroe to Calhoun, May 24, 1851, in Abel, *Official Correspondence*, 352; Calhoun, Executive Journal, May 21, 23, 24, roll 21, TANM; Allen to Calhoun, Secretary of State Collection, 1959–293, Series 1, subseries 1.1, TANM.

40. *National Era*, August 14, 1851.

41. *National Era*, August 14, 1851.

42. *National Era*, August 14, 1851.

43. *National Era*, August 14, 1851; Davis, 246.

44. *National Era*, August 14, 1851.

45. *National Era*, August 14, 1851.

46. Horn, 28; Bonner, 103; Phillips, 4.

47. Garrard, 227; *National Era*, January 23, 1851; Larson, 64; *Daily Union*, December 28, 1851; Hays, 253; Vasconcellos, "Out of the House of Bondage," 22.

48. Sando, 83.

49. *National Era*, August 14, 1851; Davis, 246.

50. House of Representatives and Council Chamber to Fillmore, June 30, 1851, in Abel, *Official Correspondence*, 366–68.

51. Legislature to Calhoun, July 9, 1851, in Abel, *Official Correspondence*, 386–87.

52. State Department Territorial Papers, New Mexico 1851–1872, RG 59, roll 1, NMSA; *Spectator*, September 11, 1851; *Laws of the Territory*.

53. Beaubien to Calhoun, June 11, 1851, Calhoun, Papers.

54. Calhoun to Munroe, June 14, 1851, in Abel, *Official Correspondence*, 361; Calhoun, Executive Journal, June 14–16, 1851, roll 21, TANM; McLaws to Gordon, June 24, 1851, in Abel, 360–61.

55. Calhoun to Webster, June 30, 1851, in Abel, *Official Correspondence*, 362–363; Calhoun to Lea, June 30, 1851, in Abel, 369–70; Calhoun to Stuart, April 2, 1851, in Abel, 314.

56. Calhoun to Webster, June 30, 1851, in Abel, *Official Correspondence*, 362–64; Calhoun to Lea, June 30, 1851, in Abel, 369–70; Calhoun to Stuart, April 2, 1851, in Abel, 314.

57. "To the People of New Mexico," in Abel, *Official Correspondence*, 371–72.

58. Other signers were Antonio Sandoval, Santiago Armijo, Julian Tenorio, Mariano Yrisarri, A. W. Reynolds, Antonio José Otero, T. S. J. Johnson, William Mc-Grorty, Ceran St. Vrain, J. L. Collins, J. M. Giddings, Juan José Sanchez, Francisco Ortiz y Delgado, Robert Brent, M. Ashurst, Hugh N. Smith, Serafino Ramirez, Rafael Armijo, Diego Archuleta, Candido Ortiz, John R. Tullis, Alexander Duvall, Reverend McCutcheon, E. J. Vaughn, Juan Cruz Baca, William Curtis Skinner, Thomas Ortiz, John Kelly, Joab Houghton. "To the People of New Mexico," in Abel, *Official Correspondence*, 375.

59. Signing the statement were Antonio José Martínez, Vicente Martínes, José Manuel Gallegos, José Francisco Leyva, Seledonio Valdes, José Perea, Miguel Sena y Romero, J. F. Ortiz, Juan Cristóbal Chaves, Antonio J. Ortiz, Theodore Wheaton, F. T. Cabesa de Baca, Geronimo Jaramillo, José Ramón Vigil, José Pablo Gallegos, Florentino Castillo, George Gold, Esquipula Vigil, Hilario Gonzáles, Monsignor Sena y Quintana, Juan Torres, Spruce Baird, Pascual Martínez, Dionicio Gonzáles, Raymundo Córdova, Francisco Antonio Otero, José Andres Sandoval, Diego Salazar,

Miguel Mascarena. Gonzáles, 240–42; Abel, *Official Correspondence*, 378; Calhoun to Webster, June 30, 1851, in Abel, 362–64.

60. Calhoun to Lea, June 30, 1851, in Abel, *Official Correspondence*, 365.

Chapter Fourteen

1. Fort Webster wouldn't be established for another year. Cantonment Dawson preceded Fort Webster at the site. Munroe to Jones, January 27, 1851, in Abel, *Official Correspondence*, 290.

2. Annual Report of the Commissioner, 1851, 186–87, 193; Calhoun to Lea, February 2 and 16, 1851, Arrott, Fort Union Collection; Whiting to Calhoun, February 10, 1851, in Abel, *Official Correspondence*, 291.

3. Sarracino to Calhoun, January 29, 1851, in Abel, *Official Correspondence*, 283–84; Annual Report of the Commissioner, 1851, 187–89, 195; Pino to Luna, undated, in Abel, 286; Calhoun to Lea, May 4, 1851, in Abel, 341–42, and August 22, 1851, in Abel, 401; *Weekly Missouri Republican*, February 6, 1852.

4. Benjamin J. Latz was born in 1825 and arrived in New York on July 26, 1842. The passenger list describes him as a furrier from Posen, Germany; his brother Herman was a tailor. When he volunteered, he was living in St. Louis. Latz is described as the only St. Louis Jew to participate in the Mexican War. He fought in the battle of Sacramento. Mustering out in New Orleans in 1847, he returned to New Mexico. According to the 1850 census, Latz, twenty-four, was living in La Cuesta with his wife, Maria Baronia, twenty-three, and eighteen-year-old José Pacheco, who may have been a relative since he's not listed as a servant. Maria was born in New Mexico, Latz in Poland. Latz would also serve as a special agent for Governor David Meriwether in 1855 and 1856. In 1856 he moved to La Plancha, California, and by 1858 his B. J. Latz & Company had struck gold in its mine in Calaveras County. In 1862, Latz was back in New Mexico, where he signed a petition asking for Indian agents to be appointed on the eastern frontier for the Southern Comanches, Mescaleros, and Navajos. He fought in the Civil War battle of Valverde. Latz died in Santa Fe on June 9, 1864. Ehrlich, *Zion in the Valley*, 86; der Marcus, *United States Jewry, 1776–1985*, 2:138; *Jewish Tribune*, December 21, 1883; Letter from the Secretary of the Treasury, March 3, 1857, 321; Second Auditor of the Treasury, January 16, 1857, S. Ex. Doc. 28, S. S. 880, 355; *San Francisco Bulletin*, September 26, 1856, and June 3, 1858; Secretary of the Interior to the Committee on Indian Affairs, U.S. Senate, April 2, 1862, S. Misc. Doc. 79, S. S. 1124, 18.

5. Gordon, 107; Ebright, "San Miguel del Bado Grant."

6. McLaws to Alexander, March 20, 1851, in Abel, *Official Correspondence*, 273; Calhoun, Executive Journal, March 25 and 29, 1851; McLaws to Howe, March 30, 1851, in Abel, 310; Calhoun to Latz, March 11, 1851, in Abel, 297–98; Ehrlich, 86; Michno, 173.

7. *National Era*, May 8, 1851.

8. McLaws to Alexander, March 14 and 16, 1851, in Abel, *Official Correspondence*, 303–4; Howe to McLaws, March 18, 1851, Records of US Army Commands, DNM, Selected Documents Related to the Navajo Indians, 1846–1868, RG 98, roll 1; Calhoun to Lea, March 31, 1851, in Abel, 308; *Missouri Courier*, May 22, 1851; McLaws to Howe, March 30, 1851, in Abel, 310.

9. Witnesses to the treaty included Manuel Alvarez, Manuel Chaves, John G. Jones, Hugh N. Smith, William Kephart, Horace L. Dickenson, and Reverend E. G. Nicholson, the Methodist minister.

10. Calhoun to Stuart, April 2, 1851, in Abel, *Official Correspondence*, 314–16; Mc-Laws to Howe, April 5, 1851, in Abel, 317; Calhoun to Lea, March 31, 1851, in Abel, 308.

11. Calhoun to Stuart, April 2, 1851, in Abel, *Official Correspondence*, 313–14; Munroe to Jones, March 30, 1851, in Abel, 311.

12. Calhoun to Latz, April 18 and May 8, 1851, in Abel, *Official Correspondence*, 327–28, 351–52; McLaws to Chapman, April 18, 1851, in Abel, 318; Calhoun to Lea, May 1, 1851, in Abel, 341–42; Calhoun, Executive Journal, April 17 to May 15, 1851; Tiller, 38–39; Calhoun to Munroe, in Abel, 350–51; McLaws to Alexander, May 8, 1851, in Abel, 330–31; Munroe to Jones, May 31 and June 30, 1851, in Abel 328–30, 358–59.

13. Calhoun to Lea, May 1, 1851, in Abel, *Official Correspondence*, 341–42; *Daily Missouri Republican*, June 30, 1851; McLaws to Chapman, May 30, 1851, in Abel, 342–44; Calhoun to Lea, June 1, 1851, in Abel, 355; List of Property, June 13, 1851, in Abel, 378; Calhoun to Chapman, June 9, 1851, in Abel, 356; Munroe to Jones, June 29, 1851, in Abel, 345–46; Calhoun to Webster, June 30, 1851, in Abel, 363.

14. Calhoun to Lea, July 1, 25, and 28, 1851, in Abel, *Official Correspondence*, 379, 388–91; Munroe to Jones, July 13, 1851, in Abel, 347–49; Annual Report of the Commissioner, 1851, 199–200.

15. Munroe to Calhoun, April 8, 1851, in Abel, *Official Correspondence*, 322–23; Munroe to Calhoun, April 9, 1851, in Abel, 324; Calhoun to Munroe, April 10, 1851, in Abel, 325; Conrad to Weightman, April 3, 1851, in Abel, 327–28.

16. Calhoun to Lea, April 29, 1851, in Abel, *Official Correspondence*, 337–39.

17. Calhoun to Clayton, April 27, 1851, in Abel, *Official Correspondence*, 336–37; Calhoun to Lea, May 28, 1851, in Abel, 353–54.

18. Calhoun to Lea, April 29 and May 28, 1851, in Abel, *Official Correspondence*, 337–39, 354–55; Lea to Calhoun, April 5 and 12, 1851, in Abel, 321, 326.

19. John Greiner was born September 14, 1810, in Philadelphia. He came to Ohio early and settled at Marietta, where he was a painter and dealer in painting materials. On May 4, 1837, he married Laurinda Bennett. Around 1841 they moved to Zanesville, where he was a member of the Zanesville Temperance Society. Later he moved to Columbus. For eight years Greiner was state librarian and later an editor of the *Ohio State Journal* and the *Columbus Gazette*. Active in early Whig campaigns, he wrote some of the most popular political songs of the day and sang them to crowds

of thousands. The 1850 census lists Greiner, forty, Laurinda, and six children aged twelve to one. In October 1851, Greiner's twelve-year-old son, George Woodbridge Greiner, died. "The deceased was a youth of intelligence far beyond his years and was as amiable as he was intelligent. It will be a sad stroke to his father . . . when he hears of the death of his son." *Cincinnati Commercial Tribune*, May 15, 1871; *Plain Dealer*, May 18, 1871; *Cincinnati Daily Gazette*, May 24, 1871; *Daily Ohio Statesman*, October 29, 1851.

20. Galloway, "Private Letters of a Government Official," 543–44.

21. *Ohio Statesman*, January 17, 1845, and June 6, 1851; *Cincinnati Daily Gazette*, May 24, 1871; *Plain Dealer*, May 18, 1871.

22. *Daily Commercial Register*, June 17, 1851; Jones to Sumner, March 29, 1851, Records of US Army Commands, DNM LSR, RG 98, 92, 192, roll 1; Galloway, 542–43; Sumner to Jones, October 24, 1851, in Abel, *Official Correspondence*, 416–19; *Daily Missouri Republican*, May 12, 1851.

23. Galloway, 545.

24. Woolley entered the army as a captain in 1812, served through the war with distinction, rose to major by 1825, and was brevetted to lieutenant colonel for his long and meritorious service. In 1829 he was court-martialed and found guilty of punishing a private with lashes and for having a hasty and ungovernable temper and dismissed from the service. Woolley made a claim to Congress for lost pay by his dismissal. The *Newark Daily Advertiser* on February 26, 1850, opined that Woolley was an intelligent gentleman and the pay "will tend to cheer his pathway in the decline of life." A Senate committee in 1851 found the court irregular and disagreed with the dismissal but concluded it could do nothing to change that. He died in October 1858 at age seventy-four. Reports of Committees, 31st Cong., 2nd sess., February 25, 1851; *Trenton State Gazette*, October 8, 1858.

25. Wingfield was born in 1806 and graduated from the University of Georgia in 1825. *Daily National Intelligencer*, February 21, 1850; *Columbus Enquirer*, August 23, 1834.

26. Lea to Wingfield, April 15, 1851, in Abel, *Official Correspondence*, 384–85; Lea to Greiner, April 15, 1851, in Abel, 385; Calhoun to Lea, July 30, 1851, in Abel, 392–94.

27. Gorman, *The Trouble at Round Rock*, 4.

28. *National Era*, September 11, 1851.

29. Sherman to Baker, August 30, 1851, in Abel, *Official Correspondence*, 407–8.

30. Munroe commanded the Department of Florida from 1853 to 1856 and the newly created Department of the Platte from 1858 to 1861. After a six-hundred-mile trip in an open sleigh, which overturned, Munroe suffered from exposure and injuries and died at his niece's home in New Brunswick, New Jersey, on April 26, 1861. *George W. Cullum's Biographical Register*, 2:1211; *Trenton State Gazette*, May 6, 1861; Keleher, *Turmoil*, 129 fn59.

31. Utley, *Fort Union National Monument*, 9; Conrad to Sumner, April 1, 1851, in Abel, *Official Correspondence*, 383–84.

32. Edwin Vose Sumner, born in Boston on January 30, 1797, was commissioned a second lieutenant in the Second Infantry in 1819. In the Mexican War he was major of the Second Dragoons and accompanied Kearny to New Mexico. He later joined Winfield Scott in Mexico. Thrapp, *Encyclopedia of Frontier Biography*, 1,390; Smith and Judah, 276–77.

33. In southern New Mexico Doña Ana was the only town between Socorro, in central New Mexico, and the Mexican city of Paso del Norte on the south side of the Rio Grande. Doña Ana became a post in early 1849, followed later that year by posts across from Paso del Norte and San Elizario.

34. On December 28, 1851, Brevet Major Israel B. Richardson led sixty-seven men of Company K, Third Infantry, to Cantonment Dawson at the Santa Rita copper mines, about eighty miles northwest of Fort Fillmore. Here he established Fort Webster, named for Daniel Webster, on January 23, 1852. Kiser, 112; Sumner to Bliss, August 3, 1851, in Abel, *Official Correspondence*, 382–83; Sumner to Jones, October 24, 1851, McFerran to Gordon, November 9, 1851, and General Orders No. 44, December 2, 1851, US Area Commands, LS, 9th Military Department, RG 393, NA; Prucha, 63, 67, 71, 74, 91, 111, 113, 116; Wadsworth, *Forgotten Fortress*, 11–12.

35. *National Era*, September 11, 1851; *Daily Missouri Republican*, August 28, 1851; Calhoun to Sumner, August 4, 1851, in Abel, *Official Correspondence*, 396–97.

36. Rodriguez et al. to Calhoun, August 8, 1851, in Abel, *Official Correspondence*, 402–3; Petition to Sumner, August 4, 1851, Records of US Army Commands, LSR, DNM, RG 98, 92, 192, roll 1; Sumner to Jones, October 24, 1851, in Abel, 417.

37. Calhoun to Sumner, August 4, 1851, in Abel, *Official Correspondence*, 396–97; Sumner to Calhoun, August 8, 1851, in Abel, 398; Conrad to Stanton, April 28, 1851, in Abel, 327; Calhoun to Brooks, July 30, 1851, in Abel, 392; Buell to Calhoun, August 3, 1851, in Abel, 395.

38. *Albany Courier*, June 12, 1846; Calhoun to Lea, August 22, 1851, in Abel, *Official Correspondence*, 401; Woolley, Wingfield, and Greiner to Lea, August 29, 1851, in Abel, 421–22; Calhoun to Wingfield, September 17, 1851, in Abel, 427.

39. Ball, "The U.S. Army in New Mexico," 179; McNitt, *Navajo Expedition*, 178, 181.

40. Horgan, 108–10.

41. Mares, "The Many Faces of Padre Antonio José Martínez," 59; Gonzáles, "La Politica"; Galloway, 545.

42. Baker was concerned enough about repercussions to write directly to President Fillmore and send a copy of Sherman's letter, along with a letter from Lamy. Sherman to Baker, August 30, 1851, in Abel, *Official Correspondence*, 408–12; *Victoria Advocate*, October 25, 1851; Horgan, 114, 124; *Daily Union*, February 18, 1852.

43. Sumner to Jones, October 24, 1851, in Abel, *Official Correspondence*, 418; *Alexandria Gazette*, December 16, 1851; Bennett, 30–31.

44. Calhoun to Conrad, August 31, 1851, in Abel, *Official Correspondence*, 413; Calhoun to Lea, August 31, 1851, in Abel, 414–15.

Chapter Fifteen

1. Calhoun to Webster, June 30, 1851, in Abel, *Official Correspondence*, 363; Murphy, 38; Sumner to Conrad, December 22, 1852, in Abel, 145.

2. Los Ranchos de Albuquerque was surrounded by land owned by two of the wealthiest families in the territory, the Armijos and Yrisarris. For that reason, Los Ranchos became the first county seat of Bernalillo County in 1852. Sargeant and Davis, *Shining River Precious Land*, 17.

3. *Daily Missouri Republican*, November 5 and 13, 1851; *St. Louis Union*, October 29, 1851; Read, 481–84.

4. *Trenton State Gazette*, November 17, 1851; Weightman speech, March 15, 1852.

5. Skinner, a lawyer from Connecticut, came to New Mexico with Kearny in the Missouri Light Artillery. He got involved in Santa Fe Trail trade with Connelly and the Oteros. In the late 1840s he built a mill in Peralta, one of the first modern water mills of New Mexico, to supply flour for troops. In 1847 Skinner was clerk of the circuit court. After Skinner's death the Oteros acquired his mill and filled government contracts for grains and flour. Alexander, *Among the Cottonwoods*, 83–84.

6. *St. Louis Union*, October 29, 1851; *Daily Missouri Republican*, November 13, 1851; Larson, 66–68; *National Era*, December 18, 1851.

7. *St. Louis Union*, October 29, 1851; *Daily Missouri Republican*, November 13, 1851; Larson, 66–68; *National Era*, December 18, 1851.

8. *The Republic*, November 12, 1851.

9. Calhoun to Webster, September 15, 1851, in Abel, *Official Correspondence*, 425–26.

10. Vaughan, 188; Calhoun to Webster, September 23, 1851, in Abel, *Official Correspondence*, 428–29; Calhoun, Executive Journal, September 24, 1851, roll 21, TANM; *Spectator*, September 25, 1851; *Weekly Missouri Republican*, February 6, 1852.

11. Wheaton to Calhoun, September 20, 1851, in Abel, *Official Correspondence*, 427–28.

12. Calhoun to Webster, October 1, 1851, in Abel, *Official Correspondence*, 430–31.

13. Calhoun to Lea, October 1, 1852, in Abel, *Official Correspondence*, 432–33.

14. *National Era*, December 18, 1851; Calhoun to Webster, October 29, 1851, in Abel, *Official Correspondence*, 440–41.

15. McNitt, *Navajo Expedition*, 170–71 fn7; Frink, *Fort Defiance & The Navajos*, 19; Bowen to Bowen, October 11 and November 2, 1851, Arrott.

16. Sumner to Jones, October 24, 1851, in Abel, *Official Correspondence*, 419; Calhoun to Lea, October 1, 1851, in Abel, 433.

17. Greiner to Calhoun, October 20, 1851, in Abel, *Official Correspondence*, 438; Sumner to Calhoun, October 24, 1851, in Abel, 439–40; Calhoun to Sumner, October 31, 1851, Arrott; Calhoun to Webster, October 29, 1851, in Abel, 440–41.

18. Calhoun, Executive Journal, October 24, 1851, roll 21, TANM; Proclamation,

James S. Calhoun, October 24, 1851, Military Occupation, Roll 98, 1846–1850 and 1851–1878, NMSA; Calhoun to Sumner, November 9, 1851, in Abel, *Official Correspondence*, 444; Beck et al. to Calhoun, November 9, 1852, Abel, 445–46; Calhoun to Sumner, November 10, 1851, in Abel, 447–49.

19. McFerran to Shoemaker, November 10, 1851, in Abel, *Official Correspondence*, 446; Sumner to Calhoun, November 10, 1851, in Abel, 449–50, 452; Calhoun to Sumner, November 10, 1851, in Abel, 450–51.

20. Beck et al. to Calhoun, November 11, 1851, in Abel, *Official Correspondence*, 453–54; Calhoun to Sumner, November 11, 1851, in Abel, 454–56; Sumner to Calhoun, November 11 and 13, 1851, in Abel, 455–57.

21. Sumner to Jones, November 20, 1851, in Abel, *Official Correspondence*, 445.

22. Galloway, 546–47; *National Era*, September 11, 1851.

23. *Daily Missouri Republican*, October 28 and 30, 1851; Larson, 66; Murphy, 41–42, 47; Calhoun to Baker, October 1, 1851, in Abel, *Official Correspondence*, 431–32; Calhoun to Webster, October 29, 1851, in Abel, 440–41; Derrick to Calhoun, September 13, 1851, in Abel, 423.

24. *Daily Missouri Republican*, November 29, 1851; Larson, 68 fn30, 320.

25. *Daily Missouri Republican*, November 13, 1851; Santa Fe County Records, County Sheriff, Box 16071, 1,847–167.

26. *Semi-Weekly Union*, December 27, 1851.

27. Murphy, 44; *Daily Missouri Republican*, August 28, 1851; Greiner, July 29, 1851, in Galloway, 545; *Union*, November 7, 1851.

28. Calhoun, Executive Journal, August 9, roll 21, TANM.

29. Speech to Legislature, December 1, 1851, Secretary of State Collection, 1959–293, Series 1, subseries 1.1, TANM; Allen to Calhoun, Secretary of State Papers, Collection 1949–293, Territorial Archives, NMSA.

30. Allen to Calhoun, Secretary of State Papers, Collection 1949–293, Territorial Archives, NMSA; Calhoun to Webster, October 29, 1851, in Abel, *Official Correspondence*, 440–41; *Weekly Missouri Republican*, February 6, 1852.

31. Speech to Legislature, December 1, 1851, Secretary of State Collection, 1959–293, Series 1, subseries 1.1, TANM

32. Calhoun, Executive Journal, September 22, 1851, roll 21, TANM; Calhoun speech, December 1, 1851; Response to House, December 20, 1851, Secretary of State Collection, 1959–293, Roll 1, TANM; Mix to Calhoun, August 8, 1851, in Abel, *Official Correspondence*, 398.

33. Calhoun to Webster, June 30, 1851, in Abel, *Official Correspondence*, 362; *Weekly Missouri Republican*, February 6, 1852.

34. McNitt, *Navajo Wars*, 206–7; Sumner to Jones, January 1, 1852, in Abel, *Official Correspondence*, 433–34.

35. Annual Report of the Commissioner, 1851, 6, 9–10, 12–13.

Chapter Sixteen

1. Martha Ann Davis, wife of John H. Davis, died in Columbus on November 7, 1851. *Columbus Enquirer*, November 11, 1851, and June 27, 1875.

2. Greiner to Calhoun, January 5, 1852, in Abel, *Official Correspondence*, 463; Calhoun to Lea, January 30, 1852, in Abel, 471–72; Galloway, 547.

3. Calhoun to Lea, January 31, 1852, in Abel, *Official Correspondence*, 473–75; *Columbus Enquirer*, February 19, 1850; Galloway, 548.

4. Calhoun to Lea, February 29, 1852, in Abel, *Official Correspondence*, 486–89; Galloway, 549; Weightman to Alvarez, May 6, 1852, Alvarez Papers; Read Collections, Proclamations, March 29 and April 2, 1852, Read Collection, Territorial Archives of New Mexico, roll 98, NMSA; Calhoun to Lea, March 31, 1852, in Abel, 513.

5. Horsman, *Feast or Famine*, 129; Steele, xxii, 115, 116; Leonard to AAG, June 5, 1849, Records of US Army Commands, DNM, Letters Sent and Received, RG 98, 92, 192, roll 1; Myers, 48; *National Intelligencer*, February 7, 1851; McCall, *Letters from the Frontiers*, 495.

6. Galloway, 547–49; *Ohio State Journal*, March 9, 1852.

7. Greiner to Calhoun, January 29, 1852, in Abel, *Official Correspondence*, 466–69; Calhoun to Lea, January 31, 1852, in Abel, 473–75.

8. Calhoun to Lea, February 29, 1852, in Abel, *Official Correspondence*, 488–89; Murphy, 45, 47, 49; Greiner to Baird, April 7, 1852, in Abel, 520; Baird to Sumner, December 18, 1851, Records of US Army Commands, RUSAC DNM SDRNI, RG 98, roll 1, NMSA.

9. Fort Union; Carroll, "Before Fort Craig," 25; Sumner to Jones, January 1, 1852, in Abel, *Official Correspondence*, 433–34; Sumner to Jones, January 27, 1852, US Area Commands, LS, 9th Military Department, RG 393, NA.

10. Calhoun to Lea, January 31, 1852, in Abel, *Official Correspondence*, 474–75; *Daily Commercial Register*, April 5, 1852.

11. Petition, February 10, 1852, in Abel, *Official Correspondence*, 481–82; Calhoun to Lea, February 25 and 29, 1852, in Abel, 483, 487–88; Calhoun, Executive Journal, February 16, 1852, roll 21, TANM.

12. Calhoun to Sumner, February 11, 1852, in Abel, *Official Correspondence*, 479–80; Sumner to Calhoun, February 11, 1852, in Abel, 478.

13. Calhoun to Lea, February 29, 1852, in Abel, *Official Correspondence*, 486–89; Sumner to Calhoun, March 21, 1852, in Abel, 492–93; Calhoun to Sumner, March 28, 1852 in Abel, 509.

14. Sumner to Jones, February 3, 1852, in Abel, *Official Correspondence*, 479; Sumner to Conrad, March 27, 1852, in Abel, 516; Sumner to Morris, April 1, 1852, in Abel, 516–17.

15. Sumner to Carleton, January 28 and March 4, 1852, in Abel, *Official Correspondence*, 477.

16. Calhoun to Lea, February 29, 1852, in Abel, *Official Correspondence*, 488.

17. Greiner to Calhoun, March 25, 1852, in Abel, *Official Correspondence*, 494–97; Greiner to Calhoun, March 30, 1852, Schroeder Papers; Greiner to Lea, April 30, 1852, in Abel, 529–31.

18. Galloway, 547; *Daily Commercial Register*, April 5, 1852; *Augusta Chronicle*, June 10, 1852; *Republic*, May 21, 1852.

19. *Semi-Weekly Union*, January 3, 1852; Weightman to Alvarez, February 9, 1852, Alvarez Papers; *Daily Union*, December 28, 1851; Weightman speech.

20. *National Era*, February 26, 1852; Greiner to Lea, April 30 and May 19, 1852, in Abel, *Official Correspondence*, 529–31, 536–37.

21. Weightman speech; *Republic*, March 11, 1852.

22. Weightman speech.

23. Weightman speech.

24. Weightman speech; Larson, 72–73; Ganaway, 226.

25. Weightman speech; *National Era*, April 29, 1852.

26. *Daily American Telegraph*, April 13, 1852; *Columbus Enquirer*, April 27, 1852.

27. Weightman to Pino and Gonzales, March 20, 1852, in Twitchell, *History of Military Occupation*, 386–90.

28. On December 26, 1850, Weightman wrote to the president that appointing Smith would be "adverse to the wishes and feelings of the people of that country," who in recent elections had elected Manuel Alvarez as secretary and lieutenant governor.

29. Weightman asked Alvarez to translate portions of his last speech for Vicar Juan Felipe Ortiz and to remember him to Baird, Mower, Baker, Sheets and friends, Juan Antonio Baca y Pino, Manuel Chaves and friends, Cunnningham, Hume, and Massie. Twitchell, *History of Military Occupation*, 389; Weightman to Alvarez, May 6 and June 16, 1852, Alvarez Papers; T Chávez, *Manuel Alvarez*, 158–59, 174, 177, 180.

30. Weightman sent his respects to Baird, Greiner, West, Mower, Watts, Sheets, Richardson, Massie, and friends. Weightman to Alvarez, May 6, 1852, Alvarez Papers.

31. "The captain was either a hopelessly disorganized keeper of records or a brazen embezzler," wrote William Marvel. Franklin Pierce dismissed him in 1855 for what the US Comptroller described as "great irregularity and palpable fraud." He won reinstatement to the army in 1857. Reynolds served under General Twiggs at San Antonio and was a party to his surrender to the Confederates in 1861, when President Lincoln dropped Reynolds from army rolls a second time. A Virginian, he served as a general in the Confederacy throughout the war and then joined the Khedive's Army in Egypt. There he died on May 26, 1876. Thomas worked for a railroad and then coal-mining companies in Pennsylvania and Virginia. He became a Confederate officer and died in the Battle of Bull Run on July 21, 1861 at age thirty-seven. *Times-Picayune*, April 16, 1852; *Boston Courier*, October 15, 1855; *New York Times*, July 2, 1876; Marvel, *Burnside*, 11; McCall, *Letters from the Frontiers*, 196; George W. Cullum's *Biographical Register*.

32. Galloway, 549; Harwood, 371; Murphy, 49; *Ohio State Journal*, March 9, 1852.

33. They were Samuel Craton, Bernardo Ordoner, Clemente Martin, Antonio Jose Trujillo, Calistro Garcis, José Miguel Ortiz, Thomas Evans, Morris Tegardner, John Young, Thomas Jones, Luisa Campos, Russell Williams, Juan Cruz Sanchez, and Jose Antonio Borrego.

34. Calhoun to Alvarez, Calhoun Papers; *Weekly Messenger*, May 26, 1852.

35. *Newark Daily Advertiser*, May 11, 1852.

36. Wingfield to Lea, February 6 and May 22, 1852, in Abel, *Official Correspondence*, 469–70, 538.

37. Calhoun to Lea, April 6, 1852, in Abel, *Official Correspondence*, 514–15; Greiner to Sumner, April 4, 1852, in Abel, 519–20; Whiteley, "Reconnoitering Pueblo Ethnicity," 458.

38. Calhoun to Sumner, April 7, 1852, in Abel, *Official Correspondence*, 517–19.

39. Sumner to Calhoun, April 8, 1852, in Abel, *Official Correspondence*, 520–21.

40. Sumner to Jones, April 9, 1852, in Abel, *Official Correspondence*, 521–22.

41. Sumner to Jones, April 9, 1852, in Abel, *Official Correspondence*, 521–22; *Weekly Messenger*, May 26, 1852; Calhoun, Executive Journal, April 10,; *Weekly Union*, March 5, 1853.

42. Calhoun to Dawson, April 12, 1852, in Abel, *Official Correspondence*, 523–24; *Ohio State Journal*, June 8, 1852.

43. Calhoun to Sumner, April 12, 1852, in Abel, *Official Correspondence*, 524–25; Sumner to Calhoun, April 14, 1852, in Abel, 526–27; Greiner, order, April 15, 1852, in Abel, 532; Calhoun to Sumner, April 18, 1852, in Abel, 527.

44. Proclamation, April 21, 1852, in Abel, *Official Correspondence*, 528; Sumner to Jones, April 22 and 28, 1852, in Abel, 525–26, 532.

45. Merritt to Stuart, April 30, 1852, in Abel, *Official Correspondence*, 533.

46. *Daily National Intelligencer*, June 8, 1852; *Ohio State Journal*, June 8, 1852.

47. Carleton to Sumner, May 1 and 24, and Sumner to Carleton, May 3, 1852, US Area Commands, LR, 9th Military District, RG 393, NA; Katie Bowen to Father & Mother, November 30, 1851, Arrott.

48. Greiner to Lea, April 30, 1852, in Abel, *Official Correspondence*, 529–31; Galloway, 550–51; Sumner to Calhoun, May 2, 1852, in Abel, 546.

Chapter Seventeen

1. *Weekly Union*, March 5, 1853; Abel, "The Journal of John Greiner," 205; Murphy, 43–44; Greiner to Lea, April 30, 1852, in Abel, *Official Correspondence*, 531; *San Antonio Ledger*, July 1, 1852.

2. Sumner to Carleton, May 5, 1852, in Abel, *Official Correspondence*, 534; Carleton to Sumner, May 13, 1852, Arrott; Russell, 27; Katie Bowen undated letter, Bowen Letters, Arrott.

3. The liquor sellers were Morris Miller, Hugh Hutchinson, John Woland, Calvin

Scofield, Arthur Morrison, Samuel Sims, William Reynolds, Samuel Morey, Jacob Meador, and William Halstead.

4. Carleton to Calhoun, April 26, 1852, and Carleton to Sumner, May 13, 1852, RG 98, 92 and 192, roll 1; Calhoun to Jones, May 1, 1852, in Abel, *Official Correspondence*, 544.

5. Katie Bowen undated letter, Bowen Letters, Arrott; Calhoun, Executive Journal, May 21.

6. Sumner to Carleton, May 20, 1852, in Abel, *Official Correspondence*, 537; Sumner to Calhoun, May 20, 1852, in Abel, 537; Sumner to Lea, May 26, 1852, in Abel, 549; Whiting to Calhoun, May 26, 1852, in Abel, 550.

7. McParlin served at Fort Union from 1851 to 1852; Byrne, from 1852 to 1855.

8. Carleton to Sumner, May 24, 1852, RG 98 Roll 1 Records of U. S. Army Commands, Department of New Mexico, selected documents related to the Navajo Indians, 1846–1868; Sumner to Calhoun, May 20, 1852, in Abel, *Official Correspondence*, 548; M. Cook, "Governor James S. Calhoun Remembered," 7.

9. Abel, "Journal of John Greiner," 206–7; Katie Bowen to her mother, May 28, 1852, Bowen Letters, Arrott.

10. Carleton to Sumner, May 24 and August 30, 1852, LR, DNM, Records of U.S. Army Commands, Selected Documents Related to the Navajo Indians, 1846–1868, RG 98, roll 1, NMSA; *Times-Picayune*, July 22, 1852.

11. *Times-Picayune*, July 21, 1852; *Daily American Telegraph*, August 13, 1852; Bieber, ed., "Letters of William Carr Lane, 1852–1854," 179; *Times Picayune*, July 2, 1852; *Daily National Intelligencer*, July 5, 1852; Connelley, *The Provisional Government of Nebraska Territory*, 8:353; Whiteley, 461.

12. *Alexandria Gazette*, July 7, 1852; Greiner to Lea, July 31, 1852, in Abel, *Official Correspondence*, 541–42; *Ohio State Journal*, February 8, 1853.

13. Whiting to Lea, July 5, 1852, in Abel, *Official Correspondence*, 540–41; Whitely, 457–58.

14. *Times Picayune*, July 22, 1852.

15. *Daily National Intelligencer*, August 6, 1852; Whiteley, 456, 463, 471–72.

16. *Times Picayune*, September 15, 1852; Whiteley, 463.

17. Whiteley, 471–72.

18. Sumner to Webster, May 8, 1852, in Abel, *Official Correspondence*, 535; *Weekly Union*, March 5, 1853.

19. Whiteley, 454.

20. Galloway, 551–53.

21. Greiner to Lea, June 30 and July 31, 1852, in Abel, *Official Correspondence*, 539–42; Abel, "Journal of John Greiner," 220–21.

22. Sweeney, 258; Abel, "Journal of John Greiner," 221–222.

23. Sweeney, 259; Abel, "Journal of John Greiner," 228.

24. Greiner to Lea, July 31, 1852, in Abel, *Official Correspondence*, 541–42; Galloway, 553–54; Greiner to Lea, August 30, 1852, Schroeder Papers.

25. Whiting to Lea, July 5, 1852, in Abel, *Official Correspondence*, 540–41; Keleher, *Turmoil*, 130 fn65; *Charleston Mercury*, December 21, 1859.

26. *El Hispano American*, February 10, 1906; Bradford Prince Papers.

27. *Albuquerque Journal*, November 18, 1911, and July 15, 1915; *Baltimore Sun*, March 12, 1915.

28. M. Cook, "Calhoun Remembered"; "Union Cemetery: A Walking Tour."

29. McNitt, *Journal of a Military Reconnaissance*, lxiii.

30. Loyola, 277.

Epilogue

1. Carleton to Sumner, August 30, 1852, RG 98, 92, 192, Roll 1; *Times-Picayune*, February 15, 1853.

2. *Republic*, September 2, 1852; *Baltimore Sun*, November 5, 1852; *Weekly Chronicle & Sentinel*, December 13, 1854; *Temperance Crusader*, October 1, 1857; Michno, 161; Abel, "Indian Affairs in New Mexico under the Administration of William Carr Lane," 221.

3. Kiser, 90.

4. *Weekly Union*, March 5, 1853.

5. La Mesilla, citizens wrote, was settled early in 1850 by Americans and New Mexicans who believed it was New Mexico Territory. The town then had upward of 1,500 inhabitants. The Mexican government had established a custom house there to collect duties and was taking lands from Americans and others and giving them to Mexican citizens. The US Surveyor said the initial point was just north of El Paso. Boundary commissioners placed the cornerstone six or seven miles below Doña Ana. Citizens of Mesilla to Calhoun, August 25, 1851, in Abel, *Official Correspondence*, 404–5; *Republic*, May 27, 1851.

6. *Missouri Courier*, May 26, 1853; Abel, "Indian Affairs," 349, 356; Garland to Cooper, October 28, 1853, US Area Commands, LS, 9th Military Department, RG 393, 9:74, NA.

7. Galloway, 554; Abel, "Journal of John Greiner," 243; *Santa Fe Gazette*, March 19, 1853.

8. Galloway, 554; Abel, "Indian Affairs," 343; *Galliopolis Journal*, August 4, 1853; *Daily Commercial Register*, September 12, 1853; Elder and Weber, 101 fn10.

9. His fellow investors included W. F. M. Arny, J. M. Gallegos, H. S. Johnson, Ambrosio Armijo, Henry Connelly, Simon Delgado, and Anastacio Sandoval. *Rio Abajo Weekly Press*, April 17, 1866.

10. *Daily Commercial Register*, June 7, 1861; *Rio Abajo Weekly Press*, October 3, 1865, and June 19, 1866; *Boston Herald*, June 19, 1869.

11. In 1866 he married Maria Willey. *Cincinnati Commercial Tribune*, May 15, 1871.

12. Hendricks.

13. *Republic*, August 27, 1853; Elder and Weber, 4.

14. Reports of Explorations and Surveys; *Missouri Courier*, May 26, 1853.

15. *Times Picayune*, August 3, 1853; *Texas State Gazette*, September 17, 1853; *Sacramento Daily Union*, December 31, 1853; *Cleveland Leader*, October 8, 1853; Gonzáles, "La Politica."

16. *Daily Pennsylvanian*, December 2, 1853.

17. *Republic*, July 12, 1853.

18. Chaput, 155.

19. Chaput, 157–59; *Weekly Union*, December 3, 1853.

20. *Boston Herald*, October 3, 1854; Chaput, 160, 163, 178; *New York Times*, September 19, 1854; *Daily National Intelligencer*, September 26, 1854.

21. According to the 1860 Census, their children were Louisa Serena, seventeen; Richard Coxe, fifteen; Rodger, thirteen; Susan, seven; Charles Hanson, four; and Emilee, two.

22. Chaput, 171; *Baltimore Sun*, November 8, 1854; *Weekly Champion and Press*, May 7, 1859, and February 9, 1861; *Atchison City Directory*, Ancestry.com.

23. Twitchell, *History of Military Occupation*, 392–93; *The Crisis*, August 29, 1861; *Biographical Directory of the American Congress*.

24. *Atchison Weekly Globe*, March 19, 1914.

25. Chávez, 162–63, 177, 185, 190; *Times Picayune*, September 5, 1856.

26. Kephart became a pastor and missionary and served as a chaplain during the Civil War. He spent his last years with a daughter in Deming, New Mexico, where he died May 29, 1894. Murphy, 7–9, 50.

27. Clever, who was from Cologne in Prussia, was an attorney and merchant in Santa Fe doing business as Clever & Seligman & Co. Gottschalk, 11.

28. Elder and Weber, 27; McNitt, *Navajo Wars*, 282–84, 301.

29. McNitt, *Navajo Wars*, 327, 366, 385; *Daily Illinois State Journal*, July 31, 1857; *Daily Union*, December 6, 1857; Bailey, *The Long Walk*, 106 fn14; *Commercial Advertiser*, November 7, 1859; Hunt, *Kirby Benedict*, 149–50.

30. *Sacramento Daily Union*, April 14, 1857; *Daily Missouri Democrat*, March 29, 1861; *Rio Abajo Weekly Press*, December 27, 1865.

31. Watrous was one of New Mexico's wealthiest merchants and stock raisers and one of the original grantees of the La Junta land grant. He was born in Montpelier, Vermont, around 1810, to Erastus Watrous. As a young man he came to New Mexico and lived for years at Fort Union. When the railroad was completed, he moved to Watrous, a station on the Atchison, Topeka, and Santa Fe Railroad. *Argus and Patriot*, April 7, 1886; *Evening News*, March 18, 1886.

32. *Daily Missouri Democrat*, September 18, 1861.

33. Reeve, "The Federal Indian Policy," 58–59.

34. Johnson was later a judge in New Mexico's Second Judicial District. In September 1869, John T. Russell sold the *Gazette* to A. P. Sullivan, who gave it a new name and new politics. It would now be the *Post*. M. Simmons, *Albuquerque*, 197; *Cincinnati Daily Gazette*, October 5, 1869.

35. *Rio Abajo Weekly Press*, January 3, 1865, June 19 and September 25, 1866, February 16, 1867; *Commercial Advertiser*, June 7, 1869.

36. Elder and Weber, 26 fn34, 264; T. Chávez, *Manuel Alvarez*, 178–79; *New Mexican*, February 1, 1876; Twitchell, *Leading Facts*, 2:273 fn197 and 2:399 fn324.

37. *Columbus Enquirer*, October 11, 1859; *Columbus Daily Enquirer*, March 22, 1866, and June 4, 1867; *Macon Weekly Telegraph*, October 9, 1862; *Columbus Tri-Weekly Enquirer*, December 5, 1857; *Baltimore Sun*, November 16, 1850; Quaife, ed. *Kit Carson's Autobiography*, 140–41; 1864 Census for Reorganizing the Georgia Militia, ancestry.com.

38. The first sheriff of Doña Ana County in 1852 was a different John Jones, who served until he was removed in 1854. Ball, *Desert Lawmen*, 367 fn4.

39. John G. Jones married Mary Blakely in Galveston in 1869. A year before, he was registered to vote in Marion County, Texas, where he had lived since 1860. In 1880 he was appointed election supervisor in Galveston County. Calhoun to Brown, July 15, 1850, in Abel, *Official Correspondence*, 227; *Santa Fe Gazette*, May 28 and August 13, 1853; US Marshals Service; *Commercial Appeal*, April 26, 1864; Texas Voter Registry, January 1868, ancestry.com; *Flake's Weekly Galveston Bulletin*, June 16, 1869; *Galveston Weekly News*, October 28, 1880; Ball, *U.S. Marshals*, 25, 32.

40. *Columbia Enquirer*, July 23, 1850, November 25, 1856, and February 9, 1858; *Southern Recorder*, September 23, 1851; *Daily Constitution*, August 19–20, 1853; *Columbus Daily Enquirer*, July 10, 1867; 1864 Census for Reorganizing the Georgia Militia, ancestry.com.

41. *Tri-Weekly Times and Sentinel*, May 21, 1853; *Albany Courier*, June 26, 1855.

42. *Albany Courier*, November 12, 1850; *Daily Constitutionalist*, August 14, 1863.

43. Goulding married twenty-nine-year-old Jane E. Bryan when he was thirty-three, and they had two children by 1860. *Macon Weekly Telegraph*, April 23, June 21, and July 8, 1861; *Charleston Mercury*, April 10, 1862.

44. *Charleston Courier*, March 29, 1851; *Columbia Daily Phoenix*, July 19, 1865; *Charleston Daily News*, September 14, 1870.

45. *Evening Star*, February 22, 1853; *Columbus Tri-Weekly Enquirer*, April, 26, 1856; *Columbus Enquirer*, July 24, 1855; Martin, 80, 86, 87, 107.

46. *Columbus Enquirer*, January 10, 1854; Martin, 116; *Columbus Daily Enquirer*, July 25, 1859.

Appendix Three

1. Elder and Weber, 34.
2. Cutts, 225.
3. M. Simmons, *Little Lion*, 34.
4. Gottschalk, 27.
5. Twitchell, *Leading Facts*, 102 fn71.
6. Larson, 31, 82; M. Simmons, *Albuquerque*, 147.

7. J. Thompson, 372.

8. Crutchfield, 75–76.

9. Messervy, William S. Social Networks and Archival Context.

10. *Augusta Chronicle*, November 12, 1849.

11. Elder and Weber, 4.

12. Larson, 14–15; M. Simmons, *Albuquerque*, 157.

13. Kraemer, 2–3; Cutts, 217.

14. M. Simmons, *Little Lion*, 245 fn28; *Salt Lake Telegram*, November 29, 1902.

15. M. Simmons, *Little Lion*, 114.

16. Elder and Weber, 26 fn36.

17. Daves, "Cura José Francisco Leyva," 1–2.

18. Chaput, 196.

19. M. Simmons, *Little Lion*, 243 fn7; Gottschalk, 28.

20. Alexander, 133.

21. Gonzáles, *Politica*, 104, 130, 211.

22. Hunt, 146 fn14.

23. Twitchell, *Leading Facts*, 2:292.

24. Hunt, 149 fn15.

25. *Boston Courier*, August 9, 1849; *Augusta Chronicle*, November 12, 1849; Elder and Weber, 40 fn11.

26. Alexander, 95, 101.

27. Michno, 267; Twitchell, *Leading Facts*, 2:269.

28. Alexander, 83–84.

29. Gonzáles, *Politica*, 214.

30. Alexander, 111, 112.

31. Michno, 267.

32. Michno, 267.

33. Meketa, 15.

34. Sanchez and Miller, 15, 42, 50.

35. Keleher, *Turmoil*, 203 fn38.

36. Sargeant and Davis, 17.

Appendix Six

1. Elder and Weber, 34 and 34 fn73.

2. M. Simmons, *Little Lion*, 64.

3. Gonzáles, *Politica*, 244; M. Simmons, *Little Lion*, 157.

4. Elder and Weber, 35 fn85.

5. Owen, 20–21.

6. Michno, 101; Espinosa, 6; Laumbach, 260–61.

7. M. Simmons, *Little Lion*, 112–13; Baca, "Sheriffs of Valencia County," 114.

8. Gordon, 247.

9. M. Simmons, *Little Lion*, 245 fn28; *Salt Lake Telegram*, November 29, 1902.
10. Espinosa, 7.
11. Sánchez and Miller, 104.
12. Arellano, 33–34.
13. Lecompte, 35.
14. Elder and Weber, 3.
15. Sargeant and Davis, 17.
16. Weber, 203.
17. Gonzáles, *Politica*, 52.
18. Espinosa, 7.
19. Gottschalk, 25–26.
20. Gonzáles, *Politica*, 104, 130, 211.
21. Gonzáles, *Politica*, 497.
22. Daves, "Abreu Family," 1–2.

BIBLIOGRAPHY

Abbott, Martin. "Memoirs of a Milledgeville Native, Augustin H. Hansell." *Georgia Historical Quarterly* 57 (Fall 1973): 430–38.

Abel, Annie, ed. *The Official Correspondence of James S. Calhoun While Indian Agent at Santa Fé and Superintendent of Indian Affairs in New Mexico.* Washington, DC: Government Printing Office, 1915.

Abel, Annie Heloise. "Indian Affairs in New Mexico Under the Administration of William Carr Lane." *New Mexico Historical Review* 16 (July 1941): 328–58.

———. "The Journal of John Greiner." *Old Santa Fe* 3 (July 1916): 189–243.

Abert, James W. *Abert's New Mexico Report: 1846–1847.* Albuquerque, NM: Horn & Wallace, 1962.

Acts of the General Assembly of the State of Georgia, Passed in Milledgeville at an Annual Session in November and December, 1836, vol. 1.

Adams, William Y. *Indian Policies in the Americas from Columbus to Collier and Beyond.* Santa Fe: School for Advanced Research Press, 2014.

Alexander, Francelle E. *Among the Cottonwoods: The Enduring Rio Abajo Villages of Peralta & Los Pinos, New Mexico Before 1940.* Albuquerque, NM: Rio Grande Books, 2012.

Alleged Frauds on Creek Indians. Message of the President of the United States, Transmitting Information in Relation to Alleged Frauds on the Creek Indians in the Sale of Their Reservations, July 3, 1838. H. Ex. Doc. 452. S. S. 331–1.

Allen, Mrs. H. D., and Louis H. Andrews. Index of City of Milledgeville, Memory Hill Cemetery. 1938.

Alvarez, Manuel. Papers. New Mexico State Library and Archives, Santa Fe.

The American Revolution in North Carolina. http://www.carolana.com/NC /Revolution/revolution_continental_army.html.

Ancestry. https://www.ancestry.com.

Angélico Chávez History Library. Palace of the Governors, Santa Fe, NM.

Annual Report of the Commissioner of Indian Affairs, 1851. Washington, DC: Government Printing Office, 1851. http://digital.library.wisc.edu/1711.dl/History .AnnRep51.

Annual Report of the Commissioner of Indian Affairs, 1852. Sen. Ex. Doc. 1. 32nd Cong., 2nd sess. S. S. 658.

Annual Report of the Commissioner of Indian Affairs, for the year 1849. Sen. Ex.
Doc. 1. 31st Cong., 1st sess. S. S. 550.

Annual Report of the Commissioner of Indian Affairs, for the years 1846–1850.
Washington, DC: Government Printing Office, 1846–1850. http://digicoll
.library.wisc.edu/cgi-bin/History/History-idx?type=header&id=History.Ann
Rep4650.

Annual Report of the Missionary Society of the Methodist Episcopal Church. New
York: James Collord Printer, 1950.

Arellano, Anselmo F. *La Tierra Amarilla: The People of the Chama Valley*. Tierra
Amarilla, NM: Chama Valley Independent Schools, 1978.

Arrott, James, W. Fort Union Collection. Donnelly Library, New Mexico Highland
University, Las Vegas, NM.

Austin, Jeanette Holland. *Georgia Intestate Records*. Baltimore: Genealogical
Publishing, 1986.

Baca, Elmo. "Pecos Valley Villages Stand Proud." *New Mexico Magazine* (October
1990): 87–98.

Bailey, Lynn R. *The Long Walk: A History of the Navajo Wars, 1846–1868*. Tucson,
AZ: Westernlore, 1988.

Balch, Alfred. Report on the Sales of Indian Reservations, November 1838. Message
from the President of the United States, February 20, 1839. H. Doc. 209, S. S. 347.

Baldwin County Court of Ordinary, Book B, March 14, 1810, and Georgia Probate
Records, 1742–1975. FamilySearch. https://FamilySearch.org.

Baldwin County, GA, Will Book A, 1806–1829. http://files.usgwarchives.net/ga
/baldwin/wills/willbka.txt.

Ball, Durwood. *Army Regulars on the Western Frontier, 1848–1861*. Norman:
University of Oklahoma Press, 2001.

———. *Desert Lawmen: The High Sheriffs of New Mexico and Arizona, 1846–1912*.
Albuquerque: University of New Mexico Press, 1992.

———. *The United States Marshals of New Mexico and Arizona Territories, 1846–
1912*. Albuquerque: University of New Mexico Press, 1978.

———. "The U.S. Army in New Mexico, 1848–1886." In *Telling New Mexico: A
New History*, edited by Marta Weigle, Frances Levine, and Louise Stiver, 173–89.
Albuquerque: University of New Mexico Press, 2009.

Bancroft, Hubert H. "The Financial Panic of 1837." *The Great Republic by the Master
Historians*. Vol. 3. http://www.publicbookshelf.com/public_html/The_Great
_Republic_By_the_Master_Historians_Vol_III/thepanic_ce.html.

Bancroft, Hubert Howe. *History of Arizona and New Mexico, 1530–1888*.
Albuquerque, NM: Horn & Wallace, 1962.

Barbour, Barton H. *Reluctant Frontiersman: James Ross Larkin on the Santa Fe Trail,
1856–57*. Albuquerque: University of New Mexico Press, 1990.

Bauer, K. Jack. *The Mexican War 1846–1848*. Lincoln & London: University of
Nebraska Press, 1974.

Bell, Peter Hansbrough. General Correspondence, 1849–1853. Texas State Archives, Austin.

Benham, Priscilla Myers. "Rusk, Thomas Jefferson (1803–1857)." *Handbook of Texas Online*. Texas State Historical Association. https://www.tshaonline.org/handbook/browse?handbook_entries%5Bquery%5D=Rusk%2C%20Thomas%20Jefferson%20%281803–1857%29.

Bennett, James A. *Forts and Forays: A Dragoon in New Mexico, 1850–1856*. Albuquerque: University of New Mexico Press, 1996.

Berrien, John M. *Speech of Mr. Berrien of Georgia, on the Bill Appropriating Three Millions of Dollars to be Expended Under the Direction of the President in Negotiating a Peace with Mexico*. Delivered in the Senate of the United States, February 5, 1847. Washington, DC: John T. Towers, 1847.

Bieber, Ralph P. "Letters of William Carr Lane, 1852–1854." *New Mexico Historical Review* 3 (April 1928): 179.

Binkley, William Campbell. "The Question of Texan Jurisdiction in New Mexico Under the United States, 1848–1850." *Southwestern Historical Quarterly* 26 (July 1920): 1–38.

Biographical Directory of the United States Congress. https://bioguideretro.congress.gov/.

Boatwright, Eleanor Miot. *Status of Women in Georgia, 1783–1860*. Brooklyn, NY: Carlson, 1994.

Boney, F. N. "The Politics of Expansion and Secession, 1820–1861." In *A History of Georgia*, edited by Kenneth Coleman, 129–52. Athens: University of Georgia Press, 1977.

Bonner, James C. "The Georgia Penitentiary at Milledgeville 1817–1874." *Georgia Historical Review* 55 (Fall 1971): 303–28.

———. *Milledgeville: Georgia's Antebellum Capital*. Athens: University of Georgia Press, 1978.

Boyd, E. "The First New Mexico Imprint." *Princeton University Library Chronicle* 33 (Autumn 1971): 30–40.

Boyle, Susan Calafate. *Los Capitalistas: Hispano Merchants and the Santa Fe Trade*. Albuquerque: University of New Mexico Press, 1997.

Brantley, J. Kenneth. *Hancock County, Georgia, Court of Ordinary Minutes, 1799–1817*. Powder Springs, GA: Brantley Association of America, 1998.

Brooks, Nathan C. *A Complete History of the Mexican War: Its Causes, Conduct, and Consequences, Comprising an Account of the Various Military and Naval Operations from its Commencement to the Treaty of Peace*. Chicago: Rio Grande, 1965.

Bullock, Alice. *Mountain Villages*. Santa Fe, NM: Sunstone, 1974.

Burnett, Lonnie A. "John Forsyth, Jr." *The Encyclopedia of Alabama*. http://encyclopediaofalabama.org/article/h-1381.

Burt, Jesse, and Robert B. Ferguson. *Indians of the Southeast: Then and Now*. Nashville & New York: Abingdon, 1973.

Butler, Steven R. "Alfred Butler in the Mexican War." Steven Butler's Family History Website. http://www.watermelon-kid.com/family/bios/butler-mexican_war1 .htm.

Caffey, David L. *Chasing the Santa Fe Ring: Power and Privilege in Territorial New Mexico*. Albuquerque: University of New Mexico Press, 2014.

Calhoun, James S. Letters. Western Americana Collection. Beinecke Rare Book and Manuscript Library, Yale University.

Calhoun, James S. Papers, 1851–1852. New Mexico State Library and Archives, Santa Fe.

Campbell, Davine V., and William R. Henry. *Land Records of Houston County, 1836–1840*. Warner Robins, GA: Central Georgia Genealogy Society, 1991–1994.

Candler, Allen, and Clement Evans. *Cyclopedia of Georgia*. Atlanta: State Historical Association, 1906.

Carroll, Charles. "Before Fort Craig." In *Fort Craig: The United States Fort on the Camino Real*. US Department of the Interior, Bureau of Land Management, 2000.

Causes of Hostilities of the Creek and Seminole Indians in Florida. Instruction to Brevet Major General T. S. Jesup and Other Officers of the Army for Their Removal to the West, June 6, 1836. American State Papers 021, Military Affairs, Vol. 6, No. 691.

Chance, Joseph E., ed. *The Mexican War Journal of Captain Franklin Smith*. Jackson & London: University Press of Mississippi, 1991.

Chaput, Donald. *Francois X. Aubry: Trader: Trailmaker and Voyageur in the Southwest, 1846–1854*. Glendale, CA: A. H. Clark, 1975.

Chávez, Fray Angelico. *But Time and Change: The Story of Padre Martinez of Taos*. Santa Fe, NM: Sunstone, 1981.

Chávez, Thomas E. *Manuel Alvarez, 1794–1856: A Southwestern Biography*. Niwot: University Press of Colorado, 1990.

———. "The Trouble with Texans: Manuel Alvarez and the 1841 'Invasion.'" *New Mexico Historical Review* 53 (April 1978): 133–44.

Cobb, KyL T. *Griffin, Georgia: We Could Have Been Famous . . . .* Vol. 1, Glory. Charleston, SC: Last GASPS, 2015–2016.

Coleman, Philip, James Byrne, and Jason King, eds. *Ireland and the Americas: Culture, Politics and History*. Santa Barbara, CA: ABC-CLIO, 2008.

Colonial and State Records of North Carolina. Documenting the American South. University of North Carolina at Chapel Hill. https://docsouth.unc.edu/csr/.

Columbus, Georgia and the Counties of Marion, Muscogee, Chattahoochee, Talbot, Harris Compiled from the Historical Writings of Rev. George White, George G. Leckie and the WPA Writers. New York: Pudney & Russell, 1854

The Congressional Globe: Containing the Debates and Proceedings of the Second Session of the Thirty-Fifth Congress. February 18, 1859. University of North Texas Digital Library. http://digital.library.unt.edu/ark:/67531/metadc30802/.

Connelley, William E. *The Provisional Government of Nebraska Territory and the Journals of William Walker.* Vol. 8. State Journal Co., 1899.

Contract: General Jesup, Creek chiefs, &c. Letter from the Secretary of War, Transmitting a Report from the Commissioner of Indian Affairs, March 23, 1838. H. Doc. 274, S. S. 328.

Cook, Anna Maria Green. *History of Baldwin County, Georgia.* Anderson, SC: Keys Hearn, 1925. Reprint, Spartanburg, SC: Reprint Co. 1992.

Cook, James F. *The Governors of Georgia, 1754–2004.* 3rd ed. Macon, GA: Mercer University Press, 2005.

Cook, Mary Jean. "Governor James S. Calhoun Remembered." *Wagon Tracks* 8 (February 1994): 7–9.

Cooksey, Elizabeth B. "Burke County." *New Georgia Encyclopedia.* October 31, 2018. http://www.georgiaencyclopedia.org/.

Coulter, E. Merton. "John Jordan Crittenden." *Crisis at Fort Sumter.* Tulane University. https://www.tulane.edu/~sumter/Crittenden.html.

——— . "The Nullification Movement in Georgia." *Georgia Historical Review* 5 (March 1921): 3–39.

Crane, Leo. *Desert Drums: The Pueblo Indians of New Mexico, 1540–1928.* Glorieta, NM: Rio Grande, 1972.

Creider, Lawrence S. "The Publications of Padre Antonio José Martínez, 1834–1846." *New Mexico Historical Review* 95 (Spring 2020): 159–211.

Crumpton, Daniel. *Burke County, Georgia Land Records: Boundaries as of 1777.* Warrenton, GA: D. N. Crumpton, 2009.

——— . *Jefferson County, Georgia, and Some Surrounding Areas: Land Records, mid-1700s-mid-1800s.* Warrenton, GA: D. N. Crumpton, 2003.

Crutchfield, James A. *Revolt at Taos: The New Mexican and Indian Insurrection of 1847.* Yardley, PA: Westholme, 2015.

Cutts, James Madison. *The Conquest of California and New Mexico, by the Forces of the United States, in the Years 1846 & 1847.* Albuquerque: Horn & Wallace, 1965.

Dary, David. *The Santa Fe Trail: It's History, Legends and Lore.* New York: Penguin Putnam, 2000.

Daves, Doyle. "The Abreu Family: Movers and Shakers in Nineteenth Century New Mexico." *La Crónica de Nuevo México* 107 (Summer 2017), 1–2.

——— . "Cura José Francisco Leyva, Activist Priest and the Founding of Las Vegas." *La Cronica* (Winter 2016): 1–2.

Davidson, Victor. *History of Wilkinson County.* Macon, GA: Genealogical Publishing, 2009.

Davis, Charles L. *A Brief History of the North Carolina Troops of the Continental Establishment in the War of the Revolution with a Register of Officers of the Same.* Philadelphia: Pennsylvania Historical Society, 1896.

Davis, Robert S. and Silas E. Lucas. *The Georgia Land Lottery Papers, 1805–1914.* Easley, SC: Southern Historical Press, 1979.

Davis, W. W. H. *El Gringo: New Mexico & Her People*. Santa Fe, NM: Rydal, 1938.

Dawson, William C. *A Compilation of the Laws of the State of Georgia Passed by the Legislature, 1819–1829*. Milledgeville, GA: Grantland & Orme, 1831.

Debo, Angie. *The Road to Disappearance: A History of the Creek Indians*. Norman: University of Oklahoma Press, 1941.

DeKalb County, Georgia, Military Indian Wars. USGenWeb Archives. http://files .usgwarchives.net/ga/military/indian/ezzard.txt.

de Lamar, Marie, and Elizabeth N. Rothstein. *The Reconstructed 1790 Census of Georgia*. Baltimore: Genealogy Publishing, 1985.

———. *Records of Washington County, Georgia*. Baltimore: Genealogical Publishing, 1985.

Delaney, Robert W. *The Southern Ute People*. Phoenix, AZ: Indian Tribal Series, 1974.

DeVoto, Bernard. *The Year of Decision: 1846*. New York: Truman Talley Books, 1942.

Dickerman, Carolyn. "Mid-Nineteenth-Century Botanical Exploration in New Mexico." *New Mexico Historical Review* 60 (April 1985): 160–71.

Dodd, Jordan R. *Georgia Marriages, 1801 to 1825*. Orem, UT: Lihona Research, 1993.

Duffus, R. L. *The Santa Fe Trail*. Albuquerque: University of New Mexico Press, 1930.

Duniway, Clyde A. "Daniel Webster and the West." *Minnesota History* 9 (March 1928): 3–15.

Dunlay, Tom. *Kit Carson and the Indians*. Lincoln & London: University of Nebraska Press, 2000.

The Early Marriages of Baldwin County, Georgia. The USGenWeb Project. http:// theusgenweb.org/ga/baldwin/earlymarriages.html.

Ebel, Carol. "Louisville." *New Georgia Encyclopedia*. September 28, 2020. https:// www.georgiaencyclopedia.org/articles/counties-cities-neighborhoods/Louisville.

Ebright, Malcolm. "San Miguel del Bado Grant." New Mexico History, Office of the New Mexico State Historian. http://newmexicohistory.org/places/san -miguel-del-bado-grant.

Edrington, Thomas S. "Military Influence on the Texas–New Mexico Boundary Settlement." *New Mexico Historical Review* 4 (October 1984): 371–93.

Edwards, Frank S. *A Campaign in New Mexico with Colonel Doniphan*. Albuquerque: University of New Mexico Press, 1996.

Ehle, John. *Trail of Tears: The Rise and Fall of the Cherokee Nation*. New York: Anchor Books Doubleday, 1988.

Ehrlich, Walter. *Zion in the Valley: The Jewish Community of St. Louis*. Columbus: University of Missouri Press, 1997.

Eisenhower, John S. D. *Agent of Destiny: The Life and Times of General Winfield Scott*. New York: Free Press, 1997.

———. *So Far from God: U.S. War with Mexico, 1846–1848*. New York: Random House, 1989.

Elder, Jane Lenz, and David J. Weber, eds. *Trading in Santa Fe: John M. Kingsbury's Correspondence with James Josiah Webb, 1853–1861.* Dallas: Southern Methodist University Press, 1996.

Ellis, William Arba. *Norwich University, 1819–1911: Her History, Her Graduates, Her Roll of Honor.* Montpelier, VT: Capital City, 1911.

Ellisor, John T. *The Second Creek War: Interethnic Conflict and Collusion on a Collapsing Frontier.* Lincoln & London: University of Nebraska Press, 2010.

Emory, William Hemsley, et al. *Notes of a Military Reconnaissance: From Fort Leavenworth, in Missouri, to San Diego, in California, Including Parts of the Arkansas, Del Norte, and Gila Rivers.* Washington, DC: Wendell & Van Benthuysen, 1848.

Espinosa, J. Manuel. "Memoir of a Kentuckian in New Mexico, 1848–1884." *New Mexico Historical Review* 13 (January 1937): 1–13.

Finlay, Mark R. "Central of Georgia Railway." *New Georgia Encyclopedia.* September 3, 2014. https://www.georgiaencyclopedia.org/articles/business-economy/central-georgia-railway.

Fischer, David Hackett. *Albion's Seed: Four British Folkways in America.* New York & Oxford: Oxford University Press, 1989.

Foote, Cheryl J. "'American Ladies' in Early Territorial New Mexico, 1846–1879." In *Sunshine and Shadows in New Mexico's Past.* Vol. 2, *The U.S. Territorial Period, 1848–1912,* edited by Richard Melzer, 127–42. Los Ranchos, NM: Rio Grande Books, 2011.

———. *Women of the New Mexico Frontier, 1846–1912.* Albuquerque: University of New Mexico Press, 2005.

Foreman, Grant. *Indian Removal.* Norman: University of Oklahoma Press, 1972.

Fort Union: Historic Resource Study. US National Park Service. https://www.np.gov/parkhistory/online_books/foun/chap2n.htm#71.

Frink, Maurice. *Fort Defiance & the Navajos.* Boulder, CO: Fred Pruett, 1968.

Furber, George C. *The Twelve Months Volunteer, or, Journal of a Private, in the Tennessee Regiment of Cavalry, in the Campaign, in Mexico, 1846–7.* Cincinnati, OH: J. A. & U. P. James, 1847.

Galer, Mary Jane. *Columbus, Georgia: List of People, 1828–1852.* Columbus, GA: Iberian, 2000.

Galloway, Tod B. "Private Letters of a Government Official in the Southwest." *Journal of American History* 3 (January 1909): 540–54.

Gambrell, Herbert. "Lamar, Mirabeau Buonaparte (1798–1859)." *Handbook of Texas Online.* Texas State Historical Association. https://www.tshaonline.org/handbook/entries/lamar-mirabeau-buonaparte.

Ganaway, Loomis Morton. "New Mexico and the Sectional Controversy, 1846–1861." *New Mexico Historical Review* 18 (April 1943): 215.

Gardner, Mark L. *Wagons on the Santa Fe Trail: 1822–1880.* Santa Fe, NM: Long Distance Trails Group Office, National Park Service, 1997.

Garrard, Lewis H. *Wah-to-yah & the Taos Trail*. Palo Alto, CA: American West, 1968.

Gaissert, Margarette Goldsby. *Some Church Members and Records and Some History of Some Hancock County, Georgia, Churches*. Sparta: Self-published, 1982.

Garstka, Katharine. "The Scots-Irish in the Southern United States: An Overview." October 16, 2009. Archives.com. http://www.archives.com/experts/garstka-katharine/the-scots-irish-in-the-southern-united-states-an-overview.html.

Gates, Frederick B. "Canals." *New Georgia Encyclopedia*. July 15, 2020. https://www.georgiaencyclopedia.org/articles/business-economy/canals.

GenealogyBank. https://www.genealogybank.com/.

Gentry, Leila Thornton. *Historical Collections of the Georgia Chapter of the Daughters of the American Revolution*. Atlanta, GA: C. P. Byrd.

George W. Cullum's Biographical Register of the Officers and Graduates of the United States Military Academy at West Point, New York, Since Its Establishment in 1802. Bill Thayer's website. http://penelope.uchicago.edu/Thayer/E/Gazetteer/Places/America/United_States/Army/USMA/Cullums_Register/.

Georgia Archives. University System of Georgia, Morrow. https://www.georgiaarchives.org/.

Georgia Historic Newspapers. https://gahistoricnewspapers.galileo.usg.edu/.

Georgia River Network. https://garivers.org/.

Goff, John H. *Place Names of Georgia*. Athens: University of Georgia Press, 2007.

Gonzáles, Phillip B. "Mexican Party, American Party, Democratic Party: Establishing the American Political Party in New Mexico, 1848–1853." *New Mexico Historical Review* 88 (Summer 2013): 253–85.

——— . *Política: Nuevomexicanos and American Political Incorporation, 1821–1910*. Lincoln & London: University of Nebraska Press, 2016.

——— . "La Politica: Stories of Politics and Nuevomexicanos in the Nineteenth Century." Lecture given at National Hispanic Cultural Center, September 5, 2015.

Gordon, Mary McDougall, ed. *Through Indian Country to California: John P. Sherburne's Diary of the Whipple Expedition, 1853–1854*. Stanford, CA: Stanford University Press, 1988.

Gorenfeld, William. "The Snively Affair: Land Pirates of the Santa Fe Trail." *New Mexico Historical Review* 91 (Winter 2016): 27–56.

Gorman, Howard. *The Trouble at Round Rock*. Phoenix: Department of the Interior, 1952.

Gott, Richard. *Cuba: A New History*. New Haven & London: Yale University Press, 2004.

Gottschalk, Marcus C. *Pioneer Merchants of Las Vegas*. Las Vegas, NM: M. C. Gottschalk, 2004.

Graham, Paul K. *1805 Georgia Land Lottery Fortunate Drawers and Grantees*. Decatur, GA: Genealogy, 2010.

Green, Fletcher M. "James S. Calhoun: Pioneer Georgia Leader and First Governor of New Mexico." *Georgia Historical Quarterly* 39 (December 1955): 309–35.

Gregg, Josiah. *The Commerce of the Prairies.* Lincoln & London: University of Nebraska Press, 1926.

Greiner, John. "Overawing the Indians." Collection 1972–033, Schroeder Papers, Folder 1148, Box 10787, Serial 10787, NMSA.

Hamilton, Holman. *Zachary Taylor: Soldier in the White House.* Indianapolis, IN: Bobbs-Merrill, 1951.

Hardy, Janice A., and Harold Lawrence. *Milledgeville, Georgia, Methodism, 1810–1869.* Milledgeville: Boyd, 2004.

Harwood, Thomas. *History of New Mexico Spanish and English Missions of the Methodist Episcopal Church from 1850 to 1910.* Albuquerque, NM: El Abogado, 1910.

Hays, John P. "The Curious Case of New Mexico's Pre–Civil War Slave Code." *New Mexico Historical Review* 92 (Summer 2017): 251–83.

Hayward, John. *Gazetteer of the United States of America.* Hartford, CT: Case, Tiffany, 1853.

Hendricks, Rick. "David V. Whiting." New Mexico Office of State Historian. https://newmexicohistory.org/2013/10/29/david-v-whiting/.

Historic Markers Across Georgia. http://lat34north.com/HistoricMarkersGA /GA_Index.

Historic Sites of the US–Mexican War. http://www.dmwv.org/mexwar/mwsites /cameron.htm#belknap.

"History of the Southern Utes." Southern Ute Indian Tribe. https://www.souther nute-nsn.gov/history/.

Hitz, Alex M. "Georgia Bounty Land Grants." *Georgia Historical Quarterly* 38 (December 1954): 337–48.

Holmes, Yulssus Lynn. *Those Glorious Days: A History of Louisville as Georgia's Capital, 1796–1807.* Macon, GA: Mercer University Press, 1996.

Holtby, David V. *Forty-Seventh Star: New Mexico's Struggle for Statehood.* Norman: University of Oklahoma Press, 2012.

Horgan, Paul. *Lamy of Santa Fe: His Life and Times.* New York: Farrar, Straus & Giroux, 1975.

Horn, Calvin. *New Mexico's Troubled Years: The Story of the Early Territorial Governors.* Albuquerque, NM: Horn & Wallace, 1963.

Horney, Kylie A. "W. T. Wofford (1824–1884)." *New Georgia Encyclopedia.* July 15, 2020. https://www.georgiaencyclopedia.org/articles/history-archaeology/w-t -wofford-1824-1884.

Horsman, Reginald. *Feast or Famine: Food and Drink in American Westward Expansion.* Columbia: University of Missouri Press, 2008.

Houston, Martha Lou. *Marriages and Land Lottery List of Hancock County, Georgia, 1806–1850.* Baltimore: Genealogical Publishing, 1977.

Hubbell, John T. "Three Georgia Unionists and the Compromise of 1850." *Georgia Historical Quarterly* 51 (September 1967): 307–23.

Hull, A. L. *A Historical Sketch of the University of Georgia*. Atlanta: Foote & Davies, 1894.

Hunt, Aurora. *Kirby Benedict: Frontier Federal Judge*. Washington, DC: Beard Books, 1961.

Hutton, Paul Andrew. "Kit Carson's Ride." *Wild West* (April 2007): 28–37.

Huxford, Judge Folks. *Marriages and Obituaries from Early Georgia Newspapers*. Easley, SC: Southern Historical, 1989.

An Index to Georgia Tax Digests. Vols. 3–4. Atlanta: R. J. Taylor Jr. Foundation, 1886.

Indian Depredations. Message from the President, Transmitted Report of Agents Appointed to Inquire What Depredations Were Committed by Seminole and Creek Indians on the Property of Citizens, January 29, 1838. H. Doc. 127, S. S. 326.

Iverson, Peter. *Diné: A History of the Navajos*. Albuquerque: University of New Mexico Press, 2002.

Jackson, Mrs. Alexander M. (Cordelia). "Mrs. Alexander M. Jackson Letters." *New Mexico Historical Review* 31 (October 1956): 338–46.

Jaehn, Tomas. "The Unpolitical German in New Mexico, 1848–1914." *New Mexico Historical Review* (January 1996): 1–24.

Jenkins, John S. *History of the War Between the United States and Mexico from the Commencement of Hostilities to the Ratification of the Treaty of Peace*. Auburn, NY: Derby & Miller, 1851.

Jensen, Joan M., and Darlis A. Miller. *New Mexico Women: Intercultural Perspectives*. Albuquerque: University of New Mexico Press, 1986.

Johnson, Timothy D. *A Gallant Little Army: The Mexico City Campaign*. Lawrence: University Press of Kansas, 2007.

———. *Winfield Scott: The Quest for Military Glory*. Lawrence: University Press of Kansas, 1998.

Kattell, Camilla. *At the Confluence of Two Cultures: William and George Bent Confront Manifest Destiny, 1829–1918*. Albuquerque, NM: Light Horse, 2017.

Keleher, William A. Papers. Center for Southwest Research, University of New Mexico, Albuquerque.

———. *Turmoil in New Mexico, 1846–1868*. Albuquerque: University of New Mexico Press, 1952.

Kenly, John R. *Memoirs of a Maryland Volunteer: War With Mexico, in 1846–48*. Philadelphia: J. P. Lippincott, 1873.

Kilbourne, Elizabeth E. *Columbus, Georgia, Newspaper Clippings*. Vols. 1–4. Savannah, GA: E. E. Kilbourne, 1997.

King, Thomas Butler. Papers. Southern Historical Collection, University of North Carolina Library, Chapel Hill.

Kiser, William S. *Dragoons in Apacheland: Conquest and Resistance in Southern New Mexico, 1846–1861*. Norman: University of Oklahoma Press, 2012.

Kraemer, Paul M. "Donaciano Vigil, 'The Gifted Giant'—But Was He a Traitor?" *La Crónica de Nuevo México* 85 (October 2010): 1–3.

Kurtz, Wilbur G. "The First Regiment of Georgia Volunteers in the Mexican War." *Georgia Historical Quarterly* 27 (December 1948): 301–23.

La Farge, Oliver. *Santa Fe: The Autobiography of a Southwestern Town*. Norman: University of Oklahoma Press, 1959.

Lamar, Howard R. *The Far Southwest, 1846–1912: A Territorial History*. New Haven & London: Yale University Press, 1966.

Larson, Robert W. *New Mexico's Quest for Statehood, 1846–1912*. Albuquerque: University of New Mexico Press, 1968.

Laumbach, Verna. "Las Vegas Before 1850." *New Mexico Historical Review* 8 (October 1933): 241–64.

Laws of the Territory of New Mexico: Passed by the First Legislative Assembly in the City of Santa Fe and to Which Are Prefixed the Constitution of the United States, and the Act of Congress Organizing New Mexico as a Territory. Santa Fe, NM: James L. Collins, 1852.

Lecompte, Janet, "The Independent Women of Hispanic New Mexico, 1821–1846." In *New Mexico Women: Intercultural Perspectives*, edited by Joan M. Jensen and Darlis A. Miller, 71–93. Albuquerque: University of New Mexico Press, 1986.

Lera, Thomas. "The Palace of the Governors Stamp Designs." *New Mexico Historical Review* 89 (Fall 2014): 459–80.

Letter from the Secretary of the Treasury, Transmitting Statements in Relation to the Condition of Certain State Banks, March 3, 1835. H. Ex. Doc. 190. S. S. 275.

Letter from the Secretary of War, Transmitting a Report from the Commissioner of Indian Affairs, March 23, 1838. H. Ex. Doc. 274. S. S. 328.

Letters Received by Office of Adjutant General, Record Group 94, roll 432. New Mexico State Archives.

Livingston-Little, D. E., ed. *The Mexican War Diary of Thomas D. Tennery*. Norman: University of Oklahoma Press, 1970.

Loyola, Sister Mary. "The American Occupation of New Mexico, 1821–1852." *New Mexico Historical Review* 14 (July 1939): 34–75, 274–86.

Lucas, S. Emmett. *Some Georgia County Records*. Vols. 1 & 5. Easley, SC: Southern Historical Press, 1978.

Luckett, Robert E. "Charles McDonald (1793–1860)." *New Georgia Encyclopedia*. September 5, 2014.

Lupold, John S. "Columbus." *New Georgia Encyclopedia*. September 9, 2019. https://www.georgiaencyclopedia.org/articles/counties-cities-neighborhoods/columbus.

Magoffin, Susan. *Down the Santa Fe Trail and into Mexico: The Diary of Susan Shelby Magoffin, 1846–1847*. Lincoln & London: University of Nebraska Press, 1926.

Mahan, Joseph B. *Columbus: Georgia's Fall Line Trading Town*. Northridge, CA: Windsor, 1986.

Marcus, Jacob Rader. *United States Jewry, 1776–1985*. Vol. 2, *The Germanic Period*. Detroit, MI: Wayne State University Press, 2018.

Mares, E. A. "The Many Faces of Padre Antonio José Martínez: A Historiographic Essay." In *Padre Martinez: New Perspectives from Taos*, 18–47. Taos, NM: Millicent Rogers Museum, 1988.

———. "Padre Martínez, Defender of the People." *New Mexico Magazine* (June 1985): 57–60.

Martin, John H. *Columbus, Georgia, 1827–1865*. Columbus, GA: Thomas Gilbert, 1874.

"Martin Van Buren—The Independent Treasury." World Biography, U.S. Presidents. https://www.presidentprofiles.com/Washington-Johnson/Martin-Van-Buren -The-independent-treasury.html.

Marvel, William. *Burnside*. Chapel Hill: University of North Carolina Press, 2009.

McCaffrey, James M. *Surrounded by Dangers of All Kinds: The Mexican War Letters of Lieutenant Theodore Laidley*. Denton: University of North Texas Press, 1997.

McCall, George A. *Letters from the Frontiers: Written During a Period of Thirty Years' Service in the Army of the United States*. Philadelphia: American Law, 1868.

———. *New Mexico in 1850*. Norman: University of Oklahoma Press, 1968.

McCrary, Royce C. "Georgia Politics and the Mexican War." *Georgia Historical Quarterly* 60 (Fall 1976): 211–27.

McNitt, Frank, ed. *Journal of a Military Reconnaissance from Santa Fe, New Mexico, to the Navajo Country Made in 1849 by Lieutenant James H. Simpson*. Norman: University of Oklahoma Press, 1964.

———. *Navajo Wars: Military Campaigns, Slave Raids, and Reprisals*. Albuquerque: University of New Mexico Press, 1972.

Meketa, Jacqueline Dorgan. *Louis Felsenthal: Citizen-Soldier of Territorial New Mexico*. Albuquerque: University of New Mexico Press, 1982.

Mellichamp, Josephine. "William Dawson." In *Senators From Georgia*, 127–30. Huntsville, AL: Strode, 1976.

Message from the President of the United States, in Compliance with a Resolution of the Senate, Transmitting Documents Relating to Frauds, &c., in the Sale of Indian Reservations of Land, July 2, 1836. Sen. Doc. 425, S. S. 284.

"Messervy, William S." Social Networks and Archival Context. http://snac cooperative.org/ark:/99166/w63w2jdg.

Michno, Gregory F. *Depredation and Deceit: The Making of the Jicarilla and Ute Wars in New Mexico*. Norman: University of Oklahoma Press, 2017.

Mills, Frederick V. "Methodist Church: Overview." *New Georgia Encyclopedia*. September 29, 2020. https://www.georgiaencyclopedia.org/articles/arts-culture /methodist-church-overview.

Mueller, Edward A. *Perilous Journeys: A History of Steamboating on the Chattahoochee, Apalachicola, and Flint Rivers, 1828–1928*. Eufaula, AL: Historic Chattahoochee Commission, 1990.

Murphy, Lawrence R. *Antislavery in the Southwest: William G. Kephart's Mission to New Mexico, 1850–53.* El Paso: Texas Western, 1978.

Myers, Harry C. "The Journal of Captain Philip St. George Cooke, First U.S. Dragoons, on an Escort of Santa Fe Traders in the Year of 1843." Santa Fe Trail Association Symposium, 1995.

Neighbours, Kenneth. "The Taylor-Neighbors Struggle over the Upper Rio Grande Region of Texas in 1850." *Southwestern Historical Quarterly* 61 (April 1958): 431–63.

Neil, William M. "The Territorial Governor as Indian Superintendent in the Trans-Mississippi West." *Mississippi Valley Historical Review* 43 (September 1956): 213–37.

"Nicholas Philip Trist." Monticello. http://www.monticello.org/site/research-and -collections/nicholas-philip-trist.

Nichols, David A. "Land, Republicanism, and Indians: Power and Policy in Early National Georgia, 1780–1825." *Georgia Historical Quarterly* 85 (Summer 2001): 199–226.

Northern, William J. *Men of Mark in Georgia.* Vol. 2. London: Forgotten Books, 2016.

"Notes on the Population of New Mexico, 1846–1849." *New Mexico Historical Review* 34 (July 1959): 200.

Nusbaum, Rosemary. *The City Different and the Palace: The Palace of the Governors: Its Role in Santa Fe History, Including Jesse Nusbaum's Restored Journals.* Santa Fe, NM: Sunstone, 1978.

Ober, Frederick A. *Travels in Mexico and Life Among the Mexicans.* Boston: Estes & Lauriat, 1887.

Opler, Morris E. "The Apachean Culture Pattern and Its Origins." In *Handbook of North American Indians*, Vol. 10, *Southwest*, edited by Alfonso Ortiz and William C. Sturtevant, 368–92. Washington, DC: Smithsonian, 1979.

———. "Chiricahua Apache." *Handbook of North American Indians*, Vol. 10, *Southwest*, 401–18.

Oswandel, J. Jacob. *Notes of the Mexican War, 1846–1848.* Edited by Timothy D. Johnson and Nathaniel Cheairs Hughes Jr. Knoxville: University of Tennessee Press, 2010.

Owen, Gordon. *Las Cruces, New Mexico 1849–1999: Multicultural Crossroads.* Las Cruces, NM: Red Sky, 1999.

"The Panic of 1837." The History Box. http://thehistorybox.com/ny_city/panics /panics_article5a.htm.

Paquette, Robert L. "The Everett-Del Monte Connection: A Study in the International Politics of Slavery." *Diplomatic History* 11 (January 1987): 1–22.

———. *Sugar Is Made with Blood: The Conspiracy of La Escalera and the Conflict Between Empires over Slavery in Cuba.* Middletown, CT: Wesleyan University Press, 1988.

Park, Orville A. "The Georgia Scotch-Irish." *Georgia Historical Quarterly* 12 (June 1928): 115–35.

Parkes, Henry Bamford. *A History of Mexico*. New York: Houghton Mifflin, 1960.

Phillips, Ulrich Bonnell. "Historical Notes of Milledgeville, Ga." *Gulf States Historical Magazine* (November 1903): 1–11.

Ports, Michael A. *Jefferson County, Georgia Tax Lists, 1799–1803*. Baltimore: Genealogical Publishing, 2016.

Poss, Faye Stone. *Early Jefferson County, Georgia Newspaper Abstracts, 1799–1811*. Snellville, GA: Faye Stone Poss, 2011.

Price, Vivian. *The History of DeKalb County Georgia, 1822–1900*. Fernandina Beach, FL: Wolfe, 1997.

Prince, Bradford. Papers, 1959–174. New Mexico State Library and Archives, Santa Fe.

Prucha, Francis Paul. *A Guide to the Military Posts of the United States, 1789–1895*. Madison: State Historical Society of Wisconsin, 1964.

Quaife, Milo Milton, ed. *Kit Carson's Autobiography*. Lincoln & London: University of Nebraska Press, 1966.

Rathbun, Daniel C. B., and David V. Alexander. *New Mexico Frontier Military Place Names*. Las Cruces, NM: Yucca Tree, 2003.

Read, Benjamin M. Collection. Territorial Archives. New Mexico State Library and Archives, Santa Fe.

Records of US Army Commands, Department of New Mexico, Selected Documents Related to the Navajo Indians 1846–1868, Record Group 98, roll 1. New Mexico State Archives.

Reed, Thomas W. *History of the University of Georgia*. University of Georgia Online Archives. https://www.libs.uga.edu/hargrett/archives/reedindex.html.

Reeve, Frank D. "The Federal Indian Policy." *New Mexico Historical Review* 13 (July 1938): 261–313.

Report of the Secretary of the Interior, Communicating, in Further Compliance with a Resolution of the Senate, Certain Papers in Relation to the Mexican Boundary Commission, March 22, 1853. Sen. Ex. Doc. 6, S. S. 688.

Reports of Committees, 31st Cong., 2nd sess., February 25, 1851.

Reports of Explorations and Surveys to Ascertain the Most Practicable and Economic Route for a Railroad from the Mississippi River to the Pacific Ocean, 1853–6. 33rd Cong., 2nd sess. Sen. Ex. Doc. 78.

Rhodes, Eugene Manlove. "God's Badgered Man." *Santa Fe New Mexican Centennial Edition, 1849–1949*, 12–13.

Richardson, James D. *A Compilation of the Messages and Papers of the Presidents, 1789–1897*. Vol. 5. Washington, DC: Government Printing Office, 1897.

Richardson, Rupert N. "Neighbors, Robert Simpson (1815–1859)." *Handbook of Texas Online*. Texas State Historical Association. https://www.tshaonline.org/handbook/browse?handbook_entries%5Bquery%5D=Neighbors%2C%20Robert%20Simpson%20%281815–1859%29.

Rippy, J. Fred. "The Indians of the Southwest in the Diplomacy of the United States and Mexico, 1848–1853." *Hispanic American Historical Review* 2 (August 1919): 363–96.

Robarts, William Hugh. *Mexican War Veterans: A Complete Roster of the Regular and Volunteer Troops in the War Between the United States and Mexico, from 1846 to 1848.* Washington, DC: A. S. Witherbee, 1887.

Robinson, Jacob S. *Journal of the Santa Fe Expedition Under Colonel Doniphan in 1846.* Santa Barbara, CA: Narrative, 2001.

Robinson, Sherry. *El Malpais, Mt. Taylor, and the Zuni Mountains: A Hiking Guide and History.* Albuquerque: University of New Mexico Press, 1994.

———. *I Fought a Good Fight: A History of the Lipan Apaches.* Denton: University of North Texas Press, 2013.

Russell, Marian Sloan. *Land of Enchantment: Memoirs of Marian Russell Along the Santa Fe Trail.* Albuquerque: University of New Mexico Press, 1954.

Sale of Indian Reservations, &c. Message from the President of the United States, Transmitting a Report on the Sales of Indian Reservations, Made Under Orders of the Courts of Alabama, &c., February 20, 1839. H. Doc. 209, S. S. 347.

Sánchez, Joseph P., and Larry D. Miller. *Martineztown 1823–1950: Hispanics, Italians, Jesuits & Land Investors in New Town Albuquerque.* Los Ranchos de Albuquerque: Rio Grande, 2009.

Sando, Joe S. *Pueblo Nations: Eight Centuries of Pueblo Indian History.* Santa Fe, NM: Clear Light, 1992.

Santa Fe County Records, Series 7, County Sheriff. New Mexico State Library and Archives, Santa Fe.

Sargeant, Kathryn, and Mary Davis. *Shining River Precious Land: An Oral History of Albuquerque's North Valley.* Albuquerque, NM: Albuquerque Museum, 1986.

Schroeder, Albert. Papers, Collection 1972–033. New Mexico State Library and Archives, Santa Fe.

Schubert, Frank N. *Vanguard of Expansion: Army Engineers in the Trans-Mississippi West, 1819–1879.* Washington, DC: Historical Division, Office of Administrative Services, Office of the Chief of Engineers, 1980.

Schwartzman, Grace M., and Susan K. Barnard. "A Trail of Broken Promises: Georgians and Muscogee/Creek Treaties, 1796–1826." *Georgia Historical Quarterly* 75 (Winter 1991): 697–718.

Scott, Carole E. "Banking Lessons from the Antebellum South." B>Quest. 2000. https://www.westga.edu/~bquest/2000/antebellum.html.

———. "The Troubled World of Antebellum Banking in Georgia." B>Quest. 2016. https://www.westga.edu/~bquest/2000/antebellumGAbanks.pdf.

Second Auditor of the Treasury, January 16, 1857, S. Ex. Doc. 28, S. S. 880.

Secretary of the Interior to the Committee on Indian Affairs, US Senate, April 2, 1862, S. Misc. Doc. 79, S. S. 1124.

Secretary of State Papers. Collection 1959–293 and Archives. New Mexico State Library, Santa Fe.

Segale, Sister Blandina. *At the End of the Santa Fe Trail.* Albuquerque: University of New Mexico Press, 1932.

Sherwood, Adiel. *A Gazetteer of the State of Georgia: Embracing a Particular Description of the Counties, Towns, Villages, Rivers, &c., and Whatsoever Is Usual in Geographies, and Minute Statistical Works; Together with a New Map of the State.* Washington City: P. Force, 1837.

Shewmaker, Kenneth E., ed. *The Papers of Daniel Webster: Diplomatic Papers.* Vol. 1, *1841–1843.* Hanover, NH & London: University Press of New England, 1983.

Shishkin, J. K. *The Palace of Governors.* Santa Fe: Museum of New Mexico, 1972.

Sides, Hampton. *Blood and Thunder: An Epic of the American West.* New York: Doubleday, 2006.

Simmons, Marc. *Albuquerque: A Narrative History.* Albuquerque: University of New Mexico Press, 1982.

———. "History of the Pueblos Since 1821." In *Handbook of North American Indians.* Vol. 10, *Southwest,* edited by Alfonso Ortiz and William C. Sturtevant, 206–23. Washington, DC: Smithsonian Institution, 1979.

———. "Hygiene, Sanitation, and Public Health in Hispanic New Mexico." *New Mexico Historical Review* 67 (July 1992): 205–25.

———. *The Little Lion of the Southwest: A Life of Manuel Antonio Chaves.* Chicago: Swallow, 1973.

———. *The Old Trail to Santa Fe.* Albuquerque: University of New Mexico Press, 1996.

———. "Rio Abajo Weekly Press Was Duke City's First Real Paper." *New Mexican* (October 3, 2014). https://www.santafenewmexican.com/news/trail_dust/trail -dust-rio-abajo-weekly-press-was-duke-city-s-first-real-paper/image_9bfc1c25- cb03-5729-b687-d1c708828a57.html.

Simmons, Virginia McConnell. *The Ute Indians of Utah, Colorado, and New Mexico.* Boulder: University Press of Colorado, 2000.

Skelton, Linda Worley. "The States Rights Movement in Georgia, 1825–1850." *Georgia Historical Quarterly* 50 (December 1966): 391–412.

Smith, Elbert B. *The Presidencies of Zachary Taylor & Millard Fillmore.* Lawrence: University Press of Kansas, 1988.

Smith, George Gilman. *The Story of Georgia and the Georgia People, 1732 to 1760.* Macon, GA: George G. Smith, 1900.

Smith, George Winston, and Charles Judah, eds. *Chronicles of the Gringos: The U.S. Army in the Mexican War, 1846–1848, Accounts of Eyewitnesses & Combatants.* Albuquerque: University of New Mexico Press, 1968.

Smith, Gordon Burns. *History of the Georgia Militia, 1783–1861.* Vols. 1 & 2. Milledgeville, GA: Boyd, 2000.

Smith, P. David. *Ouray: Chief of the Utes.* Ridgeway, CO: Wayfinder, 1986.

Sobel, Robert. "Panic of 1837." *Gale Encyclopedia of U.S. Economic History.* https://

www.encyclopedia.com/history/encyclopedias-almanacs-transcripts-and-maps
/panic-1837.

Spicer, Edward H. *Cycles of Conquest: The Impact of Spain, Mexico, and the United States on the Indians of the Southwest, 1533–1960.* Tucson: University of Arizona Press, 1962.

State Department Territorial Papers, New Mexico 1851–1872. New Mexico State Library, Santa Fe.

Steel Jr., Edward M. *T. Butler King of Georgia.* Athens: University of Georgia Press, 1964.

Stegmaier, Mark J. *Texas, New Mexico, and the Compromise of 1850: Boundary Dispute & Sectional Crisis.* Kent, OH & London: Kent State University Press, 1996.

Stryker's American Register and Magazine. Washington: W. M. Morrison, 1850–1853, 3:427.

Sweeney, Edwin R. *Mangas Coloradas: Chief of the Chiricahua Apaches.* Norman: University of Oklahoma Press, 1998.

The Tabb Family in the United States. tabbfamilyhistory.com.

Taylor, Zachary. *Letters of Zachary Taylor, From the Battle-fields of the Mexican War.* Rochester, NY: Genesee, 1908.

Telfair, Nancy. *A History of Columbus, Georgia: 1828–1928.* Columbus, GA: Historical Publishing, 1929.

Tiller, Veronica E. Velarde. *The Jicarilla Apache Tribe: A History.* Lincoln & London: University of Nebraska Press, 1992.

Thomas, Mrs. Z. V. *History of Jefferson County, Georgia.* Macon, GA: J. W. Burke, 1927.

Thompson, Gregory Coyne. "Southern Ute Lands, 1848–1899: The Creation of a Reservation." *Occasional Papers of the Center of Southwest Studies,* Fort Lewis College 1 (March 1972), 1–62.

Thompson, Jerry D. "With the Third Infantry in New Mexico, 1851–1853: The Lost Diary of Private Sylvester Matson." *Journal of Arizona History* 31 (Winter 1990): 349–404.

Thompson, William Y. *Robert Toombs of Georgia.* Baton Route: Louisiana State University Press, 1966.

Thrapp, Dan L. *Encyclopedia of Frontier Biography.* Glendale, CA: A. H. Clark, 1988.

Tidball, Eugene C. *Soldier-Artist of the Great Reconnaissance: John C. Tidball and the 35th Parallel Pacific Railroad Survey.* Tucson: University of Arizona Press, 2004.

Tórrez, Robert J. "Mexican Patriotism in New Mexico, 1821–1846." In *Telling New Mexico: A New History,* edited by Marta Weigle, Frances Levine, and Louise Stiver, 129–40. Albuquerque: University of New Mexico Press, 2009.

Tschanz, David W. "Yellow Fever and the Strategy of the Mexican–American War." Montana State University. http://www.montana.edu/historybug/mexwar.html.

Tucker, Spencer. *The Encyclopedia of the Mexican–American War: A Political, Social and Military History.* Santa Barbara, CA: ABC-CLIO, 2013.

Twitchell, Ralph Emerson. *The Bench and Bar of New Mexico During the American Occupation, 1846–1850*. Santa Fe, NM: New Mexican Printing, 1891.

———. *The History of the Military Occupation of the Territory of New Mexico from 1846 to 1851 by the Government of the United States*. Chicago: Rio Grande, 1909.

———. *Leading Facts of New Mexican History*. Albuquerque, NM: Horn & Wallace, 1963.

Tyler, S. Lyman. *A History of Indian Policy*. Washington, DC: US Department of the Interior, Bureau of Indian Affairs, 1973.

"Union Cemetery: A Walking Tour." Union Cemetery Historical Society, Kansas City, MO.

US Census Bureau, 1830, 1840, 1850. Ancestry.com.

US Area Commands, Ninth Military Department, Letters Sent and Received, Record Group 393. National Archives.

US Marshals Service. https://www.usmarshals.gov/district/nm/general/history .htm.

US War Department, Department of New Mexico, Letters Sent and Received, Record Group 98, 92, 192, roll 1. National Archives.

Utley, Robert M. *Fort Union National Monument*. Washington, DC: Government Printing Office, 1962.

Vasconcellos, Ramon. "Out of the House of Bondage." *Wild West* (February 2019): 22–23.

Vaughan, John H. *History and Government of New Mexico*. Self-published, 1921.

Vestal, Stanley. *The Old Santa Fe Trail*. Lincoln & London: University of Nebraska, 1939.

Vigil, Donaciano. *Arms, Indians, and the Mismanagement of New Mexico*. El Paso: Texas Western Press, 1986.

Von Abele, Rudolph. *Alexander H. Stephens, A Biography*. Westport, CT: Negro Universities Press, 1946.

Wadsworth, Richard. *Forgotten Fortress: Fort Millard Fillmore and Antebellum New Mexico, 1851–1862*. Las Cruces, NM: Yucca Tree, 2002.

Ware, Lynn Willoughby. "Cotton Money: Antebellum Currency Conditions in the Apalachicola/Chattahoochee River Valley." *Georgia Historical Quarterly* 74 (Summer 1990): 215–33.

Weber, David J. *The Mexican Frontier, 1821–1846: The American Southwest Under Mexico*. Albuquerque: University of New Mexico Press, 1982.

———. *Richard Kern: Expeditionary Artist in the Far Southwest, 1848–1853*. Albuquerque: University of New Mexico Press, 1985.

———. *The Taos Trappers: The Fur Trade in the Far Southwest, 1540–1846*. Norman: University of Oklahoma Press, 1971.

Weightman, Richard H. Speech of Hon. Richard H. Weightman of New Mexico, Delivered in the House, March 15, 1852, in Reply to the Hon. Mr. Phelps, of Missouri. Benjamin M. Read Collection, #1959–179, Box 6, Folder 310, NMSA.

Wetherington, Ronald K. *Ceran St. Vrain: American Frontier Entrepreneur.* Santa Fe, NM: Sunstone, 2012.

White, George. *Historical Collections of Georgia: Containing the Most Interesting Facts, Traditions, Biographical Sketches, Anecdotes, etc. Relating to its History and Antiquities, from Its First Settlement to the Present Time.* New York: Pudney & Russell, 1854.

Whiteley, Peter M. "Reconnoitering Pueblo Ethnicity." *Journal of the Southwest* 45 (Autumn 2003): 438–518.

Whittlesey, E. Report by Committee of Claims, July 2, 1838. House Report. 25th Cong., 2nd sess. S. S. 336.

Wilcox, Cadmus Marcellus. *History of the Mexican War.* Washington, DC: Church News, 1892.

Williams, Carolyn White. *History of Jones County, Georgia, 1807–1907.* Macon, GA: Burke, 1957.

Wilson, Robert J. "Milledgeville." *New Georgia Encyclopedia.* July 20, 2020. https://www.georgiaencyclopedia.org/articles/counties-cities-neighborhoods /Milledgeville.

Winders, Richard Bruce. *Mr. Polk's Army: The American Military Experience in the Mexican War.* College Station: Texas A&M University Press, 2000.

Winn, William W. *The Triumph of the Ecunnau-Nuxulgee: Land Speculators, George M. Troup, State Rights, and the Removal of the Creek Indians from Georgia and Alabama, 1825–38.* Macon, GA: Mercer University Press, 2015.

Wood, W. K. "The Georgia Railroad and Banking Company." *Georgia Historical Quarterly* 57 (Winter 1973): 544–61.

Worsley, Etta B. "Columbus." *Georgia Review* 1 (Fall 1947): 366–77.

Wright Jr., J. Leitch. *Creeks and Seminoles: The Destruction and Regeneration of the Muscogulge People.* Lincoln & London: University of Nebraska Press, 1986.

Wyly-Jones, Susan. "Dawson, William Crosby." *American National Biography.* https://www.anb.org/search?q=Dawson%2C+William+Crosby&searchBtn =Search&isQuickSearch=true.

Young, Mary E. "The Creek Frauds: A Study in Conscience and Corruption." *Mississippi Valley Historical Review* 42 (December 1955): 411–37.

———. *Redskins, Ruffleshirts and Rednecks: Indian Allotments in Alabama and Mississippi 1830–1860.* Norman: University of Oklahoma Press, 1961.

Newspapers

Albany Courier
Albany Patriot
Albuquerque Journal
Alexandria Gazette
Augusta Chronicle

Baltimore Sun
Boston Courier
Boston Evening Transcript
Boston Herald
Boston Traveler

Charleston Courant
Charleston Courier
Charleston Daily News
Charleston Mercury
Cincinnati Commercial Tribune
Cincinnati Daily Gazette
Civilian and Galveston Gazette
Cleveland Leader
Cleveland Plain Dealer
Columbia Daily Phoenix
Columbus Daily Enquirer
Columbus Enquirer
Columbus Times
Columbus Tri-Weekly Enquirer
Commercial Appeal
Daily American Telegraph
Daily Illinois State Journal
Daily Missouri Republican
Daily National Intelligencer
Daily Ohio Statesman
Daily Missouri Democrat
Daily Union
Federal Union
Galliopolis Journal
The Georgian
Hancock Advertiser
Hillsdale Daily News
Ledger-Enquirer
Louisville Gazette and Republican
    Trumpet
Macon Messenger
Macon Weekly Telegraph
Nashville Whig
National Banner

National Era
National Intelligencer
New Bedford Mercury
New London Weekly Chronicle
New York Daily Tribune
New York Herald
New York Post
New York Times
Newark Daily Advertiser
Ohio Statesman
Palmyra Weekly Whig
The Republic
Richmond Enquirer
Sacramento Daily Union
San Antonio Ledger
Sandusky Register
San Francisco Bulletin
Santa Fe Gazette
Savannah Daily Republican
Savannah Republican
Schenectady Reflector
Semi-Weekly Union
Southern Banner
Star of Florida
St. Joseph Times
St. Louis Republican
St. Louis Union
Temperance Crusader
Trenton State Gazette
Victoria Advocate
Washington Reporter
Weekly Arkansas Gazette
Weekly National Intelligencer
Weekly Union

INDEX

Page numbers in *italic* text indicate illustrations.

Columbus Canal and Water Company, 29, 54

Columbus Guards, 18, 19, 41, 77, 325n16

Columbus Land Company, 34, 37, 39, 42, 46, 47

Columbus Enquirer, 6, 23, 58, 60, 69, 69, 93, 173, 192, 248, 300

Compromise of 1850, 180, 184–86, 188, 192

Conklin, James, 138, 293, 335n17

Connelly, Henry, 174, 175, 195, 210, 276, 295, 305, 307, 340n19, 347n5

Conrad, Secretary of War Charles M., 187, 195, 217, 219, 222, 261, 270, 335n22

Coosa River, 27, 33, 34

cotton business, 12, 14, 21, 23, 25, 31, 33, 54–55, 67

Crawford, George W., 67, 75, 77, 94, 104, 107, 109, 167, 169, 181, 329n23

Creek Tribe, 10, 13, 19, 21, 23, 33 34, 36, 40–44; land fraud, 35, 36, 40, 43, 45, 46; women, 33, 36

Creek Indian leaders: Efau Emathla, 42; Neah Emathla, 43; Jim Boy, 44; Jim Henry, 43–44; Eneah Micco, 42, 43; Opothle Yoholo, 38, 38, 44

Cuba, 61–66, 62

Cunningham, Major Francis A., 174, 175, 293

currency, Georgia, 17, 30, 31, 48, 56, 68

Davis, William W. H., 159, 276

Davis, Arthur B., 25

Davis, John H., 106, 109, 118, 148, 149, 168, 280, 287, 324n5, 329n38, 349n1

Dawson, William C., 3, 16, 19, 21, 22, 58–60, 137, 166–69, 166, 179, 182, 184, 216, 252, 311n32, 318nn31–32; wife Henrietta Dawson, 19, 59, 168, 169, 216

Democratic Party / Democrats, 20, 31, 55, 56, 67, 70, 71, 106, 108, 110, 159, 162,

166, 173, 186, 224, 232, 270. 273, 274, 277, 312n6, 323n15, 325n11, 330n43, 330n47

disease: Georgia, 9, 12, 14, 33; Santa Fe Trail, 110–11, 215; Santa Fe, 238, 255

Echols, Josephus, 73

El Paso, TX, 132, 155, 171, 218, 219, 237, 241, 272, 279, 353n5

Evans, Thomas C., 28, 29, 351n33

Everett, Alexander, 63, 64

Ewing, Secretary of Interior Thomas, 106, 108, 164

Fillmore, President Millard, 3, 182, 185, 186, 189, 195, 196, 203, 247, 249, 257, 260, 299, 329n23, 338n29, 346n42

Flournoy, Samuel, 15, 43, 44, 69, 76

Fontaine, John, 27, 28, 32, 43, 51, 314n5, 10

Foote, Senator Henry, 167, 181, 232–33

forts, 208, 231, 235, 240; Conrad, 218, 240, 241; Defiance, 218, 222, 227–28, 230

Fillmore, 218, 240, 256, 346n34; Leavenworth, 110, 113, 215; Marcy, 220; Massachusetts, 218; Mitchell, 43; Union, 216, 218, 228, 229, 240, 254–56, 269, 277, 278, 296, 352n7, 354n31; Webster, 208, 218, 240, 269, 343n1, 346n34

Forty-niners, 110, 115, 128, 129, 136

Forsyth, John, 19, 22, 23, 63; son John Forsyth Jr., 77, 78, 80, 321n8

free people of color, 51, 61, 202

Gale, Alabama Gov. John, 39

Gallegos, José Manuel, 273, 293, 295, 301, 335n23, 336n46, 338n23, 342n59, 353n9

gambling, 14, 115, 118, 119, 175, 192, 201, 220, 235, 242

Garcia, Encarnacion, 133–34, 149–50, 158

genízaros, 145

Georgia, 11; bounty lands, 12; canals, 54,

militia: Georgia, 39, 44; New Mexico, 194, 195, 197, 203, 204, 229, 234

Milledgeville, GA, 3, 11, 15, 19, 20, 23–27, 34, 61, 72, 281, 285, 286, 311n27, 312n6; capital, 14; churches, 14–15; early history, 13–16, 23; Lafayette visit, 18; Thespian Society, 17

Mississippi, 13, 19, 21, 84, 332n22

Missouri, 6, 114, 163, 188, 275, 338n26; St. Louis, 109

Missouri Volunteers, 114, 160, 209, 343n4

Mitchell, William H., 29, 43, 54, 109, 118, 138, 279, 325n18, 327n46

Morris, Josiah, 61

Mower, Horace, 216, 261, 350nn29–30

Munroe, Col. John, 133, 135–37, 140, 144, 146, 147, 151–53, 156, 157, 162, 166, 167, 170–77, 181–83, 187, 190, 194, 195, 200, 204, 208, 211–13, 217, 246–48, 39n34, 340n19, 345n30

Native Americans. See Indian tribes

Navajo Tribe, 4, 7, 116, 120–33, 136–40, 143–47, 153, 155–57, 194, 195, 203, 208, 211–23, 226, 227, 229–46, 257, 262, 267, 276, 328n8, 343n4; Chief Armijo, 239; Chief Chapitone, 127, 129; Chief José Largo, 123–24; Chief Manuelito, 123, 125; Chief Mariano Martínez, 126, 127; Chief Narbona, 123–25, 124; Chief Sandoval, 124, 127

Neighbors, Robert S., 144, 171–73, 176, 181, 182

New Mexicans, 1–2, 7, 8, 114–15, 119, 121, 131, 171, 176, 193, 195, 197–99, 203, 220, 232–33; relations with Americans, 224, 231, 241–42, 246–49, 252, 270

New Mexico, 185; after Mexican War, 1, 106–8, 114; Americans in, 1–2, 7, 114, 119, 123, 127, 129, 131–33, 163, 196, 197, 216, 232, 239, 247, 252, 256, 266;

civil government, 261–62; climate, 117, 327n43; courts, 141–43, 165, 175, 193, 200, 204, 206, 216–17, 221, 234, 250, 261–62; elections, 198, 223, 224, 246; food, 117, 118, 273; Kearny Code, 114; land grants, 121, 131, 134, 139, 145, 156, 197, 296, 297, 303, 305, 306, 341n33, 354n31; laws, 137, 142, 204; legislature, 8, 174, 187, 196, 199–200, 203–4, 206, 220, 233–35, 270, 301; military government, 162–65, 174–75, 177, 187, 226; newspapers, 6, 130, 198, 273–74, 276, 337n56; politics, 162, 165–67, 170, 175, 206, 224; population, 114, 196, 202; printing press, 165–66, 335nn21–23; railroad, 272, 273, 275; rebellion of 1847, 114, 141; taxes, 165, 167, 201, 204, 206, 222, 225, 226, 250, 261, 270; Territory, 3, 184–87, 189, 190, 226, 235–36, 270

New Mexico counties, 235, 293–97, 301–6, 340n23; Doña Ana, 358n38; Rio Arriba, 196, 226, 235, 275; San Miguel, 109, 193, 235, 275, 301, 303–6, 341n31, 41n33; Santa Fe, 197, 275, 278, 279, 298, 340; Socorro, 241, 242; Taos, 204, 232; Valencia, 157, 162

New Mexico towns and villages: Abiquiu, 138, 140, 141, 148, 150, 153, 154, 218, 294, 295, 304, 341n30; Albuquerque, 117, 162, 176, 203, 208, 217, 218, 223, 240, 253, 272, 273, 277; Anton Chico, 212, 213, 229, 245, 263, 305; Cebolleta, 124, 136, 137, 145, 156, 157, 195, 218, 229; Doña Ana, 136, 155, 173, 197, 209, 218, 303, 346n33, 353n5; La Cuesta, 209, 213, 343n4; Las Vegas, 112, 134, 139, 151, 211, 218, 235, 254, 293, 303, 306; Los Ranchos de Albuquerque, 223, 224, 294, 298, 304, 347n2; Mesilla, 218, 270, 353n5; Mora, 254, 304; Ojo Caliente, 154; Rayado, 134,

154, 218; San Miguel del Vado, 112, 145, 146, *146*, 176, 211, 219, 295, 301; Socorro, 132, 136, 146, 203, 208, 218, 235, 241, 304, 306; Wagon Mound, 134, 151, 210, 324n24. *See also* Santa Fe; Taos

New Mexico Volunteers, 122, 135, 139, 140, 154, 157, 183, 194, 195, 203, 204, 211, 229, 242, 295, 297, 340n16

New York, 17, 27, 28, 52, 54, 303, 311n26, 316n9

newspapers, 6, 23, 60, 103, 178, 232, 233, 236, 247, 248 275, 337n56. See also *Columbus Enquirer; Santa Fe Gazette*

Nicholson, Rev. Enoch, 193, 215, 233, 250, 339n9, 344n9

North Carolina, 9, 10, 26, 284, 309n6

Ogeechee River, 9, 10, 54, 282–85, 288, 289; Ogeechee Swamp, 289

Oglethorpe House, 44, 52, 53, 60, 68

Organic Act, 187, 206, 231, 234, 340n18

Ortiz, Vicar Juan Felipe, 220, 293, 294, 335n17, 350n29

Ortiz, Candido, 223, 233, 297, 301, 342n58

Ortiz y Delgado, Francisco, 187, 296, 336n46, 342n58

Ortiz, Tomás, 250, 297, 301

Overman, Charles, 241, 262, 263, 269, 336n46, 340n23

Palace of the Governors, 114, 115, 160, 191, *199*, 200, 201, 209, 233, 238, 252, 253, 269, 271, 326n32, 327n36

Pillans, Palmer, 165, 171, 294, 301, 334n6, 335n17, 338nn22–23

Panic of 1837, 4, 48–50, *49*, 56

Pecos River, 145, 209, 212, 242

peonage, 84, 170, 201

Perry, M. W., 34, 35, 314n10

Pino, Facundo, 194, 295

Pino, Miguel, 248, 294

Poinsett, Joel R., 45

Polk, President James, 75, 79, 100, 101, 176, 185, 325n11

Point of Rocks, 133, 134, 210, 269

Presbyterian Church, 15, 192, 250, 296, 322n3, 339n9

Pueblos: 7, 118, 121, 129, 131–32, 142–46, 149, 171, 174, 175, 194, 202–3, 205, 213, 234, 245, 259–61; Acoma, 263; Cochiti, 145, 237; Isleta, 132, 194, 203, 208; Jemez, 122, 129, 132, 137, 145, 235, 240; Laguna, 129, 132, 229, 245; Nambe, 145, 237, 155; San Felipe, 145, 237, 240; San Ildefonso, 132, 145; Santa Ana, 122, 136, 145, 208, 235, 237, 240; Santa Clara, 145, 255; Santo Domingo, 122, 145, 155, 237; Taos, 114, 132, 141, 142, 143, 204, 245, 267, 295; Tesuque, 145, 251, 255, 257, 259, 261; Zia, 122, 145, 237, 240; Zuni, 128–29, 132, 145, 156, 157, 276

Quinn, James H., 231, 245, 296, 334n12, 336n46

Ragland, Thomas, 29

Read, Rev. Hiram, 220, 233

Reynolds, Captain Alexander W., 166, 167, 176, 206, 221, 223, 224, 231, 235, 245–49, 294, 297, 335n25, 342n58, 350n31

Rio Grande, 117, 139, 141

Robinson, James D., 118, 174–75, 294, 304, 334n17

Rosenstein, Simon, 162

St. Vrain, Ceran, 114, 141, 161, 165, 167, 174, 187, 194, 204, 232, 297, 307, 35, 327n34, 327n46, 336n46, 339n12, 342n58

Sanford, John W. A., 36, 37, 39, 42, 47

Sangre de Cristo Mountains, 112, 117, 134, 141

Santa Fe, NM, *113, 116*: Americans, 119; army post, 218; description, 112–13, 115, 117; gambling, 192, 218; government center, 113, 253, 327n36; Indian agency, 106, 109; mail, 168, 196, 272; market, 116–17; newspapers, 176, 198, 273, 354n 34, 357n56; politics, 170, 192, 273; trade center, 113; transportation, 119; US conquest, 114; unrest, 253

Santa Fe Gazette, 191, 198, 225, 232, 247, 273, 276–77, 296, 339n6, 354n34

Santa Fe Trail, 1, 6, 108, 110–14, 133, 145, 151, 273, 324n10, 327n34, 330n52

Santa Rita del Cobre copper mine, 136, 155, 208, 218, 240, 245, 262, 346n34

Sarracino, Francisco, 156–57, 208, 303, 334n12

Schley, Georgia Governor William, 41, 42, 51

Scots-Irish, 9

Scott, John S., 35, 314n10

Scott, Gen. Winfield, 44, 84, 99, 183

Seminole Tribe, 42–44, 125, 318n31, 329n34

Shaw, Rev. James M., 233, 250

Sherman, Caleb, 217, 221, 305, 346n42

Shorter, Eli, 26, 29, 30 34, 37, 40, 42, 45, 46, 47

Sierra Blanca, 210, 251

Simpson, James H., 122, 123, 125, 127, 128, 130, 329n23

Skinner, William C., 165, 167, 172, 224, 231, 247, 294, 297, 301, 342n58, 347n5

slavery, 107, 179, 186, 192: Cuba, 61, 63, 64; Georgia, 10, 12; among New Mexicans, 122, 156, 157, 195, 204, 230, 246, 340n16; New Mexico, 107–8, 163, 164, 170, 174, 179, 180, 184, 187, 188, 198, 202, 232, 233, 338n19; among tribes, 120, 156, 230

Smith, Hampton, 25, 28

Smith, Hugh N., 161, 164, 167, 174, 181, 187, 188, 190, 198, 237, 296, 297, 301, 304, 334n6, 338n19, 342n58, 344n9, 350n28

Smith, Rev. Louis, 215, 220, 233

South, the, 13, 19, 21, 61, 64, 70, 108, 169, 170, 176, 182, 184, 186, 248, 279

South Carolina, 3, 11, 12, 16, 21, 22, 86–88, 181, 280, 282, 286, 325n13, 325n21; Charleston, 16, 17, 73, 109

Spain: Cuba, 61, 63, 64; Mexico, 101; New Mexico, 113–14, 119,121–22, 132, 143, 145, 156, 221

State Rights Party, 22, 27, 31, 54, 55, 67, 70, 319n22

statehood, New Mexico, 1, 3, 5, 108, 159–80, 184, 187, 188, 198, 235–36, 266, 267, 294

Steen, Major Enoch, 136, 155, 173, 336n44

Stephens, Alexander, 3, 6, 67, 75, 104, 105, 107, 108, 169, 179–82, *180*, 184, 186, 273

Stephens, R. M., 250, 255, 256, 279, 306

Stuart, Interior Secretary Alexander H. H., 195–96, 204, 205, 253, 260

Sumner, Col. Edwin Vose, 215, 217–23, 218, 227–30, 232, 235, 240–42, 247, 249–55, 257, 261–63, 269–71, 278, 346n32

Tallapoosa River, 33, 34

Taos, New Mexico, 114, 132, 135, 139, 141, 143, 146, 152, 176, 195, 204, 05, 216, 218, 226, 229, 232, 246, 293, 295, 296, 303, 306, 330n49

Tariff of 1828, 21

Tarrant, Leonard, 36

Tarver, Benjamin P., 28, 35, 37, 46, 314n10, 314n19, 315nn20–21

Taylor, Zachary, 79; as general, 75, 78–85, 103–6; as president, 3, 107, 108,